A WORLD BANK STUDY

Education in Sub-Saharan Africa
A Comparative Analysis

Kirsten Majgaard and Alain Mingat

THE WORLD BANK
Washington, D.C.

© 2012 International Bank for Reconstruction and Development / The World Bank
1818 H Street NW, Washington DC 20433
Telephone: 202-473-1000; Internet: www.worldbank.org

Some rights reserved

1 2 3 4 15 14 13 12

World Bank Studies are published to communicate the results of the Bank's work to the development community with the least possible delay. The manuscript of this paper therefore has not been prepared in accordance with the procedures appropriate to formally edited texts.

This work is a product of the staff of The World Bank with external contributions. Note that The World Bank does not necessarily own each component of the content included in the work. The World Bank therefore does not warrant that the use of the content contained in the work will not infringe on the rights of third parties. The risk of claims resulting from such infringement rests solely with you.

The findings, interpretations, and conclusions expressed in this work do not necessarily reflect the views of The World Bank, its Board of Executive Directors, or the governments they represent. The World Bank does not guarantee the accuracy of the data included in this work. The boundaries, colors, denominations, and other information shown on any map in this work do not imply any judgment on the part of The World Bank concerning the legal status of any territory or the endorsement or acceptance of such boundaries.

Nothing herein shall constitute or be considered to be a limitation upon or waiver of the privileges and immunities of The World Bank, all of which are specifically reserved.

Rights and Permissions

This work is available under the Creative Commons Attribution 3.0 Unported license (CC BY 3.0) http://creativecommons.org/licenses/by/3.0. Under the Creative Commons Attribution license, you are free to copy, distribute, transmit, and adapt this work, including for commercial purposes, under the following conditions:

Attribution—Please cite the work as follows: Majgaard, Kirsten and Alain Mingat. 2012. *Education in Sub-Saharan Africa: A Comparative Analysis.* Washington, D.C.: World Bank. DOI: 10.1596/978-0-8213-8889-1. License: Creative Commons Attribution CC BY 3.0

Translations—If you create a translation of this work, please add the following disclaimer along with the attribution: *This translation was not created by The World Bank and should not be considered an official World Bank translation. The World Bank shall not be liable for any content or error in this translation.*

All queries on rights and licenses should be addressed to the Office of the Publisher, The World Bank, 1818 H Street NW, Washington, DC 20433, USA; fax: 202-522-2625; e-mail: pubrights@worldbank.org.

ISBN (paper): 978-0-8213-8889-1
ISBN (electronic): 978-0-8213-8890-7
DOI: 10.1596/978-0-8213-8889-1

Cover photo: Children in front of a primary school in Maputo, Mozambique. Photo courtesy of Cornelia Jesse.

Library of Congress Cataloging-in-Publication Data

Majgaard, Kirsten.
 Education in sub-saharan Africa : a comparative analysis / by Kirsten Majgaard and Alain Mingat.
   p. cm.
  ISBN 978-0-8213-8889-1 — ISBN 978-0-8213-8890-7
  1. Education—Africa, Sub-Saharan—Finance. 2. Education—Africa, Sub-Saharan—Finance—Statistics. 3. School management and organization—Africa, Sub-Saharan. 4. Education and state—Africa, Sub-Saharan. I. Mingat, Alain. II. Title.
  LB2826.6.A34M35 2011
  370.967—dc23
                                                                 2011028218

Contents

Acknowledgments		*xv*
Acronyms and Abbreviations		*xvii*
	Overview	1
	Is Everyone Getting a Chance at Education?	2
	Are Those Given a Chance Actually Learning?	6
	Is What They Are Learning Relevant for Work and Life?	8
	Are Countries Investing Enough in Education and Achieving a Sound Balance across Levels of Education?	11
	Are the Resources Well Deployed and Managed to Ensure Efficient Functioning of Education Systems?	14
	How Is Cross-Country Diversity in Policies and Educational Outcomes Useful for Country-Specific Policy Development?	14
	Notes	16
	References	17
	Country Status Reports	18
Chapter 1	**Coverage of Education and Prospects for Expansion**	21
	Overview of the Pattern of Coverage	21
	Relationship between Education Coverage and Per Capita GDP	27
	Prospects for the Expansion of Education Coverage	30
	Issues for Policy Development	40
	Notes	41
	References	43
Chapter 2	**Socioeconomic Disparities in Education**	45
	Gender Disparities: Analysis of Administrative Data	45
	Socioeconomic Disparities beyond Gender: Analysis of Household Surveys	52
	Issues for Policy Development	54
	Notes	55
	References	55

Chapter 3	**Out-of-School Children**	**57**
	Estimating the Number of Out-of-School Children	58
	Profile of Out-of-School Children	63
	Reaching Out-of-School Children	66
	Issues for Policy Development	78
	Notes	80
	References	82
Chapter 4	**Patterns of Spending on Education**	**87**
	Aggregate Spending	87
	Patterns in the Distribution of Spending	95
	Relationship between Resources and Coverage	103
	Prioritizing Spending among School Inputs	104
	Management of Resources	111
	Issues for Policy Development	114
	Notes	116
	References	117
Chapter 5	**Learning Outcomes**	**121**
	Status of Learning Outcomes in Sub-Saharan Africa	121
	How Can Students' Learning Outcomes Be Improved?	126
	Issues for Policy Development	145
	Notes	148
	References	150
Chapter 6	**Social Outcomes**	**155**
	Relationship between Education and Social Outcomes in Sub-Saharan African Countries	155
	Relationship between Education and Social Outcomes by Level of Education	163
	Cross-Country Variations in the Relationship between Education and Social Outcomes	165
	Effectiveness of Education Systems at Generating Social Outcomes	166
	Issues for Policy Development	169
	Notes	169
	References	170
Chapter 7	**Education and Employment**	**171**
	Cross-Country Analysis of the Pattern of Employment	171
	Labor Productivity by Economic Sector	177
	Quantitative Match between Demand and Supply in the Labor Market	179

	Relationship between Higher Education Enrollment and	
	Unemployment	185
	Issues for Policy Development	188
	Notes	190
	References	190
Appendix A	Definitions and Background Information	193
	References	196
Appendix B	Enrollment Data	197
	References	199
Appendix C	Social Disparities	201
	References	203
Appendix D	Out-of-School Children	205
	References	208
Appendix E	Education Expenditure	209
	References	213
Appendix F	Gross Enrollment Rate (GER) and Its Underlying Components	215
Appendix G	Student Learning	217
Appendix H	Social Outcomes	219
	On Including Wealth in Regressions	219
	Reference	219
Appendix I	Education and Employment	235
	Reference	240
Appendix J	Lists of Surveys	241
Appendix K	The Millennium Development Goals	243
	References	244

Boxes

Box 1.1: Benin School Construction through Community-Driven Development: A Decade of Lessons Learned — 29

Box 1.2: Mauritania: Community Management of Primary School Construction — 32

Box 1.3: Zimbabwe: Increased Access to Secondary Education through Government–Community Partnerships and School-Based Management — 40

Box 3.1: The Central African Republic, The Gambia, Lesotho, and
    Malawi: Enhancing Teacher Deployment to Rural Areas ... 69
Box 3.2: Malawi: Impact of Conditional Cash Transfers on Girls'
    Secondary School Attendance ... 72
Box 3.3: Kenya: Girls' Scholarship Program ... 72
Box 4.1: Madagascar, Niger, and Senegal: Contract Teacher Recruitment to
    Expand Primary School Coverage ... 107
Box 4.2: Madagascar: Improvement in the Allocation of Teachers to
    Schools ... 114
Box 5.1: Ghana: Leaping in Quality from "Poor" to "Fair" ... 134
Box 5.2: Senegal: Better Management of Instructional Time to Improve
    Student Learning ... 138
Box 5.3: Madagascar: School Management Impact Evaluation ... 142
Box 5.4: The Gambia: Reducing Teacher Absenteeism by Strengthening
    Supervision ... 144
Box 5.5: Uganda: Public Access to Information Increases Effective Arrival
    of Grants to Schools ... 145
Box 5.6: Kenya: Teacher Incentive Pilot Program ... 146

Tables
Table O.1: Social Outcomes by Average Education Level in Sub-Saharan
    African Countries, ca. 2003 ... 9
Table O.2: Randomness in Teacher Allocation to Primary Schools,
    Selected Sub-Saharan African Countries, 2000–08 ... 16
Table 1.1: Education Coverage in Low-Income Countries, by World
    Region, ca. 2009 ... 23
Table 1.2: Secondary Education Coverage in Selected Sub-Saharan
    African Countries, ca. 2009 ... 26
Table 1.3: Absolute Gains in Coverage, by Education Level, in 33
    Low-Income Sub-Saharan African Countries, 1990–2009 ... 30
Table 1.4: Scenarios for the Expansion of Lower Secondary Enrollment by
    2020 in 33 Low-Income Sub-Saharan African Countries ... 37
Table 2.1: Gender Disparities at All Levels of Education, Sub-Saharan
    African Countries, Selected Years ... 46
Table 2.2: Comparison of Sub-Saharan African Gender Disparities in
    Education with Those of Low-Income Countries in Other World
    Regions, 2008 ... 46
Table 2.3: Distribution of Population Aged 5–24 by Gender, Location,
    Income, and Level of Schooling in Sub-Saharan African Countries,
    ca. 2005 ... 52
Table 2.4: Disparities by Social Group and Level of Education,
    Sub-Saharan African Countries, ca. 2005 ... 53
Table 3.1: Primary Entry and Attainment Rates Based on Different Data
    Sources, 33 Low-Income Sub-Saharan African Countries, ca. 2003 ... 59

Table 3.2: Estimated Number of Out-of-School Children in 33 Low-Income Sub-Saharan African Countries, ca. 2003 — 60

Table 3.3: Correlation of Distance to School and Probability of Grade One Enrollment, Simulated for Aggregate of Eight Sub-Saharan African Countries, ca. 2003 — 67

Table 3.4: Education Policies to Increase Access to, and Participation in, Primary Schooling — 73

Table 3.5: Impact of Proportion of Female Teachers on Primary-School Repetition and Retention Rates in Sub-Saharan African Countries — 74

Table 3.6: Impact on Primary School Retention of Reduced Repetition and Increased Share of Schools with Full Primary Cycle — 76

Table 3.7: Education Policies to Increase Retention in Primary Education — 77

Table 4.1: Comparison of Public Spending on Education (Capital and Recurrent), ca. 2005 — 88

Table 4.2: Average Tax Revenues and ODA Relative to Total Public Spending, Sub-Saharan African Countries, 2005–07 — 90

Table 4.3: Household Spending on Education in Selected Sub-Saharan African Countries, ca. 2003 — 94

Table 4.4: Comparison of Education Spending Distribution, by Level, 2006 or Latest Available Year — 95

Table 4.5: Public Recurrent Spending Per Student by Educational Level in Sub-Saharan African Countries, ca. 2003 — 97

Table 4.6: International Comparison of Per-Student Public Spending by Educational Level, ca. 2005 — 100

Table 4.7: Concentration of Public Education Spending within a Cohort, by Sub-Saharan African Country Income Level — 102

Table 4.8: School Inputs in Primary Education in Sub-Saharan African Countries, ca. 2003 — 105

Table 4.9: Decomposition of Variables' Relative Influence to Explain Variability in Primary GER across Sub-Saharan African Countries — 110

Table 4.10: Comparison of Randomness in Teacher Allocation to Primary Schools in Selected Sub-Saharan African Countries — 113

Table 4.11: Scope for Increasing Education Spending in Selected Low-Income Sub-Saharan African Countries — 115

Table 5.1: Test Scores and Index of Student Learning in Primary Education in Selected Sub-Saharan African Countries, 1996–2009 — 123

Table 5.2: Variance Decomposition of PASEC Learning Scores in 10 Sub-Saharan African Countries — 130

Table 5.3: School Management and Accountability Tools in Selected Sub-Saharan African Countries, 2007 — 143

Table 6.1: Logit Regression Results: Relation between Risk of Poverty and Educational Attainment in Benin, 2001 — 156

Table 6.2: Social Outcomes by Level of Education, Sub-Saharan African Average — 164

Table 6.3: Contribution to Social Outcomes by Year of Education,
Sub-Saharan African Average — 165

Table 7.1: Employment Status Distribution per 100 Working-Age
Population, Aggregate for 23 Sub-Saharan African Countries, ca. 2003 — 172

Table 7.2: Simulation of Employment by Sector as a Function of Per
Capita GDP, Average Low-Income Sub-Saharan African Country — 176

Table 7.3: Apparent Labor Productivity by Sector, Sub-Saharan African
Average, 1985–2003 — 178

Table 7.4: Employment Status by Age Group and Highest Level of
Schooling Attended, Aggregate for 23 Sub-Saharan African Countries,
ca. 2003 — 183

Table 7.5: Employment and Unemployment by Level of Education and
Age Group in 23 Sub-Saharan African Countries, ca. 2003 — 185

Table 7.6: Determinants of Unemployment Rate in 25–34 Age Cohort of
Higher-Education Graduates: Cross-Country Analysis, ca. 2003 — 186

Table 7.7: Modeling Higher Education Enrollment and Share of Skilled
Formal Sector Jobs — 187

Table A.1: Classification of Sub-Saharan African Countries Used in This
Report — 193

Table A.2: Definitions of Student Flow Indicators — 194

Table A.3: Duration of Primary and Secondary Cycles (Standardized)
in 47 Sub-Saharan African Countries, 2005 — 195

Table B.1: Education Coverage by Level of Education in 47 Sub-Saharan
African Countries, ca. 2009 — 197

Table B.2: Development in Education Coverage over Time in Sample of 33
Low-Incomea Sub-Saharan African Countries, 1990, 1999, and 2009 — 198

Table C.1: Gender Disparities by Level of Education and Sub-Saharan
African Country, ca. 1990 and 2008 — 201

Table D.1: Number and Proportion of Out-of-School Children in 33
Low-Income Sub-Saharan African Countries, 2003 — 205

Table D.2: Characteristics of Out-of-School Children in 30 Low-Income
Sub-Saharan African Countries, ca. 2003 — 206

Table D.3: Extent of Social Disparities between Children In and Out of
School in 30 Sub-Saharan African Countries, ca. 2003 — 207

Table E.1: Public Spending (Capital and Recurrent) on Education in
Sub-Saharan African Countries, ca. 2005 — 209

Table E.2: Public Recurrent Spending per Student per Year in
Sub-Saharan African Countries, by Education Level, ca. 2003 — 210

Table G.1: PASEC and SACMEQ Scores and Their Transformation to the
MLA Scale in Sub-Saharan African Countries, 1996–2009 — 217

Table H.1: Education and Risk of Being Poor in Sub-Saharan African
Countries, without Wealth as Control — 220

Table H.2: Education and Childbearing Behavior in Sub-Saharan African
Countries, with and without Wealth as Control — 220

Table H.3: Education and Maternal Health in Sub-Saharan African
Countries, with and without Wealth as Control ... 220
Table H.4: Education and Child Health and Development in Sub-Saharan
African Countries, with and without Wealth as Control ... 221
Table H.5: Education, Knowledge about HIV/AIDS, and Use of
Information Media in Sub Saharan Africa Countries, with and without
Wealth as Control ... 221
Table H.6: Relation between Education and Probability of Being in the 40
Percent Poorest, by Country ... 221
Table H.7: Relation between Education and Woman's Age at First Birth,
by Country ... 222
Table H.8: Relation between Education and Months between Last Two
Consecutive Births, by Country ... 223
Table H.9: Relation between Education and Number of Live Births to
Date, by Country ... 224
Table H.10: Relation between Education and Probability of Using any
Contraceptive Method Frequently, by Country ... 224
Table H.11: Relation between Education and Number of Prenatal
Consultations during Pregnancy, by Country ... 225
Table H.12: Relation between Education and Number of Tetanus
Vaccinations during Last Pregnancy, by Country ... 226
Table H.13: Relation between Education and Probability of Receiving
Vitamin A during Last Pregnancy, by Country ... 226
Table H.14: Relation between Education and Probability that Last
Delivery Was Assisted by Skilled Attendant, by Country ... 227
Table H.15: Relation between Education and Probability that Children
Sleep under a Bed Net, by Country ... 228
Table H.16: Relation between Education and Probability that Children
Are Fully Vaccinated by Age 2, by Country ... 228
Table H.17: Relation between Education and Mortality Rate of Children
under 5, by Country ... 229
Table H.18: Relation between Education and Probability that Children
Aged 9–11 Have Ever Attended School, by Country ... 230
Table H.19: Relation between Education and Index of Knowledge of
HIV/AIDS, by Country ... 230
Table H.20: Relation between Education and Probability of Reading
Newspapers Frequently, by Country ... 231
Table H.21: Relation between Education and Probability of Listening to
the Radio Frequently, by Country ... 232
Table H.22: Relation between Education and Probability of
Watching TV Frequently, by Country ... 232
Table H.23: Construction of Index of Improvement in Social
Outcomes from Six Years of Primary School, 36 Sub-Saharan African
Countries ... 233

Figures

Figure O.1: Sub-Saharan Africa's Educational Pyramid, ca. 2009	3
Figure O.2: Projected Primary Completion Rates by 2015 in Low-Income Sub-Saharan African Countries	5
Figure O.3: Correlation of Reading Ability and Length of Schooling, Selected Sub-Saharan African Countries	7
Figure O.4: Public Spending on Education in Sub-Saharan African Countries (Capital and Recurrent), ca. 2005	12
Figure O.5: Tradeoff between Teacher Salary and Pupil-Teacher Ratio at Primary Level in Selected Sub-Saharan African Countries, ca. 2003	13
Figure O.6: Number of Schools by Per-Student Spending, Burundi and Malawi, ca. 2004	15
Figure 1.1: Sub-Saharan Africa's Educational Pyramid, ca. 2009	22
Figure 1.2: Primary School Entry and Retention Rates in Sub-Saharan African Countries, ca. 2009	25
Figure 1.3: Relationship between Per Capita GDP and School-Life Expectancy in Low-Income Sub-Saharan African Countries, 1990–2009	28
Figure 1.4: Growth in Primary Education Coverage in 33 Low-Income Sub-Saharan African Countries, 1990–2009	31
Figure 1.5: Relative Gains in Education Coverage, by Education Level, in 33 Low-Income Sub-Saharan African Countries, 1990–2009	33
Figure 1.6: Average Annual PCR Growth in 33 Low-Income Sub-Saharan African Countries, 1999–2009	34
Figure 1.7: Projected Primary Completion Rates through 2015 in Low-Income Sub-Saharan African Countries	35
Figure 1.8: Projected Enrollment in Lower Secondary Education by 2020 as a Multiple of Enrollments in 2003	39
Figure 2.1: Gender Gap in the Primary Completion Rate, by Sub-Saharan Africa Country, 2008	47
Figure 2.2: Comparison of Gender Disparities in Three Groups of Sub-Saharan Africa Countries, 2008	48
Figure 2.3: Relationship between Education Coverage and Gender Disparity in Primary Education Sub-Saharan Africa Countries, 2008	49
Figure 2.4: Difference between Actual and Model-Predicted Gender Parity Index in Primary Education, by Sub-Saharan Africa Country, 2008	50
Figure 2.5: Comparison of Gender Disparities in Education by Data Source, Sub-Saharan Africa Countries, ca. 2005	53
Figure 3.1: Typical Schooling Profile in a Low-Income Country	58
Figure 3.2: Proportion of Out-of-School Children in 33 Low-Income Sub-Saharan African Countries, ca. 2003	61
Figure 3.3: Relationship between the Proportion of Out-of-School Children at Beginning and End of the Primary Cycle, in 33 Low-Income Sub-Saharan African Countries, 2003	62

Figure 3.4: Risk of Being Out of School by Gender, Location, and Wealth, Aggregate for Low-Income Sub-Saharan African Countries, 2003 — 63

Figure 3.5: Distribution of Out-of-School Children by Gender, Location, and Wealth, Aggregate for Selected Low-Income Sub-Saharan African Countries, ca. 2003 — 64

Figure 3.6: Distribution of Out-of-School Children by Gender, Location, and Wealth in Selected Low-Income Sub-Saharan African Countries, ca. 2003 — 65

Figure 3.7: Extent of Differences between Out-of-School and Enrolled Children in 30 Low-Income Sub-Saharan African Countries — 79

Figure 3.8: Suggested Targeting to Reach 35 Million Out-of-School Children in 33 Low-Income Sub-Saharan African Countries — 80

Figure 4.1: Public Spending on Education in Sub-Saharan African Countries (Capital and Recurrent), ca. 2005 — 89

Figure 4.2: Trend in ODA to Sub-Saharan Africa, 1990–2007 — 92

Figure 4.3: Growth in Government Revenue and ODA in Sub-Saharan Africa, 1997–2007 — 92

Figure 4.4: Ranking of Sub-Saharan African Countries by Per-Student Spending on Primary Education — 98

Figure 4.5: Patterns of Coverage and Per-Student Spending by Educational Level in Sub-Saharan African Countries, ca. 2005 — 101

Figure 4.6: Relation of School-Life Expectancy and Education Spending in Selected Sub-Saharan African Countries, ca. 2005 — 102

Figure 4.7: Per-Student Spending and GER at the Primary Level in Low-Income Sub-Saharan African Countries, ca. 2003 — 104

Figure 4.8: Comparison of Average Teacher Salary and Pupil-Teacher Ratio at Primary Level in 16 Sub-Saharan African Countries with Similar Per-Student Spending, ca. 2003 — 106

Figure 4.9: School Distribution in Burundi and Malawi, by Per-Student Spending, ca. 2004 — 111

Figure 4.10: Relation between Numbers of Students and Teachers at Primary Level in Benin and Madagascar, 2005/06 — 112

Figure 5.1: Correlation of ASLI Scores with GDP per Capita and Primary Completion Rate in 31 Sub-Saharan African Countries, ca. 2005 — 125

Figure 5.2: Literacy and Length of Studies, Selected Sub-Saharan African Countries — 125

Figure 5.3: Relationship between Per-Student Spending on Primary Level and the Africa Student Learning Index, 31 Sub-Saharan African Countries. ca. 2005 — 127

Figure 5.4: Relationship between Public Per Student Spending on Education and Performance on the 2009 PISA Mathematics Test, 27 OECD Countries — 127

Figure 5.5: Relation between Primary Schools' National Exam Pass Rates and Per-Student Spending — 128

Figure 5.6: Relationship between Primary Teacher Salary and GER in
  Selected Sub-Saharan African Countries 141
Figure 6.1: Relationship between Educational Attainment and the Risk
  Poverty, Benin 2001, and Sub-Saharan African Average 157
Figure 6.2: Relationship between Women's Educational Attainment and
  Childbearing, Sub-Saharan African Average 158
Figure 6.3: Relationship between Women's Educational Attainment and
  Prenatal Health Care, Sub-Saharan African Average 159
Figure 6.4: Relationship between Mothers' Educational Attainment and
  Child Health and Development, Sub-Saharan African Average 160
Figure 6.5: Relationship between Educational Attainment and Awareness
  of HIV/AIDS, Sub-Saharan African Average 162
Figure 6.6: Relationship between Educational Attainment and Exposure
  to Information Media, Sub-Saharan African Average 163
Figure 6.7: Cross-Country Variation in the Relationship between
  Education, Live Births and Child Vaccination in Selected Sub-Saharan
  African countries 166
Figure 6.8: Relationship between Effectiveness at Generating Social
  Outcomes and the ASLI Scores in Sub-Saharan African Countries 167
Figure 6.9: Relationship between National Average Level Social Outcome
  Indicators and Change in Indicators from Six Years of Primary
  Education, Sub-Saharan African Countries 168
Figure 7.1: Employment by Sector in 23 Sub-Saharan African Countries,
  Circa 2003 173
Figure 7.2: Farm Employment by Per Capita GDP in 23 Sub-Saharan
  African Countries, Circa 2003 174
Figure 7.3: Formal and Public Sector Employment by Per Capita GDP in
  23 Sub-Saharan African Countries, Circa 2003 175
Figure 7.4: Relation between Employment in Informal Non-Farm Sector
  Employment and Unemployment Rate in 23 Sub-Saharan African
  Countries, Circa 2003 177
Figure 7.5: Highest Level of Schooling among Working-Age Population in
  23 Sub-Saharan African Countries, Circa 2003 179
Figure 7.6: Relationship between Share of Population with Upper
  Secondary or Higher Education and Per Capita GDP in 23 Sub-
  Saharan African Countries, Circa 2003 180
Figure 7.7: Comparison of Educational Attainment of Two Generations in
  Ghana, Mozambique, Zambia and Aggregate for 23 Sub-Saharan
  African Countries, Circa 2003 180
Figure 7.8: Share of WorkForce Employed in the Formal and Informal
  Sectors, by Highest Level of Education Attended, Circa 2003 181
Figure 7.9: Shares Working in Farm vs. Non-Farm Sectors, and in
  Public vs. Modern Private Sectors, by Education Level, Circa 2003 182

Figure 7.10: Simulation of Higher Education Enrollment Associated with 25% Unemployment among 25-34 Year Olds with Higher Education, by Per Capita GDP, in Selected Sub-Saharan African Countries   187

Maps
Map 1.1: Primary School Completion Rates in Sub-Saharan Africa, 2009   24

Acknowledgments

This report was prepared by a team led by Ramahatra Rakotomalala. The report was authored by Kirsten Majgaard and Alain Mingat. Cornelia Jesse, Francis Ndém, Meng Zhao, Juan Carlos Rodriguez, and Koffi Segniagbeto assisted with first-rate background analyses. Kiong Hock Lee helped with careful editing. Jee-Peng Tan launched the study and provided general guidance to the team.

Over the years, many people—too many to name individually—have contributed to the preparation of the education Country Status Reports for African countries, which constitute the foundation for this work. They include representatives from African ministries of education and other national agencies in the respective countries, staff and consultants from the World Bank and the Pôle de Dakar (UNESCO-BREDA) and other development agencies.

Many other individuals contributed to the study. At the concept note stage, the team benefited from guidance from Carlos Rojas, Yaw Ansu and Jean-Claude Balmes (*Agence Française de Développement*). Dung-Kim Pham and Elizabeth Ninan provided comments to an initial draft. Peer reviewers were Amit Dar, Laurent Cortese and Punam Chuhan-Pole. Linda English, Mathieu Brossard and Shwetlena Sabarwal also provided valuable comments. Christopher Thomas, Peter Materu, Cristina Santos, Maureen Lewis and Michel Welmond ensured management oversight. This report could not have been completed without the valuable contributions and support of everyone.

The Team also acknowledges the generous financial support received from the Education Program Development Fund of the Global Partnership for Education (formerly EFA FTI), a multi-donor trust fund established in 2004 to help low-income countries accelerate progress towards universal primary completion.

Acronyms and Abbreviations

AGEMAD	Amélioration de la Gestión de l'Education à Madagascar
AFTHD	Africa Technical Families Human Development
AIDS	Acquired Immune Deficiency Syndrome
ASLI	African Student Learning Index
BREDA	Regional Office for Education in Africa [of UNESCO]
CAR	Central African Republic
CCT	conditional cash transfer
CDC	Centers for Disease Control and Prevention
CDD	community-driven development
CONFEMEN	Conference of Ministers of Education of French-Speaking Countries
CR	completion rate
CSR	Country Status Report
CWIQ	Core Welfare Indicators Questionnaire
DAC	Development Assistance Committee (OECD)
DHS	Demographic and Health Survey
EFA	Education For All
FTI	Fast Track Initiative (Education For All)
GDP	gross domestic product
GER	gross enrollment rate
GIR	gross intake rate
GNI	gross national income
GPI	Gender Parity Index
HIV	Human Immunodeficiency Virus
IBRD	International Bank for Reconstruction and Development
IDA	International Development Association
LAY	latest available year
LS	lower secondary

MDG	Millennium Development Goal
MICS	Multiple Indicator Cluster Survey
MLA	Measurement of Learning Achievement
MoE	Ministry of Education
NA	not available
ODA	Overseas Development Assistance
OECD	Organization for Economic Cooperation and Development
PASEC	Program for the Analysis of Education Systems of CONFEMEN
PCR	primary completion rate
PETS	Public Expenditure Tracking Survey
PIRLS	Progress in International Reading Literacy Study
PTA	Parent-Teacher Association
PTR	pupil teacher ratio
R^2 / R-square	coefficient of determination in statistical analysis
SACMEQ	Southern Africa Consortium for Monitoring Educational Quality
SLE	school life expectancy
TVET	technical and vocational education and training
UIS	UNESCO Institute of Statistics
UNCTAD	United Nations Conference on Trade and Development
UNESCO	United Nations Educational, Scientific, and Cultural Organization
UNESCO-BREDA	UNESCO Regional Office for Education in Africa, Pôle de Dakar
UNICEF	United Nations Children's Fund
UPC	universal primary completion
US	upper secondary

Overview

As in most countries worldwide, Sub-Saharan African countries are striving to build their human capital so they can compete for jobs and investments in an increasingly globalized world. In this region—which includes the largest number of countries that have not yet attained universal primary schooling—the ambitions and aspirations of Sub-Saharan African countries and their youth far exceed this basic goal. Over the past 20 years, educational levels have risen sharply across Sub-Saharan Africa. Already hard at work to provide places in primary schools for all children, most countries of the region are also rapidly expanding access to secondary and tertiary levels of education.

Alongside this quantitative push is a growing awareness of the need to make sure that students are learning and acquiring the skills needed for life and work. Achieving education of acceptable quality is perhaps an even greater challenge than providing enough school places for all. Thus, Sub-Saharan African countries are simultaneously confronting many difficult challenges in the education sector—and much is at stake.

Policy makers need to balance conflicting objectives when crafting education policies and making spending decisions. Having access to information about choices and development paths taken by other countries in and around the region—and to data about their outcomes—can be a valuable aid. This book gives those concerned with education in Sub-Saharan Africa an analysis of the sector from a cross-country perspective, aimed at drawing lessons that individual country studies alone cannot provide. A comparative perspective is useful not only to show the range of possibilities in key education policy variables but also to learn from the best performers in the region. (Although the report covers 47 Sub-Saharan African countries whenever possible, some parts of the analysis center on the region's low-income countries—in particular, a sample of 33 low-income countries.)[1]

Drawing on the collective knowledge of country-specific education studies prepared over the past decade, the report focuses on fundamental questions such as these:

- Is everyone getting a chance at education?
- Are those given a chance actually learning?
- Is what they are learning relevant for work and life?
- Are countries investing enough in education and achieving a sound balance across levels of education?
- Are the resources well deployed and managed to ensure efficient functioning of education systems?
- How is the cross-country diversity in policies and educational outcomes useful for country-specific policy development?

Although countries in Sub-Saharan Africa are highly diverse in the many dimensions that describe an education system, these questions are pertinent for most, if not all, of the region's countries.

Is Everyone Getting a Chance at Education?

For the past decade, school enrollments in the low-income Sub-Saharan African countries have risen sharply at all levels of education. The primary gross enrollment rate (GER) grew by an average of 3.1 percentage points per year between 1999 and 2009, compared with only 0.8 percentage points per year in the 1990s in the sample of 33 low-income Sub-Saharan African countries. Enrollments in secondary and higher education are also growing rapidly, although from a smaller base.

As a result, there has been an upward shift in the relationship between school-life expectancy and per capita gross domestic product (GDP). School-life expectancy, for instance, has more than doubled between 1990 and 2009 in countries with a per capita GDP of around US$150 (in constant prices).[2] Richer countries have also experienced increases in school-life expectancy, though the gains have been more modest. Declining unit costs and more favorable demographics explain part of the gains in school-life expectancy. Increased funding for primary education in the region's low-income countries has also contributed to this positive development. Still another push may have come from the United Nations (UN) Millennium Development Goals and the 2000 World Education Forum in Dakar sponsored by the UN Educational, Scientific and Cultural Organization (UNESCO).

Low Pupil Retention Erodes Progress

Despite some encouraging developments, however, low retention levels are eroding progress, and most countries in Sub-Saharan Africa are not on track to achieve universal primary completion (UPC) by 2015. The average primary completion rate (PCR) gained 20 percentage points between 1999 and 2009 in the sample of 33 low-income Sub-Saharan African countries—an average of 2 percentage points per year. Yet, average primary completion reached only 63 percent in the sample group by 2009 (and 67 percent across the region as a whole), indicating that most of these countries are still far from UPC.

Each country's PCR reflects the combined influence of two principal factors: (a) intake into grade one and (b) retention of pupils until the end of the primary cycle. However, retention is low in most Sub-Saharan African countries because of high dropout rates, as the shape of the educational pyramid in figure O.1 illustrates.

In fact, dropping out from within a cycle of education is the dominant exit route from the education system. A high dropout rate could be an indication that the type and quality of schooling provided is inadequate or does not meet the expectations and needs of students and parents. This volume classifies Sub-Saharan African countries within four groups for a more detailed assessment of the nature of the challenges facing each country in their quest for UPC. Six countries, including Côte d'Ivoire and Niger, face the greatest challenges to attaining UPC because they must simultaneously raise both intake and retention rates.

A Third of Children Are Out of School

An estimated 35 million primary-school-age children are out of school across the sample of 33 low-income Sub-Saharan African countries. This corresponds to

Figure O.1 Sub-Saharan Africa's Educational Pyramid, ca. 2009

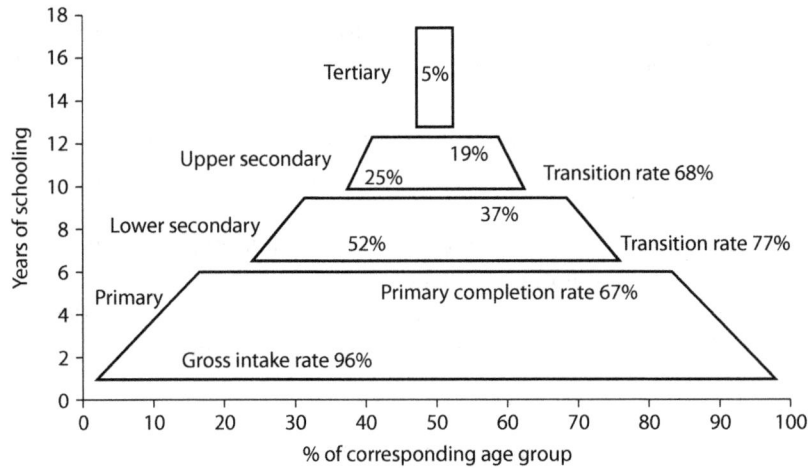

Source: Authors' illustration, based on 2006–10 UNESCO Institute for Statistics data (UIS Data Centre). Whenever recent UIS data were unavailable, data were used from Pôle de Dakar UNESCO-BREDA 2005, 2006, 2007; or from Country Status Reports (CSRs), listed in chapter references. All data from 2005 or later. For the full data set, see appendix B, table B.1.
Note: The pyramid is based on all Sub-Saharan African countries for which data are available. All figures are simple averages of country-specific data. For primary education, the gross intake rate (GIR) reflects the average of values truncated at 100. For tertiary education, the figure shows only the gross enrollment ratio (GER) because of the lack of data on dropout rates within this cycle of education.

about a third of the total primary-school-age population—ranging from 8 percent in Zimbabwe to 58 percent in the Central African Republic.

The set of policies needed to reach and keep all children in school, at least until the end of the primary cycle, is likely to vary from country to country. Also, policy prescriptions for children who have never been in school (20 million of the 35 million) differ from those for children who dropped out of school before the end of the primary cycle (15 million of the 35 million). The available empirical evidence points to the importance of policies such as these:

- Making schooling more accessible by bringing schools closer to home—including, in some settings, the use of multigrade teaching to help contain costs
- Offering a complete cycle of primary schooling to all children, even in small schools
- Reducing grade repetition, which increases the risk of students dropping out
- Increasing the proportion of female teachers to strike a better gender balance among the teaching faculty
- Reducing the school fees and other costs borne by parents, including opportunity costs.

Out-of-School Children Most Likely Rural or Poor

Living in a rural area or being poor are both strong predictors of a child being out of primary school. As educational coverage has expanded since 1990, however, the disadvantage to girls in terms of primary school participation has diminished. Geographic and income-based disparities are now much wider than gender-based disparities, as these data for children ranging in age from 9 to 11 show:

- Girls are 6 percentage points more likely to be out of school than boys.
- Rural children are 23 percentage points more likely to be out of school than urban children.
- Children from the two poorest income quintiles are 27 percentage points more likely to be out of school than children from the two richest quintiles.

The more that is known about the out-of-school children, the better equipped policy makers and practitioners will be to design and implement appropriate policy prescriptions for their respective countries. The report provides data on the number of out-of-school children in each country and on their socioeconomic characteristics.

Primary Completion Rates on the Rise

Under current trends, the average primary completion rate could reach 75 percent by 2015 in the sample of 33 low-income Sub-Saharan African countries. Further, assuming that all countries follow an accelerated trend of improvement (equal to that of the best performers), the average primary completion rate may reach 82 percent by 2015 in the low-income countries. Figure O.2 shows the two

Figure O.2 Projected Primary Completion Rates by 2015 in Low-Income Sub-Saharan African Countries

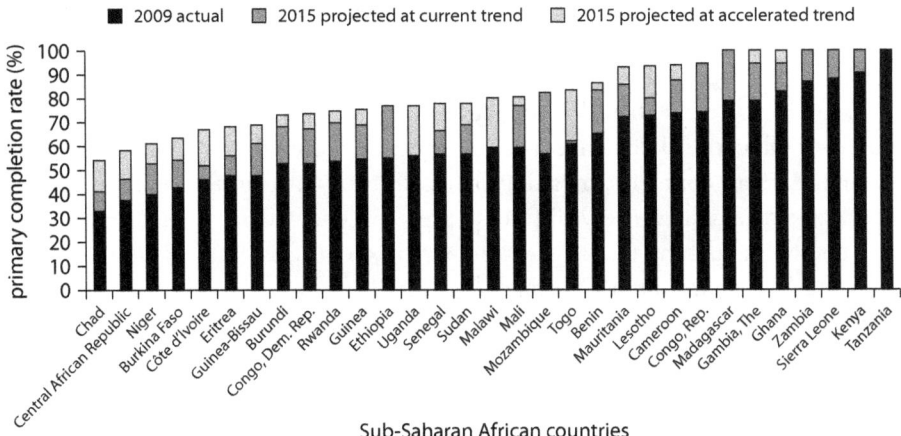

Source: Authors' calculations based on UIS Data Centre for the years shown, supplemented with data from Pôle de Dakar UNESCO-BREDA 2007 and selected CSRs. For the full data set, see appendix B, table B.2.
Note: The figure includes 31 of the 33 low-income countries in the sample; Nigeria and Zimbabwe are omitted for lack of data. The primary completion rate (PCR) is the number of students in the last grade of primary school, minus the number of repeaters, as a share of the population of official age for attending that grade.
a. The 2009 value of the PCR is shown when the 1999–2009 trend was negative (Malawi).
b. If the PCR grew more than 3.5 percentage points per year in 1999–2009, this higher growth rate is used instead of 3.5 (Ethiopia, Madagascar, Mozambique, and Tanzania).

projections of the primary completion rate by 2015 for each country in the sample except Nigeria and Zimbabwe, for which data were unavailable.

Rising PCR Increases Demand for Secondary Education

The strong increase in the primary completion rate, coupled with the region's high population growth rate, have increased pressures for countries in the region to expand secondary school coverage. Many Sub-Saharan African governments now consider lower secondary education to be part of a basic education cycle, consistent with trends elsewhere in the world. The pressure to expand secondary school coverage will continue for some years to come, but there are still relatively few initiatives to help these countries prepare for and respond to the increasing demand.

Knowing how to respond requires understanding of the scope of the challenge. Projections show that the number of primary school completers will likely more than double by 2020 compared with 2003 and that lower secondary enrollments will likely increase even more as a greater share of primary completers seek to continue their education. The expansion of secondary school coverage will, in turn, increase the demand for tertiary education.

Gender Disparities Widen at Higher Levels

Gender disparities widen as students move up the educational ladder, but there are broad differences across countries, even when taking into account different levels of coverage. On average, the regional average gender parity index in 2008 drops from 0.95 in the first grade of primary education to 0.91 at the end of the primary cycle, to 0.85 in lower secondary education, to 0.78 in upper secondary education, and finally to 0.65 in higher education.[3]

Given the cumulative nature of gender disparities, it is necessary to address the issue in the early stages of education. Gender disparities tend to be smaller wherever educational coverage is higher, but the correlation is loose across Sub-Saharan African countries, meaning that countries with similar levels of educational coverage achieve very different levels of gender equity. This report finds that countries such as Benin, Cameroon, the Central African Republic, Chad, and Guinea-Bissau—all in Central or West Africa—have the highest gender disparities in the region, even after taking their low educational coverage into account. There is, clearly, a need to focus attention on reducing the disadvantages to girls by addressing the obstacles that limit girls' school participation in these countries.

Are Those Given a Chance Actually Learning?

Primary school students in low-income Sub-Saharan African countries have, on average, learned less than half of what is expected of them. School attendance in and of itself is not sufficient to achieve the expected gains of education, such as enhanced cognitive skills and higher productivity in the workplace. Students need to be learning, but international test score data show that student learning outcomes are often poor in Sub-Saharan African countries.

This report combines test scores from three international learning assessment programs to create a comparable Africa Student Learning Index (ASLI) for the region. The average value of the index across the region's low-income countries is low—45, within a general range of 27–66—implying that students absorb and comprehend only 45 percent of the curriculum at the time of testing (typically during fourth or fifth grade). Across the region, richer countries perform better, but the average ASLI score for the middle-income Sub-Saharan African countries[4] of 54 percent is still lower than that of most other countries that have participated in international student learning assessments.

Only 75 Percent Can Read after Six Years of School

Likewise, across the region, only three out of four adults who completed six years of schooling can read. In the best-performing countries, almost everyone reads after completing a six-year cycle. However, there are broad differences in the number of years of schooling needed to provide children with lifelong literacy skills, as shown in figure O.3. Countries that perform at the lower end of the range of this indicator would probably be better off improving student learning in the first six years of schooling before they lengthen the basic cycle.

Figure O.3 Correlation of Reading Ability and Length of Schooling, Selected Sub-Saharan African Countries

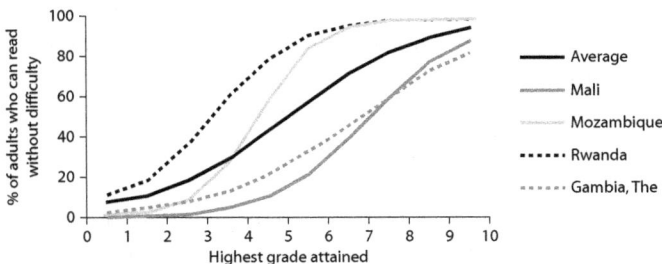

Source: Authors' construction based on 2000–05 household survey data, listed by country in appendix J, table J.1.
Note: The "average" line designates the average reading-schooling correlation among 32 Sub-Saharan African countries.

More Spending Is Not Sufficient to Boost Learning Outcomes

There is no simple way of improving learning outcomes; in particular, just spending more is not sufficient. Raising learning outcomes is turning out to be more difficult than merely providing school places.

In particular, there is no evidence that more resources result, on the average, in more learning in Sub-Saharan African countries: a cross-country analysis of the correlation between per-student spending in primary schools and their ASLI scores finds no relationship between the two. This finding is consistent with numerous other studies of both developed and developing countries.

What Factors Do Improve Learning?

Although per-student spending seems to bear little relationship to learning, other factors do matter. Vast differences in learning outcomes remain after controlling for observable school inputs and differences in student background, implying that what goes on in classrooms matters more than the mere provision of more school inputs.

Educational resources are clearly necessary but not sufficient to produce higher levels of student learning. Under the right conditions, increasing inputs that are in scarce supply can yield a high marginal return in terms of student learning, but some best practice policies in the following areas can improve student learning:

- *Preschool education* appears to be important for educational attainment and learning later in life, and community-based provision can be an option for expanding preschool coverage at a low cost.
- *School infrastructure* can affect student learning but, in view of the high cost of infrastructure, a fairly basic-quality infrastructure is probably sufficient in most low-income countries.
- *Textbooks* are among the most cost-effective inputs to student learning. Recent evidence suggests that a student-textbook ratio of 1 to 1 works well, and students from poor families need free textbooks.
- *Class-size reduction* does not, contrary to a priori expectations, lead to better learning outcomes unless classes are excessively large (more than 60 students)

and should therefore probably not be a priority in most of the region's low-income countries.
- *Single-shift teaching* with larger class sizes is probably better for learning than multishift teaching, which tends to reduce instructional time while often not saving much money.
- *Multigrade classes* can be beneficial for educational attainment and learning, especially in areas with low population densities, but they must be implemented with care.
- *Community involvement and increased accountability* can help raise attendance and thereby effective instructional time, which has been shown to be crucial for student learning.
- *In-service teacher education programs* may lead to better student learning than longer and more costly preservice training programs.
- *Appropriate teacher salaries*, set at suitable levels for local labor market conditions, coupled with performance incentives, can also contribute to better student learning.

Teacher Presence and Effectiveness Are Paramount

Most important, teachers must be present at work and make the best use of their skills and the resources available to them for effective learning to take place. Current high rates of teacher absenteeism represent a serious problem that calls upon governments and donors to place greater emphasis on accountability structures to ensure that children are being taught well.

The first set of tools available to promote accountability includes interventions that address community control or involvement in school monitoring and management. The second category consists of performance-based incentives that hold teachers and school principals accountable for their students' learning. These two are not mutually exclusive and may be combined in different ways. Although evidence on the effectiveness of specific interventions is still scarce, this should not deter policy makers from experimenting with different policy instruments and thus adding to the pool of knowledge about the most cost-effective ways to improve student learning.

Is What They Are Learning Relevant for Work and Life?

Despite weak learning outcomes, empirical evidence suggests that education, particularly of girls, is correlated with significant health and social benefits for future generations, as table O.1 shows.

More Education Associated with Desired Social Outcomes

Analysis, based on household surveys, of the relationship between educational attainment and various social outcomes finds that additional years of education are positively (or negatively, in the case of child mortality and other metrics) associated with desired social outcomes.

Table O.1 Social Outcomes by Average Education Level in Sub-Saharan African Countries, ca. 2003

	Highest grade attained[a]	
	No formal education	Completed upper secondary education
Childbearing		
Age at first birth (years)	18.3	20.1
Months between consecutive births	36.9	40.2
Number of live births by approx. age 30	3.3	2.2
Use of any contraceptive method (%)	27.9	55.2
Prenatal health		
Number of prenatal consultations	3.2	5.3
Number of tetanus vaccines during pregnancy	1.2	1.6
Women getting vitamin A in pregnancy (%)	12.5	19.4
Delivery assisted by skilled personnel (%)	24.9	50.9
Child health and development		
Children sleep under a bed net (%)	14.4	30.2
Children fully vaccinated by age 2 (%)	24.7	39.7
Under-5 mortality rate (per thousand)	159.5	77.2
Children enrolled in school (%)	68.0	95.5
Poverty, HIV/AIDS, and use of media		
Risk of being poor (%)	45.6	13.3
Knowledge about HIV/AIDS (index)	4.9	7.5
Use of radio (%)	43.3	76.0
Use of television (%)	4.9	35.6
Use of newspapers (%)	0.7	38.3

Source: Authors' construction based on household survey data for up to 36 Sub-Saharan African countries, listed in appendix J, table J.1.

a. In the childbearing and prenatal health categories, "highest grade attained" refers to the grade attained by the woman herself. For child health and development, it refers to educational attainment of the child's mother; for poverty and so on, it refers to the educational attainment of the head of household.

For example, women with higher educational attainment are more likely to seek and receive prenatal care during pregnancy, and their children are more likely to receive childhood immunizations and survive beyond their fifth birthdays. Although not a proof of causality, these results suggest that education provides a good foundation for improving family health and welfare.

Each additional year spent in school, whether in primary or secondary school, appears to be associated with more or less the same improvement in social outcomes. Because a year in primary school costs less than a year in secondary school but the two contribute the same improvement in social outcomes, it follows that primary education in particular can be a cost-effective means of achieving desired social outcomes.

Effects of Education on the Labor Market Are Less Apparent
In terms of labor market outcomes, the rise in educational attainment of the labor force in the region appears to have had little impact on average labor productivity. The weighted average labor productivity for Sub-Saharan Africa, across all sectors, has remained at practically the same level since 1985. At the same time, the average level of schooling has been increasing across the region. That rising education has had such little impact suggests poor use of human capital.

Rapid expansion of higher education in recent years, coupled with only moderate growth in suitable employment opportunities, have resulted in considerable unemployment among graduates in low-income Sub-Saharan African countries. Most of these countries are dualistic economies with small, slow-growing formal or modern sectors—traditionally the employer of first resort among highly skilled workers. Currently, almost 80 percent of workers who attended higher education are working in the modern sector, but young workers with similar educational profiles are now less likely to find formal sector jobs than in the past. The relatively faster-growing informal sector, on the other hand, cannot effectively absorb the rapidly growing numbers of graduates from higher education or other levels of postbasic education.

Unemployment Suggests Mismatch between Education and Needed Skills
Beyond a possible quantitative mismatch, there may be other, more fundamental reasons for the high rates of unemployment among young workers with postbasic education. Shortages of high-skilled workers within certain fields of study—medicine and engineering, for example—may coexist with high unemployment rates in other fields because the composition of the output of postbasic educational institutions by specialization does not reflect the demands of the labor markets.

Beyond the mismatch between supply and demand, the region's rapid increase in tertiary-level enrollment, coupled with the drop in per-student spending, has eroded learning conditions over time; thus, students graduate without the required marketable skills. If most recent graduates cannot find gainful employment or jobs that match their skills, it may be an indication that the education system needs some form of rebalancing such as shifting its emphasis on quantity to an emphasis on quality. Further expansion of higher education may need to be more selective to ensure a better match with labor market needs and to avoid further downward pressure on per-student spending.

Education Policy Is Important to Growth and Job Creation
The above also underscores the importance of policies that can foster economic growth and create jobs, especially well-paid jobs, though these policies are largely beyond the control of the ministries of education. These recommended education policies emerge from the analysis:

- Collection and dissemination of relevant labor market information may help reduce some labor market mismatches.
- Alignment of higher education programs with employers' needs may help to produce more employable students whose expectations match available job opportunities.
- Strategic use of public funding may improve postprimary education by focusing more on high-quality inputs and by directing spending (a) to areas where there are shortages of skilled workers or (b) into fields of specialization that can be potential drivers of economic growth, such as in science and technology.

Are Countries Investing Enough in Education and Achieving a Sound Balance across Levels of Education?

The simultaneous expansion of enrollments at all three levels of education translates into steep financial challenges for most, if not all, Sub-Saharan African countries. Low-income Sub-Saharan African countries—despite their low tax base—are already spending more than 4 percent of their GDP on education on average, a level comparable to that of low-income countries in other parts of the world. During the growth years of the past decade, many Sub-Saharan African countries experienced strong growth in their public revenues as a result of strong macroeconomic growth combined with better tax collection and larger aid flows. In recent years, however, these salutary trends may have slowed or reversed because of the global economic downturn.

Regional Education Funding Is High, but Some Countries Lag Behind

This report finds that low-income Sub-Saharan African countries spend 4.3 percent of GDP on education—a level comparable with low-income countries in other regions—but they are outspent by middle-income Sub-Saharan African countries, which spend as much as 5.7 percent of their GDP on education on average, as well as by Organisation for Economic Co-operation and Development (OECD) countries, which spend an average of 5.5 percent.

Because most low-income Sub-Saharan African countries have a low tax base given the small size of their formal sectors, they spend a higher proportion on education of their total government budgets (17 percent) than virtually any other country group. In particular, they spend a higher proportion of their budgets on education than either low-income countries elsewhere in the world (14 percent) or high-income OECD countries (12 percent).

Overall, this already high allocation somewhat limits the scope for further increases in education funding; in some Sub-Saharan African countries, however, current allocations to education are still modest, as shown in figure O.4, and there is still ample scope to allocate more public revenues to the sector. Figure O.4 also shows a wide diversity in public spending choices, with public spending on education (as a percentage of GDP) varying from 0.6 percent in Equatorial

Figure O.4 Public Spending on Education in Sub-Saharan African Countries (Capital and Recurrent), ca. 2005

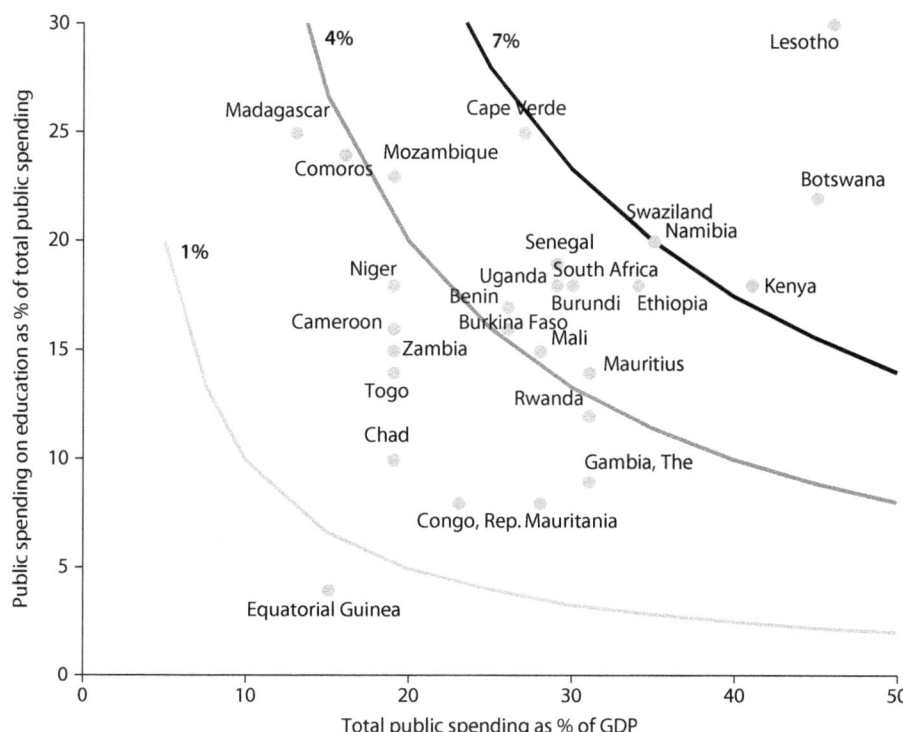

Source: Author's construction, based on education spending data from UIS Data Centre. For full data set, see appendix E, table E.1.
Note: GDP = gross domestic product. The three curved lines show the data points consistent with a fixed level of public spending on education corresponding to 1 percent, 4 percent, and 7 percent of GDP, respectively. For lack of expenditure data, the figure does not include the Democratic Republic of Congo, Gabon, Guinea-Bissau, Liberia, Nigeria, São Tomé and Príncipe, the Seychelles, Somalia, Sudan, Tanzania, and Zimbabwe.

Guinea to 13.4 percent in Lesotho. These variations are substantial and are larger than those observed in other regions of the world.

Education Allocations Have Implications for Key Goals

This book presents empirical evidence showing that countries that use their education budgets and resources efficiently can, for instance, achieve higher levels of educational coverage and longer school-life expectancy. Also, within a given budget, countries with very high average teacher salaries are less able to provide acceptable pupil-teacher ratios than countries with lower average teacher salaries, as figure O.5 shows. Spending decisions are clearly interrelated.

High Per-Student Spending at the Secondary Level Limits Educational Coverage

As an increasing number of the low-income Sub-Saharan African countries approach universal primary education at the same time that secondary education

Figure O.5 Tradeoff between Teacher Salary and Pupil-Teacher Ratio at Primary Level in Selected Sub-Saharan African Countries, ca. 2003

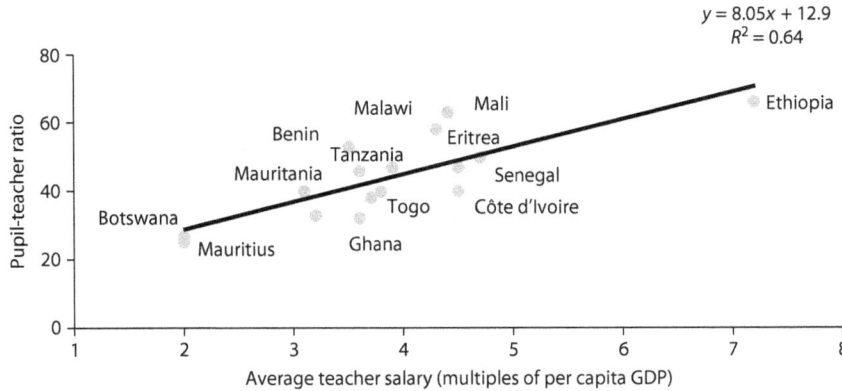

Source: Authors' construction based on data from CSRs and other country studies.
Note: pc = per capita, GDP = gross domestic product. The chart displays data for 16 countries, selected because they have similar levels of per-student spending relative to GDP per capita.

enrollments are growing, these countries will need to allocate increasingly larger shares of their education budgets to the secondary cycle. The extent of this shift will, however, depend on their individual policy choices. In this context, it is worth noting that middle-income countries outside the Sub-Saharan African region still allocate most of their education budgets to primary education. This may be explained, in part, by their relatively lower levels of per-student spending in secondary education.

Sub-Saharan African countries spend more on each student in postbasic education, relative to per capita GDP, than most other developing nations. Primary education spending per student in the region is quite similar to the levels found in other developing countries. In secondary and higher education, however, Sub-Saharan African countries generally have much higher levels of per-student spending relative to per capita GDP than other developing countries.

Unless the high levels of per-student spending, particularly among the middle-income Sub-Saharan African countries, are reduced as enrollment expands, they effectively limit the possibilities for expanding coverage of postbasic education. Options for cutting per-student spending may include taking advantage of economies of scale, tapping into students' willingness to pay, and developing new models of service delivery that may lower per-student cost, including new models for delivery to students in rural areas where most of the unserved population reside.

Inequities Have Decreased, but Poor Families Are Still Burdened

Inequalities in the distribution of public education spending have diminished over time, but they are higher in the region's low-income countries than in the middle-income countries. Although low-income Sub-Saharan African countries still suffer from fairly large inequities in the distribution of public education spending, these inequalities have diminished significantly over the past 30 years. The 10 percent most educated in the population received 63 percent of the resources in 1975, 56 percent in 1992, and 43 percent in 2003. This apparent decline in structural disparities is a result of the significant expansion in enrollments during the period coupled with the leveling out of per-student spending across educational levels as coverage expanded.

Household spending on primary education is still high. Although most countries have formally abolished primary school fees, the ratio of household spending to government spending is nearly as high in primary education (37 percent) as in the education sector as a whole (42 percent). When school fees are abolished, they tend to be replaced by other forms of user charges, particularly where schools were not fully compensated for the loss of revenue. Paying for community teachers where the public supply is inadequate, for instance, places a heavy burden on poor families in many countries in the region. When making spending allocations, policy makers should carefully consider the impact on households, particularly on poor families.

Are the Resources Well Deployed and Managed to Ensure Efficient Functioning of Education Systems?

There are large disparities in the allocation of resources across schools within countries. For example, per-student spending varies widely across primary schools in Burundi and Malawi, as figure O.6 illustrates. This pattern is common across the region. The uneven pattern of per-student spending reflects that, at the school level, there is often a weak relationship between number of teachers and number of students, a result of poor practices regarding teacher deployment.

Sub-Saharan African Countries Show Wide Disparities in Teacher Allocation

Education Country Status Reports (CSRs, listed in chapter references) have systematically documented large degrees of randomness in the allocation of teachers to primary schools across Sub-Saharan African countries. Table O.2 shows these large differences clearly.

Disparities in schooling conditions are not, however, confined to the allocation of teachers. The degree of randomness in the distribution of classrooms, textbooks, and school furniture is sometimes higher than that of the distribution of teachers. Fortunately, disparity in teacher allocation can be reduced rapidly through improved resource management practices, as in the case of Madagascar, which achieved a significant reduction in this indicator over the course of a single school year.

How Is Cross-Country Diversity in Policies and Educational Outcomes Useful for Country-Specific Policy Development?

This book brings together valuable, comparable cross-country data about education systems in the Sub-Saharan African region. Since 1999, more than 40 CSRs on education have been completed for more than 25 Sub-Saharan African

Figure O.6 Number of Schools by Per-Student Spending, Burundi and Malawi, ca. 2004

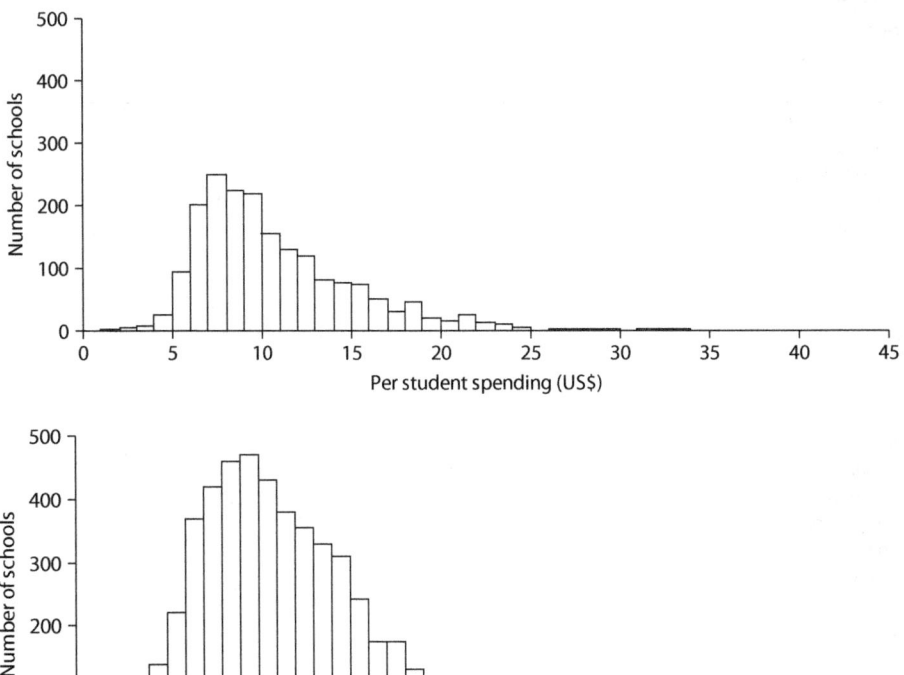

Source: Authors' analysis of Malawi School Census 2003/04 and Burundi School Census 2004/05.

countries (as some countries have been the subject of more than one report).[5] Often prepared by World Bank teams with the support of the countries' respective ministries of education and the Pôle de Dakar (UNESCO-BREDA), the CSRs follow a similar structure, thus enabling cross-country comparisons of their results. The collection of CSRs therefore constitutes a valuable knowledge asset for the Sub-Saharan African region that has been explored for this volume. Other sources of data used in the book include education statistics from the UNESCO Institute for Statistics (UIS Data Centre); household and labor market surveys (listed in appendix J, tables J.1 and J.2); and international student learning assessments, including the Program for the Analysis of Education Systems of CONFEMEN (PASEC) and Southern Africa Consortium for Monitoring Educational Quality (SACMEQ).

The findings and data presented in this volume can help Sub-Saharan African countries to situate themselves using a regional comparative perspective and can encourage those countries to get ideas and learn from other countries' experiences. It finds a large variability in policies and educational outcomes across the 47 Sub-Saharan African countries, which are not only at different stages of education system

Table O.2 Randomness in Teacher Allocation to Primary Schools, Selected Sub-Saharan African Countries, 2000–08

percent

	Degree of randomness [$1-R^2$]
São Tomé and Príncipe	3
Guinea	9
Mozambique	15
Namibia	15
Guinea-Bissau	16
Madagascar	19
Niger	19
Senegal	19
Mauritania	20
Zambia	20
Rwanda	21
Gabon	26
Mali	27
Burkina Faso	28
Ethiopia	29
Côte d'Ivoire	33
Chad	34
Malawi	34
Uganda	34
Congo, Rep.	38
Cameroon	45
Central African Republic	46
Burundi	50
Togo	53
Benin	54
Simple average	28.3

Sources: Authors' compilation from indicated countries' CSRs, listed in chapter references.

development but also widely different in their responses to conflicting objectives, such as when trading off educational coverage with per-student spending.

Although countries ultimately must make their own policy choices and decide what works best in their particular circumstances, Sub-Saharan African countries can benefit from learning about the experiences of other countries that are faced with, or have gone through, similar development paths. Given the large number of countries included in the analysis, the book finds that Sub-Saharan African countries have more choices and more room for maneuver than would appear if attention were focused on only one or a few country experiences.[6]

Countries can make better choices when understanding the breadth of policy choices available to them. They are well advised, however, to evaluate the applicability of policy options to their contexts and to pilot and evaluate the results for performance and subsequent improvement.

Notes

1. The sample of 33 low-income countries (selected in Bruns, Mingat, and Rakotomalala 2003) comprises the Sub-Saharan African countries eligible for lending from the World

Bank Group's International Development Agency (IDA) except those with very small populations (Cape Verde, the Comoros, and São Tomé and Príncipe) or highly incomplete data (Angola, Liberia, and Somalia). (The IDA threshold changes every year, as do the countries' gross national incomes [GNI] per capita, so there may be small changes from year to year in this group.) Based on a 2006 GNI per capita of less than US$1,065, the 33 countries in the sample are Benin, Burkina Faso, Burundi, Cameroon, the Central African Republic, Chad, the Democratic Republic of Congo, the Republic of Congo, Côte d'Ivoire, Eritrea, Ethiopia, The Gambia, Ghana, Guinea, Guinea-Bissau, Kenya, Lesotho, Madagascar, Malawi, Mali, Mauritania, Mozambique, Niger, Nigeria, Rwanda, Senegal, Sierra Leone, Sudan, Tanzania, Togo, Uganda, Zambia, and Zimbabwe.

2. "School-life expectancy" is the number of years a child of school entrance age is expected to spend in school, from primary to tertiary levels, including years spent on repetition. It is the sum of the age-specific enrollment rates for the levels specified (definition adapted from the UNESCO Institute for Statistics Glossary, http://glossary.uis.unesco.org/glossary).

3. The gender parity index is calculated as follows: (a) in the first grade of primary education, as the gross intake rate (GIR) of females to males; (b) at the end of the primary cycle, as the primary completion rate (PCR) of females to males; and (c) in the secondary and tertiary cycles, as the gross enrollment rate (GER) of females to males.

4. "Middle-income" Sub-Saharan countries (whose 2006 GNI per capita exceeded US$1,065) include Botswana, Equatorial Guinea, Gabon, Mauritius, Namibia, the Seychelles, South Africa, and Swaziland.

5. A list of the Country Status Reports completed to date is provided in the reference list.

6. The large variability across Sub-Saharan African countries also provides for a rich cross-country data set that is used throughout the book to search for links between policies and desirable educational outcomes.

References

Bruns, B., A. Mingat, and R. Rakotomalala. 2003. *Achieving Universal Primary Education by 2015: A Chance for Every Child*. Washington, DC: World Bank.

Pôle de Dakar UNESCO-BREDA (United Nations Educational, Scientific and Cultural Organization, Regional Office for Education in Africa). 2005. "Education for All in Africa: Paving the Way for Action." Dakar+5 Report, Pôle de Dakar UNESCO-BREDA, Dakar.

———. 2006. "Education for All in Africa: Sub-regional Statistics and Analysis." Dakar+6 Report, Pôle de Dakar UNESCO-BREDA, Dakar.

———. 2007. "Education for All in Africa: Top Priority for Integrated Sector-Wide Policies." Dakar+7 Report, Pôle de Dakar UNESCO-BREDA, Dakar.

UIS (United Nations Educational, Scientific and Cultural Organization, Institute for Statistics) Data Centre (database). UIS, Montreal. http://stats.uis.unesco.org.

Country Status Reports

The titles listed below are education Country Status Reports (CSRs)—products of collaboration among national teams of government representatives and staff from the World

Bank and other development partners, particularly the Pôle de Dakar UNESCO-BREDA. In French, this series is known as *Rapports d'état des systèmes éducatifs nationaux* (RESEN). Most of the reports can be downloaded at http://www.worldbank.org/afr/education.

Das, J., S. Dercon, J. Habyarimana, and P. Krishnan. 2004. "Public and Private Funding of Basic Education in Zambia: Implications of Budgetary Allocations for Service Delivery." Africa Region Human Development Working Paper 62, World Bank, Washington, DC.

Kamano, P. J., R. Rakotomalala, J.-M. Bernard, G. Husson, and N. Reuge. 2010. *Les défis du système éducatif Burkinabé en appui à la croissance économique*. Africa Human Development Series, Africa Region Human Development Working Paper 196. Washington, DC: World Bank.

Marope, M. Toka. 2005. "Namibia: Human Capital and Knowledge Development with Equity." Africa Region Human Development Working Paper 84, World Bank, Washington, DC.

Pôle de Dakar UNESCO-BREDA (United Nations Educational, Scientific and Cultural Organization, Regional Office for Education in Africa). 2006. "Elements d'analyse du secteur éducatif au Togo." Country Status Report, Pôle de Dakar UNESCO-BREDA, Dakar.

World Bank. 2000a. "Contraintes et espaces de liberté pour le développement en quantité et en qualité de l'education au Niger." Country Status Report, World Bank, Washington, DC.

———. 2000b. "Coûts, financement et fonctionnement du système éducatif du Burkina Faso: Contraintes et espaces pour la politique éducative." Country Status Report, World Bank, Washington, DC.

———. 2001a. "Education and Training in Madagascar: Towards a Policy Agenda for Economic Growth and Poverty Reduction." Africa Region Human Development Working Paper 12, World Bank, Washington, DC.

———. 2001b. "Le système éducatif Mauretanien: Eléments d'analyse pour instruire des politiques nouvelles." Africa Region Human Development Working Paper 15, World Bank, Washington, DC.

———. 2002. "Le système éducatif Béninois: Performance et espaces d'amélioration pour la politique éducative." Africa Region Human Development Working Paper 19, World Bank, Washington, DC.

———. 2003a. "Cost and Financing of Education: Opportunities and Obstacles for Expanding and Improving Education in Mozambique." Africa Region Human Development Working Paper 37, World Bank, Washington, DC.

———. 2003b. *Education in Rwanda: Rebalancing Resources to Accelerate Post-Conflict Development and Poverty Reduction*. Country Study Series. Washington, DC: World Bank.

———. 2003c. "Rapport d'état du système éducatif national Camerounais: Elèments de diagnostic pour la politique éducative dans le contexte de l'EPT et du DSRP." Country Status Report, World Bank, Washington, DC.

———. 2003d. "Le système éducatif Togolais: Eléments d'analyse pour une revitalisation." Africa Region Human Development Working Paper 35, World Bank, Washington, DC.

———. 2004a. "Cost, Financing and School Effectiveness of Education in Malawi: A Future of Limited Choices and Endless Opportunities." Africa Region Human Development Working Paper 78, World Bank, Washington, DC.

———. 2004b. "La dynamique des scolarisations au Niger: Evaluation pour une développement durable." Africa Region Human Development Working Paper 40, World Bank, Washington, DC.

———. 2004c. "School Education in Nigeria: Preparing for Universal Basic Education." Africa Region Human Development Working Paper 53, World Bank, Washington, DC.

———. 2004d. "Strengthening the Foundation of Education and Training in Kenya: Opportunities and Challenges in Primary and General Secondary Education." Country Status Report, World Bank, Washington, DC.

———. 2005a. *Education in Ethiopia: Strengthening the Foundation for Sustainable Progress.* Country Study Series. Washington, DC: World Bank.

———. 2005b. "Primary and Secondary Education in Lesotho: A Country Status Report for Education." Africa Region Human Development Working Paper 101, World Bank, Washington, DC.

———. 2005c. "Rapport d'état du système éducatif Ivoirien: Eléments d'analyse pour instruire une politique éducative nouvelle dans le contexte de l'EPT et du PRSP." Africa Region Human Development Working Paper 80, World Bank, Washington, DC.

———. 2005d. "Le système éducatif Guinéen: Diagnostic et perspectives pour la politique éducative dans le contexte de contraintes macro-économiques fortes et de réduction de la pauvreté." Africa Region Human Development Working Paper 90, World Bank, Washington, DC.

———. 2005e. "Le système éducatif de la République Démocratique du Congo: Priorités et alternatives." Africa Region Human Development Working Paper 68, World Bank, Washington, DC.

———. 2006a. "Mauritania: rapport d'état sur le système éducatif national (RESEN)— Elements de diagnostic pour l'atteinte des objectifs du millenaire et la réduction de la pauvreté." Unpublished Country Status Report, World Bank, Washington, DC.

———. 2006b. "Swaziland: Achieving Education for All; Challenges and Policy Directions." Africa Region Working Paper 109, World Bank, Washington, DC.

———. 2007a. *L'éducation au Mali: Diagnostic pour le renouvellement de la politique éducative en vue d'atteindre les objectifs du millénaire.* Africa Human Development Series. Washington, DC: World Bank.

———. 2007b. *Education in Sierra Leone: Present Challenges, Future Opportunities.* Africa Human Development Series. Washington, DC: World Bank.

———. 2007c. *Le système éducatif Burundais: Diagnostic et perspectives pour une nouvelle politique éducative dans le contexte de l'éducation primaire gratuite pour tous.* Africa Human Development Series, World Bank Working Paper 109. Washington, DC: World Bank.

———. 2007d. *Le système éducatif Tchadien: Eléments de diagnostic pour une politique éducative nouvelle et une meilleure efficacité de la dépense publique.* Africa Human Development Series, World Bank Working Paper 110. Washington, DC: World Bank.

———. 2008a. "Eléments de diagnostic du système éducatif Malagasy: Le besoin d'une politique éducative nouvelle pour l'atteinte des objectifs du millénaire et de la réduction de la pauvreté." Unpublished Country Status Report, World Bank, Washington, DC.

———. 2008b. *Le système éducatif Centrafricain: Contraintes et marges de manœuvre pour la reconstruction du système éducatif dans la perspective de la réduction de la pauvreté.*

Africa Human Development Series, World Bank Working Paper 144. Washington, DC: World Bank.

———. 2009. *Le système éducatif Béninois: Analyse sectorielle pour une politique éducative plus equilibrée et plus efficace*. Africa Human Development Series, World Bank Working Paper 165. Washington, DC: World Bank.

———. 2010a. "Angola Education Policy Note: Quality Education for All." Unpublished Country Status Report, World Bank, Washington, DC.

———. 2010b. *The Education System in Malawi*. Working Paper 182. Washington, DC: World Bank.

———. 2010c. *The Education System in Swaziland: Training and Skills Development for Shared Growth and Competitiveness*. Africa Human Development Series, World Bank Working Paper 188. Washington, DC: World Bank.

———. 2010d. "Out of the Ashes: Learning Lessons from the Past to Guide Education Recovery in Liberia." Country Status Report, World Bank, Washington, DC.

———. 2010e. *Le système éducatif Congolais: Diagnostic pour une revitalisation dans un contexte macroéconomique plus favorable*. Africa Human Development Series, World Bank Working Paper 183. Washington, DC: World Bank.

———. 2010f. *Le système éducatif Malien: Analyse sectorielle pour une amélioration de la qualité et de l'efficacité du système*. Africa Human Development Series, World Bank Working Paper 198. Washington, DC: World Bank.

———. 2011a. "Education in Ghana: Improving Equity, Efficiency, and Accountability of Education Service Delivery." Country Status Report, World Bank, Washington, DC.

———. 2011b. "The Gambia Education Country Status Report." World Bank, Washington, DC.

———. 2011c. "Rwanda Education Country Status Report: Toward Quality Enhancement and Achievement of Universal Nine Year Basic Education; An Education System in Transition, a Nation in Transition." Education Sector Review, World Bank, Washington, DC.

———. 2011d. *The Status of the Education Sector in Sudan*. Africa Human Development Series. Washington, DC: World Bank.

———. 2011e. "Le système éducatif de la Côte d'Ivoire: Comprendre les forces et les faiblesses du système pour identifier les bases d'une politiqe nouvelle et ambitieuse." Country Status Report, World Bank, Washington, DC.

———. 2012. "Education in South Sudan: Status and Challenges for a New System." Country Status Report, World Bank, Washington, DC.

CHAPTER 1

Coverage of Education and Prospects for Expansion

Over the past 15 years, the countries of Sub-Saharan Africa have achieved considerable progress in expanding educational coverage, particularly in basic education. Yet many of them have still not attained universal primary school completion—a Millennium Development Goal (MDG) prioritized by nearly all governments with support from their donor partners—and most lag behind other low-income countries in enrollments at the secondary and tertiary levels.

This chapter takes stock of the current status of educational coverage in Sub-Saharan Africa and its diversity across countries by

- Documenting the pattern of recent growth
- Analyzing the relation between coverage and country income
- Evaluating the prospects for and challenges of attaining universal primary school completion
- Examining the scale of the concomitant challenges at subsequent levels, particularly in secondary education
- Reflecting on the priorities for policy development in light of the quantitative dimensions of the emerging educational landscape.

Overview of the Pattern of Coverage

The snapshot presented below relies mainly on administrative data on enrollments collected from school censuses that are supplied to and subsequently published by the United Nations Educational, Scientific, and Cultural Organization (UNESCO) Institute for Statistics (UIS).[1] For a few countries, the published data are adjusted to take account of differences across countries in the structure of their education systems.[2]

Figure 1.1 Sub-Saharan Africa's Educational Pyramid, ca. 2009

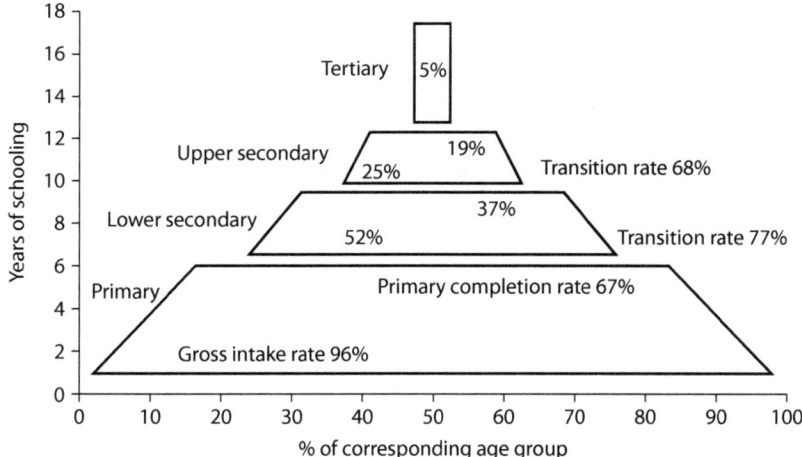

Source: Author's illustration, based on 2006–10 UNESCO Institute for Statistics data (UIS Data Centre). Whenever recent UIS data were unavailable, data from Pôle de Dakar UNESCO-BREDA 2005, 2006, 2007; or from Country Status Reports (CSRs), listed in chapter references. All data are from 2005 or later. For the full data set, see appendix B, table B.1.
Note: The pyramid is based on all Sub-Saharan African countries for which data are available. All figures are simple averages of country-specific data. For primary education, the gross intake rate (GIR) reflects the average of values truncated at 100. For tertiary education, the figure shows only the gross enrollment ratio (GER) because of the lack of data on dropout rates within this cycle of education.

The educational pyramid for Sub-Saharan Africa, shown in figure 1.1, has a wide base but narrows dramatically after grade one.[3] The gross intake rate (GIR) in grade one averages 96 percent, implying that most children in the region do have the opportunity to start primary schooling. But a large number of the entrants leave the system in subsequent grades, leading to completion rates that average only 67 percent at the end of the primary cycle, 37 percent at the end of the lower secondary cycle, and 19 percent at the end of the upper secondary cycle. The gross enrollment ratio (GER) averages 26 percent at the preprimary level and 5 percent at the tertiary level.

Weak Student Retention Warrants Attention

As the pyramid shows, dropping out within a cycle of education is the dominant route of exit from primary and secondary education in most African countries.[4] Of the 44 percentage point loss in enrollment between grade one and the starting grade in lower secondary education, 29 points (or nearly two-thirds) are associated with dropping out in primary school, while the remaining 15 points are lost in the transition between the two cycles of schooling. And of the 33 percentage point loss in enrollment between the starting grade in lower secondary education and the final grade in upper secondary education, 21 points (or 64 percent) relate to dropping out within either of the two cycles, and only 12 points from the loss in the transition between the two cycles.

The dominance of within-cycle exits in Sub-Saharan African countries contrasts sharply with the pattern in more mature education systems such as those of wealthier countries, where entrants to a cycle of schooling typically persist to the end of the cycle so that exits from the system are concentrated between cycles through some formalized mechanism (for example, end-of-cycle examinations that may be used as a basis for selection for the next cycle).

The weak retention of students in primary and secondary education warrants close attention in most Sub-Saharan African countries. Addressing it will require, as a first step, an understanding of its possible causes; this task is attempted in subsequent chapters. Suffice it to say here that the policies that have helped to boost enrollments so effectively in the past—among them building more schools, hiring more teachers, and abolishing school fees—are unlikely to be sufficient to improve retention. Progress on this front is likely to require additional measures to relieve demand-side constraints and to improve the quality of services and learning outcomes, so as to convince parents and their children that remaining in the system would yield enough longer-run benefits to justify the costs involved.

Sub-Saharan African Education Coverage Trails Other World Regions

Table 1.1 shows regional averages for low-income countries in four regions outside of Sub-Saharan Africa. Europe and Central Asia and Latin America and Caribbean countries are closest to achieving universal primary school completion, with completion rates at or close to 100 percent in 2009, compared with 86 percent in East Asia and Pacific, 86 percent in South Asia, and 63 percent in Sub-Saharan Africa.

As the level of education rises, the gaps between Sub-Saharan African countries and the other four regions widen, reaching their widest in tertiary education where Sub-Saharan Africa's average coverage, measured in enrollments per 100,000 inhabitants,[5] is far below that of low-income countries in any other region.

Table 1.1 Education Coverage in Low-Income Countries, by World Region, ca. 2009

	Median GDP per capita in country sample	Preprimary	Primary			Lower secondary	Upper secondary	Higher
	(Current US$)	GER (%)	GIR (%)	PCR (%)		GER (%)	GER (%)	(Students per 100,000 pop.)
East Asia and Pacific	1,257	33	114	86		76	52	2,140
Europe and Central Asia	1,982	33	100	100		97	91	3,072
Latin America and the Caribbean	1,960	73	114	99		103	74	3,317
South Asia	1,058	53	106	86		75	30	903
Sub-Saharan Africa	508	15	119	63		45	21	450

Source: Authors' calculations based on UIS data (UIS Data Centre).
Note: GER = gross enrollment ratio, GIR = gross intake rate, PCR = primary completion rate, GDP = gross domestic product. To increase sample size, the GER is used rather than the intake and completion rates to compare coverage in secondary education. "Low-income" countries are those eligible for lending from the World Bank's International Development Association (IDA); see appendix A, table A.1.

Primary Education across Sub-Saharan African Countries

Primary school completion rates range widely across Sub-Saharan African countries—from 33 percent in Chad to more than 95 percent in Botswana, the Seychelles, and Tanzania. The latter three countries have attained or are close to universal primary completion (UPC). The remaining countries in our sample fall into three groups:

- Eleven countries are within striking distance of the goal of UPC, with rates of 80–95 percent.
- Nine countries are reasonably close to the goal, with rates of 60–79 percent.
- Twenty-one countries are still a long way off, with rates below 60 percent.

Map 1.1 color-codes the countries according to their UPC rates, with the darker shades indicating closer proximity to UPC.

Map 1.1 Primary School Completion Rates in Sub-Saharan Africa, 2009

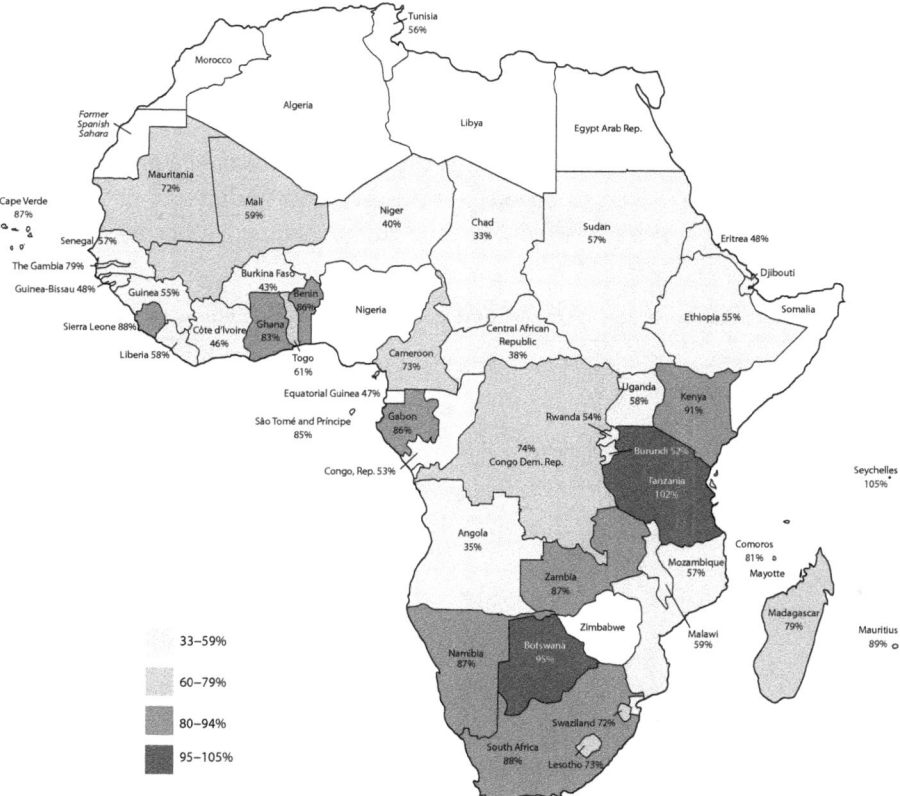

Source: Author's construction, based on 2006–10 data from UIS Data Centre. When recent UIS data were unavailable, data were used from Pôle de Dakar UNESCO-BREDA 2005, 2006, 2007; Country Status Reports (CSRs); or World Bank databases. All data are from 2005 or later. For the full data set, see appendix B, table B.1.
Note: Nigeria, Somalia, and Zimbabwe are omitted for lack of data.

Measuring Sub-Saharan African Countries' Distance from UPC

Each country's completion rate reflects the combined influence of two factors: (a) intake into grade one and (b) retention to the end of the primary cycle.[6] Because UPC requires both variables to approach 100 percent, a country's distance from UPC can be described in terms of how far short it falls on these two variables. Figure 1.2 provides a basis for distinguishing four groups of countries, as follows:

- *Group 1 (UPC achieved).* Nine Sub-Saharan African countries (Botswana, the Comoros, Gabon, Kenya, Mauritius, Namibia, the Seychelles, South Africa, and Tanzania) are in this group, having near-universal intake and completion.
- *Group 2 (UPC unachieved: low intake, low retention).* Six countries (including Côte d'Ivoire and Niger) belong in this group, with intake rates below 95 percent and retention rates no higher than 80 percent.
- *Group 3 (UPC unachieved: high intake, low retention).* In 26 countries (including Guinea-Bissau and Mauritania), intake rates exceed 95 percent, but retention rates are no higher than 80 percent.

Figure 1.2 Primary School Entry and Retention Rates in Sub-Saharan African Countries, ca. 2009

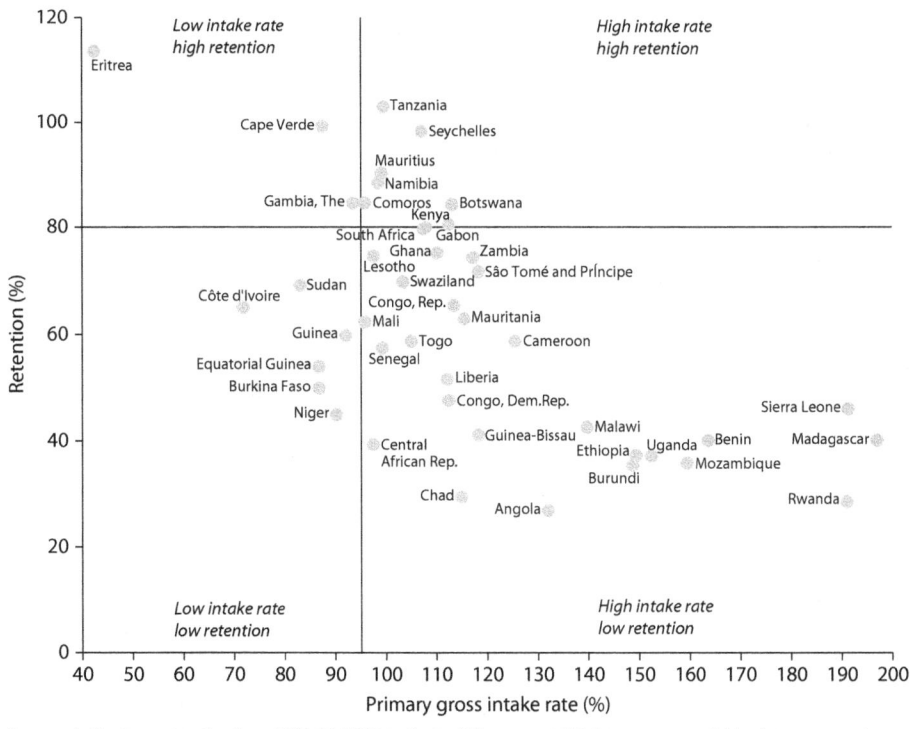

Sources: Author's construction from 2006–10 UIS Data Centre. When recent UIS data were unavailable, data were used from Pôle de Dakar UNESCO-BREDA 2005, 2006, 2007 or World Bank databases. All data are from 2005 or later. For the full data set, see appendix B, table B.1.
Note: Nigeria, Somalia, and Zimbabwe are omitted for lack of data.

- *Group 4 (UPC achieved: low intake, high retention).* In three countries (Cape Verde, Eritrea, and The Gambia), intake to grade one is still not universal, although retention rates are around 90 percent.

Group 2 countries would require the greatest effort to attain UPC because they must simultaneously raise both intake and retention rates. By differentiating across countries, the typology provides a more granular assessment of the nature of the challenges facing Sub-Saharan African countries in their quest for UPC. As an added benefit, the typology also facilitates targeting of countries for cross-country learning or capacity-building activities.

Secondary Education across Sub-Saharan African Countries

Many Sub-Saharan African governments now consider lower secondary education as part of basic education, consistent with trends elsewhere in the world.[7] Nonetheless, in only Botswana, Cape Verde, Mauritius, and South Africa is entry to lower secondary education nearly universal, with GIRs exceeding 80 percent. As table 1.2 indicates, intake rates range widely across countries, from just 13 percent in Rwanda to 91 percent in Botswana. Completion rates are similarly diverse, leading to large gaps among countries in the share of each age cohort that completes lower secondary education.

In upper secondary education, completion rates are, as expected, highest among the middle-income countries, but the variation among them is still substantial,

Table 1.2 Secondary Education Coverage in Selected Sub-Saharan African Countries, ca. 2009

	Lower secondary (%)		Upper secondary (%)	
	GIR	CR	GIR	CR
Low-income countries[a]				
Congo, Rep.	52	44	21	19
Eritrea	44	34	30	12
Mozambique	35	20	10	7
Niger	27	10	4	3
Rwanda	29	22	17	13
Middle-income countries[b]				
Botswana	95	88	56	54
Cape Verde	96	81	78	52
Gabon	74	48	43	25
Mauritius	82	83	81	44
South Africa	82	86	71	43
Sub-Saharan African average	52	37	25	19

Source: Author's construction from 2006–10 UIS Data Centre. When recent UIS data were unavailable, data were used from Pôle de Dakar UNESCO-BREDA 2005, 2006, 2007 or World Bank databases. All data are from 2005 or later. For the full data set, see appendix B, table B.1.
Note: GIR and CR refer, respectively, to the gross intake ratio to the cycle and the completion rate in that cycle.
a. Countries eligible for lending from the World Bank Group's International Development Association (IDA); see appendix A, table A.1.
b. Countries eligible for lending from the International Bank for Reconstruction and Development (IBRD) of the World Bank Group; see appendix A, table A.1.

ranging from more than 50 percent in Botswana and Cape Verde to only 25 percent in Gabon.

Countries also differ in their underlying patterns of student flow. In Botswana, more than a third of those who complete lower secondary education do not continue to the upper secondary cycle and, of those who do, practically everyone completes the cycle. By contrast, in Mauritius, practically all completers of lower secondary school go on to upper secondary school, but only about half of those who do so persist to the end of the cycle. Among low-income Sub-Saharan African counties, completion rates as well as the underlying processes are similarly diverse.

Higher Education across Sub-Saharan African Countries

Given the cross-country diversity in coverage at earlier levels of education, the gaps at this level are unsurprising. Still, the scale of the differences is dramatic: the number of students per 100,000 inhabitants enrolled in higher education institutions ranges from less than 100 in Malawi to more than 1,000 in Gabon and Nigeria, and even exceeding 1,500 in Cape Verde, Mauritius, and South Africa.

Relationship between Education Coverage and Per Capita GDP

The vast differences across Sub-Saharan African countries prompt three related questions:

- Is there a systematic relationship between education coverage and the level of economic development?
- Does that relationship differ by level of education?
- Has the relationship changed over time?

Primary Education Coverage Unrelated to Per Capita Income

In primary education, there is no longer any statistically significant relationship between a country's level of coverage, as measured by the GER, and its level of economic development, as measured by per capita GDP (R^2 is only 0.09).[8] This was not always the case. In 1990, there was a statistically significantly relationship between primary education coverage and per capita GDP across the region (R^2 of 0.44). From 1999, however, the level of per capita GDP is no longer a good predictor of primary education coverage.

Postprimary Education Coverage Strongly Linked to Per Capita Income

In lower secondary, upper secondary, and higher education, there is quite a strong positive relationship between educational coverage and per capita GDP. In the case of lower secondary education, the coefficient of determination (R^2) is 0.49.

In lower secondary education, the middle-income countries in the region do tend to have much higher coverage than the low-income countries. In upper secondary education, countries with higher per capita GDP also have significantly higher coverage (R^2 is 0.53). In higher education, there is also a significant positive relationship between student enrollment (per 100,000 inhabitants) and per capita GDP (R^2 is 0.60).

Upward Shift in the Relationship between School-Life Expectancy and Per Capita GDP

Countries at the same level of income are providing more primary education coverage than before. Figure 1.3 shows the relationship between school-life expectancy (SLE)—a measure of overall educational coverage[9]—and income at four different points.

The upward shift in the SLE–GDP relationship indicates that Sub-Saharan African countries have been able to raise the bar in education coverage from 1990 to 2009. In 1990, a country with a per capita GDP of US$150 (in constant prices) could be expected to provide, on the average, 3.6 years of schooling per person. In 1999, SLE for the same level of per capita GDP had risen to 5.4 years; in 2005, to 6.5 years; and in 2009, to 8.4 years.

In other words, SLE has more than doubled over the 20-year period in countries with a per capita GDP of US$150. Richer countries have also experienced SLE increases over the same period, but the gains have been more modest and realized only after 1999.

Demographic, Other Factors Contribute to Gains in School-Life Expectancy

Three key factors, including declining unit costs and more favorable demographics, explain the rise in SLE at all levels of development:

- *Teacher salaries have declined relative to GDP.* Between 1975 and 2000, average primary school teacher salaries—the principal component in the cost of

Figure 1.3 Relationship between Per Capita GDP and School-Life Expectancy in Low-Income Sub-Saharan African Countries, 1990–2009

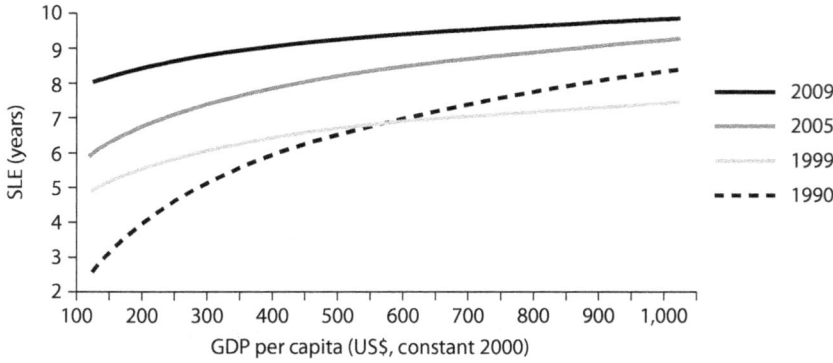

Sources: Authors' construction. SLE data are calculated based on enrollment data (GER and cycle lengths) from UIS Data Centre. GDP data are from World Bank, DDP (Development Data Platform).
Note: SLE = school-life expectancy, GDP = gross domestic product. The graph depicts the statistical relationships (logarithmic) between the two variables in the years shown. "Low-income" countries are those eligible for lending from the International Development Association (IDA); see appendix A, table A.1.

Box 1.1

Benin School Construction through Community-Driven Development: A Decade of Lessons Learned

During the 2000–04 period, most new classrooms in Benin were built by communities with funding from the World Bank's Social Fund (SF) Project. In all, the communities built more than 1,800 classrooms during this period (twice as many as built by the Ministry of Education [MoE]) and at a unit cost 20 percent lower than ministry-managed construction projects.

A follow-up community-driven development (CDD) project in 2005–11 was conceptualized soon after Benin's first election of local governments in 2003. The decentralization law transferred to the local governments the responsibility for managing basic social infrastructure, including schools. Building on lessons learned from the SF, the government supported the new local governments by adopting the CDD approach. The local governments began fulfilling their responsibilities for basic social infrastructure through two implementation modalities: (a) direct management of large-scale, complex projects; and (b) delegation to communities to manage small-scale, low-cost, basic local infrastructure projects. Education remained a top priority, with 73 percent of communities choosing education as their infrastructure project, completing a total of 1,680 classrooms and sanitation facilities to date. The communities outperformed the MoE by building schools of the same design and quality at 30 percent less than the MoE's cost.

In 2008, the MoE received funds from Education for All's Fast-Track Initiative (FTI) and three other donors to support its 10-year sector program (2006–15), which includes the construction of about 2,000 classrooms and related sanitation facilities. To speed up implementation, the MoE broke down the first phase of the school construction program (1,000 classrooms) into three components, which were then entrusted to two contract management agencies (CMAs) and the CDD project. Again, the communities outperformed the agencies. After 18 months of implementation, the CMAs fulfilled less than half of their contracts, while the CDD project delivered almost all. The unit cost of classrooms built by microcontractors under contract with the communities averaged €112 per square meter in 2009—26 percent less than similar classrooms built by medium-size contractors under contracts with the CMAs (at €152 per square meter). In 2011, learning from this rich past experience, the MoE decided to fully integrate the CDD approach into its regular modus operandi for the construction of schools.

Sources: World Bank 2004; Theunynck 2009.

primary education—have been declining in real terms, relative to per capita GDP, in all regions of the world (Mingat 2004). The decline was particularly steep in the Sub-Saharan African region: from 8.6 times per capita GDP in 1975 to 4.4 in 2000. Countries have also found novel ways to reduce the cost of constructing classrooms (see box 1.1).

- *Demographic pressures have eased.* Children up to age 14 now make up 41 percent of the region's population, compared with 45 percent in 1990 (EdStats).
- *Funding for primary education has increased.* Greater international focus on primary education in recent years has increased donor funding to expand primary education in low-income Sub-Saharan African countries. In addition, many of the low-income countries have increased their own funding for primary education (discussed further in chapter 4 of this volume, "Patterns of Spending in Education").

Prospects for the Expansion of Education Coverage

Turning to the prospects for expanding coverage, this section focuses on the following aspects:

- Which countries are likely to achieve UPC by 2015?
- How quickly must secondary education expand to accommodate the growing numbers of primary school completers?
- Is this rate of expansion feasible?

Education Coverage Growth, 1990–2009

In absolute terms, coverage has grown faster at the primary level than at the secondary and tertiary levels, particularly since 1999. Table 1.3 compares the absolute percentage point gains in coverage across different levels of schooling.

Primary Coverage Growth

This pattern of growth, however, will not continue as most countries in the region move toward UPC. The primary GER will stabilize, and further growth in primary enrollment will be driven largely by demographic factors.

Primary education coverage has clearly improved steadily throughout the period, but the spurt began around 1999. Figure 1.4 shows the primary GER

Table 1.3 Absolute Gains in Coverage, by Education Level, in 33 Low-Income Sub-Saharan African Countries, 1990–2009

	Average coverage gain per year (%)				
				Higher	
Period	Primary (GER)	Lower secondary (GER)	Upper secondary (GER)	(GER)	(Students per 100,000 pop.)
1990–99	0.8	0.8	0.4	0.04	5
1999–2009	3.1	1.9	0.9	0.20	25
Overall (1990–2009)	2.0	1.4	0.7	0.10	15

Sources: Authors' calculation based on UIS data for the years shown (UIS Data Centre), supplemented with data from Pôle de Dakar UNESCO-BREDA 2007 and selected CSRs. Some data are calculated by interpolation from other years' data. For the full set of enrollment data for 1990, 1999, and 2009, see appendix B, table B.2.
Note: GER = general enrollment rate. "Low-income" countries are eligible for lending from International Development Association (IDA); see appendix A, table A.1.

Figure 1.4 Growth in Primary Education Coverage in 33 Low-Income Sub-Saharan African Countries, 1990–2009

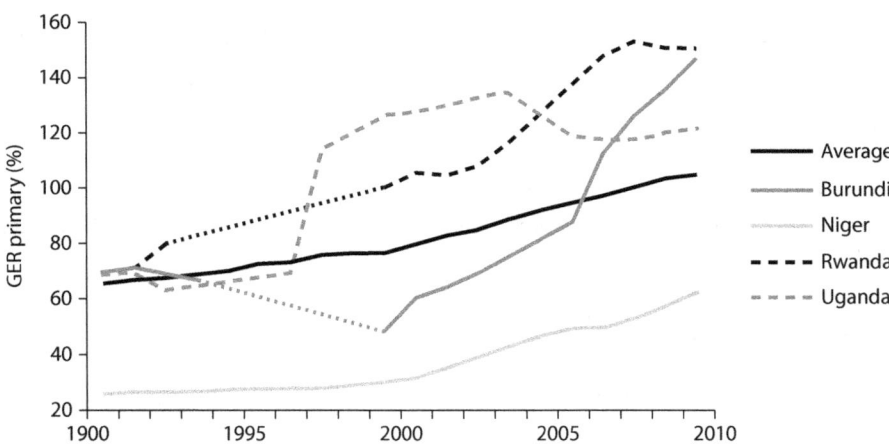

Sources: Based on data from UIS Data Centre, Pôle de Dakar UNESCO-BREDA 2007, and selected CSRs. Some data are calculated by interpolation from other years' data. For the full set of enrollment data for 1990, 1999, and 2009, see appendix B, table B.2. There is a break in the data for Rwanda and Burundi between 1993 and 1998.
Note: GER = general enrollment ratio. The average shown is the simple average, not the truncated average. "Low-income" countries are those eligible for lending from International Development Association (IDA); see appendix A, table A.1.

trends in a sample of 33 low-income Sub-Saharan African countries from 1990 to 2009.[10] Rates increased, on average, from 66 percent in 1990 to 77 percent in 1999 and to 105 percent in 2009.

Figure 1.4 shows widely different trends across the countries in the region. In Niger, for example, there was virtually no improvement in the GER during the 1990s. In Burundi, civil war in the early to mid-1990s saw a dramatic drop in the GER (World Bank 2007b). In Uganda, on the other hand, primary school coverage surged in 1997 following the abolition of school fees (Avenstrup, Liang, and Nellemann 2004) but has dropped since 2003 as the system moved past its multicohort effects.

Overall, primary education coverage has improved significantly since 1999 in most low-income countries in the region. This increase came with a rapid expansion in the supply of classrooms and school capacity. In some countries, this was accomplished by delegating the management of school construction to local communities (see box 1.2).

Overall Coverage Growth Since 2000

Because coverage also increased significantly in secondary and higher education, as shown in figure 1.5, educational coverage has grown at all levels of education since around the turn of the century. Interestingly (although there is not necessarily a cause-and-effect correlation), the improvement coincided roughly with some important events that may have pushed the scaling-up of education coverage: the Dakar Forum on education in early 2000 and the UN Millennium Summit later that year when the MDGs were adopted.

Box 1.2

Mauritania: Community Management of Primary School Construction

In 1989, in response to high unmet demand for schooling, Mauritania became the first Sub-Saharan African country to fully delegate the management of school construction to local communities. At that time, many communities were already building their own classrooms using local materials and traditional techniques (at an estimated cost of US$2,000 per classroom). The community-built classrooms were, however, temporary or substandard structures.

The community-managed classroom construction program first tested by the MoE (1989–95) was implemented on the following premises:

- Appraisal of communities' (parents associations') requests based on simple school-mapping criteria
- Delegation of construction responsibility to the communities, including contractor selection and payment
- Prefinancing by the communities (about 40 percent of total construction cost, with the balance borne by the government) to finance standard-design, modern classrooms using simple technology at an estimated cost of US$5,000 equivalent.

Although the project started slowly, it took off as soon as trust was built between the MoE and the first participating communities. It rapidly surpassed its initial 250-classrooms objective, delivering 1,020 classrooms at the end of the project as a result of additional support from other donors, such as the Agence Française de Développement (AFD). The capacity of communities to construct classrooms and schools continued to increase over time—doubling during the five years (1995–2000) of the subsequent project with the delivery of 2,200 classrooms.

The expansion of school facilities had a positive impact on the GER. In particular, since the delegation of school construction management to local communities began in 1989, the GER has risen sharply—from 48 to 95 percent.

A few modifications have been made since the program began, particularly (a) reduction of communities' share of the construction cost to 30 percent to foster participation from the poorest communities and (b) replacement of iron-sheet roofing by more expensive storm-resistant concrete slab roofing. Unit costs of construction by contractors hired by the communities remain low at US$140 per square meter (2006), compared with US$210 per square meter for classrooms constructed by the contract management agency, AMEXTIPE (Agence Mauritanienne d'Exécution des Travaux d'Intérêt Public pour l'Emploi), hired by municipalities to manage urban infrastructure construction. Subject to technical control by a team of three mobile civil engineers, technical audits of the community-managed projects indicate that construction is of acceptable quality.

Sources: Theunynck 2009; World Bank 1996, 2003.

Figure 1.5 Relative Gains in Education Coverage, by Education Level, in 33 Low-Income Sub-Saharan African Countries, 1990–2009

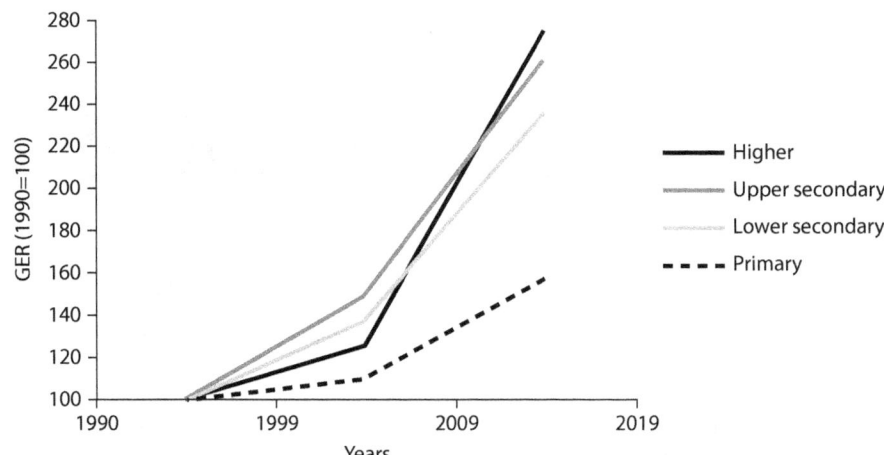

Sources: Author's construction, based on data from UIS Data Centre. See also appendix B, table B.2.
Note: GER = general enrollment ratio. The enrollment rates are presented as indices, the 1990 value being set to 100. For higher education, the index is created based on students per 100,000 inhabitants, not GER. "Low-income" countries are those eligible for lending from International Development Association (IDA); see appendix A, table A.1.

After those two summits, government and donor funding (further detailed in chapter 4) increased for the education sector—including through the Education for All (EFA) Fast-Track Initiative—as did changes in the institutional framework for the coordination and monitoring of the EFA goals.[11] Although most of the international focus has been on primary education, the impact has been on all levels of education.

Higher Education Growth

In relative terms, higher education has grown faster than other levels of education since 1999. Figure 1.5 provides a comparison of the relative growth rates, showing that higher education has led the way, followed by secondary education, and with primary education growing at a relatively slower pace.

These differences are due primarily to differences in initial levels of coverage—primary education having had a much higher initial level of coverage in 1990 than secondary and higher education had.[12] In the years ahead, a continuation of higher relative growth in secondary and higher education may be expected, together with a slowing in the growth of primary education coverage.

Prospects for Achieving UPC by 2015

The average primary completion rate (PCR) gained a total of 20 percentage points between 1999 and 2009. In the sample of 33 Sub-Saharan African countries, the PCR improved by 20 percentage points over the past decade, rising

Figure 1.6 Average Annual PCR Growth in 33 Low-Income Sub-Saharan African Countries, 1999–2009

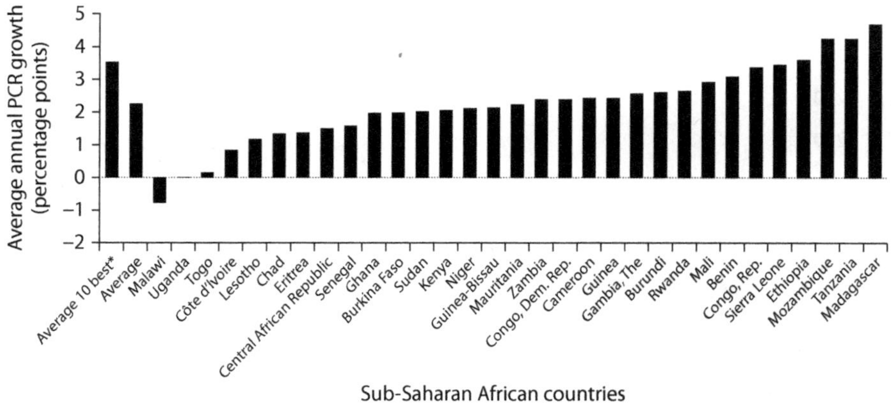

Sources: Authors' calculations from UIS Data Centre for the years shown, supplemented with data from Pôle de Dakar UNESCO-BREDA 2007 and selected CSRs. Some data are calculated by interpolation from other years' data.
Note: PCR = primary completion rate. "Low-income" countries are those eligible for lending from International Development Association (IDA); see appendix A, table A.1. Nigeria and Zimbabwe are omitted for lack of data.
a. Average of the 10 countries with the fastest improvement in the PCR is 3.5 percentage points per year.

from 43 percent in 1999 to 63 percent by 2009—an average gain of 2 percentage points per year.

Figure 1.6 shows the annual PCR gain in each of the 33 Sub-Saharan African countries. Only in Malawi did the PCR decline during the period, while most countries experienced rapid PCR increases. The fastest average annual improvement was a 4.7 percentage point gain in Madagascar.

Current Trend: Average PCR Reaches 75 Percent by 2015

Figure 1.7 shows two projections of the PCR for the year 2015, the target year for achieving UPC under the UN MDGs. The first projection assumes that countries will maintain the rate of improvement attained during the 1999–2009 period. Under this scenario, the PCR will increase from 63 percent in 2009 to 75 percent by 2015, a 12 percentage point increase over six years.

This gain would represent a significant improvement, particularly compared with the trend observed during the 1990s. But many countries will still be far from UPC. Assuming no change in the rate of improvement, only 8 of the 31 countries shown are projected to achieve the UPC goal (a PCR of 95 percent or more) in 2015.

Accelerated Trend: PCR Reaches 82 Percent by 2015

Assuming an accelerated improvement in trend growth, the average PCR may reach 82 percent by 2015. The second projection shown in figure 1.7 assumes that all countries can attain the rate of improvement of the top 10 countries in 1999–2009 (previously shown in figure 1.6). Among the top 10 countries, the PCR gained an average of about 3.5 percentage points per year.

Figure 1.7 Projected Primary Completion Rates through 2015 in Low-Income Sub-Saharan African Countries

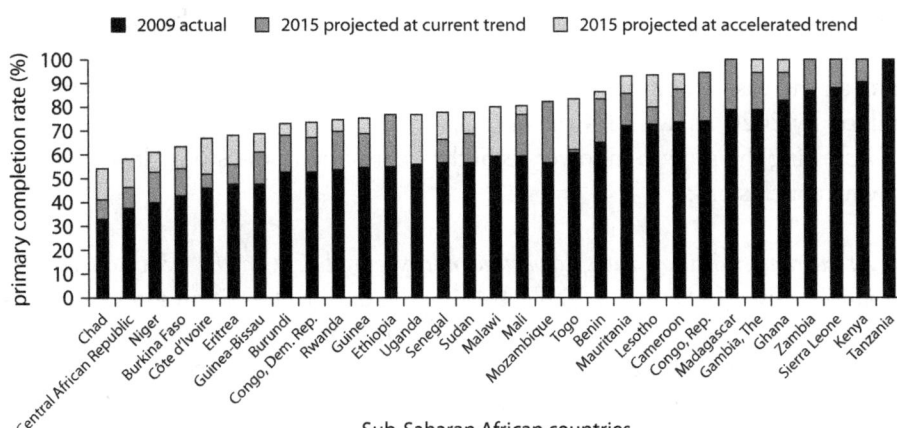

Sources: Authors' calculations from UIS Data Centre for the years shown, supplemented with data from Pôle de Dakar UNESCO-BREDA 2007 and selected CSRs. For the full data set, see appendix B, table B.2. Some data are calculated by interpolation from other years' data.
Note: PCR = primary completion rate. "Low-income" countries are those eligible for lending from International Development Association (IDA); see appendix A, table A.1. Nigeria and Zimbabwe are omitted for lack of data.
a. The 2009 value of the PCR is shown when the 1999–2009 trend was negative (Malawi).
b. If the PCR grew more than 3.5 percentage points per year in 1999–2009, this higher growth rate is used instead of 3.5 (Ethiopia, Madagascar, Mozambique, and Tanzania).

It may not be realistic to assume that all 31 countries can achieve such a high rate of improvement during the projection period, but the scenario provides a useful benchmark for what these countries can expect to achieve under the best of conditions. The average PCR could reach 82 percent under this assumption, bringing the region's low-income countries closer to achieving UPC by 2015.

Prospects for Expanding Secondary Education Coverage

The strong PCR increase, coupled with the region's high population growth rate, have increased pressures for the countries in the Sub-Saharan African region to expand secondary school coverage. This trend will continue for some years to come, but there are still relatively few initiatives to help these countries prepare for, and respond to, the increasing demand for secondary education.[13] Knowing how to respond requires understanding of the scope of the challenge.[14]

How Big Is the Challenge?

The number of primary school completers will likely more than double by 2020. A recently completed simulation study for the Africa region projects the number of primary school completers and the increase in secondary enrollment under different assumptions about the transition rates (Mingat, Ledoux, and

Rakotomalala 2010). Assuming that all the Sub-Saharan African countries will achieve a 95 percent PCR, the study projects that the number of primary school completers will more than double between 2003 and 2020. For the 33 low-income countries in the sample most discussed here, this projection translates into an increase from 9.4 million primary school completers in 2003 to 22.2 million by 2020, as table 1.4 shows.

Assessing the growth in lower secondary enrollment, the study draws the following conclusions:

- *At current transition rates, lower secondary enrollment in the 33 countries will increase by a factor of 2.5.* Table 1.4 lists the current transition rates from primary to lower secondary education. The transition rates range from 30 percent to 100 percent, with a sample average of 63 percent. If each country maintains its current transition rate, Mingat, Ledoux, and Rakotomalala (2010) project that lower secondary enrollment in the 33 countries will grow from 14.9 million students in 2003 to 37.2 million in 2020.
- *If the transition rate is raised to 100, the number of students will more than quadruple by 2020.* If transition rates increase to 100 percent by 2020 (implying the establishment of a nine-year basic education program in all 33 countries), lower secondary enrollment in the region could rise to as many as 62.9 million students by 2020—more than four times the current number.

Key Issues: Financial and Practical Feasibility and Sustainability

As discussed above, in relative terms, secondary enrollment is already increasing relatively faster than primary enrollment in the region (as previously shown in figure 1.5). Crucial questions at this point include the following:

- What secondary enrollment growth rate can different countries sustain in the coming years?
- Can all countries maintain the current transition rates from primary to secondary education?
- Will these countries be able to raise their transition rates?

There are two important issues to take into account when considering the feasibility of different policies for the expansion of secondary education: The first is financial sustainability. Each country needs to explore the issue using a sector-wide financial simulation model.[15] The second is practical feasibility in terms of educational facilities and human resource needs.

The Greater the Expansion, the Bigger the Challenge

The magnitude of the projected expansion provides an indication of its practical feasibility. Figure 1.8 shows the projected lower secondary enrollment in 2020 as a multiple of current enrollment for each of the 33 lower-income Sub-Saharan African countries.

Table 1.4 Scenarios for the Expansion of Lower Secondary Enrollment by 2020 in 33 Low-Income Sub-Saharan African Countries

		Primary				Secondary			
	Base year	2020 (PCR of 95%)		Base year		2020 (transition rate of base year)		2020 (transition rate of 100%)	
						Enrollment		Enrollment	
	Base year	Number of completers (000)	Number of completers (000)	Transition rate P-LS (%)	Enrollment (000)	(000)	(Multiple of base year)	(000)	(Multiple of base year)
Benin	2004	102	303	73	291	812	2.8	1,112	3.8
Burkina Faso	2004	106	514	58	231	1,078	4.7	1,859	8.1
Burundi	2004	65	318	52	122	551	4.5	1,055	8.7
Cameroon	2003	231	439	56	560	945	1.7	1,718	3.1
Central African Republic	2004	31	116	56	58	251	4.3	445	7.7
Chad	2004	91	384	72	211	974	4.6	1,353	6.4
Congo, Dem. Rep.	2005	728	2,354	39	615	1,683	2.7	4,314	7.0
Congo, Rep.	2005	74	165	79	259	467	1.8	589	2.3
Côte d'Ivoire	2000	243	514	63	643	1,253	1.9	1,986	3.1
Eritrea	2005	58	163	74	137	344	2.5	462	3.4
Ethiopia	2002	1,050	2,641	79	2,579	7,783	3.0	9,889	3.8
Gambia, The	2001	19	44	74	38	96	2.5	129	3.4
Ghana	2001	340	589	99	941	1,704	1.8	1,725	1.8
Guinea	2005	128	317	75	318	882	2.8	1,176	3.7
Guinea-Bissau	2002	14	64	84	35	146	4.2	174	5.0
Kenya	2005	585	1,177	—	—	—	—	—	—
Lesotho	2005	33	38	76	65	87	1.3	115	1.8
Madagascar	2003	168	623	65	422	1,533	3.6	2,359	5.6

(table continues on next page)

Table 1.4 Scenarios for the Expansion of Lower Secondary Enrollment by 2020 in 33 Low-Income Sub-Saharan African Countries *(continued)*

		Primary				Secondary			
	Base year		2020 (PCR of 95%)	Base year		2020 (transition rate of base year)		2020 (transition rate of 100%)	
						Enrollment		Enrollment	
	Base year	Number of completers (000)	Number of completers (000)	Transition rate P-LS (%)	Enrollment (000)	(000)	(Multiple of base year)	(000)	(Multiple of base year)
Malawi	2002	201	429	30	117	250	2.1	829	7.1
Mali	2004	144	533	80	347	1,186	3.4	1,474	4.2
Mauritania	2004	36	106	62	72	243	3.4	394	5.4
Mozambique	2001	102	598	54	155	940	6.1	1,725	11.1
Niger	2002	69	573	66	147	1,370	9.3	2,075	14.1
Nigeria	2005	2,595	4,135	52	3,706	6,212	1.7	11,850	3.2
Rwanda	2003	112	295	35	117	290	2.5	821	7.0
Senegal	2003	143	357	54	279	735	2.6	1,361	4.9
Sierra Leone	2004	68	183	63	125	321	2.6	509	4.1
Sudan	2003	293	974	—	—	—	—	—	—
Tanzania	2002	555	1,096	28	453	1,194	2.6	4,265	9.4
Togo	2005	114	201	80	359	612	1.7	765	2.1
Uganda	2002	344	1313	45	508	2,004	3.9	4,493	8.8
Zambia	2005	227	367	62	271	437	1.6	705	2.6
Zimbabwe	2003	282	308	70	724	847	1.2	1,209	1.7
Aggregate		9,355	22,235	67	14,909	37,228	2.5	62,934	4.2

Source: Mingat, Ledoux, and Rakotomalala 2010.

Note: PCR = primary completion rate, P-LS = primary to lower secondary, — = not available. Some data presented in this table may differ slightly from data presented in other tables of this chapter because of the different source. The analysis is based on actual cycle length, not standardized. "Low-income" countries are those eligible for lending from International Development Association (IDA); see appendix A, table A.1.

Figure 1.8 Projected Enrollment in Lower Secondary Education by 2020 as a Multiple of Enrollments in 2003

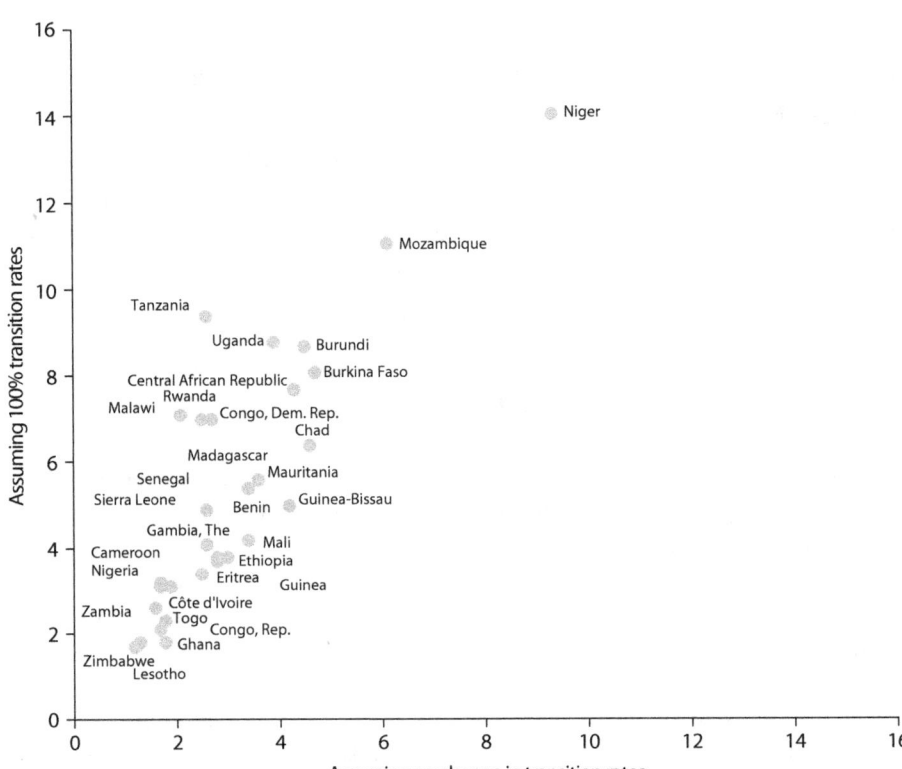

Source: Authors' construction based on calculations in table 1.4.
Note: Kenya and Sudan are not included because their single secondary cycle is considered to be upper secondary education for the purposes of this analysis. For some countries, the base year is not 2003, as indicated in table 1.4.

The horizontal axis shows the projections of lower secondary enrollment if current transition rates from primary to secondary education persist. Under that assumption, lower secondary enrollment could increase by a factor of 6 in Mozambique and by a factor of 9 in Niger. The vertical axis shows the projections if the transition rates rise to 100 percent. Under that assumption, lower secondary enrollment could grow by a factor of 11 in Mozambique and by a factor of 14 in Niger.

Countries for which the projected expansions are high—as measured by the number of times enrollments may be expected to increase—are likely to face more practical challenges in implementing the projected expansions. Figure 1.8 can therefore be interpreted as showing the extent of the practical feasibility of implementing expansion in lower secondary education under the two different scenarios for each of the countries shown.[16]

The graph shows a clear dispersion of countries in terms of the potential difficulty in implementing the expansion in lower secondary education under the two scenarios. Some countries, such as Ghana and Lesotho, may find it relatively easy (without considering the financial implications) to implement expansion

> **Box 1.3**
>
> **Zimbabwe: Increased Access to Secondary Education through Government–Community Partnerships and School-Based Management**
>
> In 1980, less than 4 percent of children of secondary school age in Zimbabwe were enrolled in secondary education. Within three years, secondary school coverage rose to more than 65 percent. The surge in secondary education is attributed to partnerships formed between the government and communities to build and equip secondary schools, most notably the following collaborations:
>
> - Parents and communities built the school infrastructure with technical and material (for example, prefabricated roofing and pillars) assistance from the government to ensure that safety standards were met.
> - The government provided trained teachers at the fixed ratio of 1 teacher for every 30 students, a per capita grant for teaching and learning materials, and free in-service training and pedagogical materials for the teachers.
> - Among other responsibilities, parents and communities paid and controlled fees for additional teachers, furniture, and construction; managed the schools; and ensured attendance.
>
> Among the results was an increase in the number of secondary schools from 200 to more than 1,600. The program also enabled pupils to attend day secondary schools close to their homes, at significantly lower unit costs than the traditional urban boarding schools.
>
> *Source:* Verspoor and SEIA Team 2008.

under either of the two scenarios. The same would not be true for Mozambique and Niger, for instance, because both are likely to encounter serious difficulty in affording and managing the projected expansions. Box 1.3 looks at how secondary education was expanded in Zimbabwe in the 1980s by partnering with communities, and that country's experience may offer some insights into how this difficulty can be eased.

Issues for Policy Development

Despite considerable progress, most of the low-income countries in the Sub-Saharan Africann region are not on track to achieve UPC by 2015. Across the region's low-income countries, the PCR gained an average of 20 percentage points between 1999 and 2009. The progress achieved thus far by many of these countries is impressive and most countries are moving in the right direction, but with the current rate of growth in enrollments, only one in four of the region's low-income countries is set to achieve UPC by the 2015 MDG deadline.

The region is also struggling with growing demand for postprimary education. Although primary school enrollment is expanding faster than enrollments at other levels of education when measured in absolute terms, secondary and higher education coverage are growing faster relative to their initial lower levels. This trend is in large part a response to the increasing demand for continuing education from the growing numbers of youths completing primary school. The region is therefore facing a dual challenge in terms of expanding educational coverage: to keep raising the PCR while, at the same time, increasing secondary and higher education coverage at a manageable rate.

Expansion at all three educational levels translates into both financial and practical challenges; the scope of these challenges differs greatly across countries. The discussion in this chapter has highlighted the scope of the challenges and how they vary greatly from one country to another. Each country's response and its pace of expansion at each level should be calibrated with care to ensure that expectations meet with reality at all levels. Niger, for instance, cannot realistically be expected to reach UPC by 2015 and is even less likely to achieve universal lower secondary education by 2020. Education policies should reflect these differences by taking into account the specific implementation and financial challenges confronting each country.

Notes

1. In later chapters, household survey data for a more limited sample of countries are used to complement the analysis presented in this chapter.
2. This adjustment was needed in only a few instances (for example, Kenya and Malawi) where the country's education structure departs substantially from the typical arrangement in the region: a primary cycle of six or seven years, followed by a secondary cycle of five to seven years, for a total duration of 11–13 years. (For country-specific details, see appendix A, table A.3).
3. Figure 1.1 reflects simple averages of country-specific data for the following indicators: the gross intake rate (GIR) and completion rates in primary, lower secondary, and upper secondary education; and the gross enrollment ratio (GER) in higher education. For a full explanation of how the different indicators are computed, see appendix A, table A.2.
4. Comparable cross-country data are unavailable to document the extent of dropout in tertiary education across Sub-Saharan African countries. However, country studies suggest that graduation rates are often low compared with overall enrollments, suggesting that dropping out is common also at the tertiary level (World Bank 2007a).
5. This measure is probably more appropriate as a measure of tertiary education coverage than the gross enrollment ratio in such settings as Sub-Saharan African where tertiary education consists of a range of degrees of varying lengths, which makes it difficult to define the appropriate reference population for computing the GER.

6. To include as large a sample as possible, rates were computed using administrative data collected through school censuses. These data offer an imprecise, though still broadly reliable, measure of entry and retention rates. Household survey data (available for a smaller number of countries) suggest that the GIR may be overestimated in some countries. In chapter 3, the survey data are analyzed in greater detail.
7. Di Gropello (2006), for example, reports that many countries in East Asia and Latin America have extended compulsory education to include lower secondary grades, delaying decisions on optional course specialization to upper secondary education or later.
8. In a logarithmic relationship, the explanatory variable in the regression is ln (per capita GDP).
9. School-life expectancy (SLE) is the average number of years of schooling of a given cohort. Estimates of SLE are derived from GERs by level (primary, secondary, and tertiary) and cycle lengths, taking years spent in repetition into account. The same method was used for all four years.
10. The sample of 33 low-income countries (selected in Bruns, Mingat, and Rakotomalala 2003) comprises the Sub-Saharan African countries eligible for lending from IDA except those with very small populations (Cape Verde, the Comoros, and São Tomé and Príncipe) or incomplete data (Angola, Liberia, and Somalia). (The IDA threshold changes every year, as do the countries' gross national incomes [GNI] per capita, so there may be small changes from year to year in this group.) The 33 countries in the sample had a 2006 GNI per capita of less than US$1,065. For the full list of the countries included in the sample of 33, and a list of IDA as well as the middle-income Sub-Saharan African countries eligible for lending from IBRD countries, see appendix A, table A.1.
11. See Pôle de Dakar UNESCO-BREDA (2007) for a description of some of the institutional changes that have occurred since the 2000 Dakar Forum.
12. For example, a gain of 5 percentage points is large if the initial level of the indicator is 10 percent, but modest if the initial level is 50 (a 50 percent increase in the first case, against a 10 percent in the second).
13. One of these initiatives is the World Bank Secondary Education in Africa (SEIA) program, launched in 2003 to promote dialogue and knowledge sharing among countries and development partners about the development of secondary education in the region. SEIA has financed a series of studies on secondary education and organized regional conferences on the topic.
14. Di Gropello (2006) reviews the situation of secondary education in Latin America and East Asia, two regions that have also experienced a period of significant growth in the number of children seeking secondary education. The report looks at how countries can address the multiple challenges they face in secondary education and grow their education systems responsibly and efficiently. The lessons gleaned from the Di Gropello report could be useful to policy makers in Sub-Saharan Africa.
15. See Mingat, Ledoux, and Rakotomalala (2010) for an initial assessment of the financial implications of expanding enrollments in secondary and higher education.
16. This analysis is conducted only on the basis of the logistical feasibility of implementation (building schools, recruiting teachers, and so on); however, it is likely that an

analysis of the financial sustainability would produce similar results because logistical and financial feasibility are linked.

References

Avenstrup, R., X. Liang, and S. Nellemann. 2004. *Free Primary Education and Poverty Reduction: The Case of Kenya, Lesotho, Malawi, and Uganda.* Case study. Washington, DC: World Bank.

Bruns, B., A. Mingat, and R. Rakotomalala. 2003. *Achieving Universal Primary Education by 2015. A Chance for Every Child.* Washington, DC: World Bank.

DDP (Development Data Platform) (database). World Bank, Washington, DC. http://databank.worldbank.org/ddp/home.do.

Di Gropello, E., ed. 2006. *Meeting the Challenges of Secondary Education in Latin America and East Asia: Improving Efficiency and Resource Mobilization.* Directions in Development Series. Washington, DC: World Bank.

EdStats (Education Statistics) (database). World Bank, Washington, DC. http://www.worldbank.org/education/edstats.

Mingat, A. 2004. "La rémunération/le statut des enseignants dans la perspective de l'atteinte des objectifs du millénaire dans les pays d'Afrique subsaharienne francophone en 2015." Discussion Paper, World Bank, Washington, DC.

Mingat, A., B. Ledoux, and R. Rakotomalala. 2010. *Developing Post-Primary Education in Sub-Saharan Africa: Assessing the Financial Sustainability of Alternative Pathways.* Africa Human Development Series. Washington, DC: World Bank.

Theunynck, S. 2009. *School Construction Strategies for Universal Primary Education in Africa: Should Communities Be Empowered to Build Their Schools?* Africa Human Development Series. Washington, DC: World Bank.

Pôle de Dakar UNESCO-BREDA (United Nations Educational, Scientific and Cultural Organization, Regional Office for Education in Africa). 2005. "Education for All in Africa: Paving the Way for Action." Dakar+5 Report, Pôle de Dakar UNESCO-BREDA, Dakar.

———. 2006. "Education for All in Africa: Sub-regional Statistics and Analysis." Dakar+6 Report, Pôle de Dakar UNESCO-BREDA, Dakar.

———. 2007. "Education for All in Africa: Top Priority for Integrated Sector-Wide Policies." Dakar+7 Report, Pôle de Dakar UNESCO-BREDA, Dakar.

UIS (United Nations Educational, Scientific, and Cultural Organization, Institute for Statistics) Data Centre (database). UIS, Montreal. http://stats.uis.unesco.org.

Verspoor, Adriaan, and SEIA (Secondary Education in Africa) Team. 2008. *At the Crossroads: Choices for Secondary Education in Sub-Saharan Africa.* Africa Human Development Series. Washington, DC: World Bank.

World Bank. 1996. "Mauritania: Education Sector Restructuring Project." Implementation Completion and Results Report 15739, World Bank, Washington, DC.

———. 2003. "Mauritania: General Education V Project." Implementation Completion and Results Report 27290, World Bank, Washington, DC.

———. 2004. "Benin: Social Fund Project." Implementation Completion and Results Report 29078, World Bank, Washington, DC.

———. 2007a. "Malawi Public Expenditure Review 2006." Report 40145-MW for Malawi Ministry of Finance, World Bank, Washington, DC.

———. 2007b. "Le système éducatif Burundais: Diagnostic et perspectives pour une nouvelle politique éducative dans le contexte de l'éducation primaire gratuite pour tous." Africa Human Development Series, World Bank Working Paper 109. Washington, DC: World Bank.

CHAPTER 2

Socioeconomic Disparities in Education

Despite the progress of recent years, Sub-Saharan Africa as a whole is not on track to achieve universal primary completion (UPC) by 2015. Nor are many Sub-Saharan African countries on track to achieve the second educational Millennium Development Goal (MDG): the elimination of gender disparity at all levels of education by 2015.

This chapter examines the region's progress toward eliminating gender disparities and highlights other disparities that are equally, if not more, important—disparities between rich and poor, and between urban and rural children across different levels of education in the region.

Gender Disparities: Analysis of Administrative Data

Gender disparities in education have received much attention over the past 20 years. Researchers, practitioners, and policy makers are concerned with gender disparities not only from the perspective of education as a fundamental human right but also from the perspectives of the efficient use of limited resources and the economic and social benefits of education. The direct and proven benefits of women's education on fertility, child nutrition and health, women's labor force participation, and economic growth can hardly be overemphasized.

Despite Great Progress, Enrollment Gaps Remain

The disadvantage to girls in terms of school participation has greatly diminished since 1990. Drawing on administrative data for selected years between 1990 and 2008,[1] table 2.1 shows steady and continuous improvements in gender equity across all levels of education in Sub-Saharan African countries. The largest improvement occurred in upper secondary and higher education, where the disparities are also the widest. Despite this remarkable progress, there were still gaps between girls' and boys' school enrollment at all levels of education in 2008.

Table 2.1 Gender Disparities at All Levels of Education, Sub-Saharan African Countries, Selected Years

	Primary			Lower secondary	Upper secondary	Higher
Year	GER F/M	GIR F/M	PCR F/M	GER F/M	GER M	GER F/M
1990	0.80	0.84	0.78	0.73	0.56	0.42
1999	0.86	0.90	0.82	0.78	0.67	0.54
2002	0.88	0.92	0.87	0.79	0.72	0.54
2005	0.90	0.94	0.88	0.82	0.75	0.60
2008	0.92	0.95	0.91	0.85	0.78	0.65

Sources: Author's calculations based on data from the UNESCO Institute for Statistics (UIS) Data Centre or, for a few countries, from Pôle de Dakar UNESCO-BREDA 2007. For all 1990 and 2008 data on individual countries, see appendix C, table C.1.
Note: GER = gross enrollment ratio. GIR = gross intake rate. PCR = primary completion rate. A value of less than 1 indicates a disadvantage to girls; a value of more than 1 signals a disadvantage to boys.

Table 2.2 Comparison of Sub-Saharan African Gender Disparities in Education with Those of Low-Income Countries in Other World Regions, 2008

	Primary			Lower secondary	Upper secondary	Higher
	GER F/M	GIR F/M	PCR F/M	GER F/M	GER F/M	GER F/M
East Asia and Pacific	0.96	0.97	1.01	0.98	1.03	1.02
Europe and Central Asia	0.98	0.99	0.98	0.99	0.98	0.99
Latin America and the Caribbean	0.98	0.97	1.04	1.01	1.18	1.68
Middle East and North Africa	0.78	0.85	0.69	0.58	0.52	0.55
South Asia	0.92	0.92	0.92	0.94	0.82	0.81
Sub-Saharan Africa	0.92	0.95	0.91	0.85	0.78	0.65

Source: Data for Africa are from table 2.1. Data for other regions are from UIS Data Centre for 2008 or latest year available.
Note: GER = gross enrollment ratio, GIR = gross intake rate, PCR = primary completion rate. "Low-income" countries are eligible for lending from the World Bank's International Development Association (IDA); see appendix A, table A.1.

Gender Disparity Widens at Higher Levels

In 2008—the latest year shown in table 2.1—the regional average gender parity index (GPI)[2] dropped from 0.95 in the first grade of primary education to 0.91 at the end of the primary cycle, to 0.85 in lower secondary education, to 0.78 in upper secondary education, and finally to 0.65 in higher education. The ratio (not shown in the table) in technical and vocational education is 0.75. This pattern shows that the disadvantage to girls relative to boys increases through each succeeding level of education.

Comparing Sub-Saharan Africa with Other World Regions

Sub-Saharan Africa is one of the few remaining global regions where girls remain disadvantaged in school participation. The region's GPIs are better than those of low-income countries in the Middle East and North Africa and are comparable to low-income countries in South Asia (table 2.2). However, low-income countries in other parts of the world have achieved greater gender equity in school participation (East Asia and Pacific, Europe and Central Asia) or are now experiencing a disadvantage to boys (Latin America and the Caribbean).

Sub-Saharan Africa Cross-Country Differences

Girls are generally at an educational disadvantage, but there are wide differences across Sub-Saharan African countries. Figure 2.1 shows the GPI in the last year of primary school in all Sub-Saharan African countries for which this statistic is available.

The ratio ranges from 0.54 in Chad to 1.36 in Lesotho, the latter indicating a much higher primary completion rate (PCR) among girls than boys.[3] Based on this indicator, the region may be divided into the three groups of countries shown in figure 2.1:

- *Group 1.* Thirteen countries, mainly from Central and West Africa, have ratios below 0.80, indicating a significant disadvantage to girls.
- *Group 2.* Fifteen countries display moderate disadvantage to girls.
- *Group 3.* At the other extreme, 16 countries, mainly from southern Africa, have ratios above 0.97, indicating little or no disadvantage to girls. Ten of those countries (Botswana, Cape Verde, Gabon, The Gambia, Lesotho, Mauritania, Namibia, Rwanda, São Tomé and Príncipe, and the Seychelles) have ratios higher than 1.03, indicating moderate disadvantage to boys.

Overall, only 6 out of the 44 Sub-Saharan African countries shown (all in Group 3) have parity at the end of the primary cycle (GPI between 0.97 and 1.03).

Figure 2.1 Gender Gap in the Primary Completion Rate, by Sub-Saharan African Country, 2008

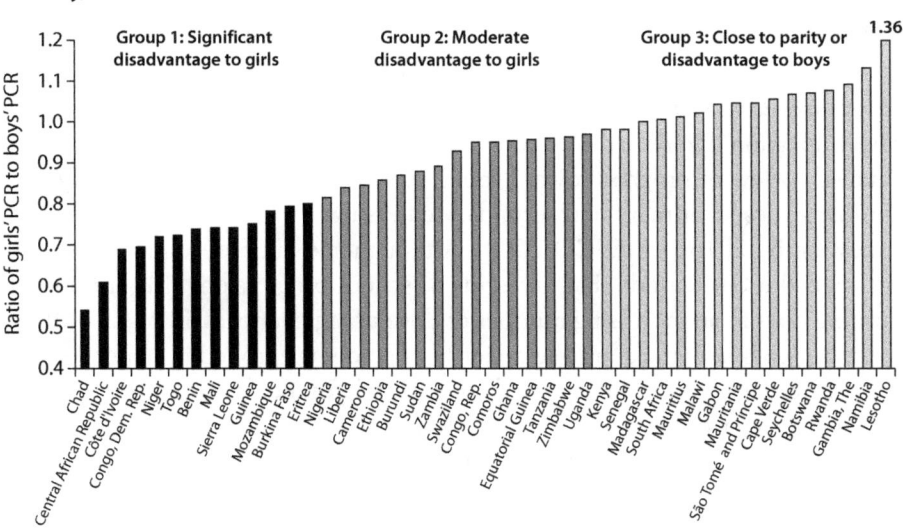

Source: Authors' construction from UIS Data Centre for 2008 or latest year available.
Note: PCR = primary completion rate. The chart is based on girls' PCR relative to boys' PCR. The cutoff points for the three groups are 75 percent and 95 percent. Angola, Guinea-Bissau, and Somalia are omitted because of lack of data.

Figure 2.2 Comparison of Gender Disparities in Three Groups of Sub-Saharan African Countries, 2008

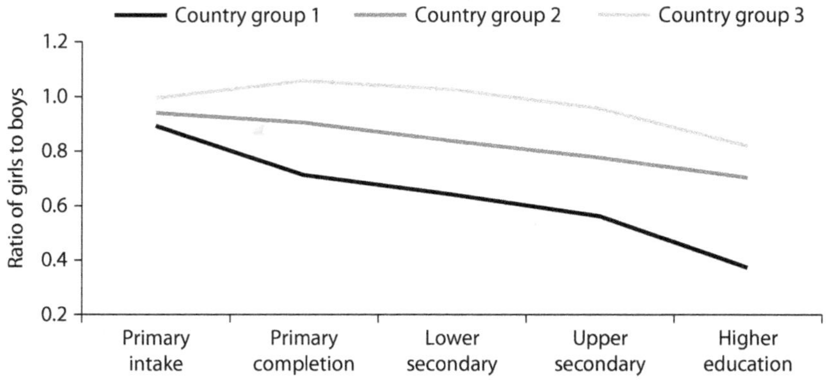

Source: Authors' construction from the UIS Data Centre for 2008 or the latest year available.
Note: GPI = Gender Parity Index, GIR = gross intake rate, PCR = primary completion rate, GER = gross enrollment ratio. The chart depicts the GPI at each level of education, calculated as follows: (a) in the first grade of primary education, the GIR of girls relative to boys; (b) at the end of the primary cycle, as PCR of girls relative to boys; and (c) in the secondary and tertiary cycles, as the GER of girls relative to boys. See figure 2.1 for the countries included in each group.

Girls' Disadvantages Increase with Grade Level in Most Countries

In nearly two-thirds of the countries (groups 1 and 2), gender disparities begin in primary education and progressively worsen the higher the grade level. A third of the countries (group 3, except Lesotho) are close to gender parity at all levels of education except higher education, where there is still a gap. This pattern of a widening gender disparity as the level of education rises highlights the importance of addressing even seemingly small disparities at the primary level.

Figure 2.2 compares gender disparities in school participation across the whole education system for the three country groups identified.

Exceptions to the Rule: Where Girls Outperform Boys

The Education for All (EFA) Global Monitoring Report (GMR) provides a detailed review of progress toward the EFA and MDG goal of eliminating gender disparities in primary and secondary education by 2005 and at all levels of education by 2015 (UNESCO 2008). Although the 2005 deadline was clearly not met, the GMR finds that, in terms of school progression, girls are outperforming boys in an increasing number of developing countries. In many of those countries, girls now make up the majority of students enrolled in upper secondary and tertiary education, except in science-related fields. In the Sub-Saharan African region, women made up the majority of higher education students in six countries in 2008: Cape Verde, Lesotho, Mauritius, Namibia, South Africa, and Sudan.

Extent of Gender Disparities after Controlling for Education Coverage

The higher the education coverage, the smaller the gender disparities. Figure 2.3 explores the relationship between education coverage and the extent of gender

Figure 2.3 Relationship between Education Coverage and Gender Disparity in Primary Education Sub-Saharan African Countries, 2008

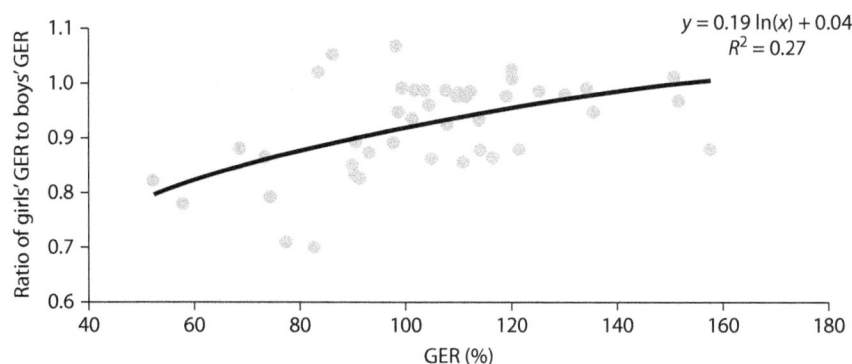

Source: Authors' construction based on data from the UIS Data Centre for 2008 or the latest year available.
Note: GER = gross enrollment ratio. The units of observation in the scatterplot represent Sub-Saharan African countries. The line depicts the statistical relationship between the GER and the ratio of girls' GER to boys' GER, corresponding to the formula shown in the chart.

disparities in the Sub-Saharan African region's primary schools. If education coverage were complete, there would be no disparities in school participation because all children would be enrolled and complete primary schooling. On the other hand, when coverage is low, there is a large potential for social disparities in school participation.

The graph in figure 2.3 shows that the GPI tends to be lower where education coverage is lower. Coverage, however, explains only a fourth of the cross-country variability in the GPI (R^2 is 0.27). Other country-specific factors clearly also play significant roles in gender disparities, at least at the primary level.

Ranking of Countries by Gender Gap Severity

Figure 2.4 illustrates the difference between the actual GPI (primary education GER of girls relative to boys) in Sub-Saharan African countries and the predicted GPI based on the regression in figure 2.3 (based on the individual country's level of education coverage). The calculation of this difference enables the identification of countries that are performing better than average in terms of reducing disadvantages to girls (top of the chart) as well as the countries that are underperforming on this count (bottom of the chart).

Factors Contributing to Severe Gender Gaps

In the underperforming countries, obstacles to girls' school participation may be particularly severe (Kane 2004; World Bank 2006). These diverse obstacles include:

- Traditions that limit the economic role of women
- Longer work hours for girls than boys outside of school (Allen 1988; Kane and de Brun 1995)
- Higher direct costs of schooling for girls (Mason and Khandker 1996; World Bank 2000).

Figure 2.4 Difference between Actual and Model-Predicted Gender Parity Index in Primary Education, by Sub-Saharan African Country, 2008

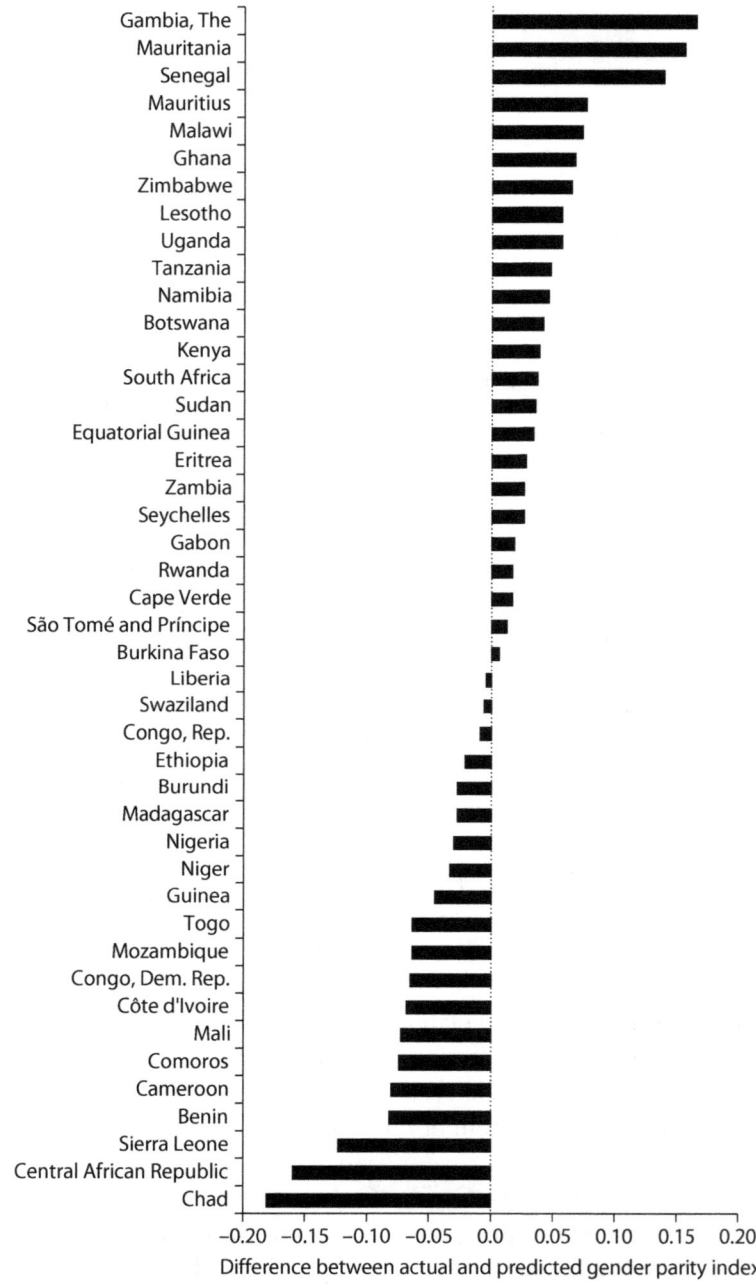

Source: Authors' construction based on data from the UIS Data Centre for 2008 or the latest year available.
Note: GPI = Gender Parity Index, GER = gross enrollment ratio. The chart shows the actual GPI in primary education (GER F/M) minus its predicted value, given the country's primary education GER. The prediction is based on a regression between the two.

Higher safety concerns for girls and traditions of early marriage or childbearing are also often cited as reasons for girls dropping out of school, though the risk of leaving school for these reasons has declined over time (Lloyd and Mensch 2006). School environmental factors such as the presence of female teachers to serve as role models or whether the school has boundary walls or latrines for girls have also been found to be important for girls' school participation (World Bank 2006).

Primary School Gender Gap Largest in Central and West African Countries

The Gambia is the best performer in terms of reducing disadvantages to girls in primary education. It has a very high GPI of 1.06 (indicating some disadvantage to boys) compared with the predicted ratio of 0.89 for its relatively modest education coverage reflected by its primary education GER of only 86 percent. Countries such as the Central African Republic, Cameroon, Benin, Guinea-Bissau, and Chad—all in Central or West Africa—are the poorest performers after taking education coverage into account. There is, clearly, a need to focus further on reducing disadvantages to girls' school participation by addressing the obstacles that play an important role in limiting girls' schooling in these countries.

Relationship between Education coverage and Gender Disparity across All Levels

The relationship explored above may help to explain why gender disparities are almost always wider at the secondary level than in primary education. To test whether there is a single relationship between education coverage and gender disparities across primary and the two cycles of secondary education, a cross-country data set[4] relates the GPI[5] to education coverage[6] in all three cycles. Dummy variables indicate whether the observation pertains to lower or upper secondary education, with primary education serving as the control level. The regression results appear as equation (2.1):

$$GPI = 26.3 + 13.9 \times Ln(GER) + 3.9 - \text{If lower sec} + 11.1 \times \text{If upper sec}$$
$$(t = 5.0)\ (t = 0.7)\ (t = 1.6)\ R^3 = .24 \quad (2.1)$$

The regression shows that the same relationship between education coverage and gender disparity prevails in all of primary, lower, and upper secondary education (the coefficients to the two dummy variables are not statistically significant). For the region as a whole, therefore, gender disparities in primary and secondary education are of the same order of magnitude, after controlling for the education coverage. At the country level, however, this may not be the case. The relatively low R^2 (0.24) implies that factors besides education coverage affect gender disparities. Nevertheless, even at the country level, we can attribute a portion of the difference between primary and secondary school gender disparities to differences in education coverage.

Socioeconomic Disparities beyond Gender: Analysis of Household Surveys

The availability of internationally comparable household surveys makes possible the analysis of other dimensions of socioeconomic disparities in education in the region. Table 2.3 presents income, rural–urban, and gender disparities for the region as a whole, based on household survey data. Each column shows the breakdown of the population enrolled at a given level of education by income, geographic location, and gender.

The last column provides the breakdown of the total population to highlight the magnitude of each type of socioeconomic disparity. For example, although 65 percent of children and youth live in rural areas, only 29 percent of the students enrolled in upper secondary education are from rural areas. Similarly, although 40 percent of all children and youth come from the two poorest income quintiles of households, they account for only 11 percent of upper secondary students.[7]

Two Data Sources Show Similar Gender Disparity Levels

Figure 2.5 compares the 2005 GPIs presented earlier in this chapter (in table 2.1, based on administrative data) with the equivalent ratios derived from household survey data. The results from the two sources of data are slightly different, particularly concerning higher education (where the household survey sample is also relatively small), but the overall pattern is the same in both cases: First, the two sources are consistent in indicating a GPI of around 0.90 in primary education in

Table 2.3 Distribution of Population Aged 5–24 by Gender, Location, Income, and Level of Schooling in Sub-Saharan African Countries, ca. 2005

percent

	Level of schooling at time of survey					
	Not enrolled	Primary	Lower secondary	Upper secondary	Higher	Total
Income quintile						
Q1	23.7	16.5	7.2	3.6	2.2	20.0
Q2	21.7	19.0	12.0	7.2	3.5	20.0
Two bottom quintiles	45.4	35.5	19.2	10.8	5.8	40.0
Q3	20.6	20.1	15.7	10.8	6.7	20.0
Q4	18.8	21.8	22.3	18.2	16.4	20.0
Q5	15.3	22.6	42.8	60.1	71.1	20.0
Two top quintiles	34.1	44.4	65.1	78.3	87.5	40.0
Geographical location						
Rural	70.8	62.2	38.1	28.8	25.9	65.3
Urban	29.2	37.8	61.9	71.2	74.1	34.7
Gender						
Female	54.0	48.5	47.1	41.8	42.5	50.9
Male	46.0	51.5	52.9	58.2	57.5	49.1

Sources: Authors' calculation based on the analysis of household survey data for 26 countries (see appendix J, table J.1): Angola, Benin, Burkina Faso, Cameroon, Central African Republic, Congo, Rep., Côte d'Ivoire, Ethiopia, Gabon, Gambia, The, Ghana, Guinea, Equatorial Guinea, Kenya, Malawi, Mali, Namibia, Niger, Nigeria, Rwanda, Senegal, Sudan, Tanzania, Uganda, Zambia, and Zimbabwe.

Figure 2.5 Comparison of Gender Disparities in Education by Data Source, Sub-Saharan African Countries, ca. 2005

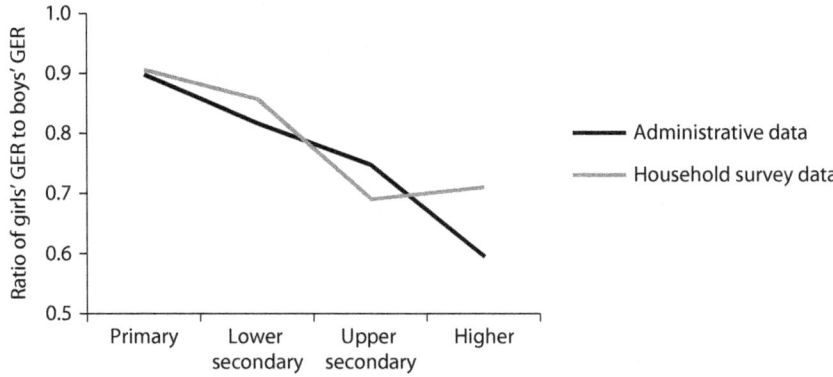

Source: Authors' construction from data in tables 2.1 and 2.3.
Note: GER = gross enrollment ratio. The gender ratio from administrative data is an unweighted average of data from about 45 countries; the similar statistic based on household survey data is a weighted average of 26 countries in the region.

Table 2.4 Disparities by Social Group and Level of Education, Sub-Saharan African Countries, ca. 2005

		Ratio of GER for disadvantaged group to GER for comparison group			
Disadvantaged group	Comparison group	Primary	Lower secondary	Upper secondary	Higher
Bottom 40% by income	Top 40%	0.80	0.29	0.14	0.07
Rural	Urban	0.87	0.33	0.22	0.19
Female	Male	0.91	0.86	0.69	0.71

Source: Author's calculations based on data in table 2.3 (for 26 Sub-Saharan African countries).
Note: GER = gross enrollment ratio.

2005. Second, both data sources show that gender disparities tend to increase with each successive level of education.

Disparities Much Wider by Income and Location than by Gender

Table 2.4 provides a more succinct comparison of the magnitude of the disparities in terms of the three socioeconomic dimensions. As can be seen, the disparities, as defined by the ratio of the GER of the disadvantaged group to the GER of the advantaged group, are far larger across income and geographic location[8] than are the disparities across gender. At the primary level, for instance, the ratio across income groups is only 0.80, compared with the ratio across gender of 0.91.

Disparities across Income and Location Rise Sharply after Primary Education

Although access to primary education is relatively high for all groups, access to secondary and higher education is severely limited for children from rural areas and even more so for children from poor households.

As seen in table 2.4, at the lower secondary level, the GER of children in rural locations is only 0.33 times that of children in urban locations. For the same level of education, the GER of children from poor households is only 0.29 times that of children from richer households. In higher education, the GER of youths from rural locations is only 0.19 times that of youths from urban locations, and the GER of youths from poor households is a mere 0.07 times that of youths from richer households.

Socioeconomic Disparities Likely to Rise when Unfavorable Factors Combine

When several unfavorable factors come together, such as being a girl from a poor household in a rural location, their combined effect is likely to be far greater than the cumulative effects of each factor on its own. Filmer (2000), for instance, finds that gender and income often interact, leading to much larger gender disparities among the economically disadvantaged than in the rest of the population.[9]

Issues for Policy Development

Reducing social disparities requires addressing both the supply of and demand for education. Girls' access to schooling remains an issue in Sub-Saharan Africa. The region remains one of the few in the world where girls still have lower rates of school participation than boys. Equally pressing in the region are the disparities between children in poor and rich households as well as between those in rural and urban households. Although these disparities have declined as a result of the expansion of school places over the years, much remains to be done. Addressing the remaining disparities will require a combination of policies: particularly continued expansion of the supply of education and policies that foster higher demand for education, particularly in rural areas and among the poor.

Increasing the supply of education requires substantial financial resources. On the supply side, the pace at which education coverage can increase will be limited mainly by financial constraints. This issue will be addressed in chapter 4, which deals with the financing of education.

Increasing the demand for education requires providing services that meet the needs of the target population. Chapter 3 looks at strategies for reaching children who are currently not receiving the full cycle of primary education. Many of these out-of-school children do have a school nearby, but they are not attending school for reasons that shall be examined. To keep these children in school until the end of the primary cycle may require both the adjustment of educational services to better meet their needs and, in some cases, some form of compensation to the families for the opportunity cost incurred in sending their children to school.

Given the cumulative nature of these socioeconomic disparities, it is necessary to address these issues beginning from the bottom of the educational pyramid. An important finding from this analysis is the importance of addressing disparities as early as possible in the education system because of their cumulative effects.

Although the disparities at higher levels of education may be wider and may attract more attention, disparities that begin at the primary level often carry over to succeeding levels of schooling.

Notes

1. Administrative or school censuses provide information on students' gender, while household surveys provide information on other socioeconomic characteristics of the students.
2. The gender parity index is calculated as follows: (a) in the first grade of primary education, as the gross intake rate (GIR) of females to males; (b) at the end of the primary cycle, as the PCR of females to males; and (c) in the secondary and tertiary cycles, as the gross enrollment ratio (GER) of females to males.
3. The Country Status Report (CSR) for Lesotho explains that the traditional economic activity for men from Lesotho is work in the gold mines of South Africa (World Bank 2005). That requires little education, so many boys are taken out of school, especially after third grade, to work as herders at home until they are old enough to work in the gold mines. As a result, the PCR was 62 percent for boys and 84 percent for girls in 2007, according to UIS.
4. The data set includes three observations for each of the about 40 countries: one for primary education, one for lower secondary education, and a third for upper secondary education, resulting in a data set totaling about 120 observations.
5. In this case, gender disparity is calculated as the ratio of girls' GER to boys' GER.
6. Measured by the GER. The logarithmic relationship is used to get the best fit (higher R^2).
7. In the case of household income, we can choose which two groups to compare. This analysis opted to compare two fairly wide income groups—the 40 percent richest to the 40 percent poorest—for better comparability with the disparities according to the other two dimensions: girls to boys (51 percent to 49 percent, respectively) and rural to urban (65 percent to 35 percent, respectively). A choice of smaller groups of income, such as the 20 percent richest to the 20 percent poorest, would have led to stronger differentiations.
8. These two groups are closely related, of course, so the disparities by location and the disparities by income in many ways measure the same thing.
9. Filmer (2000) finds strong interactions between wealth and gender in the Arab Republic of Egypt, India, Morocco, Niger, and Pakistan. For example, in India, he finds that there was a 2.5 percentage point difference in the enrollment of boys and girls among the wealthiest, while the gender gap in enrollment was 34 percentage points among the poorest households.

References

Allen, J. 1988. "Dependent Males: The Unequal Division of Labor in Mabumba Households." Labor Study Report 2, Adaptive Research Planning Team (ARPT), Luapula Province, Zambia.

Filmer, D. 2000. "The Structure of Social Disparities in Education: Gender and Wealth." Policy Research Working Paper 2268, World Bank, Washington, DC.

Kane, E. 2004. "Girls' Education in Africa: What Do We Know About Strategies That Work?" Africa Region Human Development Working Paper 73, World Bank, Washington, DC.

Kane, E., and M. de Brun. 1995. "Bitter Seeds: Girls' Participation in Primary Education in The Gambia." In *The Gambia: Why Gambian Households Underinvest in Education of Girls.* Country Economic and Sector Report 14536, World Bank, Washington, DC.

Lloyd, C., and B. Mensch. 2006. "Marriage and Childbirth as Factors in School Exit: An Analysis of DHS Data from Sub-Saharan Africa." Policy Research Division Working Paper 219, Population Council, New York.

Mason, A., and S. Khandker. 1996. "Measuring the Opportunity Costs of Children's Time in a Developing Country: Implications for Education Sector Analysis and Interventions." Human Capital Development Working Paper 72, World Bank, Washington, DC.

Pôle de Dakar UNESCO-BREDA (United Nations Educational, Scientific and Cultural Organization and Regional Office for Education in Africa). 2007. "Education for All in Africa: Top Priority for Integrated Sector-Wide Policies." Dakar+7 Report, Pôle de Dakar UNESCO-BREDA, Dakar.

UIS (United Nations Educational, Scientific and Cultural Organization, Institute for Statistics) Data Centre (database). UIS, Montreal. http://stats.uis.unesco.org.

UNESCO (United Nations Educational, Scientific and Cultural Organization). 2008. "Education for All by 2015: Will We Make It?" Education for All (EFA) Global Monitoring Report, UNESCO, Paris.

World Bank. 2000. "Contraintes et espaces de liberté pour le développement en quantité et en qualité de l'education au Niger." Country Status Report, World Bank, Washington, DC.

———. 2005. "Primary and Secondary Education in Lesotho: A Country Status Report for Education." Africa Region Human Development Working Paper 101, World Bank, Washington, DC.

———. 2006. *World Development Report 2006: Equity and Development.* Washington, DC: World Bank.

CHAPTER 3

Out-of-School Children

Much has been accomplished in the past two decades, but with a regional average primary school completion rate of only 59 percent, the Sub-Saharan African region still has a high proportion of school-age children who did not begin schooling at all or who dropped out before the end of the primary cycle. This chapter draws on household survey data to estimate the total number of out-of-school children in the region and their distribution by urban or rural location, income group, and gender. The chapter then examines selected empirical work to identify strategies that hold the most promise for reducing the number of out-of-school children.

An estimated 35 million primary-school-age children are out of school across the sample of 33 low-income Sub-Saharan African countries.[1] This corresponds to about a third of the total primary-school-age population. Of the 35 million, some 20 million have never been in school, and the remaining 15 million children have dropped out of school.

The set of policies needed to reach and keep all children in school, at least until the end of the primary cycle, is likely to vary from country to country. One key question is whether emphasis should be placed on (a) increasing or adjusting the *supply* of education, or (b) stimulating the *demand* for schooling. The available empirical evidence points to the importance of policies that

- Make schooling more accessible by bringing schools closer to home—including, in some settings, multigrade teaching that helps to contain the social costs of schooling
- Offer a complete cycle of primary schooling to all children
- Manage grade repetition, which increases the risk of students dropping out
- Increase the proportion of female teachers to strike a better gender balance among the teaching faculty and
- Reduce the school fees and other costs of schooling, including opportunity costs, borne by parents.

The chapter also examines other strategies that may be effective in reaching out-of-school children, including efforts to stimulate the demand for education by offsetting the opportunity cost of schooling.

Estimating the Number of Out-of-School Children

Methodology

There are two categories of out-of-school children, and figure 3.1 illustrates those categories within the typical schooling profile found in the region's low-income countries.

Estimating the Proportion of Out-of-School Children

Typically, less than 100 percent of children enter grade one (shown by point A), and even fewer attain grade six (point B).[2] The chart distinguishes between two categories of out-of-school children: The first category comprises children who have never been enrolled in primary education (area X); they are out of school for the entire duration of primary education. The second category consists of children who enrolled in school but dropped out before grade six (area Y); they are out of school for a part of the primary cycle.

It follows from figure 3.1 that we can estimate the proportion of a cohort that is out of school if we have measures of the grade one entry rate (A) and the grade six attainment rate (B).

Calculating Cohort Measures of Grade One Entry and Grade Six Attainment Rates

The grade one entry rate can be estimated as the proportion of, for example, 10- and 11-year-old respondents who report ever having been enrolled in school. Similarly, the cohort grade six attainment rate can be calculated as the proportion of 16- and 17-year-olds who report ever having attained grade six.

Figure 3.1 Typical Schooling Profile in a Low-Income Country

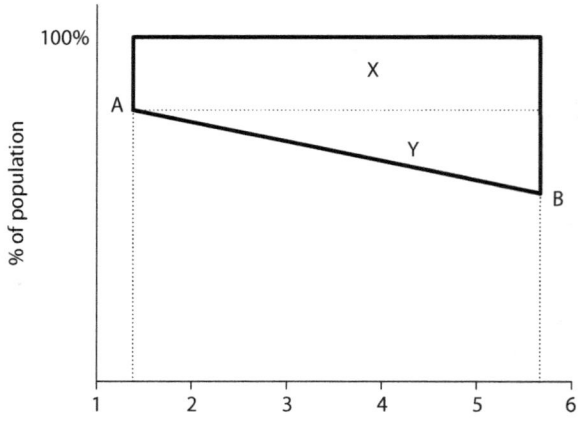

Source: Authors' construction.
Note: A "low-income" country is eligible for lending from the World Bank's International Development Association (IDA); see appendix A, table A.1.

Table 3.1 Primary Entry and Attainment Rates Based on Different Data Sources, 33 Low-Income Sub-Saharan African Countries, ca. 2003
percentage

Household survey data (cohort measures)		Administrative data (cross-sectional measures) GIR		
Grade 1 entry	Grade 6 attainment	Simple average	Truncated at 100%	PCR
80.9	50.4	98.2	87.6	49.9

Sources: UIS Data Centre for administrative data; authors' compilation of rates from household survey data from Country Status Reports (CSRs), Demographic and Health Surveys (DHS), Multiple Indicator Cluster Surveys (MICS), and Core Welfare Indicators Questionnaires (CWIQ); see appendix J, table J.1.
Note: GIR = gross intake rate, PCR = primary completion rate. Household surveys are carried out in different years in different countries, but the results presented here are all adjusted to 2003. Averages are unweighted. "Low-income" countries are those eligible for lending from IDA; see appendix A, table A.1.

Table 3.1 provides the average values of these two statistics across the sample of 33 low-income countries in the region. The table compares these values with the corresponding cross-sectional measures (gross intake rate [GIR] and primary completion rate [PCR]) obtained from administrative data.

The comparison reveals a gap of almost 7 percentage points between the GIR and the cohort grade one entry rate.[3] Such a wide difference occurs because the former is often overinflated.[4] For grade six, however, there is little difference between the PCR and the cohort grade six attainment rate. This comparison illustrates the reliability of the household survey data for estimating the out-of-school population.[5]

Thirty-Five Million Out-of-School Children

We can estimate the proportion of out-of-school children in a country based on its cohort entry and attainment rates.[6] The number of out-of-school children in a country is then calculated by applying the percentage of out-of-school children to the size of the school-age population.[7]

Table 3.2 provides the consolidated result. Based on the schooling profile observed in 2003, a total of about 35 million children are out of school in the 33 low-income Sub-Saharan African countries. This constitutes about a third of the school-age population in these countries.

Twenty Million Never Enrolled, and an Additional 15 Million Dropped Out

The cohort grade one entry rate is used to estimate the number of children who have never been enrolled in school. Applying this percentage share (18.5 percent) to the school-age population, an estimated 20 million children have never been enrolled in school.

The number of children who enrolled but dropped out can be calculated as the residual of the 35 million who are out of school. This yields an estimate of more than 15 million primary school dropouts (or 14.7 percent of the school-age

Table 3.2 Estimated Number of Out-of-School Children in 33 Low-Income Sub-Saharan African Countries, ca. 2003

	Number of children (million)	School-age population, average across countries[a] (%)
Out-of-school children	35.2	33.3
Never enrolled	19.6	18.5
Dropped out	15.5	14.7
School-age population[b]	105.8	100.0

Source: Authors' calculations based on population data from UN 2007 and access rates from household surveys, as reported in the CSRs.
Note: "Low-income" countries are eligible for lending from IDA; see appendix A, table A.1.
a. Population-weighted average.
b. Based on the population of 6- to 11-year-olds (six-year cohort).

population) in the 33 countries. Clearly, each country should address both school access and retention issues to ensure that all children complete the primary cycle.

Comparison with Other Estimates and Regions

Estimates of the share of out-of-school children in Sub-Saharan African countries have varied, possibly based either on differences in methodology or the timing of the studies. However, even the lowest estimated percentage of out-of-school children in Sub-Saharan Africa is higher than that of any other global region.

Is the Share of Out-of-School Children Declining?

The share of out-of-school children has declined since 1999. In 2001/02, they made up 41.8 percent of primary-school-age children in the region, according to estimates (based on both household surveys and administrative data) by the United Nations Educational, Scientific, and Cultural Organization (UNESCO) Institute of Statistics (UIS 2005). That estimate is higher than this report's estimate of 33.3 percent for 2003.

The difference between the UIS 2001/02 estimate and the 2003 estimate here may, at least in part, be explained by (a) differences in methodology,[8] and (b) the earlier date of the UIS study during a period of significant progress in primary school enrollment that began around 1999. Different estimates aside, the fact remains that the share of the out-of-school children in the region is still large.

World's Highest Share of Out-of-School Children

The UIS study covered all developing countries, allowing Sub-Saharan Africa's situation to be seen from a global perspective. Even with the lower current estimate of 33 percent, the region has the highest proportion of out-of-school children in the world, as the following 2001/02 regional statistics show:

- South Asia: 26 percent
- Eastern Europe and Central Asia: 12 percent

- Middle East and North Africa: 10 percent
- East Asia and the Pacific: 6 percent
- Latin America and the Caribbean: 6 percent
- Industrialized countries: 4 percent.

Individual countries outside the region with high proportions of out-of-school children include Haiti (46 percent), the Republic of Yemen (45 percent), Pakistan (44 percent), the Lao People's Democratic Republic (38 percent), Cambodia (35 percent), and Nepal (34 percent). Unsurprisingly, these countries are among the poorest in their respective regions.

Proportion of Out-of-School Children, by Sub-Saharan African Country

Figure 3.2 shows the proportion of out-of-school children and the proportion of school-age children who have never enrolled in school in each of the 33 low-income Sub-Saharan African countries. The difference between the former and the latter is the proportion of school-age children who enrolled in school but subsequently dropped out of school.

This distinction is crucial to policy makers and practitioners because different policy prescriptions are required to ensure that these children are enrolled and stay in school at least until the end of the primary cycle: for children who have never enrolled, it may be necessary to focus on improving access to schooling and for children who drop out of school, it may be necessary to focus on improving retention and thereby reducing dropout rates.

Figure 3.2 Proportion of Out-of-School Children in 33 Low-Income Sub-Saharan African Countries, ca. 2003

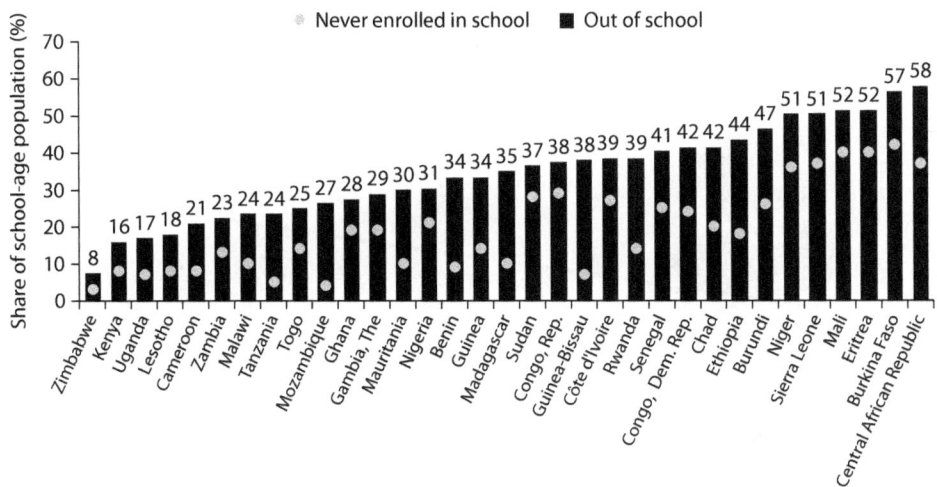

Source: Authors' calculations, based on UN 2007, GIR and PCR data from the UIS Data Centre, and access rates from household surveys reported in CSRs. For more detail, see appendix D, table D.1.
Note: "Low-income" countries are eligible for lending from IDA; see appendix A, table A.1.

Across Countries, 8 Percent to 58 Percent of Children Were Out of School in 2003

The proportion of primary-school-age children who were out of school ranged from 8 percent in Zimbabwe to 58 percent in the Central African Republic, as seen in figure 3.2. More than half of school-age children were out of school in six countries: Burkina Faso, the Central African Republic, Eritrea, Mali, Niger, and Sierra Leone. Most of these children never enrolled in school, implying that access to schooling may be a major issue in these six countries. On the other hand, in countries such as Guinea-Bissau, Mozambique, and Tanzania, the main problem is clearly one of children dropping out of school.

Access and Retention Problems Do Not Always Go Hand in Hand

Figure 3.3 shows the relationship between the proportion of a cohort that is out of school in grade one and the proportion of a cohort that is out of school in grade six. There is a positive and statistically significant relationship, implying that countries that have many children lacking access to grade one also tend to have many out-of-school children at the end of the primary cycle.

The relationship, however, is not particularly strong (the coefficient of determination, R^2, is 0.37), as is clearly reflected by the large differences between individual country observations and the trend line. For instance, among countries where less than 10 percent of children never enrolled in grade one, the trend line indicates that the proportion who do not attain grade six should be around 40 percent. However, the actual proportions of children who do not attain grade six vary between 12 percent (Zimbabwe) and 69 percent (Guinea-Bissau). This disparity underscores the need for country-specific

Figure 3.3 Relationship between the Proportion of Out-of-School Children at Beginning and End of the Primary Cycle, in 33 Low-Income Sub-Saharan African Countries, 2003

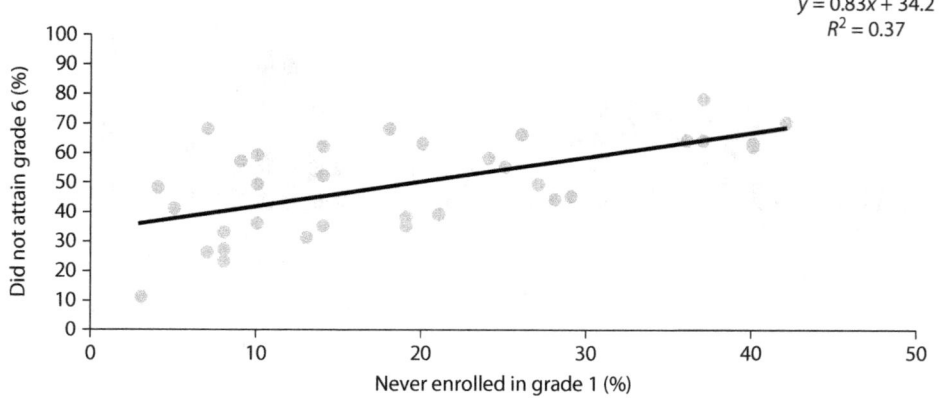

Sources: Authors' construction based on population data from UN 2007, GIR and PCR data from UIS Data Centre, and access rates from household surveys as reported in CSRs. For more country-specific detail, see appendix D, table D.1.
Note: GIR = gross intake rate, PCR = primary completion rate.

diagnostics and policy prescriptions aimed at reducing the proportion of out-of-school children in the region.

The three largest countries—Nigeria, Ethiopia, and the Democratic Republic of Congo—account for almost half of all out-of-school children in the region, with 7 million, 5 million, and 4 million out-of-school children, respectively. Together, they account for 16 million of the estimated 35 million out-of-school children in the 33 low-income Sub-Saharan African countries.

Profile of Out-of-School Children

The more that is known about the out-of-school children, the better equipped policy makers and practitioners will be to design and implement policy prescriptions that will be appropriate for their respective countries. Toward this end, the present analysis uses cross-country, comparable information from household surveys to examine the characteristics of the out-of-school children.

Aggregate Distribution by Gender, Location, and Wealth

The extent to which a child is at risk of being out of school depends on the child's socioeconomic background—the risk rising with poverty—as well as geographic location (urban or rural) and gender.

Rural and Poor Children Are Most at Risk

Among all children between the ages of 9 and 11, as figure 3.4 illustrates, the risk of being out of school is

- Higher for girls (39 percent) than for boys (33 percent), a relatively small difference of less than 6 percentage points[9]

Figure 3.4 Risk of Being Out of School by Gender, Location, and Wealth, Aggregate for Low-Income Sub-Saharan African Countries, 2003

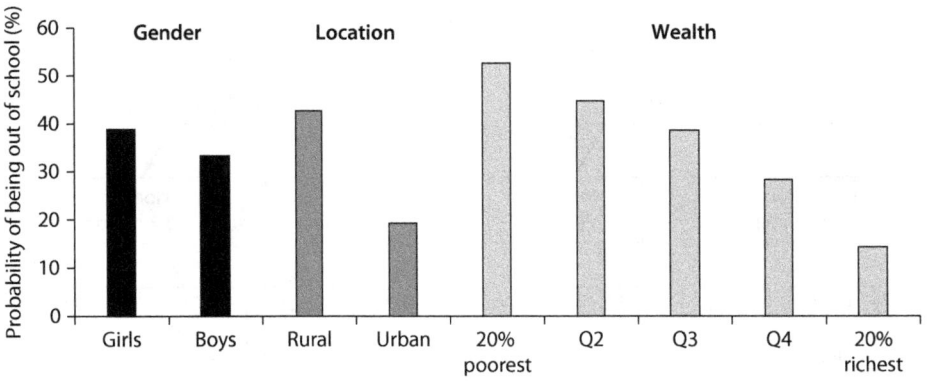

Source: Authors' construction based on population data from UN 2007, GIR and PCR data from UIS Data Centre, and access rates from household surveys as reported in CSRs. For more country-specific detail, see appendix D, table D.1.
Note: Based on data for children aged 9–11 years. The table contains the consolidated analysis for 30 low-income countries. "Low-income" countries are eligible for lending from IDA; see appendix A, table A.1.

- Higher for rural children (43 percent) than for urban children (20 percent), a 23 percentage point difference
- Higher for children from the two poorest income quintiles, who are 27 percentage points more likely to be out of school than children from the two richest quintiles.

In other words, living in a rural area or being poor are both strong predictors of a child being out of school.

The Rural Dimension. Nearly 30 million of the 35 million out-of-school children live in rural areas. Figure 3.5 presents the breakdown of the estimated 35.2 million out-of-school children in the 33 countries by location, wealth, and gender. As shown, an estimated 29.6 million of the out-of-school children live in rural areas, compared with only 5.6 million in urban areas. There is clearly a strong rural dimension to the problem that can hardly be overemphasized.

The Poverty Dimension. Nineteen million of the 35 million out-of-school children come from poor households. As shown in figure 3.5, the poorest 40 percent of households account for 55 percent (or 19.4 million) of the 35.2 million out-of-school children.

Almost half of the out-of-school children are both rural and poor. Figure 3.5 also shows the extent to which the two key dimensions overlap. More than 90 percent of out-of-school children (31.9 million) are either rural *or* poor,[10] while almost 50 percent (17.1 million) are both rural *and* poor.

Figure 3.5 Distribution of Out-of-School Children by Gender, Location, and Wealth, Aggregate for Selected Low-Income Sub-Saharan African Countries, ca. 2003

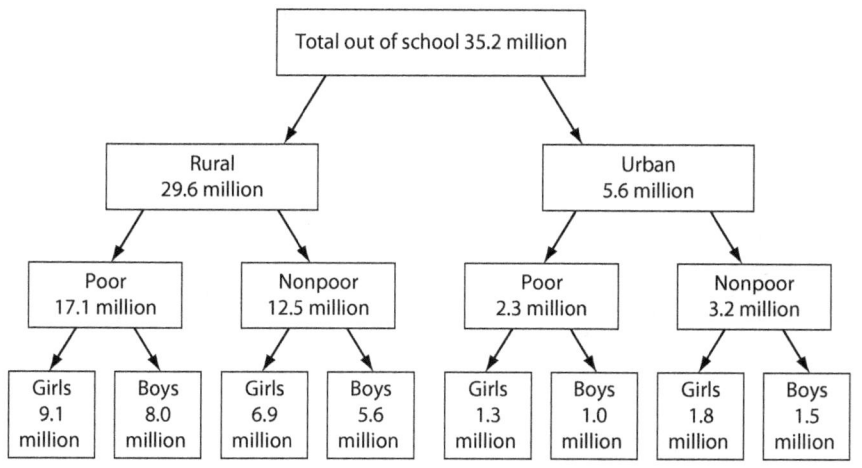

Source: Authors' construction based on population data from UN 2007, GIR and PCR data from UIS Data Centre, and access rates from household surveys as reported in CSRs; see appendix D, table D.1.
Note: "Poor" corresponds to the poorest 40 percent of the population, and "nonpoor" to the remaining 60 percent. "Low-income" countries are eligible for lending from IDA; see appendix A, table A.1.

Figure 3.6 Distribution of Out-of-School Children by Gender, Location, and Wealth in Selected Low-Income Sub-Saharan African Countries, ca. 2003

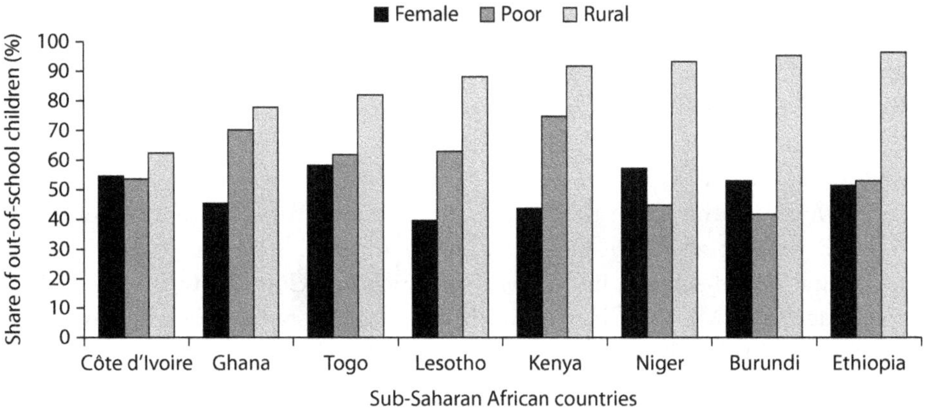

Source: Authors' construction based on population data from UN 2007, GIR and PCR data from UIS Data Centre, and access rates from household surveys as reported in CSRs; see appendix D, table D.1.
Note: "Poor" corresponds to the poorest 40 percent of the population. "Low-income" countries are eligible for lending from IDA; see appendix A, table A.1.

Profile of Out-of-School Children by Country

The distinctions by gender, location, and wealth also vary by country, as shown in figure 3.6.

Gender Disparity

In Sub-Saharan African countries where overall educational coverage is high (around 80 percent or more), more boys than girls tend to be out of school. On the other hand, where coverage is less than 80 percent, there is either gender parity or girls account for most of the out-of-school children. For example, figure 3.6 shows that in some countries (notably Burundi, Côte d'Ivoire, Niger, and Togo), most of the out-of-school children are girls, while in other countries (Ghana, Kenya, and Lesotho), most are boys.

This correlation supports the finding in chapter 2 of a close relationship between gender disparities and the level of educational coverage.

Socioeconomic Disparity

In the poorest countries, deprivation of schooling affects children from all strata of society. In some of the region's poorest countries, notably Burundi and Niger, out-of-school children are distributed almost equally across all five income quintiles—possibly indicating that even households in the upper quintiles are affected by poverty and are experiencing just as much difficulty sending their children to school as those in the lower quintiles. In the relatively richer countries, such as Ghana and Kenya, the deprivation of schooling tends to be more concentrated among the poor.

Rural–Urban Disparity

The more-urbanized countries may have large pockets of urban out-of-school children. However, throughout the 33 low-income Sub-Saharan African countries, children in rural areas have a higher risk of being out of school than urban children. In the predominantly rural countries, almost all out-of-school children live in rural areas. In Ethiopia, for example, with 84 percent of the population living in rural areas, rural children account for 96 percent of all out-of-school children (UN 2007, 115).

However, in the more urbanized Côte d'Ivoire, rural children account for only 63 percent of all out-of-school children.[11] In this case, a policy targeting only rural out-of-school children will not suffice if Côte d'Ivoire is to achieve the educational MDGs. Given their different circumstances, rural out-of-school children and urban out-of-school children will need separate policy initiatives and prescriptions.

Reaching Out-of-School Children

With only four years left to realize the MDG goals, a third of primary-school-age children are out of school in the Sub-Saharan African region's low-income countries. The central question, then, is this: what can be done to ensure that more children will not only enroll in grade one but will also complete the full cycle of primary education in the near future?[12]

There are two key parts to this question: What does it take to ensure that all children enroll in the first grade of primary education? And once the children are in school, what does it take to keep them enrolled until the end of the primary cycle?

Supply-Side Factors that Influence Access to Schooling

Over the past four decades, supply-side policies have been the cornerstone of the region's expansion in educational coverage. The most basic of these policies—building more schools in underserved areas—has greatly improved access to schooling in the past. It is a necessary, but not sufficient, condition of school attendance that the service be made available. Table 3.3, based on data from eight Sub-Saharan African countries, shows that 73 percent of school-age children now have a school within 2 kilometers from home.[13]

Distance from Home to School

Table 3.3 also shows a gradual decline in the probability of attending school as the distance between school and home increases. For example, when the nearest school is more than 5 kilometers away, only 41 percent of the children are enrolled. But when the nearest school is within 1–2 kilometers from the home, 66 percent of children are enrolled.

Table 3.3 Correlation of Distance to School and Probability of Grade One Enrollment, Simulated for Aggregate of Eight Sub-Saharan African Countries, ca. 2003
percentage

	Distance between home and nearest school						
	< 300 m	300 m-1 km	1-2 km	2-3 km	3-5 km	> 5 km	Total
Share of school-age population	40	17	16	10	9	8	100
Simulated grade one entry rate	73	69	66	61	59	41	n.a.

Sources: Authors' calculation based on household survey data from Benin, Burundi, Côte d'Ivoire, Congo, Rep., Ethiopia, Guinea, Mali, and Mauritania.
Note: n.a. = not applicable. Regression analysis was used to determine a statistical relationship, based on a consolidated data set for the eight countries, between the probability of enrollment in grade one and the distance between home and nearest school. The entry rate shown in the last row is calculated by simulation using this statistical relation. The last row may therefore present a smoother relationship between the two variables than is the case in reality.

In the sample of eight countries covered in table 3.3, 27 percent of school-age children live more than 2 kilometers away from the nearest school. If the distance to school were reduced to less than 2 kilometers for these children, their grade one enrollment rates could rise by approximately 15 percentage points (from about 54 percent to about 69 percent). This improvement would increase the grade one entry rate for the cohort as a whole from 66 percent to about 70 percent, an improvement of 4 percentage points. Countries with a large share of children living far from the nearest school—such as Burundi, Ethiopia, and Mali—can expect greater improvements in enrollment by reducing the distance to school.

Multigrade Teaching

One way to reduce the distance to school is by building more and smaller schools rather than fewer large schools. In the small schools, multigrade teaching can be used to keep costs down while offering the whole primary cycle in the same school (Theunynck 2009).

Supply of Schools

As noted in table 3.3, 27 percent of the children who live within 300 meters of the nearest school are not enrolled. This suggests that having a school nearby is a necessary but far from sufficient condition for raising school enrollment.

A study of 21 low-income countries that included some Sub-Saharan African countries, for instance, finds that reducing the distance to school generally has a significant but small effect on school enrollment (Filmer 2004). However, in countries where "distance to the nearest primary school is large there tends to be a reasonably sized impact of distance on enrollment," Filmer (2004, 8) also finds. In addition, he concludes that "other interventions, such as those that raise the quality of schooling, or those that affect the demand for schooling directly through incentives to enroll or indirectly through the expected benefits to schooling, should be included in any strategy for education for all" (2004, 22).

Schooling Supply Meets Demand by Adapting to Local Needs
Rural residents represent over 70 percent of the total population of the region, but most school systems initially served mainly urban populations, resulting in primary school curricula and textbooks that are often biased toward an urban context.

Reforming Curricula
Curriculum content has seldom focused on the skills needed for improving the livelihood of rural populations (FAO and UNESCO-IIEP 2006). A review of curriculum reforms undertaken by several Sub-Saharan African countries—conducted by the Food and Agriculture Organization (FAO) and UNESCO's International Institute for Educational Planning (IIEP)—showed how each country can bring its schools closer to its respective communities by making the curriculum more relevant to local realities.

Taylor and Muhall (1997) argue that contextualizing the curriculum—for example, by using agriculture as a unifying theme and building on children's experience from outside the school—renders the curriculum more relevant to rural students. Nevertheless, as they observe, "many community members, particularly parents, view primary education as a means of enabling their children to leave agriculture behind and to go to work in urban areas where they may earn money which can be brought home to the family" (Taylor and Muhall 1997, 31). For reasons such as these, great care must be taken to ensure that the curriculum, while incorporating the children's communities and experiences, still focuses on literacy and numeracy rather than on producing trained farmers or school completers fit only for agriculture or nonskilled jobs (Taylor and Muhall 1997, 31).

Adapting School Calendars
From the supply and demand perspectives, the school calendar and hours of instruction are policy instruments that may be used to make it more conducive for parents to send their children to school (see, for example, World Bank 2001, 2005). In rural settings where many activities—such as fetching water, planting, harvesting, and winnowing—are highly labor-intensive and time-sensitive, both school calendar and hours of instruction can be adjusted to free children for work on family farms or in the home when necessary.

When the school calendar and schedule are deliberately designed with these constraints in mind, such as in the nonformal education centers in Ethiopia (World Bank 2005), they reduce the direct and opportunity costs of school attendance, thus making schools more attractive to parents and increasing their willingness to send their children to school.

Ensuring Adequate Local Services
In many developing countries, there is increasing empirical evidence of high returns on investment in school facilities that ensure an adequate level of service (Schady and Paxson 1999; World Bank 2004b). The quality of school

infrastructure, including the availability of drinking water and toilets, greatly increases the probability of boys' enrollment in Ethiopia (Chaudhury, Christiaensen, and Asadullah 2006, 18). The availability of water and sanitation was important for the retention of girls, for instance, in Senegal (Sey 2001).

Overcrowding, on the other hand, can substantially reduce the probability of enrollment (Chaudhury, Christiaensen, and Asadullah 2006, 18). One of the major problems in ensuring an adequate level of service is the shortage of teachers who are willing to accept rural assignments. Some countries are experimenting with new ways of overcoming this problem, with varying degrees of success, as box 3.1 describes.

Box 3.1

The Central African Republic, The Gambia, Lesotho, and Malawi: Enhancing Teacher Deployment to Rural Areas

Central African Republic—Regionally Based Teacher Training and Post Assignment
Assigning teachers trained in the capital to the provinces, even the provinces of their origin, proved difficult because the teachers preferred to remain in the capital where there are more opportunities. To overcome the problem, regional teacher training institutes that recruit within the respective provinces were established. This has made it easier to assign teachers to the provinces.

The Gambia—Progressive Financial Incentives
A progressive financial incentive program for teachers in The Gambia succeeded in raising the number of teachers deployed to, and staying on in, the remotest and understaffed areas. The incentive in the form of a bonus rises with the distance from the school to the main road—varying from 30 percent to 40 percent of the basic salary. A survey of teacher trainees reports that 95 percent of the trainees would accept a rural posting upon completion of their training if it comes with an appropriate hardship allowance.

Lesotho—School-Based Posts
Lesotho has had some success in attracting teachers to previously underserved rural areas through the so-called "market" system. Teachers apply directly to the schools for vacancies, giving schools more autonomy in teacher recruitment and management and facilitating the filling of vacancies in less desirable areas. The drawbacks of this school-based recruitment approach include the potential for nepotism and difficulty recruiting more qualified teachers to areas where living conditions are less attractive.

Malawi—Self-Selection of Teacher Training Applicants
Upon applying to the teacher training institute, applicants are informed that they will be assigned to remote rural areas. The intention is to foster applicant self-selection and thus ensure that future graduates consist primarily of those who are willing to serve in remote areas.

Source: Jarousse et al. 2009.

Demand-Side Factors that Attract Parents, Children

Among the effective demand-side interventions to enroll and retain primary-school-age pupils are abolishing school fees, curbing other required parents' fees, compensating for the opportunity cost of sending children to school, and direct cash or food donations to families.

Abolishing School Fees and Limiting Required Contributions

In poor households, fees and other nonvoluntary contributions—even when they are quite small—can be a significant barrier to parents sending their children to school. The probability of nonenrollment is particularly acute in rural areas where subsistence farmers often have little monetary income.

An increasingly fewer number of countries in the region now impose school fees in public primary schools. UNESCO (2008) reports that in 2006, 13 countries still charged primary school tuition fees, down from 22 countries in 2000. There are, however, other direct costs of schooling. It is quite common, for instance, for schools to request financial contributions from parents—for example, in the form of parents' association fees—to cover some of their operating or maintenance costs. In addition, children may be required to buy textbooks, writing materials, and uniforms.

In many countries, parents may also be asked to contribute to the hiring of additional teachers for the school. This practice is quite common in community schools in Chad, Mali, and Togo (World Bank 2007a, 2007c; Pôle de Dakar UNESCO-BREDA 2006) and in public schools in Cameroon, the Republic of Congo, and Madagascar (World Bank 2001, 2003, 2010) when the government provides too few teachers to run the school.

The higher the sum of all costs and required contributions, the more likely children are to be out of school. Empirical evidence from many countries points to a very high price elasticity of demand for schooling. For example, when the governments of Uganda and Malawi abolished primary school fees in the 1990s, enrollments surged by two-thirds in both countries (Avenstrup, Liang, and Nellemann 2004). Similarly, following the lifting of the "droits exigibles" (fees) in 2001 in Cameroon, enrollments increased by 59 percent in primary grade one.[14]

When abolishing primary school fees, countries should therefore anticipate a surge in enrollment and plan accordingly to accommodate that surge. The operational guide for the abolition of school fees prepared jointly by the World Bank and United Nations Children's Fund (UNICEF 2009) provides a useful list of the steps needed in the planning process. The abolition of school fees can often be a catalyst for other longer-terms reforms of primary education.

Compensating for Opportunity Cost

Analyses of household survey data show that children contribute to the household economy, particularly in rural areas where they are often responsible for a wide variety of work such as fetching water, collecting firewood, looking after younger siblings, herding livestock, and other farm work. Therefore, there is an opportunity cost involved in going to school because the time children spend at school reduces their contribution to the household economy.

The opportunity cost rises with age because older children are generally more productive than their younger siblings. Further, the opportunity cost of children's labor weighs heavily on very poor families, particularly when the children are also the main breadwinners. Two types of interventions can offset the opportunity cost of schooling: mitigating the cost and adding benefits for school attendance.

Reducing the Opportunity Cost. The opportunity cost of schooling can be reduced, for instance, by installing a borehole in the village, providing a grinding mill, or organizing community services to care for young children, thus freeing girls who would otherwise be responsible for caring for their younger siblings to go to school.

Increasing the Benefits of School Attendance. Providing free meals at school also reduces the opportunity cost of attending school. In addition, it often improves children's nutritional health which, in turn, has a positive impact on their school attendance. In Kenya, for instance, student attendance increased by 30 percent in preschools that were provided with free school meals (Vermeersch and Kremer 2004). However, it should be emphasized that such programs, if they are not well planned, can lead to overcrowding in schools or a reduction in instructional time. Further, as the Government of Malawi and World Bank (2007b) found, feeding programs can be financially difficult to sustain.

Stimulating Demand through Conditional Cash Transfer Programs

Another way to increase the benefits of schooling is through a cash transfer program, whereby families receive periodic donations of cash or food if their children attend school. Conditional cash transfer (CCT) programs now play an increasingly important role in the poverty reduction strategies of many developing countries.

Rigorous impact evaluations in many Latin American countries have generally found these programs to be effective in raising children's school attendance (see, for example, Schultz 2001; Rawlings and Rubio 2003; Glewwe and Olinto 2004; Schady and Araujo 2006). Similarly, Malawi's pilot CCT program for teenage girls reduced the dropout rate among girls in school and increased the reenrollment rate among girls who had dropped out of school (see box 3.2). Barrera-Osorio et al. (2008), however, report a negative impact on the attendance of siblings of treated students, particularly sisters, because of a reallocation of responsibilities among family members.

Research Shows Positive Impact of Demand-Side Interventions

Aside from the Malawi case described in box 3.2, there are few impact evaluations of demand-side interventions aimed at raising student attendance in Sub-Saharan Africa. Several studies are under way, such as the Lesotho CCT pilot

Box 3.2

Malawi: Impact of Conditional Cash Transfers on Girls' Secondary School Attendance

In 2008, Malawi launched a two-year conditional cash transfer pilot program targeted at teenage girls and young women to promote their attendance and, among those who had dropped out, reenrollment in secondary school. The program consisted of two different types of cash transfers: (a) direct transfers of US$1–$5 a month to each girl, and (b) indirect transfers of US$4–$10 a month to the parents of each girl. One year after its commencement, the transfer program had had a significant impact on secondary school attendance. The reenrollment rate among girls who had already dropped out of school rose by a factor of 2.5, while the dropout rate among those in school fell by 5 percentage points, from 11 percent to 6 percent.

Source: Baird, McIntosh, and Ozler 2009.

Box 3.3

Kenya: Girls' Scholarship Program

Kremer, Miguel, and Thornton (2005) conducted a randomized evaluation of the impact on learning of a Girls Scholarship Program implemented in two districts in rural Kenya in late 2001. Out of a sample of 128 schools, half were randomly chosen to participate in the program.

The merit-based scholarships were awarded to girls in the sixth grade who scored in the top 15 percent in the program schools in each district. In the two years of the program, the winners received: (a) a grant of approximately US$6.40 paid directly to the school to cover school fees; (b) a cash grant of US$12.80 paid to their family to cover school supplies; and (c) public recognition at an awards ceremony at the school.

Girls eligible for the scholarship had higher school attendance rates in one district, and higher average test scores in all treatment schools, compared with girls in the control group. In Busia district, the program resulted in a 30 percent drop in absenteeism among girls. Test scores among girls enrolled in schools eligible for the scholarship program rose by 0.19 standard deviations. In addition, there is evidence of positive externalities on boys (who were not eligible for the awards) as well as on girls with low pretest scores (who were unlikely to win awards). On average, boys' test scores increased by 0.08 standard deviations. Schools offering the scholarship also had significantly higher teacher attendance (almost a 5 percentage point increase), indicating higher teaching effort following the introduction of the program.

Source: Kremer, Miguel, and Thorton 2005.

program for orphans and vulnerable children in school. One recent randomized evaluation in Kenya found that a merit scholarship program for girls in primary schools raised their test scores as well as attendance among both girls and boys, as described further in box 3.3.

Alternative Interventions

More research is needed on the cost-effectiveness of alternative interventions to increase school participation. School feeding programs and CCT programs are costly to implement. It is therefore important to compare the cost-effectiveness of these programs relative to other interventions. For instance, deworming, at US$3.50 per additional year of schooling, can be extraordinarily cost-effective in raising children's school participation, compared with a school feeding program costing as much as US$36 per additional year of schooling achieved (Kremer 2003).

Table 3.4 summarizes some of the education policies discussed above and compares their potential impact and costs.

Factors that Influence Retention

Parents enroll their children in school because they expect the benefits of schooling to outweigh the costs. When the child is pulled out of school early, it is an indication that a shift in the cost-benefit balance has occurred, and parents have assessed that it is no longer worth investing in schooling for that child.

Table 3.4 Education Policies to Increase Access to, and Participation in, Primary Schooling

Policy	Scope	Potential impact	Cost	Implementation
Basic supply-side policy: *Ensure all children have a school nearby*				
Bring schools closer to the children	About 1 in 4 children live > 2 km away from school, but large variations exist across and within countries.	Being close to a school is necessary for access and participation: about 27% of children do not go to school even when the school is nearby.	High	Target areas where distance to school is a problem. Use multigrade teaching, when appropriate, to reduce cost.
Qualitative supply-side policy: *Ensure better fit between schooling conditions and parental expectations and constraints*				
Adjust school calendar and schedule	To be assessed at the country level	Potentially high in some countries	Low	Allow school calendar and schedules to accommodate children's constraints.
Adjust curriculum content	To be assessed at the country level	Potentially high, depending on recipients' needs	Low	Allow adjustments of curriculum content.
Abolish primary school fees	To be assessed at the country level	Potentially high	Moderate to high depending on country	Abolish school fees and reduce or eliminate parents' payments of teachers' salaries and school materials.
Reduce the opportunity cost of schooling	All parents in poverty	Potentially high	High	Examine the costs and impact of school feeding program, cash transfers, and other alternatives.

Source: Authors' compilation.

Most of the factors that influence access to schooling are also associated with retention. There are, however, additional factors that affect retention, and they are mostly related to the child's schooling experience once enrolled. Some of these are discussed below.[15]

Late Starters at Higher Risk of Dropping Out

Although the official age of entry to primary education is 6 or 7 years, many children in Sub-Saharan Africa do not enroll until they are 8, 9, or even 10.[16] Malnutrition and long distances to school are two of the factors that cause children to start school at later ages (World Bank 2004a).

These children who start school late incur higher opportunity costs than their younger peers because children's productivity increases with age. For the same reason, over-age children are at greater risk of being taken out of school than their peers who enroll at the correct school starting age, particularly if they are not making good progress or if they have to repeat a grade. For girls, there is the added factor of parents being reluctant to let their children attend school once they reach puberty. The later they enroll, the less schooling these girls are likely to receive.

Increasing the Share of Female Teachers Increases Retention, Decreases Repetition

Mapto-Kengne and Mingat (2002) examined the impact of gender composition of the teaching faculty on student repetition and retention in a sample of 54 developing countries across Africa, the Middle East, Asia, and Latin America.[17] Based on a regression analysis using the country as the unit of observation, they find that although the proportion of female teachers does not affect access to schooling and student learning, it does have a beneficial impact on repetition rates of both boys and girls as well as on the retention rate of girls.[18] Having a more gender-balanced teaching force can, therefore, have a significant and positive impact on children's schooling careers.

Gender-Balance Simulation Shows Impact. Table 3.5 simulates what happens to repetition and retention rates when the gender composition of the teaching faculty changes. For the Sub-Saharan African region as a whole, raising the proportion

Table 3.5 Impact of Proportion of Female Teachers on Primary-School Repetition and Retention Rates in Sub-Saharan African Countries
percentage

			Scenarios				
Assumption	Proportion of female teachers		20.0	30.0	38.0[a]	40.0	50.0
Results	Simulation of repetition		17.2	15.9	14.9[a]	14.5	13.1
	Simulation of retention	Girls	51.1	55.9	59.7[a]	60.7	65.6
		Boys	66.7	66.7	66.7[a]	66.7	66.7

Source: Authors' calculation based on regression results from Mapto-Kengne and Mingat 2002.
a. Similar to current regional averages of these statistics.

of female teachers by 10 percentage points raises girls' retention rate by almost 5 percentage points while not affecting the retention rate of boys. It would also reduce the repetition rate of boys and girls by more than 1 percentage point.

Share of Female Teachers Relatively Low but Growing. Currently, female teachers make up about 38 percent of the teaching faculty in the sample of 33 low-income Sub-Saharan African countries, up from 35 percent in the mid-1990s (UIS Data Centre). In low-income countries in Asia and the Middle East, about half of the teachers are women. In Latin America, as many as three out of four teachers are women. From an international perspective, then, Sub-Saharan African countries have relatively few female teachers.

Across countries, however, the variation in the proportion of female faculty is large—from a low of 12 percent in Chad to a high of 78 percent in Lesotho. The simulation results in table 3.5 show that if the proportion of female teachers were raised from the current 38 percent to 50 percent across the region, the retention rate could be expected to improve by about 3 percentage points overall: a 6 percentage point improvement for girls without any change among boys.

Incomplete Primary Education Cycle Reduces Retention in Low-Income Countries

Equation (3.1) shows the relationship between the retention rate and the proportion of all new grade one students enrolled in schools that do not offer the full cycle of primary schooling (hereafter referred to as feeder schools):

$$\text{Retention rate} = 103 - 1.4 \times \text{Proportion of grade 1 in feeder school} - 1.3 \times \text{Proportion repeaters } (t = 2.9)\ (t = 3.2)\ R^2 = 0.55 \quad (3.1)$$

The proportion of repeaters is also included in the regression as a control for differences in the performance of the school system in general. The data come from Country Status Reports (CSRs) of 19 low-income Sub-Saharan African countries.[19] With the country serving as the unit of observation, the regression results should be interpreted with care.

The regression results show that the higher the proportion of children enrolled in feeder schools, the lower the retention rate. In particular, it indicates that a 1 percentage point increase in feeder school enrollment translates into a reduction of 1.4 percentage points in the primary school retention rate. The negative impact of enrollment in feeder schools on retention is significant and is too large to be ignored.

On average, across the low-income Sub-Saharan African countries, about 13 percent of grade-one new enrollees begin their schooling careers in schools that do not offer the full cycle of primary education. The proportion of feeder schools across the 19 countries covered by the CSRs ranges from 3 percent in the Republic of Congo to 8 percent in Cameroon and Rwanda, and to more than 20 percent in Benin and Mozambique.

Grade Repetition Reduces Retention

The above regression results also suggest that repetition has a significant negative impact on retention: a 1 percentage point increase in the proportion of repeaters leads to a 1.3 percentage point drop in the retention rate. Using a larger dataset covering 54 developing countries across the world, Mapto-Kengne and Mingat (2002) find that a 1 percentage point increase in the repetition rate produces a 0.9 percentage point drop in the retention rate for girls and a 0.7 percentage point decline in the retention rate for boys.[20] Although these estimates are lower than the regression results, they still indicate a significant negative impact of repetition on student retention.

Repetition High in Many Sub-Saharan African Countries

The proportion of repeaters averages 15 percent across the region's low-income countries (UIS Data Centre). The proportion ranges from 2 percent in Sudan to 29 percent in Burundi, the Central African Republic, and Uganda.

Although the intention of repetition is for the child to attain the required standard for his or her grade, empirical studies consistently show that repetition increases the probability that the child will drop out of school, thereby cutting short the child's schooling career. One reason for this outcome is that repetition shifts the balance between the costs and perceived benefits of education toward the former and away from the latter. When a child is required to repeat a grade, the household cost of schooling increases because the family has to do without the child's labor for an additional year. At the same time, repetition sends the signal that the child is not learning well and that the benefits of educating the child may be less than anticipated. This may tilt the balance, particularly if the parents' initial demand for schooling was not that strong, as is often the case for the most vulnerable children (those in rural locations, the poor, and girls), resulting in the child dropping out from school.

Reduced Repetition and Enrollment in Feeder Schools May Improve Retention

Table 3.6 presents a simulation of the impact of repetition and enrollment on the retention rate in incomplete schools. A comparison of three scenarios shows

Table 3.6 Impact on Primary School Retention of Reduced Repetition and Increased Share of Schools with Full Primary Cycle
percentage

		Scenario 1	Scenario 2	Scenario 3
Assumptions	Repeaters as share of enrollment	15[a]	10	10
	Share of grade-one pupils in feeder schools	13[a]	10	5
Result	Simulation of retention to grade six	65[a]	75	83

Source: Authors' calculation based on data for 19 low-income Sub-Saharan African countries. Numbers are calculated by simulation based on a regression between the three variables.
Note: "Feeder schools" are schools that do not offer a complete primary cycle of grades one through six.
a. Similar to current regional averages of these statistics.

that student retention could improve by 10 percentage points or more through a combined reduction in (a) grade repetition and (b) enrollment in feeder schools. The simulation is based on the above regression equation (3.1).

The simulation estimates the following under three scenarios:

- *Scenario 1* corresponds to the current average situation in low-income Sub-Saharan African countries where the proportion of repeaters is 15 percent, the proportion of grade-one children in feeder schools is 13 percent, and the retention rate is 65 percent.
- *Scenario 2* represents a region wide average reduction, to 10 percent, in both the repetition rate and the proportion of students enrolled in feeder schools. Under this scenario, the retention rate may be expected to improve by more than 10 percentage points, to 75 percent.
- *Scenario 3* represents a further reduction in the proportion of students enrolled in feeder schools to, say, 5 percent. That scenario may be expected to raise the retention rate to 83 percent.

The results suggest that the repetition rate and the proportion of students enrolled in feeder schools can be important policy instruments for increasing retention rates in the region.[21] Further, if the proportion of female teachers were raised to 50 percent, the overall retention rate may rise to as much as 78 percent—or even to 86 percent under the more optimistic scenario.[22]

Table 3.7 summarizes some of the education policies discussed above.

Table 3.7 Education Policies to Increase Retention in Primary Education

Policy	Scope	Potential impact	Cost	Implementation
Ensure provision of full education cycle	Large variation across countries	Potentially high in some countries	May be high	Address school supply deficits Use multigrade teaching where appropriate
Reduce grade repetition	To be assessed at country level	Potentially high in some countries	May lead to savings	Automatic grade promotion Use subcycles, student assessment, remedial measures
Use more female teachers	Large variation across countries (7%–60%) in the proportion of female teachers	Potentially significant	Low	Work with communities to facilitate placement of female teachers, particularly in rural areas
Ensure that children start school at the right age	To be assessed at country level	Potentially significant	Low	Information, regulation, and monitoring

Source: Authors' compilation.

*Civil Conflict, Hunger, and Other Adverse Shocks Can Shift the
Cost-Benefit Balance*
A host of factors beyond the reach of education policies can also have a strong, negative impact on school retention rates:

- *Civil conflicts or wars* often lead to school closures or stop parents from sending their children to school (World Bank 2007c)
- *Strife and hunger* cause many children to stay home from school, either to look for food or because they are too weak to walk to school (World Bank 2004b)
- *Disease or even death in the family* is another leading reason why children drop out from school. Evans and Miguel (2005) find a substantial drop in school participation in Kenya following a parent's death.

In particular, one major consequence of the human immunodeficiency virus/acquired immunodeficiency syndrome (HIV/AIDS) pandemic in the region is the large increase in the number of children orphaned (defined as those who have lost one or both parents) by the disease. The World Bank (2007b), for instance, reports that 12 percent of primary school pupils in Malawi are orphans—70 percent because of HIV/AIDS. In this light, the importance of political stability, food security, and disease control in creating environments that are conducive to children attending school can hardly be overemphasized.

Issues for Policy Development

At this juncture, despite recent years of rapid increases in primary school enrollment, many children are still out of school in Sub-Saharan Africa. In particular, an estimated 35 million children remain out of school in the sample of 33 low-income Sub-Saharan African countries.

Figure 3.7 provides an overall assessment of the extent to which out-of-school children differ from children who are enrolled in school in 30 low-income Sub-Saharan African countries, based on comparable household survey data on the characteristics of the out-of-school children.[23] Figure 3.7 helps to identify whether the main differences between out-of-school and enrolled children have to do with urban or rural location, wealth, or gender differences. In Lesotho, for example, the main difference between the two groups of children has to do primarily with the level of poverty, as shown in the right column of figure 3.7.

Adaptation of School Supply Needed for at Least Half of Out-of-School Children
Based on the classification of the 30 countries, as shown in figures 3.7 and 3.8 provides estimates of the number of the region's 35 million out-of-school children who are: (a) very similar, somewhat different, or very different from enrolled children; and (b) either never-enrolled or dropouts.

Figure 3.7 Extent of Differences between Out-of-School and Enrolled Children in 30 Low-Income Sub-Saharan African Countries

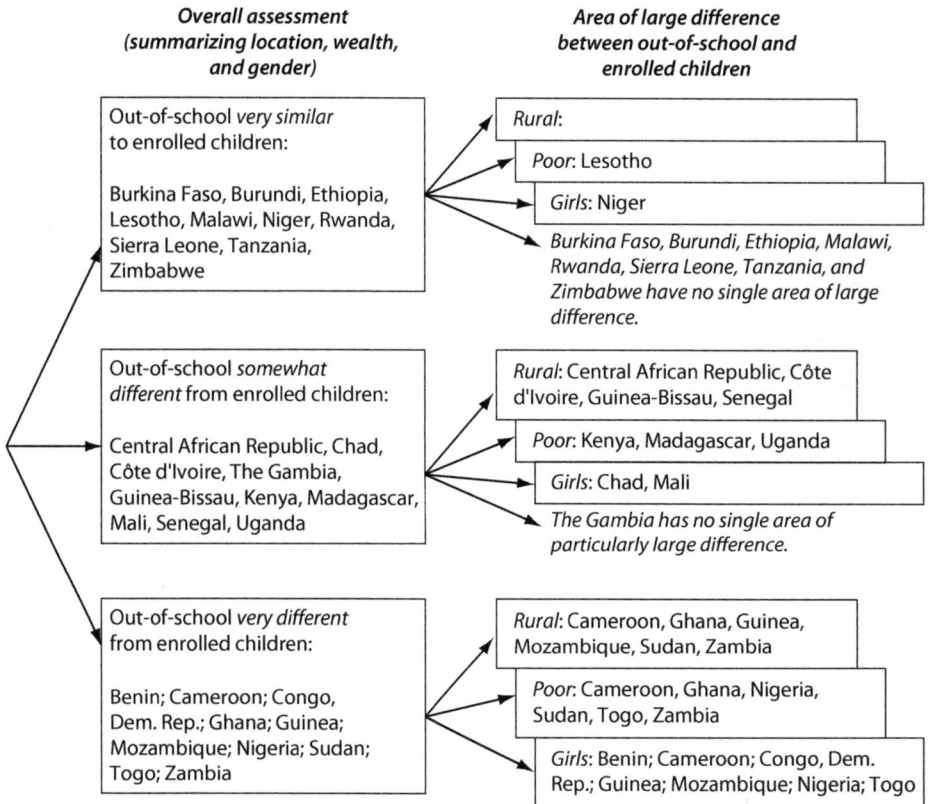

Source: Authors' construction based on analysis of household survey data for 30 low-income Sub-Saharan African countries; see appendix J, table J.1. For the full country-specific data set concerning social disparities between out-of-school and in-school children, see appendix D, table D.3.
Note: "Low-income" countries are eligible for lending from IDA; see appendix A, table A.1. Based on household survey data, the authors have calculated indicators of rural–urban disparities, wealth disparities, and gender disparities. For example, the gender disparities indicator is calculated as the ratio between the share of girls among the out-of-school and the share of girls in the total school-age population. An indicator of overall disparities has been computed as the product of these three indicators. The chart's left side is based on the overall indicator: countries in the bottom third with respect to this indicator fall in the *very similar* category; the middle third are *somewhat different*; while the top third are *very different*. The right side of the chart is constructed in a similar way based on the rural–urban, wealth, and gender disparity indexes, respectively.

The chart in figure 3.8 provides a sense of the magnitude of the problem and the solutions that may be required in the different countries. In countries such as Burundi and Niger, for instance, the out-of-school children are "very similar" to the enrolled children. In countries such as these, supply-side policies that provide "more of the same" can still play an important role in bringing the former category of children to school.

However, in countries such as Benin, Guinea, and Mozambique, the out-of-school children are so different from the enrolled children in terms of their socioeconomic characteristics that some modification of supply is likely needed.

Figure 3.8 Suggested Targeting to Reach 35 Million Out-of-School Children in 33 Low-Income Sub-Saharan African Countries

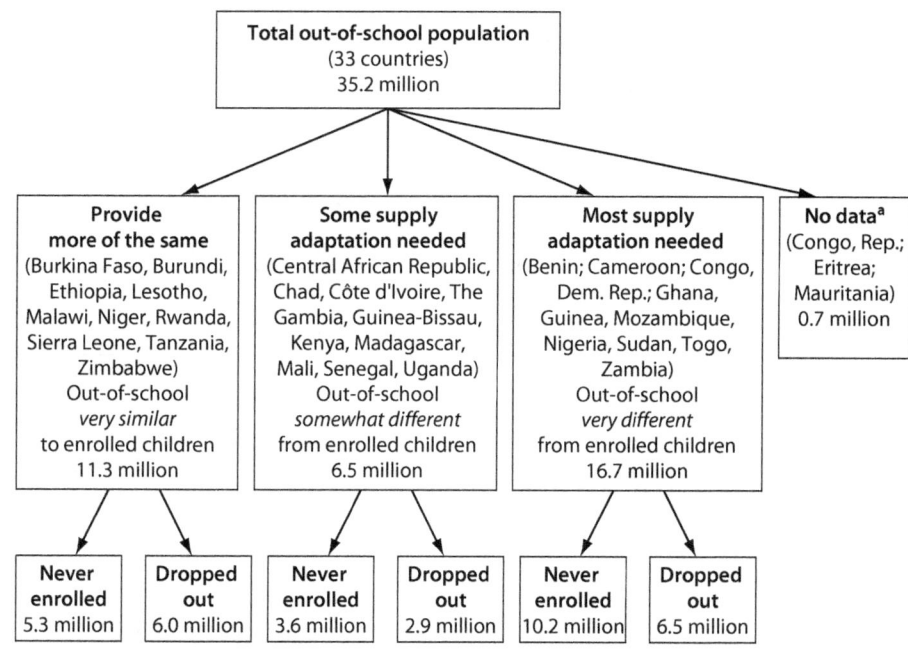

Source: Authors' construction based on categorization of countries in figure 3.7.
Note: "Low-income" countries are eligible for lending from IDA; see appendix A, table A.1.
a. No information is available on the composition of out-of-school children in these three countries.

Countries in this group account for about 17 million, or almost half, of all out-of-school children. In the remaining group of 10 countries, some modification of supply is also likely needed.

More Research Needed on Impact, Cost-Effectiveness of Policies to Raise Attendance

The discussion above referred to a number of specific policy interventions that hold promise or have proven to be effective in raising primary school access and retention. Policy makers and practitioners need to carefully evaluate the costs and benefits of each policy intervention before deciding on the way forward.

Beyond the education policies discussed above, other interventions not mentioned here could be equally effective in raising school attendance. More impact evaluations are also needed to examine the impact of different interventions and to weight their relative cost-effectiveness.

Notes

1. The sample of 33 low-income countries comprises the Sub-Saharan African countries eligible for lending from the International Development Association (IDA) except those with very small populations (Cape Verde, the Comoros, and São Tomé

and Príncipe) or highly incomplete data (Angola, Liberia, and Somalia). (The IDA threshold changes every year, as do the countries' gross national income(s) [GNI] per capita, so there may be small changes from year to year in this group.) Based on a 2006 GNI per capita of less than US$1,065, the 33 countries in the sample are Benin, Burkina Faso, Burundi, Cameroon, the Central African Republic, Chad, the Democratic Republic of Congo, the Republic of Congo, Côte d'Ivoire, Eritrea, Ethiopia, The Gambia, Ghana, Guinea, Guinea-Bissau, Kenya, Lesotho, Madagascar, Malawi, Mali, Mauritania, Mozambique, Niger, Nigeria, Rwanda, Senegal, Sierra Leone, Sudan, Tanzania, Togo, Uganda, Zambia, and Zimbabwe.

2. A six-year cohort is used for this analysis because the duration of the primary cycle is, on average, close to six years in the region.
3. The difference between 81 and 88 may seem small, but it results in highly different estimates of the number of out-of-school children.
4. In systems with a rapidly expanding supply of education, the GIR is likely inflated due to multicohort effects—that is, the admission of children of different ages in grade one in the same year, usually because no school was available earlier.
5. Administrative data is used only for the few countries for which no survey data are available.
6. The percentage of out-of-school children is computed, for each country, as the average of the cohort grade one entry rate and the cohort grade six attainment rate.
7. Calculation of the school-age population is based on the cohort aged 6–11 years for all countries. The cohort aged 7–12 years could have been used as the reference population, but it would have made only a small difference to the results. The important point here is to have a six-year age group to reflect a six-year cycle.
8. The UIS (2005) study estimated the number of out-of-school children in 2001/02 by subtracting the number of primary-school-age pupils enrolled in either primary or secondary school from the total population of the official primary school age range, usually 6–11 years old. The method may overestimate the number of out-of-school children because it includes children over the official age range who are still enrolled in primary school.
9. In absolute terms, however, there were three million more out-of-school girls than boys in the region in 2003.
10. Calculated by adding the 2.3 million urban poor to the 29.6 million rural children.
11. In Côte d'Ivoire, only 58.5 percent of the population lived in rural areas in 1998, the latest year for which this figure is available in United Nations *Demographic Yearbook* (UN 2007).
12. Until we reach the point when all children complete the primary cycle, countries should also have a strategy for offering basic skills training to the adolescents and adults who have not completed primary education. Local organizations and communities could play a role in organizing such training.
13. Calculated by adding the percentages of children who live less than 2 kilometer from school (40 + 17 + 16).
14. The fee was only about US$4 per child per year, but the large increase in grade one enrollment proved that it had been a barrier to access for a significant portion of the population. The new school entrants consisted of both (a) six- and seven-year-olds who would otherwise not have entered school, and (b) older children who had not entered school in previous years.

15. Other factors, beyond those presented here, are likely to play a role in the decision to stay or leave school, but the evidence needed to demonstrate their impact is not yet available.
16. In Tanzania, because of the school system's limited capacity, many children in rural areas had to wait to be enrolled in school in the late 1990s. This delay led to a proliferation of over-age children in and out of the school system. In collaboration with UNICEF, the government implemented an interim community-based basic education initiative, Complementary Basic Education in Tanzania (COBET), to provide basic education to over-age children. The program targeted 11- to 13-year-olds who were integrated into regular primary schools after attending COBET for three years. This program allowed the government to increase the share of children who enrolled in regular primary schools at the right age.
17. All these countries had a gross domestic product (GDP) per capita of less than US$2,000 and a population greater than 2 million.
18. More specifically, the study found a statistically significant relationship between the share of female teachers and the average repetition rate, after controlling for differences in pupil-teacher ratios. The impact on retention is the same for boys and girls. The study also found that the share of female teachers has an impact on the retention of girls, even when controlling for GDP per capita (R^2 is 0.32).
19. See the Overview chapter's reference list for a full list of Country Status Reports consulted for this volume.
20. Mingat and Sosale (2003) report a similar result. They also found no relation between repetition and student achievement.
21. Automatic promotion can also be effective in lowering high repetition rates. It can be introduced, for instance, by organizing the primary cycle into several subcycles, with repetition being allowed only between the subcycles, not within.
22. This estimate assumes that the effects of these different policies are additive, which may not be the case.
23. For full details of the analysis, see appendix D, table D.3, which compares out-of-school children and enrolled children based on geographical location, wealth, and gender.

References

Avenstrup, R., X. Liang, and S. Nellemann. 2004. *Free Primary Education and Poverty Reduction: The Case of Kenya, Lesotho, Malawi, and Uganda*. Case study. Washington, DC: World Bank.

Baird, S., C. McIntosh, and B. Ozler. 2009. "Designing Cost-Effective Cash Transfer Programs to Boost Schooling among Young Women in Sub-Saharan Africa." Policy Research Working Paper 5090, World Bank, Washington, DC.

Barrera-Osorio, F., M. Bertrand, L. Linden, and F. Perez-Calle. 2008. "Conditional Cash Transfers in Education: Design Features, Peer and Sibling Effects; Evidence from a Randomized Experiment in Colombia." Policy Research Working Paper 4580, World Bank, Washington, DC.

Chaudhury, N., L. Christiaensen, and M. Asadullah. 2006. "Schools, Household, Risk, and Gender: Determinants of Child Schooling in Ethiopia." Paper presented at the Centre for the Study of African Economies (CSAE) Annual Conference, "Reducing Poverty and Inequality: Can Africa Be Included?" University of Oxford, March 20.

Evans, D., and E. Miguel. 2005. "Orphans and Schooling in Africa: A Longitudinal Analysis." Working Paper 69208, Center for International and Development Economics Research (CIDER), University of California, Berkeley.

FAO (Food and Agriculture Organization) and UNESCO-IIEP (United Nations Educational, Scientific and Cultural Organization–International Institute for Educational Planning). 2006. "Education for Rural People in Africa." Report of the Ministerial Seminar on Education for Rural People in Africa sponsored by the FAO, the Association for the Development of Education in Africa (ADEA), and UNESCO-IIEP, Addis Ababa, September 7–9, 2005.

Filmer, D. 2004. "If You Build It, Will They Come? School Availability and School Enrollment in 21 Poor Countries." Policy Research Working Paper 3340, World Bank, Washington, DC.

Glewwe, P., and P. Olinto. 2004. "Evaluating the Impact of Conditional Cash Transfers on Schooling: An Experimental Analysis of Honduras' PRAF Program." Final program report of the International Food Policy Research Institute for the United States Agency for International Development, Washington, DC.

Jarousse, J.-P., J.-M. Bernard, K. Améléwonou, D. Coury, C. Demagny, B. Foko, G. Husson, J. Mouzon, B. Ledoux, F. Ndem, and N. Reuge. 2009. *Universal Primary Education in Africa: The Teacher Challenge. Pôle de Dakar Education Sector Analysis.* Dakar: United Nations Educational, Scientific and Cultural Organization (UNESCO) Regional Office for Education in Africa (BREDA).

Kremer, M. 2003. "Randomized Evaluations of Educational Programs in Developing Countries: Some Lessons." *American Economic Review* 93 (2): 102–06.

Kremer, M., E. Miguel, and R. Thornton. 2005. "Incentives to Learn." Policy Research Working Paper 3546, World Bank, Washington, DC.

Mapto-Kengne, V., and A. Mingat. 2002. "Analyse comparative internationale de la féminisation du corps enseignant et de l'impact du sexe de l'enseignant sur la performance des systèmes éducatifs primaires en Afrique." Communication, French Association of Comparative Education (AFEC) conference, Caen, May 23–25.

Mingat, A., and S. Sosale. 2003. "Primary Education Grade Repetition and Policy Implications: An International Comparative Perspective." Unpublished manuscript, World Bank, Washington, DC.

Pôle de Dakar UNESCO-BREDA (United Nations Educational, Scientific and Cultural Organization, Regional Office for Education in Africa). 2006. "Elements d'analyse du secteur éducatif au Togo." Country Status Report, Pôle de Dakar UNESCO-BREDA, Dakar.

Rawlings, L. B., and G. M. Rubio. 2003. "Evaluating the Impact of Conditional Cash Transfer Programs: Lessons from Latin America." Policy Research Working Paper 3119, World Bank, Washington, DC.

Schady, N., and M. C. Araujo. 2006. "Cash Transfers, Conditions, School Enrollment, and Child Work: Evidence from a Randomized Experiment in Ecuador." Policy Research Working Paper 3930, World Bank, Washington, DC.

Schady, N., and C. Paxson. 1999. "Do School Facilities Matter? The Case of the Peruvian Social Fund (FONCODES)." Policy Research Working Paper 2229, World Bank, Washington, DC.

Schultz, T. P. 2001. "School Subsidies for the Poor: Evaluating the Mexican Progresa Poverty Program." *Journal of Development Economics* 74 (1): 199–250.

Sey, H. 2001. "Quality Education for All in Senegal: Including the Excluded." Background paper, Quality Education for All Project, World Bank, Washington, DC.

Taylor, P., and A. Muhall. 1997. "Contextualising Teaching and Learning in Rural Primary Schools: Using Agricultural Experience." Volume 1, Education Research Paper 20, Department for International Development (DFID), London.

Theunynck, S. 2009. *School Construction Strategies for Universal Primary Education in Africa: Should Communities Be Empowered to Build Their Schools?* Africa Human Development Series. Washington, DC: World Bank.

UN (United Nations). 2007. *Demographic Yearbook*. New York: UN.

UIS (UNESCO Institute for Statistics). 2005. *Children Out of School: Measuring Exclusion from Primary Education*. Montreal: UIS and UNICEF.

UIS Data Centre (database). UIS (UNESCO Institute for Statistics), Montreal. http://stats.uis.unesco.org.

UNESCO (United Nations Educational, Scientific and Cultural Organization). 2008. "Education for All by 2015: Will We Make It?" Education for All (EFA) Global Monitoring Report, UNESCO, Paris.

Vermeersch, C., and M. Kremer. 2004. "School Meals, Educational Achievement and School Competition: Evidence from a Randomized Evaluation." Policy Research Working Paper 3523, World Bank, Washington, DC.

World Bank. 2001. "Education and Training in Madagascar: Towards a Policy Agenda for Economic Growth and Poverty Reduction." Africa Region Human Development Working Paper 12, Country Status Report, World Bank, Washington, DC.

———. 2003. "Rapport d'état du système éducatif national camerounais: Elèments de diagnostic pour la politique éducative dans le contexte de l'EPT et du DSRP." Country Status Report, World Bank, Washington, DC.

———. 2004a. "Books, Buildings and Learning Outcomes: An Impact Evaluation of World Bank Support to Basic Education in Ghana." Impact Evaluation Report, Operations Evaluations Department, World Bank, Washington, DC.

———. 2004b. "Cost, Financing and School Effectiveness of Education in Malawi: A Future of Limited Choices and Endless Opportunities." Africa Region Human Development Working Paper 78, Country Status Report, World Bank, Washington, DC.

———. 2005. *Education in Ethiopia: Strengthening the Foundation for Sustainable Progress.* Country Study Series. Washington, DC: World Bank.

———. 2007a. *L'éducation au Mali: Diagnostic pour le renouvellement de la politique éducative en vue d'atteindre les objectifs du millénaire*. Africa Human Development Series. Washington, DC: World Bank.

———. 2007b. "Malawi Public Expenditure Review 2006." Report 40145-MW for the Malawi Ministry of Finance, World Bank, Washington, DC.

———. 2007c. *Le système éducatif tchadien: Eléments de diagnostic pour une politique éducative nouvelle et une meilleure efficacité de la depense publique*. Africa Human Development Series. World Bank Working Paper 110, World Bank, Washington, DC.

———. 2010. *Le système éducatif Congolais: Diagnostic pour une revitalisation dans un contexte macroéconomique plus favorable.* Africa Human Development Series. World Bank Working Paper 183, World Bank, Washington, DC.

World Bank and UNICEF (United Nations Children's Fund). 2009. *"Six Steps to Abolishing Primary School Fees." Operational Guide for the School Fee Abolition Initiative.* Washington, DC: UNICEF and World Bank.

CHAPTER 4

Patterns of Spending on Education

This chapter documents and compares patterns of spending on education across the countries of Sub-Saharan Africa. The discussion focuses on the trends in aggregate spending on education, the allocation of spending across levels of education, and the composition of spending in terms of school inputs. To provide an international, comparative perspective, the analysis draws on data from other world regions.

Throughout the region as a whole, aggregate spending on education has risen in recent years as a result of strong economic growth and an increase in aid flows to the region's low-income countries. Households also account for a large share of education spending. There are, however, large differences in the distribution of spending on education across countries in the region. These differences reflect differences in policy choices in the individual countries. How much a country spends on education and its pattern of spending are important matters for discussion because they have significant impact on educational outcomes, such as on the number of school places that can be provided and on pupil-teacher ratios. Policies regarding teachers were found to exert a particularly strong impact on the level of educational coverage.

Aggregate Spending

We begin by looking at aggregate spending on education in terms of government spending; external aid for education; and private, household spending on education.[1]

Government Spending on Education

The average level of government spending on education in low-income Sub-Saharan African countries is comparable to that of low-income countries in other parts of the world. As seen in table 4.1, the average level of public capital and recurrent spending on education as a percentage of gross domestic product (GDP) is 4.3 percent in both the low-income Sub-Saharan African countries and the low-income countries in other world regions.[2] Middle-income Sub-Saharan African countries, on the other hand, spend relatively more

Table 4.1 Comparison of Public Spending on Education (Capital and Recurrent), ca. 2005

	Public spending on education (% of gross domestic product)	Total public spending (% of gross domestic product)	Public spending on education (% of total public spending)
Low-income countries[a]			
Sub-Saharan Africa	4.3	25	17
Other regions	4.3	31	14
Middle-income countries[b]			
Sub-Saharan Africa	5.7	35	16
Other regions	4.2	25	17
High-income OECD[c]	5.6	45	12

Source: Education spending data are from the United Nations Institute for Statistics (UIS Data Centre). Total public spending as a percentage of gross domestic product (middle column) is computed from the other two columns.

Note: OECD = Organisation for Economic Co-operation and Development. Table does not include: (a) countries in the World Bank's Europe and Central Asia region, and (b) countries, mostly island states, with populations less than 300,000. See appendix E, table E.1 for the full table of Sub-Saharan African countries' expenditures.

a. "Low-income" countries are eligible for lending from the World Bank's International Development Association (IDA); see appendix A, table A.1.

b. "Middle-income" countries are eligible for lending from the International Bank for Reconstruction and Development (IBRD) of the World Bank Group; see appendix A, table A.1.

c. Member countries of the Organisation for Economic Co-operation and Development.

(5.7 percent of GDP) than the middle-income countries in other parts of the world (4.2 percent).[3] In fact, the middle-income Sub-Saharan African countries spend, on average, a higher proportion of their GDP on education than the high-income Organisation for Economic Co-operation and Development (OECD) countries (5.6 percent).

Low-Income Sub-Saharan African Countries Allocate Largest Share of Public Spending to Education

The middle column compares total public spending as a percentage of GDP, which is, on the average, comparatively smaller in the low-income Sub-Saharan African countries (25 percent) than in most other country groups. However, as the right-hand column shows, on average, the low-income Sub-Saharan African countries spend a higher proportion of total public spending on education (17 percent) than virtually any other country group. In particular, they spend a higher proportion of total public spending on education than their middle-income Sub-Saharan African counterparts (16 percent) and the high-income OECD countries (12 percent).

Sub-Saharan African Countries Show Wide Diversity in Education Spending

With reference to the horizontal axis in figure 4.1, total public capital and recurrent spending as a percentage of GDP varies from a low of 13 percent in Madagascar to a high of 46 percent in Lesotho. Similarly, and with reference to the vertical axis, the proportion of public capital and recurrent spending allocated to the education sector ranges from a low of 4 percent in Equatorial Guinea to a high of 30 percent in Lesotho.

Figure 4.1 Public Spending on Education in Sub-Saharan African Countries (Capital and Recurrent), ca. 2005

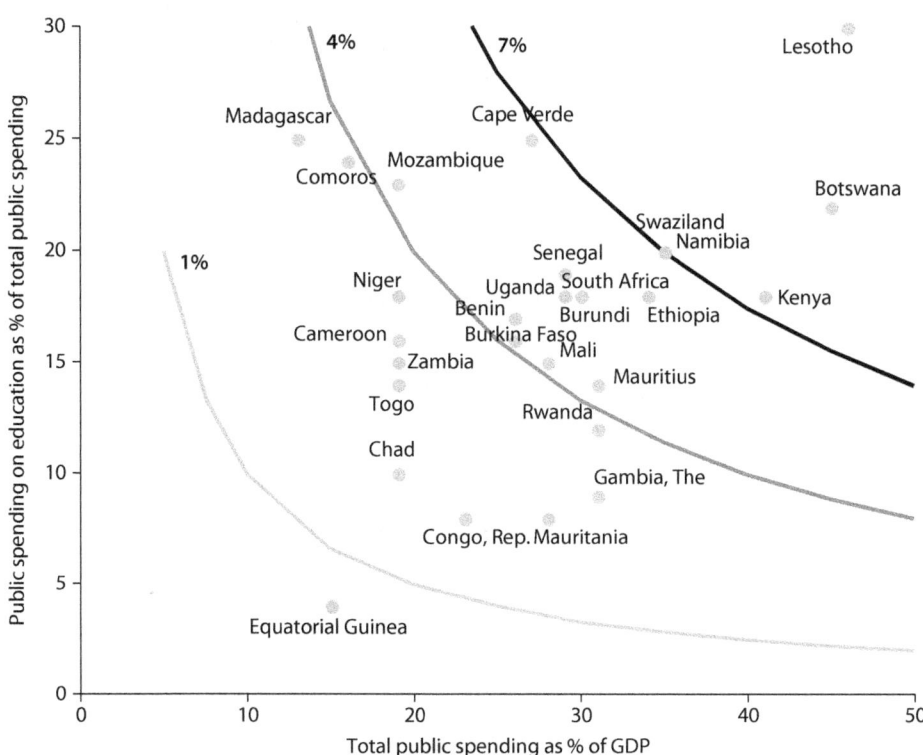

Source: Author's construction, based on education spending data from the UIS Data Centre. For full data set, see appendix E, table E.1.
Note: GDP = gross domestic product. The three curved lines show the data points that are consistent with a level of public spending on education corresponding to 1 percent, 4 percent, and 7 percent of gross domestic product, respectively. Due to lack of expenditure data, the figure does not include the Democratic Republic of Congo, Gabon, Guinea-Bissau, Liberia, Nigeria, São Tomé and Príncipe, the Seychelles, Somalia, Sudan, Tanzania, and Zimbabwe.

In general, countries with limited fiscal capacities seem to compensate by allocating larger shares of their public spending to education. This may account, at least in part, for the wide variation in public spending on education as a share of GDP across countries in the region.

This diversity in public spending on education as a percentage of GDP may be seen clearly with the aid of the three curves in figure 4.1. Each curve represents combinations of public spending on education as a percentage of total public spending, on the one hand, and total public spending as a percentage of GDP, on the other, that result in an equal percentage of total public spending on education to GDP. As seen in figure 4.1, total public spending on education as a percentage of GDP varies from less than 1 percent in Equatorial Guinea (0.6 percent) to well over 7 percent in Lesotho (13.4 percent). These variations are substantial and are larger than that observed in other regions of the world.

External Aid for Education

External aid is an important source of public spending in the Sub-Saharan African region. Table 4.2 shows tax revenues and net receipts of official development assistance (ODA) as proportions of total public spending for all Sub-Saharan African countries for which data are available.

External Aid an Important Source of Public Spending in Low-Income Countries

On average, tax revenues account for 64 percent of total public spending in the low-income countries and 78 percent in the middle-income countries.[4] ODA from bilateral donors and multilateral agencies fill much of the financing gap. In

Table 4.2 Average Tax Revenues and ODA Relative to Total Public Spending, Sub-Saharan African Countries, 2005–07

	Total public spending (% of gross domestic product)	Ratio of tax revenues to total public spending (%)	Ratio of net ODA to total public spending (%)
Angola	33	129	2
Benin	22	68	37
Botswana	31	72	2
Burkina Faso	24	49	57
Burundi	40	45	118
Cameroon	10	169	69
Cape Verde	38	54	35
Central African Republic	14	51	60
Chad	14	35	38
Comoros	22	55	36
Congo, Dem. Rep.	20	47	105
Congo, Rep.	25	155	38
Côte d'Ivoire	20	74	5
Equatorial Guinea	22	38	2
Eritrea	41	34	50
Ethiopia	22	49	61
Gabon	22	47	2
Gambia, The	27	67	47
Ghana	33	61	28
Guinea	13	88	40
Guinea-Bissau	41	29	72
Kenya	29	65	15
Lesotho	48	106	12
Liberia	17	101	357
Madagascar	20	52	72
Malawi	24	60	85
Mali	24	66	60
Mauritania	29	48	36
Mauritius	25	73	3
Mozambique	26	50	83
Namibia	35	91	7
Niger	20	51	72
Nigeria	28	—	18

(table continues on next page)

Table 4.2 Average Tax Revenues and ODA Relative to Total Public Spending, Sub-Saharan African Countries, 2005–07 (continued)

	Total public spending (% of gross domestic product)	Ratio of tax revenues to total public spending (%)	Ratio of net ODA to total public spending (%)
Rwanda	25	50	88
São Tomé and Príncipe	45	33	53
Senegal	25	76	32
Seychelles	54	72	3
Sierra Leone	22	51	131
South Africa	29	90	1
Sudan	24	28	24
Swaziland	34	106	5
Tanzania	25	43	54
Togo	18	80	23
Uganda	18	63	82
Zambia	24	71	52
Zimbabwe	46	84	16
Simple average	27	67	50
Low-income[a]	27	64	57
Middle-income[b]	29	78	3
Range	[10–54]	[28–169]	[1–357]

Sources: Authors' compilation from data on total public expenditures and tax revenues (DDP database) and data on net ODA disbursements (DAC Online database).
Note: ODA = official development assistance, — = not available.
a. "Low-income" countries are eligible for lending from International Development Association (IDA); see appendix A, table A.1.
b. "Middle-income" countries are eligible for lending from the International Bank for Reconstruction and Development; see appendix A, table A.1.

particular, ODA to low-income Sub-Saharan African countries amounted to an average of 57 percent of total public spending between 2005 and 2007. In contrast, the middle-income countries received the equivalent of 3 percent of total public spending over the same period.

ODA is therefore an important source of public spending in the low-income countries in the region.[5] Because domestic financial resources are fungible, when a government receives external funding that is tied to certain sectors, it can reallocate more of its own domestic resources to other sectors. It follows, then, that external aid is an important source of funding for all sectors, including the education sector.

Between 2005 and 2007, poor countries such as Burundi, the Democratic Republic of Congo, Rwanda, and Sierra Leone received the most aid relative to their total public spending, while the richer nations such as Botswana, Equatorial Guinea, Gabon, and South Africa were the least aid-dependent countries.

ODA to Sub-Saharan African Region Has Grown Substantially since 1999 but Declined in 2006–07

Figure 4.2 shows the trend in the total flow of ODA to Sub-Saharan African countries from 1990 to 2007.

Between 1990 and 1999, net ODA (in constant 2006 prices) to the region declined from US$24 billion to US$16 billion. From 1999, net ODA grew steadily, reaching a high of almost US$40 billion in 2006 before declining to US$32 billion in 2007.

Although donors committed (at the 2005 Gleneagles G-8 Summit) to double their aid to Sub-Saharan Africa, the 2007 narrowing of the gap between net disbursements and net disbursements excluding debt relief shows that it may be difficult to keep increasing the total volume of aid as debt relief grants taper off (IMF 2007). The global financial crisis of 2009/10 serves only to add to the uncertainty regarding the future trend in aid flows to the region.

Government Revenues Growing Faster than Aid Receipts

Figure 4.3 shows the trend in total public revenues, excluding grants, compared with that of net disbursements of ODA to the region between 1997 and 2007 (in constant 2006 prices).

Figure 4.2 Trend in ODA to Sub-Saharan Africa, 1990–2007

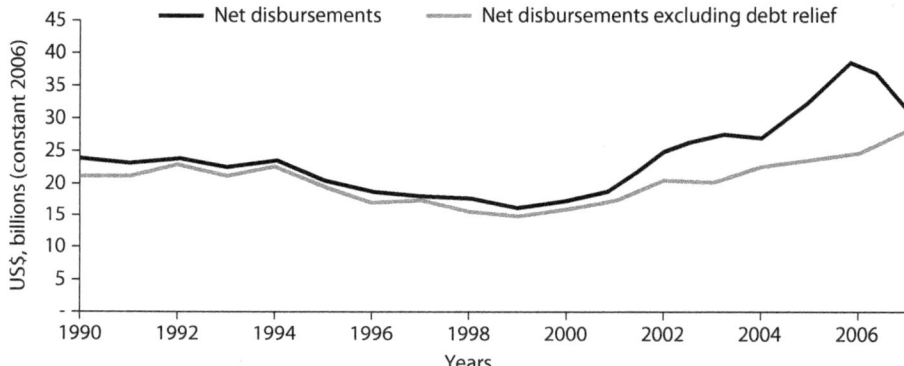

Source: DAC Online.
Note: ODA = official development assistance. Data shown reflect ODA from all donors, including those that are not members of DAC. Net disbursements are net of flows from recipient to donor countries for debt service.

Figure 4.3 Growth in Government Revenue and ODA in Sub-Saharan Africa, 1997–2007

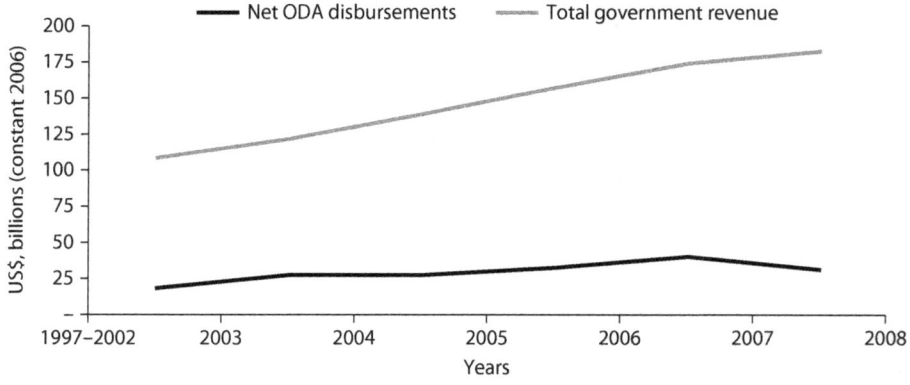

Sources: Reproduced and updated from OECD 2008, figure 1.6; data from DAC Online and DDP databases.
Note: ODA = official development assistance. Data on government revenue do not include Mauritania, São Tomé and Príncipe, and Somalia for lack of data.

Government revenues, excluding grants, increased from an average of around US$109 billion in 1997–2002 to US$184 billion in 2007. In contrast, net ODA disbursements rose from an average of US$19 billion in 1997–2002 to US$31 billion in 2007.

Since approximately 2000, domestic sources of revenues have clearly increased more than external sources. This positive development is a result of strong economic growth and greater capacity to collect taxes in the region (IMF 2007).

Education's Share of Aid Increases, but Tracking Aid Is Increasingly Problematic

External aid in the form of budget support, debt relief, and multisector programs have increased in popularity while sector-specific aid[6] has declined, from about two-thirds of total external aid in 1990 to about half in 2005. It has therefore become increasingly difficult to monitor the distribution of aid across sectors. Nevertheless, looking at aid commitments (for which more detailed sector-specific data are available), it can be seen that the share of total sector-specific aid allocated to the education sector has increased from 9 percent in 1990 to 13 percent by about 2005.

Aid Volumes and Tax Revenues Both Increased in 1999–2007

Summing up, these positive trends have enabled many Sub-Saharan African governments to increase public spending, including spending on education. Although many low-income countries still depend on external donors to finance a significant share of their public spending, one positive development is that domestic sources of revenues are growing faster than ODA for the region as a whole.

Another positive development is the increased focus on aid effectiveness in recent years, which is likely to augment the value of the aid dollar.[7] However, the next few years may see a reversal in these positive trends because the global financial crisis may result in further tapering off of debt relief for the region.

Household Spending on Education

Household spending is less documented, it's usually off the public sector budget, and it's difficult to compare across countries. Household spending on education takes several different forms, including school fees in both public and private schools that parents pay, other (often mandatory) fees such as contributions to parents' associations, and expenditures on textbooks, and school uniforms.

Fees paid by households in public schools are often spent directly by the schools or local education authorities and rarely enter into the central government accounts, but they are clearly part of household spending. The exceptions (for which the lines are less clear-cut) are spending on school meals and private tuitions that are not mandatory.

Household surveys that contain a module on expenditures are usually the main source of information about household spending on education. Such data are not, however, available for all countries. Further, even when the data are available, the surveys may not collect data on the same types of expenditures, making cross-country comparisons all the more difficult.

Bearing in mind that these data are not strictly comparable, table 4.3 provides data on the magnitude of household spending on education in selected Sub-Saharan African countries.

Household Spending on Education Is Significant, Even at Primary Level

A first observation from table 4.3 is that the aggregate amount of household spending on education is highly variable across countries but substantial in virtually all cases. In particular, household spending amounts to an average of 42 percent of government recurrent education spending in this set of countries.

A second observation is that the ratio of household financing to government spending is nearly as high in primary education (37 percent) as in the education sector as a whole (42 percent). There is some evidence that even in countries where primary education is supposed to be free, school fees tend to reappear in new shapes and forms, particularly if schools were not fully compensated for the loss of revenue when school fees were abolished (Gauthier 2006; World Bank and UNICEF 2009).

Paying for Community Teachers Burdens Poor Families

In many countries in the region, parents are funding community schools or additional teachers in public schools, often because public supply of education is inadequate. A study of 12 French-speaking countries finds that almost a third of primary school teachers were paid by parents (Mingat 2004). Although community teachers are often poorly paid, this cost poses a significant burden on poor families. Countries with particularly large numbers of community (parent-paid)

Table 4.3 Household Spending on Education in Selected Sub-Saharan African Countries, ca. 2003

		Household spending on education as a proportion of government recurrent spending on education (%)	
	Survey year	All levels	Primary education
Benin	2006	63	33
Cameroon	2002	89	74
Congo, Rep.	2005	27	29
Ethiopia	2000	28	25
Madagascar	2006	45	40
Mali	2003	11	21
Mauritania	2004	31	35
Rwanda	2000	41	25
Togo	1999	41	53
Average		42	37

Source: World Bank 2003a, 2003b, 2003c, 2005a, 2005c, 2006, 2007a, 2008, 2009.

teachers are the Republic of Congo (54 percent); Cameroon and Chad (44 percent); and Benin, Guinea, and Togo (around 30 percent) (Mingat 2004; World Bank 2002, 2003b, 2003c, 2005b, 2007b, 2009, 2010; Pôle de Dakar UNESCO-BREDA 2006).

Patterns in the Distribution of Spending

Distribution of Spending by Level of Education

Cross-country comparison of the distribution of public spending by level of education is not straightforward because the different education cycles have different durations across countries in the region. To control for these differences, table 4.4 compares public spending for a cycle of a fixed duration. The Sub-Saharan African countries are, as before, divided into two groups: low-income and middle-income. Developing and high-income countries in other parts of the world are also included in the table for comparison.

Sub-Saharan African Low-Income Countries Spend Biggest Share on Primary Cycle, Middle-Income Countries on Secondary Cycle

In the Sub-Saharan African region, low- and middle-income countries differ significantly in how they allocate education spending across different levels of education. In particular, low-income Sub-Saharan African countries spend a much larger proportion of their education budgets on primary education (averaging 47 percent for a six-year cycle) than do the middle-income Sub-Saharan

Table 4.4 Comparison of Education Spending Distribution, by Level, 2006 or Latest Available Year

	Primary		Secondary		Higher	
	(% of budget, 6-year cycle)		(% of budget, 7-year cycle)		(% of budget)	
	Average	Range	Average	Range	Average	Range
Low-income countries[a] Sub-Saharan Africa (30 countries)	47	[21–66]	30	[12–66]	18	[4–39]
Other regions (6 countries)	42	[23–59]	38	[24–44]	17	[12–23]
Middle-income countries[b] Sub-Saharan Africa (5 countries)	27	[17–38]	44	[30–68]	21	[11–32]
Other regions (20 countries)	43	[30–66]	33	[12–45]	19	[6–44]
High-income OECD[c] (22 countries)	26	[20–34]	44	[35–50]	24	[13–34]

Sources: Authors' calculation based on 2002–06 data on distribution of education spending and duration of cycles (UIS Data Centre).
Note: OECD = Organisation for Economic Co-operation and Development. Some countries have also reported spending on preprimary and postprimary, nontertiary education as well as spending unallocated by level; these were not included in the analysis. This table does not include countries in the Europe and Central Asia region or countries with populations of less than approximately 300,000.
a. "Low-income" countries are eligible for lending from International Development Association (IDA); see appendix A, table A.1.
b. "Middle-income" countries are eligible for lending from the International Bank for Reconstruction and Development (IBRD); see appendix A, table A.1.
c. OECD-member countries.

African countries (averaging 27 percent). On the other hand, the middle-income Sub-Saharan African countries allocate more of their resources to secondary education (averaging 44 percent for a seven-year cycle) than do the low-income Sub-Saharan African countries (averaging 30 percent). This pattern, at least in part, reflects the relatively higher secondary school enrollments in the middle-income countries than in low-income countries.

The spending pattern in middle-income Sub-Saharan African countries gives an indication of the potential future trend in the region's low-income countries as their education systems evolve. As an increasing number of the low-income Sub-Saharan African countries approach universal primary education, and as secondary education enrollments grow rapidly at the same time, these countries will need to allocate increasingly larger shares of their education budgets to the secondary cycle.

The extent of this shift will, however, also depend on their individual policy choices. In this context, it is worth noting that middle-income countries outside the Sub-Saharan African region still allocate most of their budgets to primary education. This may in part be explained, as noted below, by their relatively lower levels of per-student spending in secondary education. In the OECD countries where public secondary schooling is generally provided free of charge, secondary education consumes, on average, more resources than either primary or higher education.

Countries Have Large Scope to Redistribute Spending across Educational Levels

Table 4.4 above shows the range in the proportion of public spending that is allocated to the different levels of education across countries in Sub-Saharan Africa and other regions, including the OECD-member countries. There is great variability across the low-income countries in the proportion of public spending that is allocated to primary education—ranging from 21 percent to 66 percent. Similarly, the proportion allocated to secondary education ranges widely (from 12 percent to 66 percent), as it also does in higher education (from 4 percent to 39 percent). This wide range in the proportion of public spending allocated to different levels of education is present in all three income groups.

This large variability implies that countries have much room to maneuver in terms of the allocation of their public spending across different levels of education. It may take time to shift resources between levels, but the fact that different countries have made such different choices implies that countries have a large scope for redirecting resources across different levels of education.

Per-Student Spending by Educational Level

The region also shows wide variability in per-student spending, particularly in postprimary education. Table 4.5 and Figure 4.4 shows that the level of public spending per student (as a percentage of per capita GDP, for comparison) varies greatly across countries. The higher the level of education, the larger the variability.

Table 4.5 Public Recurrent Spending Per Student by Educational Level in Sub-Saharan African Countries, ca. 2003

	Primary	Secondary	Higher
	(% of per capita gross domestic product)		
Angola	7.8	—	66.0
Benin	10.8	19.3	149
Botswana	6.1	5.7	91.0
Burkina Faso	19.2	47.0	550.0
Burundi	15.1	60.2	719.0
Cameroon	7.1	33.1	84.0
Cape Verde	18.0	21.7	285.0
Central African Republic	7.3	17.0	165.0
Chad	7.1	29.2	412.0
Comoros	12.2	30.3	130.0
Congo, Dem. Rep.	2.8	14.1	57.0
Congo, Rep.	8.1	17.0	221.0
Côte d'Ivoire	17.5	48.0	137.0
Eritrea	11.8	35.7	445.0
Ethiopia	12.0	32.0	1,082.0
Gabon	4.7	13.9	52.0
Gambia, The	13.2	19.0	230.0
Ghana	17.6	43.5	372.0
Guinea	9.0	14.0	231.0
Guinea-Bissau	7.2	13.8	121.0
Kenya	9.0	22.0	266.0
Lesotho	18.0	43.0	803.0
Madagascar	8.3	35.9	189.0
Malawi	11.0	77.0	1,760.0
Mali	11.1	40.3	193.0
Mauritania	12.0	49.0	120.0
Mauritius	9.0	14.0	49.0
Mozambique	10.2	32.4	791.0
Namibia	21.0	25.2	94.0
Niger	20.0	61.0	515.0
Nigeria	14.4	21.0	111.0
Rwanda	8.1	58.6	787.0
Senegal	13.9	19.5	257.0
Seychelles	14.5	17.7	—
Sierra Leone	9.2	28.0	278.0
South Africa	14.3	17.7	53.0
Sudan	7.9	17.8	110.0
Swaziland	11.2	28.9	246.0
Tanzania	12.5	43.6	530.0
Togo	10.0	17.0	197.0
Uganda	9.8	34.9	194.0
Zambia	7.1	19.3	163.0
Zimbabwe	16.2	24.2	201.0
Simple average	11.5	30.1	322.0
Low-income[a]	11.5	32.6	359.0
Middle-income[b]	11.5	17.6	97.0
Range	[3–21]	[6–77]	[49–1,760]

Sources: Authors' compilation of data from Country Status Reports (CSRs), Pôle de Dakar UNESCO-BREDA 2007, or UIS Data Centre. Equatorial Guinea, Liberia, São Tomé and Príncipe, and Somalia are omitted for lack of data. For more details, see appendix E, table E.2. For country rankings by per-student spending in secondary and higher education, see appendix E, figure E.1.

Note: — = not available.

a. "Low-income" countries are eligible for lending from International Development Association (IDA); see appendix A, table A.1.
b. "Middle-income" countries are eligible for lending from the International Bank for Reconstruction and Development (IBRD); see appendix A, table A.1.

Figure 4.4 Ranking of Sub-Saharan African Countries by Per-Student Spending on Primary Education

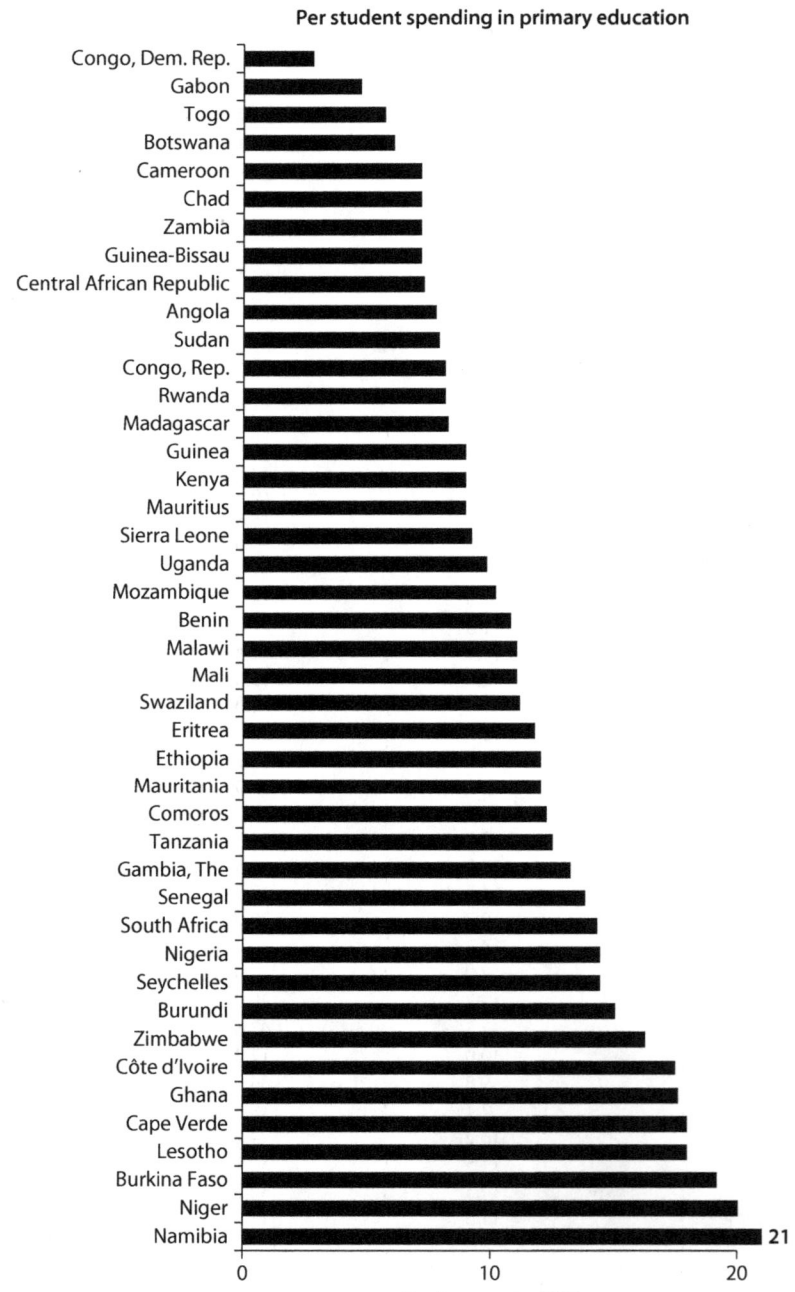

Source: Authors' construction from data shown in table 4.5.

In primary education, spending per student ranges from 3 percent of per capita GDP in the Democratic Republic of Congo to 21 percent in Namibia (a factor of seven between the highest and the lowest). On the other hand, per-student spending in secondary education varies by a factor of 13 between the highest and the lowest, while per-student spending in higher education varies by a factor of 36.

In Secondary and Higher Education, Low-Income Sub-Saharan African Countries Spend Much More Per Student than Middle-Income Countries

It is noteworthy that the average level of per-student spending in primary education, as a percentage of per capita GDP, is similar between low-income and middle-income Sub-Saharan African countries (11.5 percent in both groups). However, in secondary and higher education, the level of per-student spending relative to per capita GDP is generally much higher in the low-income countries than in the middle-income countries. The difference is particularly large in higher education, where the average among the low-income countries is more than three times the average among the middle-income countries.

In Postprimary Education, Low-Income Sub-Saharan African Countries Spend More Per Student than Developing Nations in Other Regions

Table 4.6 compares the average per-student spending of Sub-Saharan African countries, relative to per capita GDP, with that of countries at different stages of development in other parts of the world. Primary education spending per student appears to be quite similar in developing countries all across the world, with the possible exception of those in the Middle East and North Africa. In secondary and higher education, however, Sub-Saharan African countries generally have much higher levels of per-student spending relative to per capita GDP than other developing countries.

However, because universities in Sub-Saharan Africa do compete for academic staff in the global marketplace with universities in other parts of the world, a more relevant comparison may be the level of per-student spending in higher education in absolute terms, as shown in the right-hand column of table 4.6 (in 2005 US$). This comparison shows that Sub-Saharan African countries, on the average, spend about the same amount per student as other developing countries. However, when a distinction is made between low- and middle-income Sub-Saharan African countries, a striking difference emerges: although low-income Sub-Saharan African countries spend about as much per student as other developing countries, the middle-income Sub-Saharan African countries spend a much higher sum—more than twice as much as the low-income Sub-Saharan African and other developing countries.

High Per-Student Spending Limits Enrollment Expansion

The above comparison shows that Sub-Saharan African countries have a relatively high level of per-student spending in postprimary education—which is, to

Table 4.6 International Comparison of Per-Student Public Spending by Educational Level, ca. 2005

	Primary (% of gross domestic product per capita)	Secondary (% of gross domestic product per capita)	Higher	
			(% of gross domestic product per capita)	(2005 US$, current prices)
Sub-Saharan Africa	11.5	30.1	322.0	1,783
Low-income[a]	11.5	32.6	359.0	1,461
Middle-income[b]	11.5	17.6	97.0	3,713
East Asia and Pacific	12.5	13.7	59.0	1,529
Europe and Central Asia	15.0	18.3	23.0	1,040
Latin America and the Caribbean	13.0	15.3	39.0	1,447
Middle East and North Africa	16.6	19.8	40.0	1,236
South Asia	13.6	19.4	61.0	284
High-income OECD[d]	20.0	25.7	33.0	11,747

Sources: Authors' compilation from table 4.5 for Sub-Saharan African countries; from UIS Data Centre 2002–06 for other countries.
Note: OECD = Organisation for Economic Co-operation and Development. Geographic regions are those used by the World Bank for analytical purposes.
a. "Low-income" countries are eligible for lending from International Development Association (IDA); see appendix A, table A.1.
b. "Middle-income" countries are eligible for lending from the International Bank for Reconstruction and Development (IBRD); see appendix A, table A.1.
c. Data for these geographic regions include only low- and middle-income countries.
d. OECD-member countries.

some extent, justifiable. However, the high spending, particularly among the middle-income Sub-Saharan African countries, effectively limits the possibilities for expanding coverage at these levels unless these countries can reduce their per-student spending as they expand enrollment. Options for cutting per-student spending may include taking advantage of economies of scale, tapping into students' willingness to pay, and developing new models of service delivery that may lower per-student cost, including delivery to students in rural areas where most of the unserved population reside.

Equity of Expenditures

Public spending on education is not equally distributed among all children. Figure 4.5 shows the extent to which educational coverage declines with increasing levels of education, while per-student spending increases as the level of education rises in both low- and middle-income Sub-Saharan African countries.

Taken together, these contrasting patterns mean that while children who never enrolled in school receive none of the benefits of public spending on education, the relatively few children within a given cohort who succeed in climbing the educational ladder receive the largest share of the benefits of public spending on education. In the discussion that follows, the term "structural disparities" refers to differences in the amount of public education spending that is received by different members of a given cohort of children.

Figure 4.5 Patterns of Coverage and Per-Student Spending by Educational Level in Sub-Saharan African Countries, ca. 2005

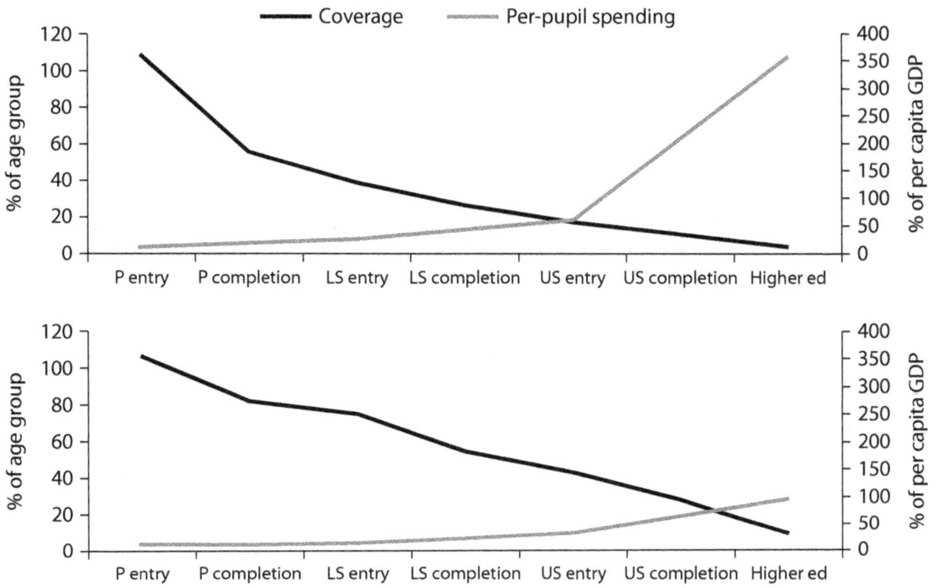

Sources: Authors' construction from UIS Data Centre for data on coverage (enrollment less repeaters as percentage of age group); CSRs for data on per-student spending whenever unit costs are broken down by lower and upper secondary. For remaining countries, data come from Pôle de Dakar UNESCO-BREDA 2005 or UIS Data Centre. For the detailed country-specific data on per-student spending, see appendix E, table E.2.
Note: P = primary, LS = lower secondary, US = upper secondary, GDP = gross domestic product.

Two Common Indicators Measure Extent of Structural Disparities

One measure of the degree of inequality in the distribution of public education spending among the members of a cohort is the Gini coefficient. An alternative, even simpler summary statistic of the extent of structural disparity in education is the share of total public education spending that is received by the 10 percent most-educated in a cohort.[8] Table 4.7 presents the average values of these two indicators for the low- and middle-income Sub-Saharan African countries.

Spending Distribution Most Inequitable in Low-Income Countries

As seen in table 4.7, the Gini coefficient in low-income countries (0.52) is higher than that in the middle-income countries (0.30), indicating a much more unequal distribution of public education spending in the former.[9] This is not surprising given that the decline in educational coverage between grade one and higher education is greater in the low-income countries than in the middle-income countries, while the increase in per-student spending relative to GDP per capita is greater in the former than the latter (as previously shown in figure 4.6).

The second indicator tells essentially the same story. On the average, 43 percent of public spending on education is received by the 10 percent most-educated in the low-income Sub-Saharan African countries, compared with only 25 percent in the middle-income countries. Table 4.7 also shows substantial differences

Table 4.7 Concentration of Public Education Spending within a Cohort, by Sub-Saharan African Country Income Level

	Average	Range
Low-income Sub-Saharan African countries[a]		
Gini coefficient	0.52	0.29–0.69
(% of public spending to 10% most-educated)		
in 2003	43	23–68
in 1992	56	—
in 1975	63	—
Middle-income Sub-Saharan African countries[b]		
Gini coefficient	0.30	—
% of public spending to 10% most-educated (2003)	25	—

Sources: Authors' consolidation of similar analyses from CSRs and other World Bank sector studies.
Note: — = not available. The methodology for calculating the two indicators is illustrated in appendix E, figure E.2 (Lorenz curve).
a. "Low-income" countries are eligible for lending from International Development Association (IDA); see appendix A, table A.1.
b. "Middle-income" countries are eligible for lending from the International Bank for Reconstruction and Development (IBRD); see appendix A, table A.1.

Figure 4.6 Relation of School-Life Expectancy and Education Spending in Selected Sub-Saharan African Countries, ca. 2005

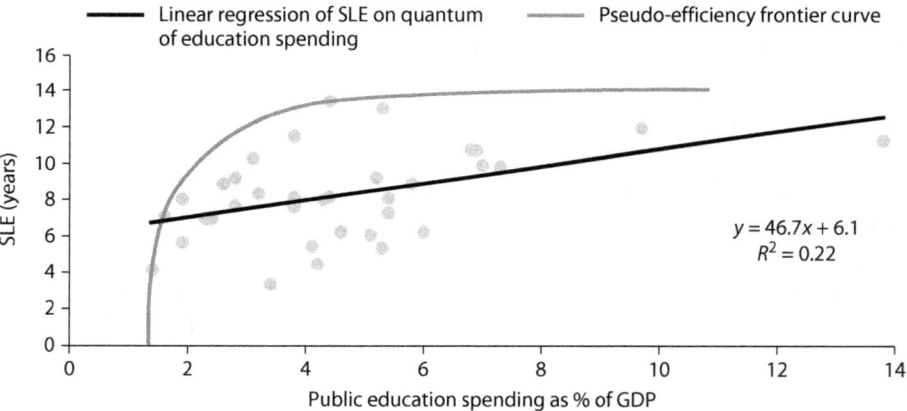

Sources: Authors' construction. SLE data are calculated based on enrollment data (GER and cycle lengths) from UIS Data Centre. Data on education spending are from UIS Data Centre. For the full data set, see appendix E, table E.1.
Note: SLE = school-life expectancy, GER = gross enrollment rate, GDP = gross domestic product. Chart is based on 35 observations. The value of the *t*-stat in the regression is 3.0, which is significant at the 1 percent level.

in the extent of inequality among the low-income countries: the Gini coefficient ranges from a low of 0.29 to a high of 0.69, while the percentage of public spending on education that is received by the 10 percent most-educated ranges from 23 percent to 68 percent.

However, Structural Disparities Have Diminished over Time

Although low-income Sub-Saharan African countries still suffer from fairly large inequities in the distribution of public education spending, these inequalities have diminished significantly over the past 30 years. The 10 percent most-educated received 63 percent of the resources in 1975, 56 percent in 1992, and

43 percent in 2003. This apparent decline in structural disparities is a result of the significant expansion in enrollments during the period, coupled with reductions in differences between per-student spending across educational levels as coverage expanded.

Relationship between Resources and Coverage

The quantum of public education spending explains little of the variability in educational coverage across Sub-Saharan African countries. School-life expectancy (SLE), defined as the total number of years of schooling that a child can expect to receive, may be used as a measure of educational coverage.[10]

Figure 4.6 relates the level of public education spending (as a percentage of GDP) to SLE, using countries as the units of observation. Along the horizontal axis, the scatterplot shows that countries differ widely in terms of the share of GDP allocated to education—between 1.4 percent and 14 percent of GDP. Along the vertical axis, the scatterplot shows that educational coverage, measured in terms of SLE, varies quite widely across the countries in the region, ranging between 3 and 14 years.

The straight line, based on the linear regression of SLE on the quantum of public education spending, shows a positive relationship: that is, the higher the quantum of public education spending, the higher the SLE. However, the quantum of total public education spending explains only 22 percent of the variance in educational coverage as measured by SLE (the coefficient of determination, R^2, is 0.22).

Some Sub-Saharan African countries achieve higher educational coverage than others for a given quantum of public education spending. That the quantum of public education spending explains only 22 percent of the variance in educational coverage suggests that factors other than the level of education spending explain the differences in educational coverage.

The pseudo-efficiency frontier curve (represented by the dotted line in figure 4.7) makes it possible to identify countries that are most efficient at achieving a higher level of educational coverage for a given volume of spending. Countries close to the curve achieve the most coverage, while the countries below the frontier are much less efficient. The Republic of Congo, Guinea, and Togo are among the most efficient countries, while Eritrea, Lesotho, and Niger produce the least coverage per 1 percent of GDP spent on education.[11]

Balancing Per-Student Spending and Coverage in Primary Education

With a given education budget, the higher the level of per-student spending, the lower the level of coverage. A priori, for a given education budget, countries with higher levels of per-student spending provide fewer student places. Using the gross enrollment ratio (GER) as an alternative measure of educational coverage, figure 4.7 shows the expected inverse relationship between per-student spending and the GER in primary education.

Figure 4.7 Per-Student Spending and GER at the Primary Level in Low-Income Sub-Saharan African Countries, ca. 2003

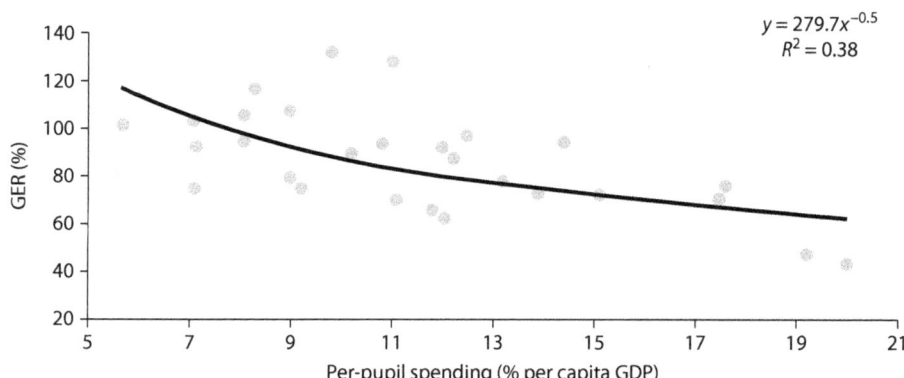

Sources: Authors' construction based on per-student spending data from CSRs and UIS Data Centre and GER data from UIS Data Centre.
Note: GER = gross enrollment rate, GDP = gross domestic product. "Low-income" countries are eligible for lending from International Development Association (IDA); see appendix A, table A.1.

Per-student spending explains 38 percent of the variance in primary GER (R^2 is 0.38). Countries represented by points above the curve provide more coverage for a given level of per-student spending than countries represented by points below the curve. One explanation for this diversity is that the countries do not face the same budgetary constraints. Thus, some countries can provide more coverage than others for a given level of per-student spending.

Prioritizing Spending among School Inputs

The previous three sections focused on the quantum of public education spending. The discussion now focuses on the composition of public education spending—in particular, on school inputs procured with the available public resources.

Composition of School Inputs

In Sub-Saharan Africa, there is large variability in pupil-teacher ratio, teacher salary, and other indicators of school inputs. Table 4.8 shows this diverse composition of school inputs in primary education among the Sub-Saharan African countries.

As shown, there are large differences in input mix across the countries:

- *Pupil-teacher ratios*, for instance, vary between 22 in Namibia and 80 in the Central African Republic.
- *Teacher salaries*, expressed in multiples of per capita GDP, range from 1.5 in Angola to 7.2 in Ethiopia.
- *Spending on goods and services* in the form of pedagogical materials, in-service teacher training, and support and administrative staff, ranges from 9 percent of total public recurrent spending in Nigeria to 46 percent in Guinea.

Table 4.8 School Inputs in Primary Education in Sub-Saharan African Countries, ca. 2003

	School inputs				School inputs				School inputs	
	Ave. teacher salary (multiples of pc gross domestic product)	Pupil-teacher ratio	Spending on goods & services (% of recur. spending)		Ave. teacher salary (multiples of pc gross domestic product)	Pupil-teacher ratio	Spending on goods & services (% of recur. spending)		Ave. teacher salary (multiples of pc gross domestic product)	Pupil-teacher ratio	Spending on goods & services (% of recur. spending)
Angola	1.5	24	19	Gambia, The	3.7	38	25	Nigeria	4.9	40	9
Benin	3.5	53	39	Ghana	3.6	32	18	Rwanda	3.8	65	28
Botswana	2.0	27	—	Guinea	2.1	44	46	Senegal	4.7	50	17
Burkina Faso	6.1	45	31	Guinea-Bissau	1.9	44	35	Sierra Leone	3.9	61	31
Burundi	6.8	52	19	Kenya	5.2	32	10	South Africa	5.0	37	10
Cameroon	3.1	61	28	Lesotho	6.6	47	31	Swaziland	3.2	33	15
Central African Rep.	4.9	80	29	Madagascar	2.8	55	43	Tanzania	3.6	46	11
Chad	3.0	70	38	Malawi	4.3	58	17	Togo	3.8	40	14
Congo, Dem. Rep.	—	33	—	Mali	4.4	63	38	Uganda	2.9	53	26
Congo, Rep.	3.2	60	20	Mauritania	3.1	40	31	Zambia	2.6	45	22
Côte d'Ivoire	4.5	40	36	Mauritius	2.0	25	15	Zimbabwe	5.5	39	22
Eritrea	4.5	47	16	Mozambique	3.9	47	20	Simple average	3.9	46	24
Ethiopia	7.2	66	15	Namibia	3.7	22	21	Low-income[a]	4.1	49	25
Gabon	2.0	36	—	Niger	5.5	43	35	Middle-income[b]	3.0	30	15

Sources: Authors' compilation from CSRs and other country studies.
Note: pc = per capita. — = not available.
a. "Low-income" countries are eligible for lending from International Development Association (IDA); see appendix A, table A.1.
b. "Middle-income" countries are eligible for lending from the International Bank for Reconstruction and Development (IBRD); see appendix A, table A.1.

Figure 4.8 Comparison of Average Teacher Salary and Pupil-Teacher Ratio at Primary Level in 16 Sub-Saharan African Countries with Similar Per-Student Spending, ca. 2003

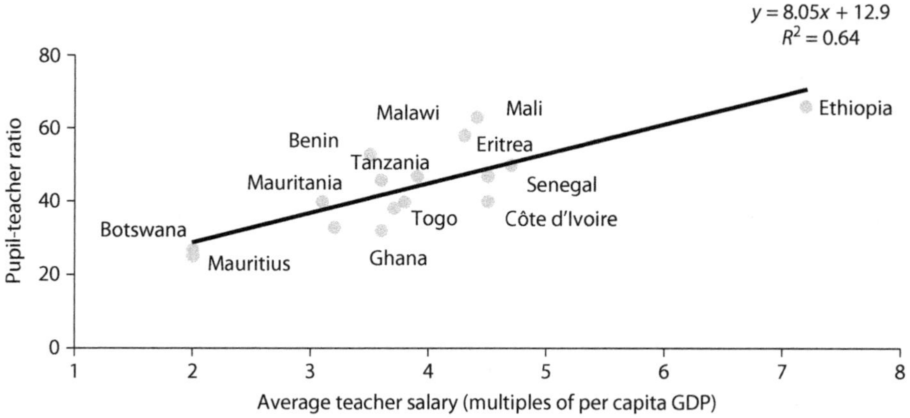

$y = 8.05x + 12.9$
$R^2 = 0.64$

Source: Authors' construction from data in table 4.8.
Note: Chart displays data for 16 countries, selected for having similar levels of per-student spending relative to gross domestic product per capita.

These differences reflect the combined effects of two factors: (a) differences in the resources available per student, as discussed above, and (b) differences in policy choices regarding input mix, as will be seen below.

Countries with similar levels of per-student spending make very different tradeoffs in terms of pupil-teacher ratio and average teacher salary. Figure 4.8 shows these tradeoffs in 16 Sub-Saharan African countries that have similar levels of per-student spending relative to per capita GDP.[12]

Some countries, Ethiopia in particular, have opted for high teacher salaries relative to GDP per capita, resulting in high pupil-teacher ratios. Other countries, such as Botswana and Mauritius, have low salaries and low pupil-teacher ratios. Clearly, different countries in the region make different tradeoffs, even when they face similar resource constraints. Madagascar, Niger, and Senegal have introduced contract teachers as a way of lowering the average teacher cost and achieving a greater expansion in education coverage (see box 4.1).

Influence of School Input Composition on Coverage

Expressing primary educational coverage as a function of education policy variables yields important insights. The impact on primary educational coverage of the choices concerning school inputs may be examined from equation (4.1) below. The equation is derived from simple accounting identities for primary education, as shown in appendix F.

$$\text{GER} = \frac{\text{PEP}}{\text{GDP}} \cdot \frac{1}{1+\alpha} \cdot \frac{1}{\text{ATSR}} \cdot \text{PTR} \cdot \frac{1}{\text{DR}} \qquad (4.1)$$

Box 4.1

Madagascar, Niger, and Senegal: Contract Teacher Recruitment to Expand Primary School Coverage

Madagascar—Community Teachers

Before 2004, the shortfall of government teachers meant that parents' associations (FRAM)[13] in Madagascar were routinely financing and recruiting their own teachers (called FRAM teachers). Beginning in 2004, the Ministry of Education responded to strong citizen demand for education and rapidly growing enrollments by subsidizing the salaries of the FRAM teachers. By the following year, 92 percent of the FRAM teachers were subsidized by the government. The number of FRAM teachers increased rapidly from 18 percent of all primary school teaching staff in 2000 to almost 50 percent in 2005.

Niger—Contract Teachers

Niger introduced a category of contract teachers in 1998, making some modifications in 2003. Since then, new teachers have been hired only as non-civil-servant teachers. Although they initially received no training—later receiving an accelerated preservice training lasting only a few weeks—new contract teachers now receive preservice teacher training that is similar to that given previously to teachers in the civil service. Between 1998 and 2003, this policy allowed the government to recruit some 10,200 new teachers, allowing it to expand student enrollment dramatically. In particular, the primary school GER increased from 30 percent in 1998 to almost 50 percent in 2005. The number of contract teachers has grown rapidly since 1998. By 2009, they accounted for 80–85 percent of all primary school teachers. This has brought about some challenges as the contract teachers gained greater bargaining power because that power enabled them to demand and receive salaries that are now approaching those of the civil servant teachers.

Senegal—From Volunteers to Contract Teachers

The primary school GER in Senegal declined from 58 percent in 1989 to 56 percent in 1994, but the high per-student cost stood in the way of expanding enrollment. Notably, the average teacher salary was comparatively high, at 7.2 times GDP per capita. In 1995, to arrest the decline in the GER and also address high unemployment among qualified school completers, the government launched the volunteer teacher initiative. Upper secondary school completers were recruited as volunteer teachers and posted to schools after a three-month preservice training course. Volunteer teachers were sent primarily to rural areas for a period of two years, renewable once, in exchange for a monthly scholarship of CFAF 50,000 (equivalent to only 1.9 times GDP per capita).

From 1995 to 1999, the volunteer teacher program recruited 1,200 new teachers annually. By 1998, volunteers represented almost 20 percent of the teaching force. At that point, with support from the trade unions, the volunteer teachers demanded and were accorded permanent

(box continues on next page)

Box 4.1 Madagascar, Niger, and Senegal *(continued)*

status within a new government contract teacher category. The change provided volunteer teachers with better career prospects in the following ways:

- After serving for two years, volunteer teachers could be recruited as (non-civil-service) contract teachers, earning 3.4 times per capita GDP, or CFAF 80,000, plus health insurance and other benefits.
- The preservice training was extended from three months to six months.
- Upon meeting certain requirements, contract teachers could join the civil service teaching corps.

In 2010, volunteer and contract teachers accounted for an estimated 56 percent of all primary school teachers. Since its introduction in 1995, the volunteer and contract teacher program has enabled Senegal to significantly expand primary school coverage: the GER has risen from 56 percent in 1994 to 77 percent in 2004 and, at the same time, the pupil-teacher ratio has fallen from 60 in 1994 to 43 in 2004.

Source: Jarousse et al. 2009.

---

where GER is the primary gross enrollment rate,
PEP is public recurrent spending on primary education,
GDP is gross domestic product,
α is the ratio of all primary education recurrent expenditures other than teacher salaries to the total teacher salary bill,
ATSR is average teacher salary relative to per capita GDP, and
DR is the ratio of the school-age population to the total population.

The equation implies that the GER would be higher,

- The larger the volume of public recurrent spending on primary education relative to GDP
- The lower the spending other than for teacher salaries as a proportion of the total teacher salary bill
- The lower the average teacher salary relative to GDP per capita
- The higher the pupil-teacher ratio
- The smaller the share of the school-age population in the total population.

From the perspective of education planners and policy makers, the last factor—the ratio of the school-age population to the total population (DR)—may be viewed as a demographic factor that is beyond the control of education planners and policy makers. The first four, however, are critical education policy variables or instruments that planners and policy makers may manipulate to attain a country's educational goals.

Above Relation Permits a Decomposition of GER Variability across Countries

Each of the variables that appear on the right side of equation (4.1) takes on different values in each of the Sub-Saharan African countries. For example, as shown in table 4.9, the pupil-teacher ratio (PTR) varies between 22 and 80 across the countries, while the share of the school-age population in the total population (DR) ranges between 10 percent and 18 percent.

The range of variation is larger for some variables than for others. Depending on their range and the functional relationship with the GER in equation (4.1), some variables explain more of the cross-country variability in the GER than others. To compare the influence of each of the variables on the variability in the GER across Sub-Saharan African countries, a log linear form of equation (4.1) is used:

$$\log(\text{GER}) = \log\left(\frac{\text{PEP}}{\text{GDP}}\right) + \log\left(\frac{1}{1+\alpha}\right) + \log\left(\frac{1}{\text{ATSR}}\right) + \log(\text{PTR}) + \log\left(\frac{1}{\text{DR}}\right) \quad (4.2)$$

Table 4.9 presents the steps and results of the decomposition. The first two columns provide, for each variable, the minimum and maximum values that are observed in the region in the latest year for which data are available. The two middle columns show which side of these ranges produce the lowest or highest value of the GER. The two columns on the right present the relative influence of the different variables in explaining the variability in the GER.

Quantum of Spending and Teacher Policy Variables Explain Most GER Variability

The last column of table 4.9 shows the following key findings: (a) the quantum of recurrent spending on primary education (PEP) accounts for 37 percent of the variability in the GER; (b) the level of spending other than on teacher salaries (α) accounts for 8 percent; while (c) the share of school-age children in the total population (DR) explains 10 percent.

The case of the average teacher salary (ATSR) and the pupil-teacher ratio (PTR) is more complex due to the interaction between the two. Discounting this interaction, these findings result: (d) ATSR explains 25 percent, and (e) PTR explains 20 percent of the variability in the GER across countries. Balancing the level of teacher salaries and the pupil-teacher ratio is therefore one of the most important decisions governments have to make because it has a large bearing on the GER or educational coverage that can be achieved with a given volume of public recurrent spending, at least at the primary level.

Cross-Country Data Useful To Illustrate Range of Policy Options

Within a given country, key education policy variables such as those in equation (4.1) above tend, in general, to change slowly over time, giving the impression

Table 4.9 Decomposition of Variables' Relative Influence to Explain Variability in Primary GER across Sub-Saharan African Countries

Variable		Range of statistic within Sub-Saharan African countries		Value from range producing lowest GER (a)	Value from range producing highest GER (b)	GER variability explained [log (b) – log (a)]	
		Min	Max			(Absolute value)	(% of total)
Public recurrent spending on primary education (% of gross domestic product)	PEP/GDP	0.5	5.2	0.5	5.2	1.01	37
Nonteacher salary recurrent spending (% of teacher salary bill)	a	10	85	0.54	0.91	0.23	8
	1/(1+ a)	0.91	0.54				
Average teacher salary relative to gross domestic product per capita	ATSR	1.5	7.2	0.14	0.67	0.68	25
	1/ATSR	0.67	0.14				
Pupil-teacher ratio	PTR	22	80	22	80	0.56	20
School-age population relative to total population	DR	10	18	5.4	10.4	0.28	10
	1/DR	10.4	5.4				

Sources: Authors' calculations based on spending data from UIS Data Centre; nonteacher salary spending, average teacher salary, and PTR data from table 4.8; and population data from DDP database.

Note: GER = primary gross enrollment rate, PEP = public recurrent spending on primary education, a = ratio of all primary education recurrent expenditures other than teacher salaries to the total teacher salary bill, ATSR = average teacher salary relative to gross domestic product per capita, PTR = pupil-teacher ratio, DR = ratio of school-age population to total population.

that there is little scope for more drastic policy changes. However, as table 4.9 shows, across countries in the Sub-Saharan African region, these policy variables may take on a wide range of values. Such cross-country data are useful in highlighting and understanding the full range of policy options that are available to education planners and policy makers.

Figure 4.9 School Distribution in Burundi and Malawi, by Per-Student Spending, ca. 2004

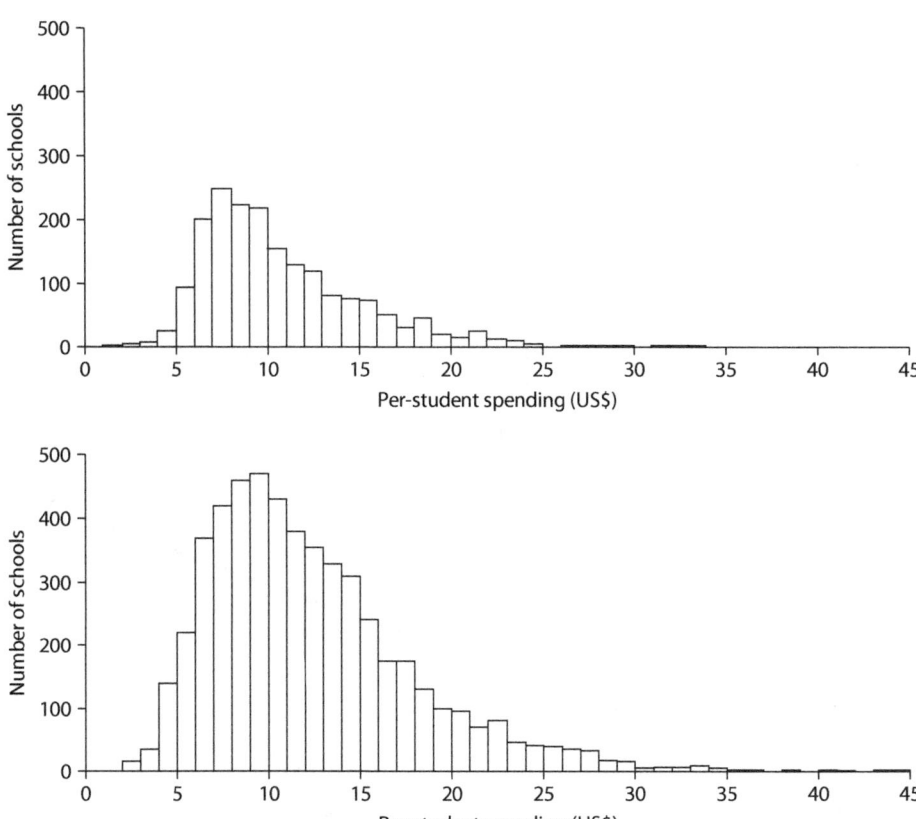

Sources: Authors' analysis of Malawi School Census 2003/04 and Burundi School Census 2004/05.
Note: The charts are constructed, based on the ministries' school census data, by estimating each school's level of per-student spending based on the number and types of staff working in the school.

Management of Resources

There are large disparities in per-student public recurrent spending across schools within a country. Figure 4.9 illustrates the wide variability in the level of per-student spending (measured in US$) across primary schools in Burundi and Malawi.

In Burundi, for the vast majority of schools (80 percent),[14] per-student spending ranges from US$8 to US$20, but some schools incur per-student spending exceeding US$30. Malawi displays an even larger variability in per-student spending: 80 percent of schools spend between US$5 and US$20 per student, indicating larger disparities across schools in Malawi.

Relationship Often Weak between Numbers of Teachers and Students

Figure 4.10 shows scatterplots of the numbers of teachers and students in all public primary schools in Benin and Madagascar. In both countries, the data

Figure 4.10 Relation between Numbers of Students and Teachers at Primary Level in Benin and Madagascar, 2005/06

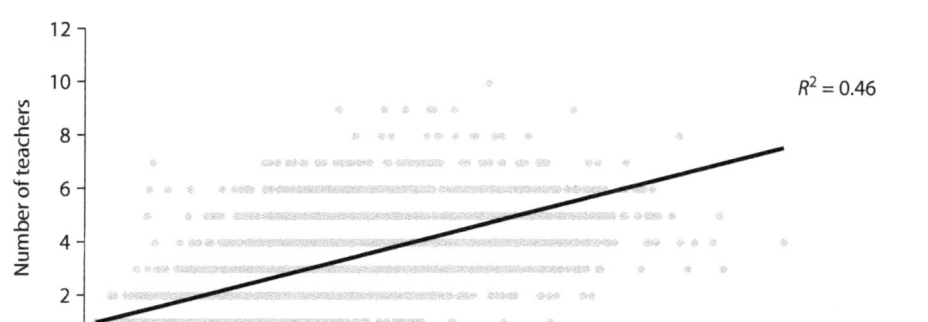

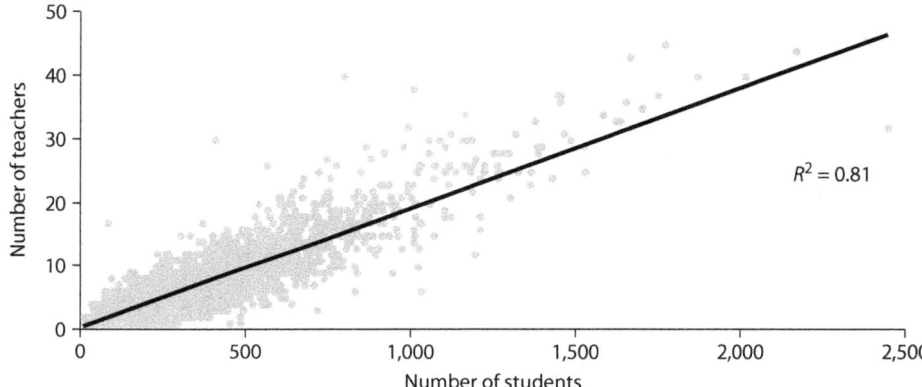

Sources: Authors' construction, based on data from the Benin and Madagascar school censuses, 2005/06; World Bank 2008, 2009.
Note: The chart for Benin is based on civil servant and contract teachers; it does not include community teachers.

suggest that schools with more students tend to have more teachers. However, the scatterplot for Benin also suggests that the relationship between the number of students and the number of teachers is not very close. A Beninese school with, say, 500 students may have as few as two teachers or as many as nine teachers.

The scatterplot for Madagascar shows a tighter relationship between the number of students and the number of teachers, but there is clearly still some inconsistency in the allocation of teachers across schools. The loose relationship between school size and teacher allocation is a reflection of the wide disparities in the level of per-student public recurrent spending discussed above because teacher salaries typically absorb more than 70 percent of the education budget.

Regression Analysis of Teacher Allocation Permits Calculation of the Degree of Randomness

In both panels of figure 4.10, the straight line corresponds to a linear regression relating the number of teachers to the number of students. For both countries, as expected, there is a positive relationship between the two variables, but the observations are much more scattered around the regression line in the case of Benin than in Madagascar.

The strength of the relationship can also be measured using the R^2 statistic.[15] R^2 is much higher in Madagascar (0.81) than in Benin (0.46), confirming the above observation of greater variability in the allocation of teachers in Benin than in Madagascar. The degree of randomness in the allocation of teachers across schools may also be measured by the proportion of the variation in the allocation of teachers that is not explained by differences in the number of students across the schools—that is, by $1 - R^2$. At 54 percent, the degree of randomness in teacher allocation across schools is clearly larger in Benin than in Madagascar, where it is only 19 percent.

Degree of Randomness Is Wide across Sub-Saharan African Countries

The World Bank's Country Status Reports (CSRs) on education systematically document the degree of randomness in the allocation of teachers in primary schools across Sub-Saharan African countries, allowing comparisons to be made.[16] Table 4.10 shows clearly the large differences in the allocation of primary school teachers across countries in the region.

Disparities in schooling conditions are not, however, confined to teacher allocation. Although analysis of the allocation of nonteacher inputs has been

Table 4.10 Comparison of Randomness in Teacher Allocation to Primary Schools in Selected Sub-Saharan African Countries

Degree of randomness $[1 - R^2]$ (%)			
São Tomé and Principe	3	Burkina Faso	28
Guinea	9	Ethiopia	29
Mozambique	15	Côte d'Ivoire	33
Namibia	15	Chad	34
Guinea-Bissau	16	Malawi	34
Madagascar	19	Uganda	34
Niger	19	Congo, Rep.	38
Senegal	19	Cameroon	45
Mauritania	20	Central African Republic	46
Zambia	20	Burundi	50
Rwanda	21	Togo	53
Gabon	26	Benin	54
Mali	27	Simple average	28

Source: Authors' calculation from CSRs for countries indicated.
Note: Data are from between 2000 and 2008.

> **Box 4.2**
>
> **Madagascar: Improvement in the Allocation of Teachers to Schools**
>
> In 2004, a Madagascar team of the "Improving Education Management in African Countries" initiative (*Amélioration de la Gestion de l'Education dans les Pays Africains*, or AGEPA), together with its partners, developed a mechanism for the distribution of teachers aimed at improving consistency and equity in the allocation of teachers across schools. The mechanism identifies schools with a severe shortage of teachers relative to the national average and gives them higher priority in the assignment of newly trained teachers based on an agreed set of transparent criteria, such as classroom availability.
>
> The Ministry of Education used this mechanism for new teacher allocation in the 2005/06 and 2006/07 school years. One year after implementation, consistency in teacher allocation improved substantially, rising from 72 percent in 2004/05 to 81 percent in 2005/06. As a result of this positive experience, the government plans to adapt the teacher allocation mechanism for future use when its reform of basic education is completed and new guidelines and standards for teacher and classroom requirements have been finalized. The downside of the allocation mechanism is the systematic deployment of new, and therefore less experienced, teachers to underserved rural areas where living conditions are less attractive to experienced teachers.
>
> *Source:* Madagascar Education for All (EFA) Plan 2008.

conducted for only a few countries, the general finding is a degree of randomness in the distribution of classrooms, textbooks, or school furniture that is in some cases higher than that in the allocation of teachers.

Large disparities in the allocation of teachers are the result of weak resource management practices, but these disparities can be reduced rapidly. In Madagascar, for example, the randomness in primary teacher allocation was reduced from 28 percent in 2004/05 to 19 percent in 2005/06—a substantial 9 percentage point reduction over the course of a single school year. The effort is further described in box 4.2.

Issues for Policy Development

What is the scope for increasing spending on education? As this chapter has shown, the region's low-income countries spend an average of about 4.3 percent of GDP, and the middle-income countries 5.7 percent of GDP, on education. These averages, however, conceal large differences across countries in the region.

Table 4.11 divides the low-income Sub-Saharan African countries into two groups based on their levels of public spending on education as a proportion of GDP: (a) countries that spend less than 4 percent of GDP on education, and (b) countries that spend 4 percent or more of GDP on education.

Table 4.11 Scope for Increasing Education Spending in Selected Low-Income Sub-Saharan African Countries

	Public spending on education (% of gross domestic product)	
	< 4 %	≥ 4 %
	Angola; Cameroon; Central African Republic; Chad; Comoros; Congo, Rep.; Gambia, The; Guinea; Madagascar; Mauritania; Niger; Rwanda; Sierra Leone; Togo; Zambia	Benin, Burkina Faso, Burundi, Cape Verde, Côte d'Ivoire, Eritrea, Ethiopia, Ghana, Kenya, Lesotho, Malawi, Mali, Mozambique, Senegal, Uganda
Total public spending (% of gross domestic product)	21.5	30.4
Public spending on education (% of total public spending)	14.5	19.7

Source: Authors' construction based on education spending data from UIS Data Centre. For the full data set, see appendix E, table E.1.

Note: "Low-income" countries are eligible for lending from International Development Association (IDA); see appendix A, table A.1.

Countries in the first group have, on average, a much lower total public spending-to-GDP ratio (21.5 percent) than countries in the second group (30.4 percent). Furthermore, countries in group one also assign, on the average, a smaller share of the public budget to education (14.5 percent) than their counterparts in group two (19.7 percent). This implies that there is scope for countries in the first group to increase education spending, even if raising total public spending as a proportion of GDP may be more difficult and require a longer time frame to achieve.

Sub-Saharan African Countries Make Very Different Decisions about Education Spending

As we have seen, there are also large differences in spending patterns within the education sector across countries in the region. Sub-Saharan African countries differ widely, for example, with respect to

- Allocation of spending across levels of education
- Level of per-student spending
- Average teacher salary
- Share of recurrent spending on goods and services.

The above regional analysis suggests that Sub-Saharan African countries have more choices and more room to maneuver than would appear if attention is focused only on individual country experiences.

Spending Choices Do Influence Educational Outcomes

How much a country spends on education and how it allocates its education spending has important implications for the attainment of key educational goals within that country. Countries that make better use of their education budgets and resources can, for instance, achieve higher levels of educational coverage and longer school-life expectancy. Within a given budget, countries with high average teacher salaries cannot provide as many school places as countries with more moderate levels of teacher salaries.

Spending decisions are, in that sense, interrelated. Decisions that affect the level of per-student spending, for instance, may also affect the level of coverage. More important, as chapter 5 will show, the composition of spending in terms of input mix also has an impact on student learning.

Notes

1. Cross-country comparisons are not always meaningful because of the differences in educational structures. These differences will be highlighted wherever they present a particular problem.
2. The sample of 33 low-income countries (selected in Bruns, Mingat, and Rakotomalala 2003) comprises the Sub-Saharan African countries eligible for lending from the International Development Agency (IDA) except those with very small populations (Cape Verde, the Comoros, and São Tomé and Príncipe) or highly incomplete data (Angola, Liberia, and Somalia). (The IDA threshold changes every year, as do the countries' gross national incomes [GNI] per capita, so there may be small changes from year to year in this group.) Based on a 2006 GNI per capita of less than US$1,065, the 33 countries in the sample are Benin, Burkina Faso, Burundi, Cameroon, the Central African Republic, Chad, the Democratic Republic of Congo, the Republic of Congo, Côte d'Ivoire, Eritrea, Ethiopia, The Gambia, Ghana, Guinea, Guinea-Bissau, Kenya, Lesotho, Madagascar, Malawi, Mali, Mauritania, Mozambique, Niger, Nigeria, Rwanda, Senegal, Sierra Leone, Sudan, Tanzania, Togo, Uganda, Zambia, and Zimbabwe.
3. "Middle-income" Sub-Saharan countries (whose 2006 GNI per capita exceeded US$1,065) include Botswana, Equatorial Guinea, Gabon, Mauritius, Namibia, the Seychelles, South Africa, and Swaziland.
4. Many African countries have a comparatively small tax base because their economies are characterized by large agriculture and nonformal sectors, and a large share of agricultural production is for own consumption.
5. Not all ODA is included in the government budget; whether ODA is included in government revenue or the expenditure budget depends, among other things, on the type of aid (debt relief, budget support, project aid, and so on) and on the government accounting rules and practices. In Malawi, for example, it has been common practice to include only grant-funded projects in the budget when domestic counterpart funds were required (World Bank 2004).
6. Funding allocated to specific sectors excludes multisector, program assistance, debt relief, humanitarian aid, and administrative expenses.
7. With the 2005 Paris Declaration on Aid Effectiveness (OECD 2005), more than 100 countries committed to continue and step up efforts to harmonize and align aid and to manage aid for results. For example, donors must increasingly align aid with national priorities, use common implementation structures, use country

procurement and financial management systems, and continue to **untie aid from conditions of purchase from suppliers based in the donor country.**

8. The method for calculating these two indexes is explained in appendix E, figure E.2.
9. The range of the Gini coefficient is between 0 and 1, and a higher value of the Gini coefficient indicates a higher degree of inequality.
10. School-life expectancy (SLE), introduced in chapter 1, is equivalent to the average number of years of schooling of a cohort and is available from the UNESCO Institute for Statistics (UIS).
11. We repeated this analysis for primary education only, relating public spending on primary education as a percentage of GDP with the primary GER. The R^2 in this regression was only a little better at 0.30.
12. It should be noted that the 16 countries have very different absolute levels of per-student spending.
13. *Fikambanan'ny Ray Amandrenin'ny Mpianatra* (FRAM) is the name of the parents' association in Madagascar.
14. This range is derived by excluding the 20 percent of the schools with the highest or lowest levels of per-student spending (that is, the 10 percent highest-spending and the 10 percent lowest-spending).
15. R^2 varies between 0 and 1. A value of 0 implies that the allocation of teachers across schools is completely independent of the number of students in the schools. On the other hand, a value of 1 implies that the teachers are being allocated to schools strictly on the basis of enrollments.
16. The method can be applied either to all schools in a country or to schools in different regions within a country. A similar analysis can be conducted for resources other than teachers—for example, for classrooms or textbooks.

References

Bruns, B., A. Mingat, and R. Rakotomalala. 2003. *Achieving Universal Primary Education by 2015: A Chance for Every Child.* Washington, DC: World Bank.

DAC (Development Assistance Committee) Online (database). Organisation for Economic Co-operation and Development, Paris. http://www.oecd.org/document/33/0,2340,en_2649_34447_36661793_1_1_1_1,00.html.

DDP (Development Data Platform) (database). World Bank, Washington, DC. http://databank.worldbank.org/ddp/home.do.

Gauthier, B. 2006. "PETS-QSDS in Sub-Saharan Africa: A Stocktaking Study." Study commissioned for the "Measuring Progress in Public Services Delivery" project. Washington, DC: World Bank.

Government of Madagascar. 2008. "Madagascar Education for All (EFA) Plan." Unpublished program document.

IMF (International Monetary Fund). 2007. "Regional Economic Outlook: Sub-Saharan Africa." World Economic and Financial Surveys. October report, IMF, Washington, DC.

Jarousse, J.-P., J.-M. Bernard, K. Améléwonou, D. Coury, C. Demagny, B. Foko, G. Husson, J. Mouzon, B. Ledoux, F. Ndem, and N. Reuge. 2009. "Universal Primary

Education in Africa: The Teacher Challenge." UNESCO-BREDA (Regional Office for Education in Africa), Dakar.

Mingat, A. 2004. "La rémunération/le statut des enseignants dans la perspective de l'atteinte des objectifs du millénaire dans les pays d'Afrique subsaharienne francophone en 2015." Unpublished discussion paper, World Bank, Washington, DC.

OECD (Organisation for Economic Co-operation and Development). 2005. "Paris Declaration on Aid Effectiveness." Adopted at the Second High Level Forum on Aid Effectiveness. Development Co-operation Directorate, OECD (Organisation for Economic Co-operation and Development), Paris. February 28–March 2.

———. 2008. "Development Co-operation Report 2007." Annual report on international aid, Development Assistance Committee, OECD, Paris.

Pôle de Dakar UNESCO-BREDA (United Nations Educational, Scientific and Cultural Organization, Regional Office for Education in Africa). 2005. "Education for All in Africa: EFA–Paving the Way for Action." Dakar+5 Report, UNESCO-BREDA Pôle de Dakar, Dakar.

———. 2006. "Elements d'analyse du secteur éducatif au Togo." Country Status Report, Pôle de Dakar UNESCO-BREDA, Dakar.

———. 2007. "Education for All in Africa: Top Priority for Integrated Sector-Wide Policies." Dakar+7 Report, UNESCO-BREDA Pôle de Dakar, Dakar.

UIS (UNESCO Institute for Statistics) Data Centre (database). UNESCO (United Nations Educational, Scientific and Cultural Organization) Institute for Statistics, Montreal. http://stats.uis.unesco.org.

World Bank. 2002. "Le système éducatif béninois: Performance et espaces d'amélioration pour la politique éducative." Africa Region Human Development Working Paper 19. Country Status Report, World Bank, Washington, DC.

———. 2003a. *Education in Rwanda: Rebalancing Resources to Accelerate Post-Conflict Development and Poverty Reduction.* Country Study Series. Washington, DC: World Bank.

———. 2003b. "Rapport d'état du système éducatif national Camerounais: Elèments de diagnostic pour la politique éducative dans le contexte de l'EPT et du DSRP." Country Status Report, World Bank, Washington, DC.

———. 2003c. "Le système éducatif Togolais: Eléments d'analyse pour une revitalisation." Africa Region Human Development Working Paper 35, World Bank, Washington, DC.

———. 2004. "Malawi: Country Assessment and Action Plan for HIPCs." Report for the Enhanced HIPC (Heavily Indebted Poor Countries) Initiative, World Bank, Washington, DC.

———. 2005a. *Education in Ethiopia: Strengthening the Foundation for Sustainable Progress.* Country Study Series. Washington, DC: World Bank.

———. 2005b. "Le système éducatif guinéen: Diagnostic et perspectives pour la politique éducative dans le contexte de contraintes macro-économiques fortes et de réduction de la pauvreté." Africa Region Human Development Working Paper 90. Country Status Report, World Bank, Washington, DC.

———. 2005c. "Le système éducatif da la république démocratique du Congo: Priorités et alternatives." Africa Region Human Development Working Paper 68. Country Status Report, World Bank, Washington, DC.

———. 2006. "Mauritania: rapport d'état sur le système éducatif national (RESEN)—Elements de diagnostic pour l'atteinte des objectifs du millenaire et la réduction de la pauvreté." Unpublished Country Status Report, World Bank, Washington, DC.

———. 2007a. *L'éducation au Mali: Diagnostic pour le renouvellement de la politique éducative en vue d'atteindre les objectifs du millénaire.* Africa Human Development Series. Washington, DC: World Bank.

———. 2007b. "Le système éducatif tchadien: Eléments de diagnostic pour une politique éducative nouvelle et une meilleure efficacité de la depense publique." Country Status Report, World Bank, Washington, DC.

———. 2008. "Eléments de diagnostic du système éducatif Malagasy: Le besoin d'une politique éducative nouvelle pour l'atteinte des objectifs du millénaire et de la réduction de la pauvreté." Unpublished Country Status Report, World Bank, Washington, DC.

———. 2009. "Le système éducatif béninois: Analyse sectorielle pour une politique éducative plus equilibrée et plus efficace." Africa Region Working Paper 165. Country Status Report, World Bank, Washington, DC.

———. 2010. "Le système éducatif congolais: Diagnostic pour une revitalisation dans un contexte macroéconomique plus favorable." Country Status Report, World Bank, Washington, DC.

World Bank and UNICEF (United Nations Children's Fund). 2009. "Six Steps to Abolishing Primary School Fees." Operational Guide for the School Fee Abolition Initiative, UNICEF and World Bank, Washington, DC.

CHAPTER 5

Learning Outcomes

This chapter focuses on learning outcomes in primary education in Sub-Saharan Africa and discusses, on the basis of the empirical evidence, the types of policies that can be effective in improving student learning. Although resources per se are necessary for schools to function, they are not sufficient to achieve satisfactory levels of learning. In most Sub-Saharan African countries, average test scores in international assessments of student learning are low, and they are not likely to improve just by increasing education spending. What does matter for learning is how resources are used to provide schools with needed inputs and, even more important, the ability of schools and teachers to transform inputs into learning.

The chapter argues that the most promising avenues to improve learning may be (a) to direct education spending to high-quality inputs that have been found to be cost-effective in improving student performance and (b) to support these policies with better systems of accountability for teachers and schools.

Status of Learning Outcomes in Sub-Saharan Africa

Why Are We Interested in Learning Outcomes?
Cognitive Skills Associated with Higher Earnings
It is well documented that higher school attainment is correlated with an increase in lifetime earnings (see, for example, Psacharopoulos and Patrinos 2002). Although data on school attainment are widely available and easy to compare across countries, student learning is more difficult to measure, and microdata linking cognitive skills with earnings are generally much harder to come by. Nevertheless, a growing body of evidence shows that the relationship between cognitive skills and earnings is probably stronger than that between school attainment and earnings (Hanushek and Wößmann 2007, 2009). This evidence strongly suggests that it is what students learn that matters most, not how many years of schooling they have completed.

Developing Countries Lag Behind
Furthermore, developing countries exhibit much larger skills deficits than generally observed from school enrollment and attainment data (Hanushek and Wößmann 2007). Although improving the quality of education is a clear Education for All

(EFA) goal, it is less explicit in the United Nations (UN) Millennium Development Goals (MDGs), which focus on educational coverage and attainment.[1] Similarly, the Independent Evaluation Group of the World Bank finds that most Bank projects supporting primary education did not specifically include the improvement of student learning in their development objectives, and even fewer projects were designed to track improvements in learning outcomes (World Bank 2006).

Reducing Disparities in Learning Can Reduce Income Inequality

Reducing differences in learning achievement between schools, and between individuals within schools, may be an objective in itself. Nickell (2004, as cited in Hanushek and Wößmann 2007) finds a relationship between the dispersion of literacy test scores and the dispersion of earnings in developed countries. This relationship implies that reducing disparities in student learning can have a beneficial impact on income distribution.

Learning achievement and incomes also have an urban-rural dimension. In particular, both are usually lower in rural than in urban areas. Chinapah (2003) reports that Monitoring of Learning Achievement (MLA) surveys conducted in the Sub-Saharan African region have consistently found an urban-rural disparity in learning achievement in all countries and in all learning areas (literacy, numeracy, and life skills).

Comparison of Learning Outcomes across Sub-Saharan African Countries

Because there is no single source of data on student learning in the Sub-Saharan African countries, it is necessary to combine several sources to create a data set with more or less comparable data on student learning that covers the largest possible number of countries. The following discussion uses bootstrapping techniques to build a comparable index on student learning for the Sub-Saharan African region.

Methodology for Constructing the Africa Student Learning Index (ASLI)

ASLI is a composite of the test scores obtained in the three learning assessment programs that have the widest application in the Sub-Saharan African region: the MLA, the Program for the Analysis of Education Systems of CONFEMEN (PASEC), and the Southern Africa Consortium for Monitoring Educational Quality (SACMEQ).[2] Table 5.1 provides the test scores from the three surveys, converted to a common scale. (For the original scores and details of the scale conversion, see appendix G, table G.1.) All test scores shown are averages of literacy and numeracy scores. The MLA also tests students in life skills, but those scores are not included here for better comparability between the three surveys.

The last column in table 5.1 calculates the ASLI score as the average of the scores provided in the three preceding columns; thus, the ASLI score for a given country may be based on one, two, or three test scores, depending on how many surveys the country has participated in. Only Mauritius has participated in all three surveys. In total, the ASLI index covers 31 Sub-Saharan African countries.[3]

Table 5.1 Test Scores and Index of Student Learning in Primary Education in Selected Sub-Saharan African Countries, 1996–2009

	MLA score	PASEC score (MLA scale)	SACMEQ score (MLA scale)	ASLI (MLA scale)
Low-income countries[a]				
Benin	n.a.	38.0	n.a.	38.0
Burkina Faso	n.a.	43.7	n.a.	43.7
Burundi	48.7	n.a.	n.a.	48.7
Cameroon	n.a.	54.0	n.a.	54.0
Chad	n.a.	38.6	n.a.	38.6
Congo, Rep.	n.a.	42.2	n.a.	42.2
Côte d'Ivoire	n.a.	54.1	n.a.	54.1
Gambia, The	40.4	n.a.	n.a.	40.4
Guinea	n.a.	48.0	n.a.	48.0
Kenya	n.a.	n.a.	62.8	62.8
Lesotho	n.a.	n.a.	39.8	39.8
Madagascar	49.2	49.2	n.a.	49.2
Malawi	39.0	n.a.	35.8	37.4
Mali	47.7	42.7	n.a.	45.2
Mauritania	n.a.	27.1	n.a.	27.1
Mozambique	n.a.	n.a.	56.0	56.0
Niger	39.2	37.1	n.a.	38.1
Nigeria	28.6	n.a.	n.a.	28.6
Senegal	43.3	46.2	n.a.	44.8
Tanzania	n.a.	n.a.	58.3	58.3
Togo	n.a.	52.0	n.a.	52.0
Uganda	53.7	n.a.	49.7	51.7
Zambia	39.5	n.a.	37.3	38.4
Zimbabwe	n.a.	n.a.	51.9	51.9
Average low-income	42.9	44.1	49.0	45.4
Middle-income countries[b]				
Botswana	49.5	n.a.	54.6	52.0
Gabon	n.a.	56.3	n.a.	56.3
Mauritius	59.8	64.0	64.1	62.6
Namibia	n.a.	n.a.	37.8	37.8
Seychelles	n.a.	n.a.	65.7	65.7
South Africa	n.a.	n.a.	48.5	48.5
Swaziland	n.a.	n.a.	55.9	55.9
Average middle-income	54.7	60.2	54.4	54.1
Average Sub-Saharan Africa	44.9	46.2	51.3	47.2
Selected non-Sub-Saharan African countries				
Morocco	62.0	n.a.	n.a.	62.0
Tunisia	69.1	n.a.	n.a.	69.1

Source: Authors' construction based on MLA, PASEC, and SACMEQ scores in literacy and numeracy. For the original scores and details of the scale conversion, see appendix G, table G.1.

Note: MLA = Measurement of Learning Achievement. PASEC = Program for the Analysis of Education Systems of CONFEMEN. SACMEQ = Southern Africa Consortium for Monitoring Educational Quality. ASLI = Africa Student Learning Index. n.a. = not applicable. MLA tests students in grade four, PASEC in grade five, and SACMEQ in grade six. MLA also tests in life skills, but those scores are not used here. All scores are from after 1995.

a. "Low-income" countries are eligible for lending from the World Bank's International Development Association (IDA); see appendix A, table A.1.
b. "Middle-income" countries are eligible for lending from the International Bank for Reconstruction and Development (IBRD) of the World Bank Group; see appendix A, table A.1.

Sub-Saharan African Learning Outcomes Are Generally Poor

The average value of the ASLI index across the region's low-income countries is 45, as seen in table 5.1. Measured on the MLA scale, the score can be interpreted as the percentage of the curriculum that students have absorbed and comprehended at the time of testing. In other words, students in low-income Sub-Saharan African countries have, on the average, learned less than half of what was expected of them.

On the other hand, the average value of this indicator for the middle-income Sub-Saharan African countries is higher, at 54 percent. In contrast, students in Morocco and Tunisia—both outside the Sub-Saharan African region—scored significantly higher averages of 62 and 69, respectively. The average score for the Organisation for Economic Co-operation and Development (OECD) countries, converted to the MLA scale, is around 80.[4]

Overall, the ASLI clearly indicates that learning outcomes in primary education are relatively poor in Sub-Saharan Africa, especially in the low-income Sub-Saharan African countries.

Learning Outcomes Vary Widely across Countries

With a score of 66, the Seychelles has the best ASLI score among the Sub-Saharan African countries listed in table 5.1. Kenya and Mauritius also have scores that are higher than 60, a level comparable to the scores of students in Morocco and Tunisia.

At the opposite end of the spectrum, students in Nigeria and Mauritania both scored less than 30—corresponding to a very low level of learning. This score is only 10 percentage points higher than the average score students obtain by randomly guessing the answers.

ASLI Scores Correlate with Income and Quantitative Schooling Outcomes

Panel A in figure 5.1 plots the ASLI score against per capita GDP and shows that richer countries tend to have higher scores. Although income (as measured by per capita GDP) is a significant determinant of learning outcomes, it explains only a small part of the cross-country variability in student learning (R^2 is 0.22 and the t-statistic 2.9).

Panel B plots the ASLI score against the primary school completion rate. As may be seen, countries with higher primary school completion rates appear to have higher average ASLI scores. Here, too, the relationship is relatively weak (R^2 is 0.14 and the t-statistic 2.1).

Literacy Varies Widely: Three Years of School in Rwanda Corresponds to Seven Years in Mali

Figure 5.2 shows the relationship between length of studies completed in youth and individuals' ability to read in selected Sub-Saharan African countries in the region, thereby illustrating the extent of the cross-country variation in literacy retention. In Rwanda, for example, 60 percent of adults with three years of

Figure 5.1 Correlation of ASLI Scores with GDP per Capita and Primary Completion Rate in 31 Sub-Saharan African Countries, ca. 2005

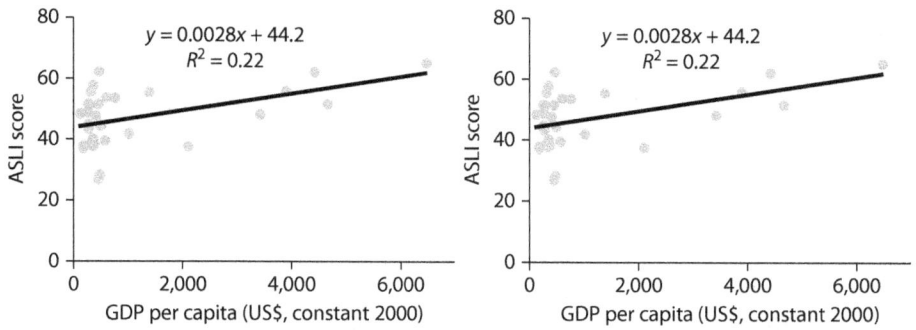

a. ASLI and GDP per Capita

b. ASLI and Primary Completion Rate

Sources: Authors' construction from ASLI scores in table 5.1 and primary completion rates from UIS Data Centre. For the full data set of primary completion rates, see appendix B, table B.1.
Note: ASLI = Africa Student Learning Index; GDP = gross domestic product. GDP per capita data are for 2005.

Figure 5.2 Literacy and Length of Studies, Selected Sub-Saharan African Countries

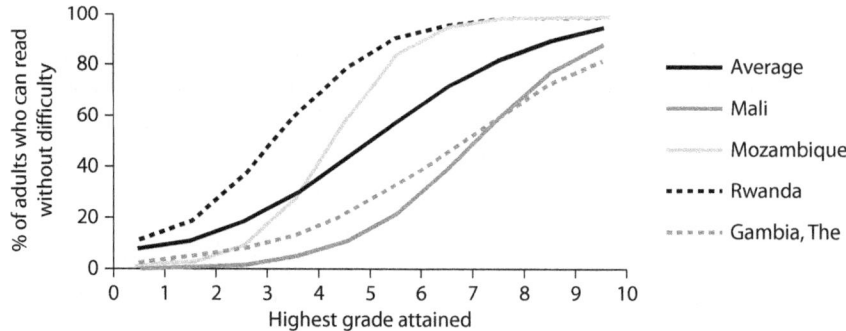

Source: Authors' construction based on household survey data from the period 2000–05. For the country-specific list of surveys, see appendix J, table J.1.
Note: "Average" is the average relation for 32 Sub-Saharan African countries.

schooling can read easily. In Mali, it takes about seven years of schooling to achieve the same outcome.

The variation is, therefore, very wide, suggesting that some school systems achieve much more in a school year than others. The results for Rwanda show that it is possible to achieve lifelong literacy for the vast majority of students with just a six-year basic cycle. This finding suggests that countries at the bottom of the ladder in terms of learning outcomes are probably better off focusing on improving student learning in the first six years of schooling than on lengthening the duration of the basic cycle.

Learning Outcomes Vary as Much within Countries as between Countries

When it comes to assessing the variations in learning achievement across schools within countries, more sources of data are available, including both national student assessment data and results from national examinations. In Côte d'Ivoire, based on a standardized test administered to a sample of 2,000 students, average test scores across schools ranged between 38 and 63 points on the MLA scale. Thus, the variability across schools in Côte d'Ivoire is of approximately the same magnitude as the variation in the ASLI index across countries in the region.

What can countries do to reduce the disparities in learning achievement across schools? Clearly, individual schools differ from one another and need different approaches depending on their particular situations. National assessments of learning achievement or the results in national examinations can be used to identify schools with the most severe problems in terms of low learning outcomes so that interventions can focus especially on those schools.

How Can Students' Learning Outcomes Be Improved?

This section reviews the evidence on policies that lead to better learning outcomes. Underlying this research is a simple conceptual model that suggests that learning outcomes are a function of student characteristics, school inputs, and the transformation of inputs into outcomes.

Student characteristics include students' innate abilities, socioeconomic backgrounds, and schooling experiences. These are important determinants of learning, but they are generally, with the possible exception of schooling experience, exogenously determined and lie beyond the direct influence of education policy and the schools. In contrast, school inputs and the transformation of inputs into outcomes can be influenced directly by education policy.

The analysis begins by examining the impact of total per-student spending on student learning outcomes. The section concludes by looking at the relationship between each of the most common school inputs and learning outcomes.

Relation between Per-Student Spending and Learning Outcomes

Per-student spending appears to have no impact on learning outcomes in Sub-Saharan Africa as well as around the world. Figure 5.3 plots the ASLI score against the level of public per-student spending on primary education as a proportion of per capita GDP in the sample of 31 Sub-Saharan African countries included in table 5.1.

Some countries with low levels of per-student spending, such as Chad and Zambia, have low learning scores. However, countries such as Niger and Namibia have high levels of per-student spending, and yet their student learning scores are no better than those of Chad and Zambia. On the other hand, Kenya and Mauritius have low levels of per-student spending like those of Chad and Zambia, but they have far higher student learning scores. A simple regression between the two variables—ASLI on per-student spending in primary education—yields a coefficient that is not statistically different from zero (the t-statistic is -1.4 and R^2 is only 0.06). There is, therefore, no evidence that more resources result, on the average, in more learning in Sub-Saharan African countries, at least in the case of primary education.

Figure 5.3 Relationship between Per-Student Spending on Primary Level and ASLI Scores in 31 Sub-Saharan African Countries, ca. 2005

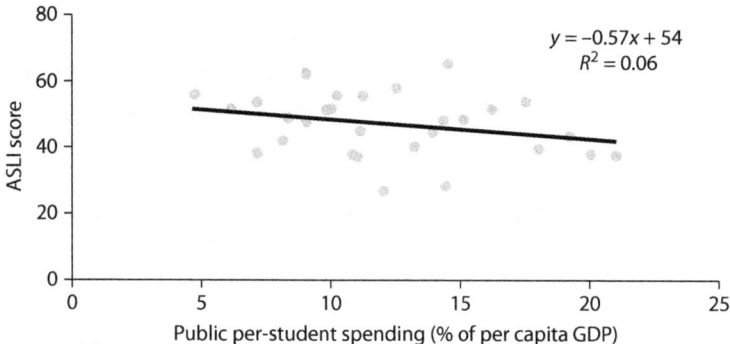

Sources: Authors' construction from ASLI scores shown in table 5.1 and per-student public spending data from Country Status Reports (CSRs), Pôle de Dakar UNESCO-BREDA 2005, or UIS Data Centre. For the country-specific data set of per-student spending, see appendix E, table E.2.
Note: ASLI = Africa Student Learning Index, GDP = gross domestic product. The *t*-statistic in the regression is -1.4, thus the relation is not statistically significant at the 5 percent level.

Figure 5.4 Relationship between Public Per-Student Spending on Education and Performance on the 2009 PISA Mathematics Test in 27 OECD Countries

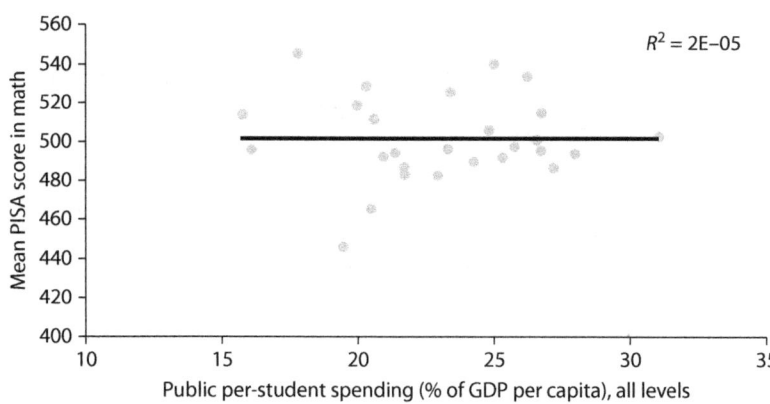

Source: EdStats. Canada, Germany, Ireland, and Luxembourg are omitted for lack of data on their per-student spending.
Note: PISA = Program for International Student Assessment. OECD = Organisation for Economic Co-operation and Development. Because PISA is administered in secondary school, the average per student spending across all levels of education is used.

This finding is consistent with the findings of numerous other studies for both developed and developing countries. For example, figure 5.4 plots the 2009 Program for International Student Assessment (PISA) mathematics score against per-student spending in all the high-income OECD countries for which these data could be compiled, and finds no correlation whatsoever between test results and spending (see also Hanushek and Wößmann 2007; OECD 2004).

More Resources Alone Do Not Improve Learning

Educational expenditures per student increased substantially in real terms between the early 1970s and the mid-1990s in a sample of OECD countries

(Wößmann 2002). In spite of the increase, there has been no substantial improvement in average scores in those countries. In his discussion on the failure of input-based schooling policies, Hanushek (2003, F94–95) concludes that "without incentives and without adequate evaluation, there should be no expectation that schools improve, regardless of the resources added to the current structure." Does this finding hold across schools with different levels of per-student spending within countries?

Similar Findings Emerge when Comparing Schools within Countries

Replicating the approach used in the cross-country analysis above, but this time using the school as the unit of observation rather than the country, figure 5.5

Figure 5.5 Relation between Primary Schools' National Exam Pass Rates and Per-Student Spending

a. Burundi

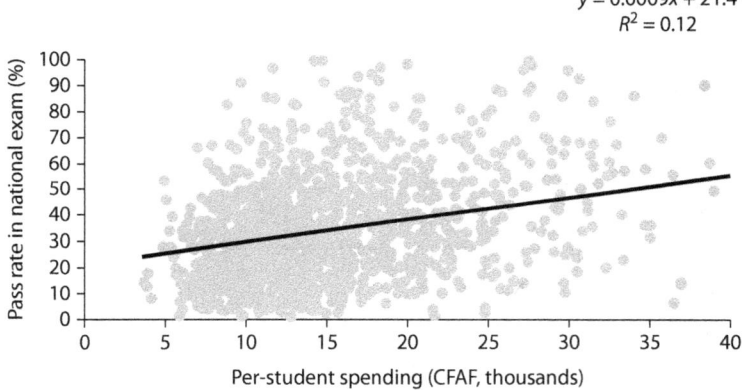

b. Niger

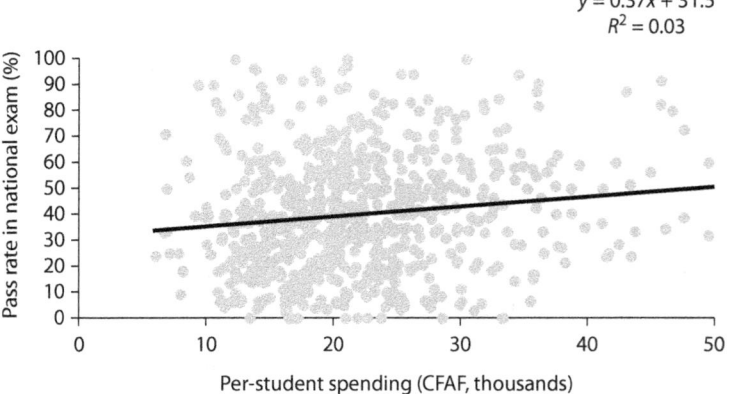

Sources: World Bank 2004b, 2007.
Note: Schools are the unit of observations in both graphs. The *t*-statistic in the regression shown is 13 for Burundi and 4 for Niger, thus statistically significant in both cases. The R^2 statistics very low, however, particularly in the case of Niger, indicating that the level of per-student spending explains little of the variation in the pass rate.

shows the results for Burundi and Niger. The chart compares each school's pass rate in national examinations with the school's level of per-student spending.[5]

Figure 5.5 shows great variations in pass rates in national exams and levels of per-student spending across schools in both countries. The latter reflects a low degree of consistency in resource allocation across schools. More important, the scatterplots show little or no statistical relationship between per-student spending and learning outcomes. The Country Status Reports (CSRs) covering more than 20 Sub-Saharan African countries find this pattern to be prevalent throughout the region.[6] Some CSRs used average test scores from student learning assessments instead of pass rates, but all CSRs have found little or no relationship between the quantity of resources and extent of student learning.

Relation between Student or School Characteristics and Learning

Although the analysis of macrodata above did not find a strong relationship between spending and student learning, it is possible that there is a relationship at the microlevel of the individual school and student.

At the level of the individual students, how much of learning is explained by school factors? To assess the relationship between school inputs and learning, individual student test scores are regressed on a set of variables describing the characteristics of the students and the schools. This analysis enables us to determine the proportion of the variation in learning achievement that is explained by either student characteristics (such as student ability and socioeconomic background) or by school characteristics.

PASEC Allows for Separation of Factors' Effects on Learning

This analysis is based on data from the PASEC learning achievement survey. The PASEC data set includes fairly detailed background data on students, such as gender, urban or rural location, and income group. The survey also includes data describing the characteristics of the schools, classes, and teachers, which are included as explanatory variables in the regression. More important, with PASEC, students are tested at the beginning and at the end of the school year. Together, these variables allow us to examine the effects of student and school characteristics on student learning while controlling for a student's initial ability.[7]

We also include a class/teacher dummy to capture the effect that students taught in the same class and by the same teacher tend to obtain scores at the end of the year that are more similar than what can be explained by the other factors included in the regression. Thus, the dummy is a measure of the effect of the pedagogical process taking place in class and the effect of student interaction—both unobservable factors of the learning environment.

Observable Schooling Conditions Account for Most Education Spending but Matter Little for Student Learning

The results of this regression analysis are quite similar for all the 10 countries covered here. Table 5.2 presents the average contribution of three *groups* of factors

Table 5.2 Variance Decomposition of PASEC Learning Scores in 10 Sub-Saharan African Countries

Regressors or variables	Role of regressors in explaining learning score variance (percentage)
Student's personal characteristics	38.6
Initial score	36.1
Social characteristics[a]	2.5
Observable schooling conditions	6.5
School (e.g., location, size)	1.6
Class (e.g., class size, textbooks)	1.7
Teacher (e.g., qualifications)	3.2
Teacher/class dummy (unobservable)	24.2
Total explained variance	69.3
Residual (not explained) variance	30.7
Total variance	100.0

Source: Authors' analysis of PASEC data for Burkina Faso, Cameroon, Côte d'Ivoire, Guinea, Madagascar, Mali, Mauritania, Niger, Senegal, and Togo.
Note: PASEC = Program for the Analysis of Education Systems of CONFEMEN (Conference of Ministers of Education of French-Speaking Countries). Results shown are the average for grades two and five.
a. "Social characteristics" include variables such as family income, location (urban or rural), gender, and family composition.

in explaining the variation in student learning scores across the 10 countries. The principal findings may be summarized as follows:

- A student's test score at the beginning of the year explains 36 percent of the variation in the learning score.
- A student's socioeconomic background explains 2.5 percent.
- Observable schooling conditions account for 6.5 percent.
- The teacher/class dummy explains 24 percent of the variation in the learning score.

The remaining 31 percent of the variation remains unexplained by the regressors. Overall, observable schooling conditions—such as (a) teachers' academic credentials and training, class size, modality of student grouping; (b) school characteristics such as location and size; and (c) the availability of textbooks and pedagogical materials (which are largely determined by available resources)—together have a relatively small impact on student learning (6.5 percent). This finding is consistent with the findings reported above based on cross-country and cross-school data.

But Pedagogy Matters a Great Deal

What matters much more for student learning are the unobservable school factors proxied by the teacher/class dummy (24.2 percent), which may be described broadly as the pedagogical processes that take place in classrooms—that is, in line with our conceptual model, the ability to transform inputs into outcomes.[8]

Overall, unobservable factors appear to explain much more than observable school inputs. This finding stresses the need to place greater focus on what goes on in classrooms rather than on the provision of more school inputs. Educational resources are clearly necessary, but not sufficient, conditions for producing higher levels of student learning.

Education Policies or School Inputs that May Enhance Learning

The following section draws from available empirical evidence to highlight the impact of specific education policies and school inputs that contribute to learning achievement. This is a vast topic, and a choice has been made to focus the discussion on the following:

- Preprimary education as an instrument to affect students' preparedness for learning (which in turn affects the initial PASEC score)
- Observable school characteristics such as the quality of school buildings and the availability of libraries
- Textbooks
- Student grouping
- Instructional time
- Teachers
- Accountability mechanisms that can influence unobservable school characteristics.

In a context of scarce resources, the focus must be on cost-effective ways to improve learning outcomes; the impact of each type of input is therefore assessed in relation to its cost.

Preprimary Education Contributes to Better Outcomes

Participation in preprimary education has been shown to improve children's cognitive skills and educational attainment later in life and, in turn, to enable higher lifetime earnings (Hyde 2006), particularly among disadvantaged children (Schady 2006). In the Sub-Saharan African region, Jaramillo and Mingat (2006) find that high preprimary gross enrollment rates are associated with lower rates of repetition and higher rates of retention to grade five in primary education. Providing preprimary education to children can also free up parents' time for work or study.

With average levels of per-student spending at the preprimary level about 40 percent higher than those of primary education, public provision of preprimary education is often expensive (Mingat 2006). Given its high cost, public provision may not be the most cost-effective use of resources in the education sector and may not be financially sustainable for most low-income countries.

However, community-based preprimary education can be provided at a much lower cost, and evaluations of such programs in Cape Verde and Guinea show that the benefits for children in terms of preparation for primary school were comparable to those of traditional, publicly provided programs. Development of community preprimary education can therefore be a useful element in the overall strategy for the education sector.

Improved School Infrastructure Also Matters but Must Be Cost-Effective
Based on a review of 96 production function studies for developing countries, Hanushek (1995) identified 34 studies that investigated the impact of physical facilities, such as quality buildings and libraries, on student learning. A large majority of the studies found a positive effect of quality school infrastructure on learning achievement. Michaelowa and Wechtler (2006) also find a positive relationship between the condition of school buildings and learning, based on a study of 14 Sub-Saharan African countries. Sey (2001) and Chaudhury, Christiaensen, and Asadullah (2006) conclude that the availability of sanitation and latrines in primary schools in Senegal and Ethiopia boosted enrollment and retention. Further, Chaudhury et al. (2006) find that teachers in schools with higher-quality infrastructure were absent less often than teachers in other schools.

However, the construction and maintenance of school buildings is costly, so infrastructure investments are usually not among the most cost-effective interventions to improve schooling outcomes. The annualized infrastructure cost in Sub-Saharan Africa amounts to about US$30 per student per year, compared with Sub-Saharan African average public recurrent spending per student per year of US$60 (Theunynck 2009). Beyond the basic level of infrastructure, available empirical evidence indicates that infrastructure improvements are worthwhile only if schools are already well equipped with textbooks and teacher manuals and have the right levels of PTRs and teacher supervision (see, for example, Hanushek 1995 or Michaelowa and Wechtler 2006).

Primary school construction cost can be reduced through harmonization and by choosing proven, cost-effective approaches. Theunynck (2009) reviews the experience gained over the past three decades with primary school construction in Sub-Saharan African countries.[9] The study finds that there has been much experimentation in the region, resulting in widely different school models, types of construction management, and levels of construction costs. It recommends that governments and donors harmonize primary school construction approaches and choose the most cost-effective implementation and procurement strategies based on experience. The study further shows that, across the region as a whole, community-managed school construction has proven to be a cost-effective approach.

Textbooks Are Among the Most Cost-Effective Investments
Based on retrospective data for 21 Sub-Saharan African countries,[10] Michaelowa and Wechtler (2006) find that a change from no textbooks to full coverage of one book per student yields improvements in student achievement of between 5 percent and 20 percent of a standard deviation. Given that textbooks are not costly compared with, for example, teachers or classrooms, the study concludes that textbooks constitute one of the most cost-effective inputs in learning.

This perspective is generally shared by much of the literature (for example, Hanushek 2003; Lockheed and Verspoor 1991). Kremer (2003), however, argues that retrospective studies tend to overestimate the impact of textbooks on learning because schools with more textbooks tend to differ from schools with fewer textbooks in ways that are not easily measured, and therefore the textbook impact really captures the effect of, for example, more resourceful parents who choose schools with more resources or organize to obtain more resources for their children's school.

Randomized trials do not suffer from this problem and may therefore provide new evidence on the best use of textbooks.[11] In a randomized study of rural primary schools in Kenya, for example, Glewwe, Kremer, and Moulin (2002) find a positive effect of textbook provision among only the top 40 percent of the students. A plausible reason was the possibility that the textbooks distributed were too difficult for most students.

Evidence Supports a Student-Textbook Ratio of 1 to 1. The student-to-textbook ratio and its impact on learning has been the subject of much study and debate over the past decades. Heyneman, Jamison, and Montenegro (1984) find no significant difference in impact between a 2 to 1 student-textbook ratio and a 1 to 1 ratio in the case of first and second graders in the Philippines, but they confirmed the impact of textbooks in general. Based on this and other similar empirical evidence, around 1990, the World Bank recommended the provision of at least one textbook per two students in each subject (Lockheed and Verspoor 1991).

However, more recent studies suggest that it is important for all students to have their own textbooks, particularly in the lower grades when it can be important to take books home for reading practice; further, teachers may not fully integrate textbooks in their instructional approach unless all students have a copy (Michaelowa and Wechtler 2006). In other words, there is more to improving student learning than merely ensuring that each child has a textbook. Ghana, for instance, improved student learning not only by reducing its 4 to 1 student-textbook ratio to a 1 to 1 ratio but also by complementing the measure with an increase in the amount of time students spend learning and the establishment of higher minimum standards in education (see box 5.1).

Subsidies Don't Guarantee Textbook Access for Disadvantaged Students. Although tuition fees for primary schools have been abolished in most countries, it is still common to find that parents have to purchase learning materials, sometimes at subsidized prices, or pay textbook fees (Kattan and Burnett 2004). Although these fees can be helpful in financing more textbooks for schools, experience shows that the most disadvantaged students cannot afford to pay and are often left without access to textbooks.

Diop (2002) reports that even with a price subsidy, most rural primary students in Togo could not afford to purchase books under a textbook sales scheme supported by the World Bank. Diop suggests the following ways in

> **Box 5.1**
>
> **Ghana: Leaping in Quality from "Poor" to "Fair"**
>
> In recent years, Ghana has made progress in raising student learning. From 2003 to 2007, eighth-grade students in Ghana improved from an average score of 276 in mathematics and 255 in science to 309 in mathematics and 303 in science in the Trends in International Mathematics and Science Study (TIMSS). Ghana placed a strong focus on the following:
>
> - Improving the learning environment by, among other things, reducing the student-textbook ratio from 4-to-1 to 1-to-1 in core subjects
> - Increasing the amount of time students spend on a given task in the classroom
> - Raising schooling standards to a minimum quality level
> - Improving student attendance, health, and nutrition by providing health care such as deworming, eyescreening, potable water, and free meals in disadvantaged schools.
>
> In 2002, Ghana established a national student assessment system to more effectively monitor student performance with greater transparency. In addition to these efforts, some teacher capacity building also took place, but it was not as systematic. In summary, Ghana focused on and succeeded in bringing all primary schools up to a minimum standard (in terms of resources and quality) and in reducing disparities between schools.
>
> *Sources:* Mourshed, Chijioke and Barber 2009; Mullis et al. 2008; Martin et al. 2008.

which governments can reduce the cost of providing textbooks to schools and improve their use:

- Encourage the development of a domestic textbook printing industry
- Seek economies of scale—for example, through cooperative textbook development and production
- Improve textbook distribution
- Train teachers in the effective use of textbooks.[12]

Student Grouping Decisions Require Careful Cost-Benefit Balance

Many schools across the region operate with very large class sizes, several shifts, or multigrade teaching. The objective is often to make the best possible use of teachers and classrooms. The question here is: when is each of these approaches appropriate? The discussion below reviews the evidence on class size, double shifts, and multigrade teaching.

Class Size Less Consequential than Teacher Management and Allocation. Available empirical studies consistently show little relationship between class size and learning outcomes when class sizes range between 30 and 60 pupils per teacher

(Behaghel and Coustère 1999; Bernard 2003; Michaelowa 2003; Verspoor 2003). In other words, other things being equal, once the PTR exceeds 30 to 1, the addition of more students, up to a maximum of 60, has little or no impact on learning outcomes.[13] Although classes with fewer than 30 students do tend to produce better learning outcomes, such small class sizes are uncommon and financially unsustainable in most countries in the region.

Reducing class sizes is costly and, in view of the evidence above, probably not a cost-effective measure for increasing student learning unless (a) current class sizes are extremely high (exceeding 60 students), or (b) all of the more cost-effective measures, such as providing schools with adequate supplies of teaching and learning materials, have already been implemented.

Further, if teachers are not proportionately distributed across schools according to student enrollment, investments to add more teachers may well be wasted because there is no guarantee that new teachers would be placed where they are most needed. This issue applies to the allocation of teachers within schools, too, because PTRs are often unacceptably high in the lower grades while upper grades enjoy much smaller class sizes (see, for example, World Bank 2004a).

Double-Shifting Eases Class Size but at a Cost to Instructional Time. In double-shift teaching, classrooms and sometimes teachers are used for two shifts of students each day as a way of dealing with shortages of available classrooms and teachers. It is a common way of organizing schools in densely populated areas. The alternative to double-shift teaching is often to raise class sizes, which, as discussed above, is not a serious drawback once class sizes have exceeded a PTR of 30, although smaller class sizes are more desirable.

One of the drawbacks of double-shifting is that the instructional time offered to each student is often reduced compared with schools that operate on only one shift. The loss of instructional time has a negative impact on learning achievement and should therefore be weighed against the potential negative impact of larger class sizes. Michaelowa (2003) estimates that double-shift schooling only results in better student learning when the alternative to double-shifting is classes with more than 100 students.

Moreover, the financial savings from double-shifting is often less than imagined. Double-shift schooling is often used in countries with rapidly expanding enrollment to provide school places for everyone within a limited budget. The extent to which double-shifting provides a low-cost solution for a large increase in student enrollment depends, however, on how it is organized. If double-shift schooling uses two groups of teachers—one in the morning and one in the afternoon—double-shifting produces a savings in capital cost but not in operating cost. On the other hand, if it uses the same set of teachers in both shifts, there are additional savings in operating cost, but the savings may be small or large, depending on how the teachers are paid. If double-shift teachers are paid a bonus for the extra work, the savings may not be large, and therefore the gain in educational coverage for a certain level of spending will not be as large as imagined. Therefore, double-shift schooling has to be used with care, balancing possible enrollment gains against the loss in instructional time suffered by the affected students.

Multigrade Schools Offer Both Benefits and Risks. Multigrade schools can be a way of providing schooling at a reasonable cost in rural areas with low population densities. This method of organizing schools was widely used in the 18th and 19th centuries in Europe and North America during the period of rapid expansion in primary education, and it remains common in many developing countries today (Birch and Lally 1995; Sigsworth and Solstad 2001).

Multigrade classrooms can be a way of containing costs in schools with low student enrollment while still providing a full cycle of education close to the children's homes. The literature on multigrade schools argues that, when done right, this format can be superior to regular teaching. In particular, there is more variability in the methods of instruction, and students learn to work independently (Sigsworth and Solstad 2001). While teachers work with one group of students, the other group works independently or in groups doing exercises or research. Teachers, however, should be trained in these techniques, and multigrade schools should have no shortage of exercise books and notebooks for this format to work well (Little 1995).

When multigrade schools only offer part of the primary cycle, however, students are at a higher risk of not completing the primary cycle. This is the case of many multigrade schools in the Sub-Saharan African region today—for example in Benin, Burkina Faso, Mauritania, and Mozambique (World Bank 2000, 2001, 2003, 2009). The benefit of providing schooling closer to home should be weighed against the increased dropout risk if the school is not offering the full primary cycle. Further, multigrade schooling should not reduce instructional time because that time has been found to be an important determinant of learning. There are, therefore, several risks associated with the implementation of multigrade schools, but when done right they can be an effective supplement to the regular system.

Instructional Time Is Crucial

Multishifting, school closures, and teacher absences effectively reduce the instructional time offered to students. Instructional time has been found to be crucial for academic achievement, especially among disadvantaged children who may not have as many opportunities for learning outside school hours (Millot and Jane 2002; Abadzi 2006). Hours of instruction received are a function of both instructional time and student attendance.

Instructional Time Varies Greatly across Countries. Mulkeen (2007) reports that planned hours of instruction per school year in seven Sub-Saharan African countries ranged from 810 hours in Eritrea to 1,599 hours in Uganda. In some countries, this number varies between schools. In Burundi, for example, students attending schools with multiple shifts received much less instructional time than students attending single-shift schools (World Bank 2007).

The effective number of hours of instruction provided to a class can be much less than the planned figure due to class cancellations, which can occur for varied reasons. For example, only 55 percent of the planned length of the school year is effectively available for instruction in Ghana after subtracting days of classes missed due to school closures and teacher absences (Abadzi 2006). In comparison, the proportion of planned school days used for instruction was much higher in Brazil, Morocco, and Tunisia: between 85 percent and 90 percent.

Effective Classroom Practices Can Raise Attendance. A second aspect of effective instructional time is student attendance. An impact evaluation of the Improving Education Management in Madagascar initiative (*Amélioration de la Gestión de l'Education à Madagascar,* or AGEMAD) concluded that certain classroom practices, such as taking daily student attendance, reduced student absenteeism in treatment schools compared with schools in the control group (World Bank 2008). Adapting the school calendar to take into account children's domestic responsibilities may also help improve children's school attendance. It may be too early to tell, but Madagascar is not alone in introducing measures aimed at increasing student attendance and learning. Senegal has adopted similar measures, and it is witnessing some improvements (see box 5.2).

Teachers

Three fundamental aspects of the relationship between teacher characteristics and student learning are teachers' educational attainment, professional teacher training, and salaries.

Teachers' Educational Attainment Not Likely to Affect Learning. Whether teachers' level of education before entering their pedagogical training has an impact on student learning has been the focus of many studies (for example, Behaghel and Coustère 1999; Bernard 2003; Jarousse and Suchaut 2001; Mingat and Suchaut 2000). All these studies conclude that although teachers need to have completed about 10–11 years of general education, additional years of academic education appear to have no impact on student learning outcomes at the primary level.

This surprising result may be explained by lower job satisfaction and potentially higher rates of absenteeism among teachers who have higher than average levels of academic qualifications. Based on PASEC data for French-speaking countries, Michaelowa (2002) concludes that teachers who have the high school degree (*baccalauréat*) were often more dissatisfied with their professional choice than teachers with lower educational attainment.

Box 5.2

Senegal: Better Management of Instructional Time to Improve Student Learning

In 2005, the head of the inspectorate in Diourbel, Senegal, conducted a study on the loss of classroom time during the school year. He found an alarming gap between official and actual instructional hours. The reasons for the difference were multifaceted and consisted of absenteeism among teachers and students, strikes, local holidays, market days, administrative and examination days, and ineffective use of instructional time. As an example, consider the teaching of French at the secondary level. Of the 196 official hours required to cover the course materials, only 124 were held; that is, one-third of the required instructional hours were lost each school year. The loss of instructional time at the primary level is thought to be even higher.

The Ministry of Education realized the severe financial and educational quality implications of the extensive loss of instructional time. It launched a communications campaign to sensitize schools, inspection personnel, and parents; increased regional and local autonomy to set the school calendar; established guidelines for monitoring and promptly dealing with teacher and student absences; and established guidelines for makeup classes. Though it is too early to tell whether the measures adopted will lead to improvements in student learning, some improvements have been observed: for instance, some school inspectorates now routinely record absences and schedule remedial classes.

Source: Adapted from Mulatu and Ndiaye 2008.

Policy makers must therefore approach the issue of raising entry requirements for the teaching profession beyond the basic 10–11 years with care: such a policy is unlikely to have much impact on student learning, but it could result in more dissatisfied teachers and a higher rate of teacher turnover. Further, such a policy change would be costly, given that the salaries of teachers with 13 years of general education is typically about 25–40 percent higher than the cost of teachers with 10 years of education (Mingat 2004).

Short Preservice Training plus In-Service Training Brings Cost-Effective Improvement. Preservice teacher training to prepare future teachers varies greatly across countries in the region with respect to both duration and content. Further, multiple programs often coexist within a given country. The duration of training ranges from very short periods for temporary teachers, contract teachers, voluntary teachers, or "parent teachers" to as long as three years for regular teachers. The content of preservice training programs also differs—for example, concerning the weight placed on pedagogical methods versus subject matter. Empirical studies have looked at the impact of preservice training on student achievement (CONFEMEN 2002, 2003, 2005a, 2005b).

Many of the studies of the impact of preservice training are not sufficiently detailed or contextualized to allow for a comparison between different preservice programs relative to no training. Nevertheless, the studies generally concur that long periods of preservice training are not necessary, as long as the training focuses on teaching skills—including how to manage a classroom, prepare lesson plans, assess pupils' learning needs, and so on. For example, studies based on PASEC data for Togo and Guinea find that teachers do need some preservice training, but a short training course of four to six months can be as good as longer preservice training programs when accompanied by additional support to the new teachers during the first year on the job and combined with the recruitment of candidates with good general education (CONFEMEN 2002, 2003). Because short training programs cost less than longer programs, preservice training programs of a relatively short duration appear to be the most promising and cost-effective option. Short programs also ease the pressure on teacher training colleges, which could otherwise form bottlenecks in the production of sufficient numbers of new teachers in some countries.

Experts strongly support in-service training as a tool for teacher development. In-service training for primary school teachers who are already working in schools includes a wide range of activities, ranging from group-based training related to the introduction of new curriculum content or textbooks to one-on-one pedagogical support that is available to teachers in some countries. In-service training may also include subject-based training—for example, to prepare primary school teachers for qualifying exams that will enable them to become qualified secondary school teachers.

Given the wide array of in-service training activities, the empirical evidence does not support any strong conclusions concerning their impact or the best ways of organizing such training. Despite the lack of empirical evidence, in-service teacher training is generally strongly supported by educators as an essential part of teacher development as long as it focuses on what goes on in the classroom. Teachers constantly develop their skills through their own teaching experiences, but this process is facilitated if they also receive opportunities for professional development through in-service training. Participating in-service training and meeting with other teachers to share experiences can also help keep teachers motivated and increase their job satisfaction.

Countries could potentially improve student learning by reallocating funds from preservice to in-service training. The evidence on preservice education of a long duration as an instrument for educational change in the Sub-Saharan African region has generally been disappointing (Mulkeen 2007). Given the high cost of long preservice programs, it appears that a program combining a relatively short preservice education with a structured program of in-service training may be the more promising approach in terms of maximizing teacher development and student learning outcomes (Lockheed and Verspoor 1991; Verspoor 2003).

As discussed above, training programs should focus on the development of teaching skills. In many countries, this would require the reallocation of resources from preservice teacher education to in-service training activities. Combined with the recruitment of graduates with 10–11 years of education, such a strategy could lead to savings in salary costs, and the savings could be used to fund additional in-service training or to establish a performance-based salary structures.

Setting of Teacher Salaries Requires a Balanced Approach. How much teachers are paid is a key aspect of teacher management that has a potentially significant impact on student learning. Setting the right level of teacher salaries is an important balancing act.

Consequences of low salaries. If teacher salaries are too low relative to comparable jobs in the local labor market, it can be difficult to recruit and retain adequately qualified teachers—as is the case, for example, in Guinea (World Bank 2005). Other adverse effects include higher rates of absenteeism, for instance, when underpaid teachers pursue other activities to generate additional income and, as a consequence, allocate less time to their teaching jobs. Chaudhury et al. (2006) find that 27 percent of primary school teachers were absent from work during unannounced visits to primary schools in Uganda. Public Expenditure Tracking Survey(s) (PETS) have documented teacher absenteeism rates of 8 percent in Kenya and 17 percent in Zambia (Gauthier 2006). And in Malawi, there is some evidence that teacher absenteeism is more frequent in remote schools, where the work atmosphere is more relaxed and visits by inspectors less frequent (Mulkeen and Chen 2008). Poorly paid teachers have also been found to impose illegal "school fees" on parents as a means of supplementing their incomes, thereby raising the private cost of education (World Bank 2005). Higher pay is no guarantee against absenteeism or corruption but may increase the financial and moral cost of being caught.

Consequences of high salaries. Higher salaries could allow for hiring of more qualified teachers, who may potentially raise student performance. On the other hand, if salaries are too high, it can become impossible for the government to pay for the number of teachers needed to provide places for all school-age children without sacrificing schooling conditions—for instance, by raising PTRs. Figure 5.6 shows that the higher the teacher salaries, the lower the primary school coverage. In addition to upward pressure on class sizes, high teacher salaries can also crowd out other needed expenditures, including spending on teaching and learning materials and other quality inputs.

Accountability Structures, Including Incentives, Can Promote Learning

Some schools are evidently better than others in transforming school inputs into learning outcomes. Hanushek and Wößmann (2007) emphasize the importance

Figure 5.6 Relationship between Primary Teacher Salary and GER in Selected Sub-Saharan African Countries

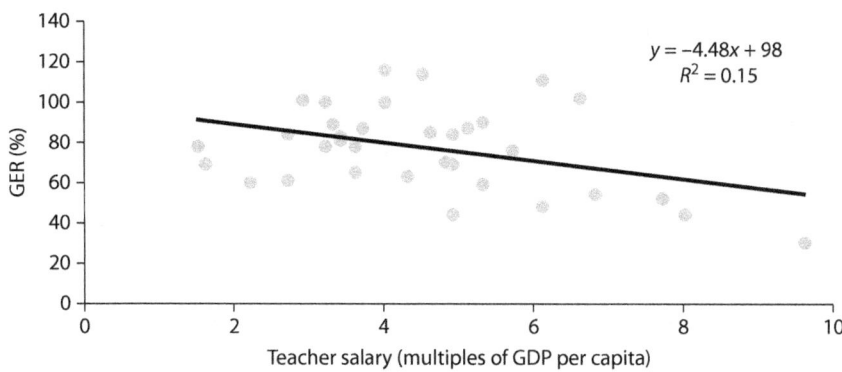

Source: Authors' construction from data in Bruns, Mingat, and Rakotomalala 2003.
Note: GER = gross enrollment rate, GDP = Gross domestic product. Chart shows data for 34 Sub-Saharan African countries.

of incentive structures in this process. They argue that if teachers, school managers, and other actors in the sector are rewarded for better student learning or penalized if they do not produce the desired results, the level of learning achievement tends to improve. That raises the question as to whether Sub-Saharan African countries have the right incentive and accountability structures in place to promote student learning.

Public School Accountability Poses Challenges. Mulkeen (2007) reports that private schools or schools managed by religious entities have lower levels of teacher absenteeism than government schools, even when teachers are paid the same. The World Bank (2004c) argues that the quality of public services often falls behind because the only way users can hold public providers accountable is through the ballot box or by speaking directly to policy makers who oversee the public providers. This implies that the chain of accountability between user and public provider is much longer and less direct than that between private providers and their clients. The chain of accountability can be shortened, however—for instance, by clarifying the duties and responsibilities of key players, simplifying supervisory and communication processes, and involving local communities in the management of schools, as the case of Madagascar illustrates in box 5.3.

At School Level, Rates of Teacher Absenteeism Indicate Level of Accountability. Teacher absenteeism is not the only problem at the school level in the Sub-Saharan African region, but it is a useful indicator of the standard of school management. A survey of World Bank task team leaders indicated that most

> **Box 5.3**
>
> **Madagascar: School Management Impact Evaluation**
>
> As part of a larger education reform, the Ministry of Education of Madagascar developed and piloted a set of interventions to enhance the management of teaching and learning. Among other things, the interventions included management tools and guides to streamline teaching and learning processes, training for teachers and school directors, school report cards, and facilitation of school-community interactions. The interventions clarified duties and responsibilities, simplified supervisory and communication processes, provided management tools to education officials, and involved communities in school management with the overall objective of increasing accountability to improve productivity and enhance learning outcomes.
>
> The government implemented the program on an experimental basis and assessed its effectiveness using a randomized impact evaluation. The study assessed the impact of the above interventions on the behavior of school staff, school functioning, and student performance. The program in its most intensive form had a positive impact on school staff behavior. Pedagogical processes are significantly better managed in the treatment group of schools than in the comparison group. After two years, 37 percent of the treatment schools were judged to be relatively well managed, compared with only 15 percent of the control schools. Better school management translated into higher student attendance rates in the treatment schools (an average of 91 percent compared with only 87 percent in the control schools), and considerably lower repetition rates (average of 18 percent compared with 23 percent, respectively), although repetition rates remained higher than the Sub-Saharan African average.
>
> *Source:* World Bank 2010.

schools in Sub-Saharan African countries have some kind of system in place to keep track of teacher attendance, as listed in table 5.3.

However, recording absenteeism may not be enough to reduce it. The impact evaluation of the AGEMAD initiative in Madagascar showed only a slight improvement in teacher attendance in schools that implemented a set of tools and procedures to improve school management, including having school directors monitor teacher attendance (World Bank 2008). The Gambia, on the other hand, has had much success with the introduction of supervision units established specifically to deal with teacher absenteeism, as described in box 5.4. Teacher attendance data are rarely used as part of teacher evaluation, and salary progressions as well as promotions are automatic in many countries or linked with characteristics such as teachers' education and length of teaching experience rather than teachers' job performance (Mulkeen 2007). In some cases, the head teachers are not even consulted regarding the promotion of teachers in their schools.[14]

Table 5.3 School Management and Accountability Tools in Selected Sub-Saharan African Countries, 2007

	Teacher attendance records	Parent-teacher associations	Direct grants to schools in previous year	School report cards
Benin	No	Some schools	Yes	Yes
Burkina Faso	Some schools	Yes	No	No
Burundi	Yes	Some schools	Yes	Yes
Central African Rep.	No	Some schools	No	No
Congo, Dem. Rep.	Yes	Yes	Yes	No
Congo, Rep.	No	Yes	No	No
Ethiopia	Yes	Yes	No	No
Ghana	—	—	Yes	Yes
Kenya	Yes	Yes	Yes	Yes
Madagascar	Yes	Yes	Yes	Yes
Malawi	Some schools	Yes	Yes	Yes
Mauritania	Yes	—	No	No
Mozambique	No	Some schools	Yes	Yes
Niger	Yes	Yes	Some schools	Some schools
Nigeria	Yes	Yes	Some schools	Some schools
Rwanda	—	Yes	Yes	Yes
Republic of South Sudan[a]	Yes	Yes	No	No
Togo	No	Some schools	Some schools	Some schools

Source: Authors' survey of World Bank task team leaders, June 2007.
Note: — = not available. No = none or very few schools. Yes = most or all schools.
a. "Southern Sudan" refers here to the autonomous region it was in 2007, now Republic of South Sudan.

At System Level, Accountability Efforts Target Governance Issues. Between 1991 and 1995, only 13 percent of grants intended for primary schools in Uganda actually reached the schools (Reinikka and Svensson 2004). The finding gave rise to a series of PETS in the Sub-Saharan African countries and elsewhere (Gauthier 2006). Lewis and Petterson (2008) identify budget leaks, whereby public education funds fail to reach intended recipients, as an important governance issue in the education sector that contributes to poor performance. Thus, problems of accountability do not apply to teachers and schools alone; it can be systemic. Uganda, however, has demonstrated that simple solutions such as public dissemination of information on funding can result in a significant increase in the proportion of funds arriving at their intended destinations, as described in box 5.5.

Accountability Interventions: Community Control and Performance-Based Incentives. The first category of interventions to address accountability includes interventions that address issues of control or involvement in school management, such as expanding community control by decreasing information asymmetries, strengthening capacity for community-based monitoring, or increasing participatory decision making. School-based management (SBM) falls in this category

> **Box 5.4**
>
> **The Gambia: Reducing Teacher Absenteeism by Strengthening Supervision**
>
> The Gambia established "cluster monitoring" supervision units to address teacher absenteeism. The supervision units systematically checked teacher attendance registers at the school level. Each unit is responsible for a limited number of schools and is equipped with adequate means of transportation to conduct regular school visits. Substantial improvements in monitoring and in teacher attendance in schools have been reported since the introduction of the supervision units.
>
> *Source:* Jarousse et al. 2009.

(Patrinos, Fasih, and Barrera 2007). The second category includes interventions focusing on the introduction of performance-based incentives, such as performance-based pay for teachers.

Benefits of community control. The World Bank's SBM work program (Patrinos, Fasih, and Barrera 2007) has yielded insights into a wide range of strategies to improve local accountability in schools. Generally, these consist of decentralizing authority to the level of the individual schools—in particular to principals, teachers, parents, sometimes students, and other school community members.[15] With a few exceptions, schools in most Sub-Saharan African countries have little autonomy. Table 5.3 above showed that many schools now have some parental involvement in school supervision through the parent-teacher associations (PTAs). However, PTAs often have limited functions and power, and parents may not feel comfortable holding teachers to account, especially in rural areas where teachers are often held in high regard in the lives of the community. Further, parents may not understand the role of the PTA and their right to demand better services and accountability. There is some indication that when schools receive "Direct Support to Schools" grants (see, for example, Muzima 2006) and the PTAs are involved in managing these grants, they become more involved in improving the school. Table 5.3 also showed that many countries now have school grants, raising the probability that PTAs are functioning and meeting regularly. In addition, improved access to information about a school's budgets and performance relative to other schools is an important tool, enabling parents to hold local officials and providers accountable (Lewis and Petterson 2008). As table 5.3 showed, many countries are now experimenting with school report cards.

Benefits of teacher incentives. Merit-based pay is one way to align teacher incentives with the objective of improving student learning outcomes. The empirical evidence on teacher incentives is somewhat mixed, however. In Kenya,

> **Box 5.5**
>
> ## Uganda: Public Access to Information Increases Effective Arrival of Grants to Schools
>
> In 1995, a Public PETS revealed that only 20 percent of the funds intended for primary schools in Uganda actually arrived at the schools. In the late 1990s, the Ugandan government launched an information campaign to address the problem and other governance issues in its school-grant program. It initiated a newspaper campaign to promote schools' and parents' ability to monitor the arrival of the grants at the schools. The information distributed included the grant amount per school and the timing of the release of funds by the central government. The outcome was a sharp increase in the proportion of grants arriving at the intended schools: up from 20 percent in 1995 to 80 percent in 2001. In the case of Uganda's school-grant program, timely public information proved to be an excellent tool for reducing and preventing fund capture by local elites.
>
> *Source:* Reinikka and Svensson 2003.

primary school teachers did not change classroom practices when promised a bonus if students improved their test scores. On the contrary, teachers merely provided students with more test preparation sessions without any change in pedagogy—an undesirable outcome resulting in only temporary test-score increases without any significant impact on lifelong learning (Glewwe, Ilias, and Kremer 2003; see box 5.6). In India, however, Muralidharan and Sundararaman (2006) find, in a randomized trial, that bonus payments to teachers in primary schools, based on average improvement in their students' test scores, did result in better learning outcomes. And incentive schools in India performed even better than control schools on subjects for which there were no incentives. Vegas (2005) reviewed several experiences with merit-based pay in Latin America and concluded that teaching quality is sensitive to incentives in the compensation structure, but only when the incentives are designed and managed right. An impact evaluation of performance-based teacher promotion is currently underway in Rwanda.

Issues for Policy Development

Because there is little or no direct relationship between total spending on education and student learning, it is clear that the mere provision of more resources is, in general, not sufficient to raise student test scores. That does not, however, necessarily mean that more resources for education are not needed. Depending on the context, and under the right conditions, increasing inputs that are in scarce supply can yield a high marginal return in terms of student learning.

Box 5.6

Kenya: Teacher Incentive Pilot Program

Glewwe, Ilias, and Kremer (2003) report on a randomized evaluation of a program in Kenya that provided a group-based incentive to teachers equivalent to about 30–40 percent of a month's salary based on performance of the school as a whole. By the second year, students in the treatment schools scored significantly higher on at least some exams than students in comparison schools.

However, the gains proved to be short-lived. One year after the program ended, there were no significant differences in test performance between the treatment and comparison schools. There is eviden ce that the teachers in the treatment schools strategized to take advantage of the program by focusing on teaching, including after-school tutoring, that concentrated on test-taking techniques to raise test scores rather than on changes in their core pedagogy or efforts to promote long-term learning.

Source: Glewwe, Ilias, and Kremer 2003.

This chapter has documented some best practice policies that can improve student learning without ignoring the cost of their implementation:

- *Preprimary education* appears to be important for educational attainment and learning later in life, and community-based provision can be an option for expanding the coverage of preprimary education at a low cost.
- *School infrastructure* can affect student learning but, in view of the high cost of infrastructure, a fairly basic-quality infrastructure is probably sufficient in most low-income countries.
- *Textbooks* are among the most cost-effective inputs in student learning, and recent evidence suggests that a student-textbook ratio of 1 to 1 works well; students from poor families need free textbooks.
- *Class size reduction* does not, contrary to a priori expectations, lead to better learning outcomes unless classes are excessively large (above 60 students) and should therefore probably not be a priority in most of the region's low-income countries.
- *Single-shift teaching* with larger class sizes is probably better for student learning than multishift teaching, which tends to reduce instructional time while often not providing much financial savings.
- *Multigrade classes* can be beneficial for educational attainment and learning, especially in areas with low population densities, but they must be implemented with care.
- *Community involvement and increased accountability* can help raise attendance and thereby effective instructional time, which has been shown to be crucial for student learning.

- *Teacher education programs* will achieve greater results from increased in-service training, which leads to better student learning, than from a longer and more costly preservice training program.
- *Teacher salaries*, set at levels appropriate to local labor market conditions and coupled with performance incentives, can also add to better student learning.

What Matters Most Is What Happens in the Classroom

Aside from the specific best practice policies listed above, what matters most for learning is the learning process—or what actually goes on in the classroom to transform inputs into learning. Building classrooms and training and hiring teachers are necessary, but not sufficient, conditions for improvements in student learning. Teachers must be present at work and make the best use of their skills and the resources made available to them for effective learning to take place. The current high rates of teacher absenteeism indicate that this is not always the case, and governments and donors must place more emphasis on these aspects of education by putting in place accountability structures that are needed to ensure that children are being taught well.

The first set of tools available to promote accountability in the sector includes interventions that address community control or involvement in school monitoring or management. The second category consists of performance-based incentives to improve student learning by holding teachers and school principals accountable for their students' learning. The two categories of tools are not mutually exclusive and may be combined in different ways. Although evidence on the magnitude of specific interventions is still scarce, this should not deter policy makers from experimenting with different policy instruments. All experiments should be accompanied by a rigorous impact evaluation to add to the pool of knowledge of the most cost-effective ways to improve student learning.

Political Economy Can Be an Obstacle to Reform

Reforms aimed at increasing accountability or implementing performance-based pay are not easy to implement because they are likely to encounter much opposition. The central government may resist decentralizing authority for the hiring of teachers, arguing that schools or communities are not ready to take on these responsibilities. Teachers' unions are likely to question changes in pay structures or changes in how teachers are hired or held accountable for student learning. Policy makers seeking to introduce accountability and performance-based reforms should anticipate likely opposition and foster fruitful dialogue to ensure successful implementation of their reforms.

More-Gradual Interventions that Increase Local Resources May Work Well

The introduction of accountability and performance-based pay measures aimed at improving student learning are likely to meet with greater success than comprehensive or systemwide reforms, particularly when they are implemented gradually and coupled with an increase in resources for the participating schools. The "Direct Support to Schools" mechanism that has been implemented in many countries across the region is an example of how to increase accountability by fostering greater PTA participation in school management issues (Ayako 2006; Muzima 2006).

If sustained, this approach can be a useful guide for the gradual introduction of an increasing number of policy tools aimed at fostering school accountability and performance. These possible tools include capacity building in school management, school report cards, and other instruments aimed at reducing information asymmetries. The Quality Education in Developing Countries program sponsored by the Hewlett and Gates foundations—which combines accountability for student learning with attention to instructional models and additional resources—is another example of success through gradual steps (Bender 2008). In Sub-Saharan Africa, the program is currently being piloted in Kenya, Tanzania, and Uganda.

Notes

1. EFA is an international initiative launched in Jomtien, Thailand, in 1990 to meet the learning needs of all children, youth, and adults by 2015. To realize this aim, a broad coalition of national governments, civil society groups, and development agencies such as the United Nations Educational, Scientific, and Cultural Organization (UNESCO) and the World Bank committed to achieving specific educational goals. The EFA goals also contribute to the global pursuit of the eight MDGs, especially MDG 2 on universal primary education and MDG 3 on gender equality in education, by 2015.

2. The Monitoring Learning Achievement (MLA) assessment was developed jointly by UNESCO and theUnited Nations Children's Fund (UNICEF) as a response to the Jomtien World Conference on Education for All, which called for the promotion of the quality of education. PASEC (Programme d'Analyse des Systèmes Educatifs de la CONFEMEN, where CONFEMEN is the Conference of Ministers of Education of French-speaking countries) is the regional program for learning assessment of French-speaking countries in Africa. SACMEQ is a regional program with participation of countries in east and southern Africa.

3. For their 2009 paper, "Do Better Schools Lead to More Economic Growth? Cognitive Skills, Economic Outcomes, and Causation," Hanushek and Wößmann constructed an internationally comparable measure of cognitive skills covering about 50 countries worldwide. The measure is based on bootstrapping results from 12 different international tests of math, science, or reading administered between 1964 and 2003. The database includes six countries in Sub-Saharan Africa: Botswana, Ghana, Nigeria, South Africa, Swaziland, and Zimbabwe; five of these countries also have an ASLI score as shown in table 5.1. When plotting the Hanushek and Wößmann score against the ASLI score, Nigeria is an outlier because it has a very poor ASLI score but a fairly good score in the Hanushek and Wößmann data set. For the remaining four countries, the Hanushek and Wößmann scores are closely correlated with the ASLI score (95 percent).

4. The OECD average is based on conversion of Progress in International Reading Literacy Study (PIRLS) and TIMSS scores to the MLA scale.
5. Per-student spending data are estimated based on information from the latest school census on the number of staff and student enrollment of each school.
6. For a complete list of CSRs consulted in this volume, see the reference list in the Overview chapter.
7. Students are tested in grades two and five. More information about PASEC can be found at www.confemen.org.
8. The effect of the teacher dummy may be inflated if data on school inputs are seriously affected by measurement errors (because the dummy is not directly observed, it absorbs the effect of any differences between teachers or classes that the other variables in the model have not already captured). Given the rigorous design and implementation of the PASEC survey instrument, however, measurement errors are likely to be small, in which case they do not substantially alter the results of the analysis.
9. Theunynck (2009) reviewed 208 construction projects, about half of which were financed by the World Bank and the remainder by governments or other development partners. Most of the projects reviewed are from Sub-Saharan Africa, but a small number of construction projects from Asia and Latin America were also included in the sample.
10. Based on SACMEQ data from 13 Sub-Saharan African countries and PASEC data from 8 Sub-Saharan African countries.
11. Several impact evaluations of textbook provision with a random experimental design are currently under way in the Sub-Saharan African region and may shed more light on the relationship between textbooks and learning, including: (a) impact evaluation of the provision of textbooks and expert teachers to schools in Sierra Leone, and (b) impact evaluation of the QIDS UP program in South Africa, which provides learning and teaching support material to schools.
12. Diop (2002) reviewed 89 World-Bank-financed education projects between 1985 and 2000 in 40 Sub-Saharan African countries. He provides useful recommendations to help countries address the issues they face in establishing sustainable systems of textbook provision.
13. Several Asian countries (such as Japan, the Republic of Korea, and Singapore) have shown that it is possible to achieve high levels of student learning even with high PTRs. Korea, for example, operates with class sizes of about 50–55 pupils, coupled with relatively high teacher salaries.
14. A notable exception is Lesotho, where schools now have the power to hire and fire teachers; thus, teachers apply and interview with the individual schools. In most Sub-Saharan African countries, teachers are hired centrally or at district-level (Mulkeen 2007).
15. One of the most-cited examples of SBM reform is El Salvador's successful EDUCO (*Educación con la participación de la Comunidad*) program (Jimenez and Sawada 1999). Vegas (2005) found that the authority of community-managed EDUCO schools to hire and fire teachers in El Salvador had a beneficial impact on student outcomes compared with traditional schools serving similar populations.

References

Abadzi, H. 2006. "The Economics of Instructional Time: How Well Are Funds Converted into Learning Activities?" Phase I Study Report, Bank-Netherlands Partnership Program, World Bank, Washington, DC.

Ayako, A. 2006. "Lessons of the Experience with Direct Support to Schools Mechanism: A Synthesis." Paper presented at the ADEA (Association for the Development of Education in Africa) Biennial Meeting, Libreville, Gabon, March 27–31.

Behaghel, L., and P. Coustère. 1999. *Les facteurs d'efficacité de l'apprentissage dans l'enseignement primaire: les résultats du programme PASEC sur huit pays d'Afrique.* Dakar: PASEC (Program for the Analysis of Education Systems of CONFEMEN).

Bender, P. 2008. "Quality Education in Developing Countries: Pratham's Read India Initiative." PowerPoint presentation, William and Flora Hewlett Foundation, Menlo Park, CA.

Bernard, J.-M. 2003. "Eléments d'appréciation de la qualité de l'enseignement primaire en Afrique francophone." Background paper for ADEA (Association for the Development of Education in Africa) study on educational quality, PASEC (Program for the Analysis of Education Systems of CONFEMEN), Dakar.

Birch, I., and M. Lally. 1995. "Multigrade Teaching in Primary Schools." Monograph, Asia-Pacific Centre of Educational Innovation for Development, UNESCO (United Nations Educational, Scientific and Cultural Organization) Principal Regional Office for Asia and the Pacific, Bangkok.

Bruns, B., A. Mingat, and R. Rakotomalala. 2003. *Achieving Universal Primary Education by 2015: A Chance for Every Child.* Washington, DC: World Bank.

Chaudhury, N., L. Christiaensen, and M. Asadullah. 2006. "Schools, Household, Risk and Gender: Determinants of Child Schooling in Ethiopia." Paper presented at the CSAE (Centre for the Study of African Economies) Annual Conference, "Reducing Poverty and Inequality: Can Africa Be Included?" University of Oxford, March 20.

Chaudhury, N., J. Hammer, M. Kremer, K. Muralidharan, and H. Rogers. 2006. "Missing in Action: Teacher and Health Worker Absence in Developing Countries." *Journal of Economic Perspectives* 20 (1): 91–116.

Chinapah, V. 2003. "Monitoring Learning Achievement (MLA) Project in Africa." Paper commissioned for the ADEA (Association for the Development of Education in Africa) Biennial Meeting, Grand Baie, Mauritius, December 3–6.

CONFEMEN (Conference of Ministers of Education of French-Speaking Countries). 2002. "Evaluation du programme de formation initiale des maîtres et de la double vacation en Guinée." Working paper, CONFEMEN, Dakar.

———. 2003. "Recrutement et formation des enseignants du premier degré au Togo: Quelles priorités?" Working paper, CONFEMEN, Dakar.

———. 2005a. "Les enseignants contractuels et la qualité de l'enseignement de base au Niger: Quel bilan?" Working paper, CONFEMEN, Dakar.

———. 2005b. "Impact du statut enseignant sur les acquisitions dans le premier cycle l'enseignement fondamental public au Mali." Working paper, CONFEMEN, Dakar.

Diop, S. 2002. "World Bank Support for Provision of Textbooks in Sub-Saharan Africa 1985–2000."Africa Region Human Development Working Paper 27, World Bank, Washington, DC.

EdStats (Education Statistics) (database). World Bank, Washington, DC. http://www.worldbank.org/education/edstats.

Gauthier, B. 2006. "PETS-QSDS in Sub-Saharan Africa: A Stocktaking Study." Study commissioned for the "Measuring Progress in Public Services Delivery" project, World Bank, Washington, DC.

Glewwe, P., M. Kremer, and S. Moulin. 2002. "Textbooks and Test Scores: Evidence from a Prospective Evaluation in Kenya." Impact Evaluation, Development Research Group. World Bank, Washington, DC.

Glewwe, P., N. Ilias, and M. Kremer. 2003. "Teacher Incentives." Working Paper 9671, National Bureau of Economic Research, Cambridge, MA.

Hanushek, E. 1995. "Interpreting Recent Research on Schooling in Developing Countries." *World Bank Research Observer* 10 (2): 227–46.

Hanushek, E. 2003. "The Failure of Input-Based Schooling Policies." *Economic Journal* 113 (485): F64–98.

Hanushek, E., and L. Wößmann. 2007. "The Role of Education Quality in Economic Growth." Policy Research Working Paper 4122, World Bank, Washington, DC.

———. 2009. "Do Better Schools Lead to More Economic Growth? Cognitive Skills, Economic Outcomes, and Causation." Working Paper 14633, National Bureau of Economic Research, Cambridge, MA.

Heyneman, S., D. Jamison, and X. Montenegro. 1984. "Textbooks in the Philippines: Evaluation of the Pedagogical Impact of the Nationwide Investment." *Education Evaluation and Policy Analysis* 6 (2): 139–50.

Hyde, K. 2006. "Investing in Early Childhood Development: The Potential Benefits and Cost Savings." Paper prepared for the ADEA (Association for the Development of Education in Africa) Biennial Meeting, Libreville, Gabon, March 27–31.

Jaramillo, A., and A. Mingat. 2006. "Early Childhood Care and Education in Sub-Saharan Africa: What Would It Take to Meet the Millennium Development Goals?" Paper prepared for the ADEA (Association for the Development of Education in Africa) Biennial Meeting, Libreville, Gabon, March 27–31.

Jarousse, J.-P. and B. Suchaut. 2001. "Evaluation de l'enseignement fondamental en Mauritanie." IREDU (Institut de Recherche sur l'Éducation), France.

Jarousse, J.-P., J.-M. Bernard, K. Améléwonou, D. Coury, C. Demagny, B. Foko, G. Husson, J. Mouzon, B. Ledoux, F. Ndem, and N. Reuge. 2009. *Universal Primary Education in Africa: The Teacher Challenge*. Dakar: Pôle de Dakar UNESCO-BREDA (United Nations Educational, Scientific and Cultural Organization, Regional Office for Education in Africa).

Jimenez, E., and Y. Sawada. 1999. "Do Community-Managed Schools Work? An Evaluation of El Salvador's EDUCO Program." *World Bank Economic Review* 13 (3): 415–41.

Kattan, R., and N. Burnett. 2004. "User Fees in Primary Education." Working paper, Education Sector, Human Development Network, World Bank, Washington, DC.

Kremer, M. 2003. "Randomized Evaluations of Educational Programs in Developing Countries: Some Lessons." *American Economic Review* 93 (2): 102–06.

Lewis, M., and G. Petterson. 2008. "Governance in Education: Raising Performance in the Sector; Overview of Issues and Evidence." Working paper, Development Economics and Human Development Network, World Bank, Washington, DC.

Little, A. 1995. "Multi-Grade Teaching: A Review of Research and Practice." Education Research Paper 12, U.K. Overseas Development Administration, London.

Lockheed, M., and A. Verspoor. 1991. *Improving Primary Education in Developing Countries.* Oxford: Oxford University Press.

Martin, M., I. Mullis, E. Gonzalez, and S. Chrostowski. 2008. *TIMSS 2007 International Science Report: Findings from IEA's Trends in International Mathematics and Science Study and the Fourth and Fifth Grades.* Chestnut Hill, MA: TIMSS & PIRLS International Study Center, Boston College.

Michaelowa, K. 2002. "Teacher Job Satisfaction, Student Achievement, and the Cost of Primary Education in Francophone Sub-Saharan Africa." HWWA (*Hamburgisches Welt-Wirtschafts-Archiv*) Discussion Paper 26273, Hamburg Institute of International Economics, Hamburg.

———. 2003. "Determinants of Primary Education Quality: What Can We Learn from PASEC for Francophone Sub-Saharan Africa?" Background paper for the ADEA (Association for the Development of Education in Africa) Biennial Meeting, Grand Baie, Mauritius, December 3–6.

Michaelowa, K., and A. Wechtler. 2006. "The Cost-Effectiveness of Inputs in Primary Education: Insights from the Literature and Recent Student Surveys for Sub-Saharan Africa." Paper presented at the ADEA (Association for the Development of Education in Africa) Biennial Meeting, Libreville, Gabon, March 27–31.

Millot, B., and J. Lane. 2002. "The Efficient Use of Time in Education." *Education Economics* 10 (2): 209–28.

Mingat, A. 2004. "La question de la rémunération des enseignants dans les pays africains." AFTHD (Africa Technical Families, Human Development) Working Paper, World Bank, Washington, DC.

———. 2006. "Early Childhood Care and Education in Sub-Saharan Africa: Towards Expansion of Coverage and Targeting of Efficient Services." Paper presented at the ADEA (Association for the Development of Education in Africa) Biennial Meeting, Libreville, Gabon, March 27–31.

Mingat, A., and B. Suchaut. 2000. *Les systèmes éducatifs africains: Une analyse économique comparative.* Brussels: De Boeck University.

Mourshed, M., C. Chijioke, and M. Barber. 2009. "How the World's Most Improved School Systems Keep Getting Better." Research report, Social Sector Office, McKinsey & Company, New York.

Mulatu, M., and M. Ndiaye. 2008. "How Smart are the Students of Senegal?" *Echos de la Banque Mondiale* 10 (April): 8–9.

Mulkeen, A. 2007. "Deployment, Utilization and Management of Teachers: The Case of Rural Schools in Africa." PowerPoint presentation, World Bank, Washington, DC.

Mulkeen, A., and D. Chen, eds. 2008. *Teachers for Rural Schools: Experiences in Lesotho, Malawi, Mozambique, Tanzania, and Uganda.* Washington, DC: World Bank.

Mullis, I., M. Martin, E. Gonzalez, and S. Chrostowski. 2008. *TIMSS 2007 International Mathematics Report: Findings from IEA's Trends in International Mathematics and Science Study at the Fourth and Eighth Grades.* Chestnut Hill, MA: TIMSS & PIRLS International Study Center, Boston College.

Muralidharan, K., and V. Sundararaman. 2006. "Teacher Incentives in Developing Countries: Experimental Evidence from India." Job Market Paper, World Bank, Washington, DC.

Muzima, J. 2006. "Lessons of the Experience with Direct Support to Schools Mechanism in Mozambique." Paper presented at the ADEA (Association for the Development of Education in Africa) Biennial Meeting, Libreville, Gabon, March 27–31.

Nickell, S. 2004. "Poverty and Worklessness in Britain." *Economic Journal* 114 (494): C1–25.

OECD (Organisation for Economic Co-operation and Development). 2004. *Learning for Tomorrow's World: First Results from PISA 2003*. Paris: OECD.

Patrinos, H., T. Fasih, and F. Barrera. 2007. *School-Based Management: Concepts and Evidence*. Washington, DC: World Bank.

Pôle de Dakar UNESCO-BREDA (United Nations Educational, Scientific and Cultural Organization, Regional Office for Education in Africa). 2005. "Education for All in Africa: EFA–Paving the Way for Action." Dakar+5 Report, Pôle de Dakar UNESCO-BREDA, Dakar.

Psacharopoulos, G., and H. Patrinos. 2002. "Returns to Investment in Education: A Further Update." Policy Research Working Paper 2881, World Bank, Washington, DC.

Reinikka, R., and J. Svensson. 2003. "The Power of Information: Evidence from a Newspaper Campaign to Reduce Capture." Policy Research Working Paper 3239, World Bank, Washington, DC.

———. 2004. "Local Capture: Evidence from a Central Government Transfer Program in Uganda." *Quarterly Journal of Economics* 119 (2): 678–704.

Schady, N. 2006. "Early Childhood Development in Latin America and the Caribbean." Policy Research Working Paper 3869, World Bank, Washington, DC.

Sey, H. 2001. "Quality Education for All in Senegal: Including the Excluded." Background paper, Quality Education for All Project, World Bank, Washington, DC.

Sigsworth, A., and K. J. Solstad. 2001. *Making Small Schools Work: A Handbook for Teachers in Small Rural Schools*. Addis Ababa: UNESCO (United Nations Educational, Scientific and Cultural Organization) International Institute for Capacity Building in Africa.

Theunynck, S. 2009. *School Construction Strategies for Universal Primary Education in Africa: Should Communities Be Empowered to Build Their Schools?* Africa Human Development Series. Washington, DC: World Bank.

UIS (United Nations Educational, Scientific and Cultural Organization, Institute for Statistics) Data Centre (database). UIS, Montreal. http://stats.uis.unesco.org.

Vegas, E., ed. 2005. *Incentives to Improve Teaching: Lessons from Latin America*. Directions in Development Series. Washington, DC: World Bank.

Verspoor, A. 2003. "The Challenge of Learning: Improving the Quality of Basic Education in Sub-Saharan Africa." Discussion paper for the ADEA (Association for the Development of Education in Africa) Biennial Meeting, Grand Baie, Mauritius, December 3–6.

Wößmann, L. 2002. *Schooling and the Quality of Human Capital*. Berlin: Springer.

World Bank. 2000. "Coûts, financement et fonctionnement du système éducatif du Burkina Faso: Contraintes et espaces pour la politique éducative." Country Status Report, World Bank, Washington, DC.

———. 2001. "Le système éducatif Mauretanien: Eléments d'analyse pour instruire des politiques nouvelles." Africa Region Human Development Working Paper 15, World Bank, Washington, DC.

———. 2003. "Cost and Financing of Education: Opportunities and Obstacles for Expanding and Improving Education in Mozambique." Africa Region Human Development Working Paper 37, World Bank, Washington, DC.

———. 2004a. "Cost, Financing and School Effectiveness of Education in Malawi: A Future of Limited Choices and Endless Opportunities." Africa Region Human Development Working Paper 78, World Bank, Washington, DC.

———. 2004b. "La dynamique des scolarisations au Niger: Evaluation pour une développement durable." Africa Region Human Development Working Paper 40, World Bank, Washington, DC.

———. 2004c. *World Development Report 2004: Making Services Work for Poor People*. Washington, DC: World Bank.

———. 2005. "Le système éducatif guinéen: Diagnostic et perspectives pour la politique éducative dans le contexte de contraintes macro-économiques fortes et de réduction de la pauvreté." Africa Region Human Development Working Paper 90, World Bank, Washington, DC.

———. 2006. *From Schooling Access to Learning Outcomes: An Unfinished Agenda; An Evaluation of World Bank Support to Primary Education*. Washington, DC: World Bank Independent Evaluation Group.

———. 2007. *Le système éducatif burundais: Diagnostic et perspectives pour une nouvelle politique éducative dans le contexte de l'éducation primaire gratuite pour tous*. Africa Human Development Series. World Bank Working Paper 109, World Bank, Washington, DC.

———. 2008. "De nouveaux modes de gestion pour accroitre les performances de l'enseignement primaire malgache." Impact evaluation of AGEMAD (Amélioration de la Gestión de l'Education à Madagascar) initiative, World Bank, Washington, DC.

———. 2009. *Le système éducatif béninois: Analyse sectorielle pour une politique éducative plus equilibrée et plus efficace*. Africa Human Development Series. Working Paper 165, World Bank, Washington, DC.

———. 2010. "Improving the Management of Primary Education in Madagascar: Results from a Randomized Impact Evaluation." Africa Human Development Working Paper, World Bank, Washington, DC.

CHAPTER 6

Social Outcomes

This chapter examines the relationship between educational attainment and various social outcomes based on recent household surveys for up to 36 countries in Sub-Saharan Africa.[1] The analysis focuses on outcomes related to child and maternal health, fertility, poverty, and knowledge of the Human Immunodeficiency Virus and Acquired Immune Deficiency Syndrome (HIV/AIDS)—all crucially important topics in the region and many of them a part of the United Nations (UN) Millennium Development Goals (MDGs).

The analysis shows that all the social indicators employed in this chapter are positively (or negatively, in the case of HIV/AIDS) associated with additional years of education. For example, women with higher educational attainment are more likely to receive prenatal care during pregnancy, and their children are more likely to receive childhood immunizations and survive beyond their fifth birthday. Although not a proof of causality, these results do suggest that education provides a good basis for improving family health and welfare.

Another interesting finding is that primary and secondary school years appear to be associated with more or less the same improvement in social outcomes. Because each year spent in primary school costs less than each year in secondary school, it follows that primary education is a more cost-effective means of achieving the desired social outcomes.

Relationship between Education and Social Outcomes in Sub-Saharan African Countries

This chapter examines the relationship between education and 17 different social outcomes that are related primarily to poverty, childbearing, and maternal and child health—a relationship that is widely documented in the literature. These social outcomes were chosen because the available empirical evidence points to a strong correlation between family health, fertility, and child welfare, on the one hand, and educational attainment, on the other. Haveman and Wolfe (1984), for instance, identify as many as 19 nonmarket benefits of education, including many that are related to better health and the ability to attain desired family size. Glewwe (1999) and Schultz (2002) find a positive link between mothers' education and children's health and education. Further, improving these social outcomes is therefore vitally important for the region—which explains, in part, the importance of gathering data on social outcomes in household surveys in Sub-Saharan African countries.

Relationship between Education and Poverty

For each social outcome, a two-step technique is used to determine its association with educational attainment. The technique is explained below for the first dimension of social outcome examined here: the risk of belonging to the poorest 40 percent of the population.

To examine the impact of educational attainment on the risk (probability) of being poor, as opposed to being nonpoor, a logit model is used. Regressions were estimated for each of the Sub-Saharan African countries in the sample.[2] The control variables included in the logit regression are age, gender, and urban/rural location.[3] Table 6.1 shows the results for only one country, Benin.

The results of the regression can also be shown graphically. The logit regression equation of table 6.1 can be used to simulate or predict the relationship between educational attainment and the risk of poverty by holding the control variables constant at the sample average. Figure 6.1 shows the relationship for Benin as well as the average relationship across all the Sub-Saharan African countries for which this analysis was done. On the horizontal axis, the educational attainment variable ranges from 0 to 12, where 0 means no education, 6 corresponds to the last grade of primary education in most countries, and 12 corresponds to attainment of the last grade of upper secondary education.

Education Is Strongly Related to Household Wealth

Figure 6.1 shows, not surprisingly, that the higher the head of household's educational attainment, the lower the risk of being poor. On the average, and for the Sub-Saharan African region as a whole, the risk of being poor declines from

Table 6.1 Logit Regression Results: Relation between Risk of Poverty and Educational Attainment in Benin, 2001

Dependent variable	Probability of belonging to poorest 40% of population
Constant	0.043
Explanatory variables (head of household)	
Educational attainment (years)	−0.233*
Age (years)	−0.0031
Female (dummy)	0.858*
Urban (dummy)	−1.333*
R^2	0.19

Source: Authors' calculation based on the DHS/MICS/CWIQ database assembled for this chapter. For a full list of the household surveys used, see appendix J, table J.1.
Significance level: * = 1 percent

Figure 6.1 Relationship between Educational Attainment and the Risk of Poverty, Benin 2001, and Sub-Saharan African Average

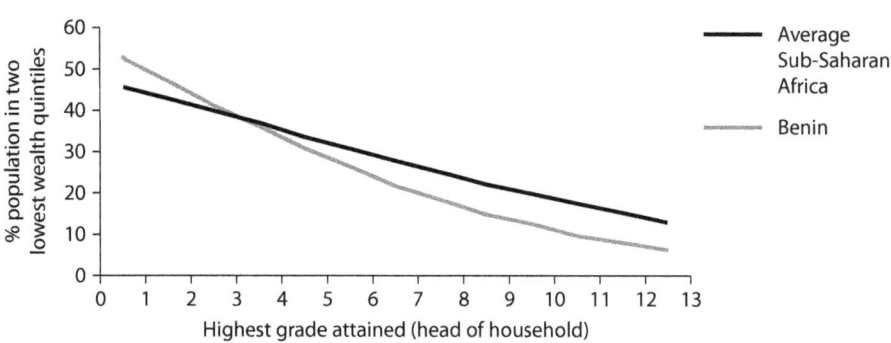

Source: Authors' calculation based on DHS/MICS/CWIQ household survey data; see appendix J, table J.1.
Note: The graph is a simulation based on logit regressions that control for age, gender, and urban/rural location.

46 percent among those with no formal education to 28 percent upon completion of 6 years of education, and to 13 percent upon completion of 12 years of education. As seen, the drop in the risk of poverty is even steeper for Benin than for the region as a whole.

Each Added Year of Schooling Correlates with Same Reduction in Poverty Risk

Although it is not surprising that there is a negative relationship between education and the risk of poverty, it is worth noting that the relationship has an almost constant gradient. In other words, each additional year of education, whether a primary or secondary year, is associated with more or less the same percentage reduction in the risk of living in poverty in adulthood.

Relationship between Education and Childbearing

Education is associated with later childbearing and longer intervals between childbirths. Many studies find that education of girls tends to delay childbearing and reduce lifetime fertility (for example, Ferré 2009; Khan et al. 2006). Education can, therefore, contribute to dampening population growth in countries with high fertility rates.

Using the same technique as described in the analysis of poverty risk above, figure 6.2 shows the relationship between the educational attainment of women and the following outcomes (on average for Sub-Saharan Africa):

- *Age at first birth.* Women who completed primary education are only a little older (18.5 years) at first birth than women with no education (18.3 years). Secondary education appears to have a greater impact in delaying age at first birth. In particular, the average age at first birth rises to 19.4 years for women who have completed lower secondary education and 20.1 years for women who completed upper secondary education. Overall, 12 years of education postpones the age at first birth by more than a year and a half.

Figure 6.2 Relationship between Women's Educational Attainment and Childbearing, Sub-Saharan African Average

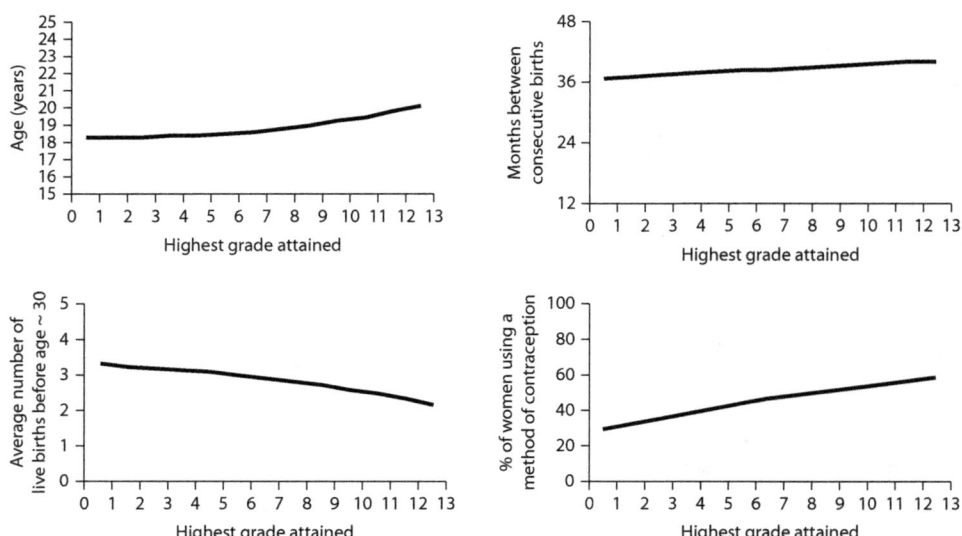

Source: Authors' calculation based on DHS/MICS/CWIQ household survey data; see appendix J, table J.1.
Note: Each graph is a simulation based on a regression that controls for age and urban/rural location.

- *Spacing interval between two latest births.* Women with more education tend to space out their pregnancies a little more than women with less education, but the difference is relatively modest. In particular, spacing between births increases from an average of 37 months for women with no education to 40 months for women with 12 years of education. The impact of an additional school year on birth spacing is about the same, whether it is a primary or secondary school year.
- *Number of live births by age 30.* As expected, the higher the educational attainment, the lower the average number of children by the age of 30 (the average age of women in the sample). The average number of live children declines from 3.3 among women with no schooling to 2.9 children among women with 6 years of schooling, and to 2.2 children among women with 12 years of schooling. The marginal impact of each additional year of education is slightly increasing. Secondary education therefore contributes a little more than half of the drop in the number of live births.
- *Use of contraceptive methods.* Contraception gives women a means to postpone childbearing and control spacing between births. Women's contraceptive use increases substantially with their level of education, rising from 28 percent for women with no formal education to 55 percent for women with upper secondary education—a difference of 27 percentage points. Primary education accounts for more than half of the impact, indicating a pattern of diminishing returns to schooling in contraceptive use.

Relationship between Education and Prenatal Health Care

Education is associated with a greater likelihood of receiving prenatal health services. Figure 6.3 shows the relationship between educational attainment and the likelihood that pregnant women will receive prenatal care and skilled assistance during delivery. Both types of care are known to reduce the risks of childbirth for mother and child and can therefore potentially contribute to a reduction in maternal and infant mortality, two of the MDG goals.[4]

As panel A of figure 6.3 shows, the more educated the woman, the more likely she is to seek and receive prenatal care during pregnancy. Women with no formal education have, on the average, only 3.2 consultations with a health care professional during their last pregnancy, compared with 5.3 consultations for women with 12 years of education.

Panel B of figure 6.3 shows that the average number of tetanus vaccines received is 1.1 among women with no education, rising to 1.6 among women with 12 years of education.[5] Likewise, as shown in panel C, women with more education are more likely to receive vitamin A supplementation during pregnancy. Only 12 percent of women without education receive vitamin A supplements, compared with 19 percent of women with upper secondary education.

Figure 6.3 Relationship between Women's Educational Attainment and Prenatal Health Care, Sub-Saharan African Average

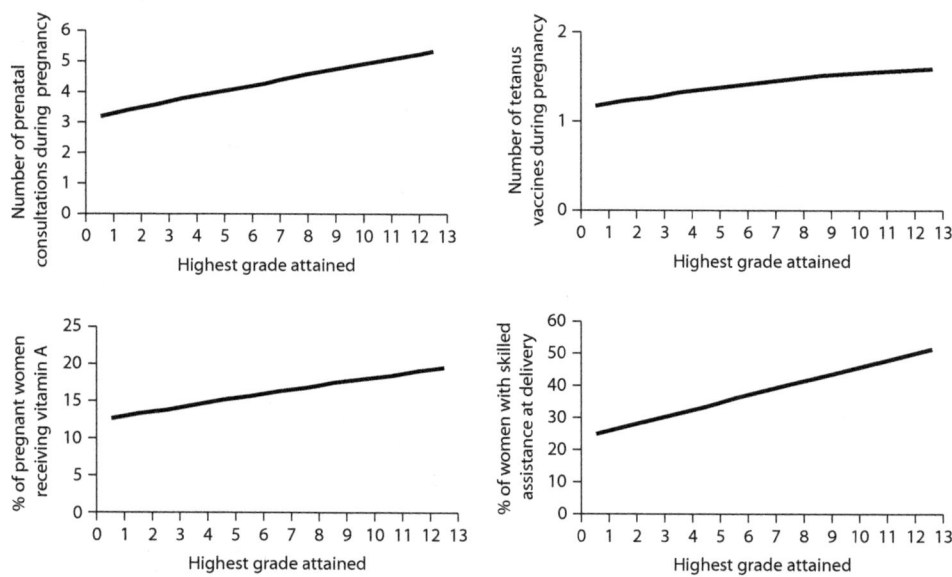

Source: Authors' calculation based on DHS/MICS/CWIQ household survey data; see appendix J, table J.1.
Note: Each graph is a simulation based on a regression that controls for age and urban/rural location.

Finally, the likelihood of receiving assistance by skilled professionals during delivery increases greatly with educational attainment, as shown in panel D of figure 6.3. Among women with no formal education, only one in four receives the service, compared with one in two among women with 12 years of education. Primary and secondary education each increases the likelihood of receiving professional assistance at delivery by about the same amount.

Relationship between Education and Child Health and Development

Mothers' education may influence child health through different pathways. Glewwe (1999) describes three possible mechanisms through which mothers' education may exert a positive influence on child health and development:

- Formal education directly imparts health knowledge to future mothers
- Literacy and numeracy skills acquired in school empower future mothers to diagnose and treat child health problems
- Increased familiarity with modern society through schooling makes women more receptive to modern medical care and treatment.

Figure 6.4 shows the relationship between mothers' education and four proxies of child health and development in Sub-Saharan Africa as a whole.

Figure 6.4 Relationship between Mothers' Educational Attainment and Child Health and Development, Sub-Saharan African Average

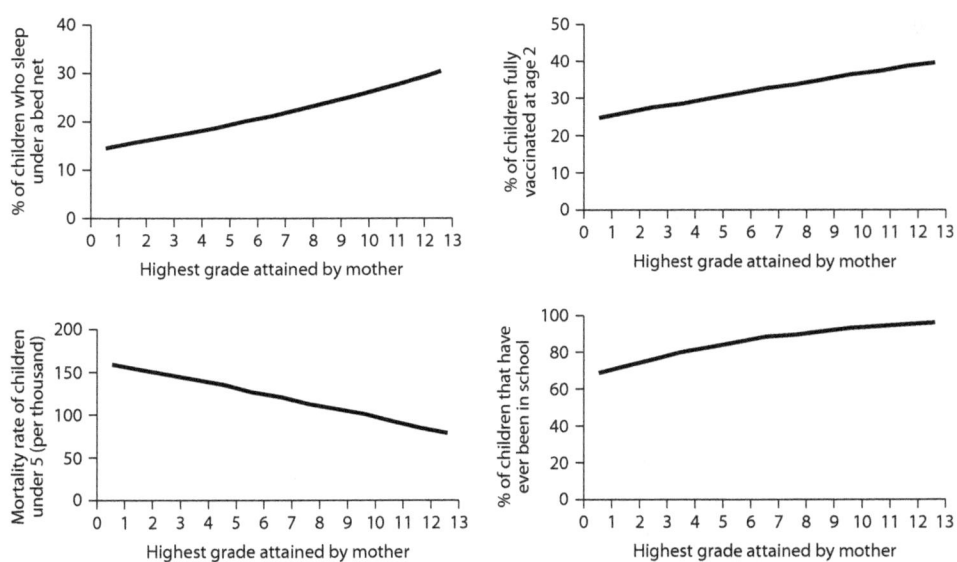

Source: Authors' calculation based on DHS/MICS/CWIQ household survey data; see appendix J, table J.1.
Note: Each graph is a simulation based on a regression that controls for mother's age, child's gender, and urban/rural location.

Mothers clearly perform much more for their children then these four proxies are able to cover. Nevertheless, the proxies indicate that a mother's level of education is positively correlated with the overall health and development of her children. On the whole, these four proxies show that educating girls has a wide-ranging impact on children's overall health and development:

- *Children's use of bed nets.* Most children in Sub-Saharan African countries still sleep without a bed net. Nevertheless, while only 14 percent of children of mothers with no education sleep under a bed net for protection against malaria and other insect borne diseases, the percentage is more than double (30 percent) among children whose mothers have 12 or more years of education.
- *Childhood immunization.* As with the use of bed nets, most children in the Sub-Saharan African region do not receive the full regimen of childhood vaccination (defined as including four polio, three DTP [diphtheria, tetanus, pertussis], one BCG [Bacillus of Calmette and Guérin, for prevention of tuberculosis], and one measles vaccine) by age two. Nevertheless, the chances that a child will receive the most important childhood vaccines in infancy increase with the level of education of the mother. Across the region, the likelihood increases from 25 percent if the mother has had no formal education to about 40 percent when the mother has had 12 years of education—a difference of 15 percentage points.
- *Child mortality.* The fourth MDG calls for a two-thirds reduction in the under-five mortality rate between 1990 and 2015. Current under-five mortality rates in most Sub-Saharan African countries are among the highest in the world. The average of 134 per 1,000 live births (in the current sample) for the Sub-Saharan African region pales even in comparison to other low-income countries. Mothers' education does, however, play an important role in reducing child mortality. The under-five mortality rate declines from 160 (per 1,000 children) among women with no education to 120 among those with 6 years of education, and 77 among those with 12 years of education. In other words, the under-five mortality rate may be reduced by over 50 percent when girls receive 12 years of schooling as opposed to no formal schooling.
- *Child development.* A mother's educational attainment is also positively correlated with her children's education. When mothers themselves have not attended school, only 68 percent of their children are or have been enrolled in primary school by the time they are 9–11 years old. The proportion climbs to 88 percent when the mother has had 6 years of education and 96 percent when the mother has had 12 or more years of education. Primary education alone contributes to more than 70 percent of the difference between mothers who have had no formal education and those who have had at least 12 years of education. Providing all girls with at least a primary education today will contribute to raising the demand for education among future generations of children.

Relation between Education and Knowledge of and Exposure to Social Issues

The higher the educational attainment, the more knowledge a person has about HIV/AIDS. The World Bank (2002) argues that a good basic education ranks among the most cost-effective means of HIV prevention, particularly among girls. Figure 6.5 shows that adults' educational attainment is positively correlated with their awareness of HIV/AIDS, as measured by a composite index of HIV/AIDS knowledge.

On a scale from 0 to 14, the HIV/AIDS knowledge index increases from about 5 for individuals with no education to 7.5 for individuals with 12 years or more of education. However, even those with 12 years of education score far less than the maximum on the HIV/AIDS knowledge index, suggesting that the general level of HIV/AIDS awareness is fairly low in the region. Primary education contributes more than half of the total impact of education on HIV/AIDS awareness.

The use of all information media also increases with educational attainment. The household surveys provide information on respondents' use of radio, television, and newspapers, as illustrated in figure 6.6.

These variables may be used as a proxy of the extent to which individuals are exposed to current information that may benefit their families or communities. Media, for example, can contribute to the spread of information concerning health threats, public programs, and the availability or lack of social services. Media use is strongly linked to informed political participation which, in turn, is crucial to social and economic development.

As expected, the most commonly used media in the Sub-Saharan African region is the radio because it is readily available everywhere at a relatively low cost. Newspapers and television—primarily because of their higher costs and limited availability, particularly in remote areas—are generally uncommon sources of information among individuals with no education or only primary

Figure 6.5 Relationship between Educational Attainment and Awareness of HIV/AIDS, Sub-Saharan African Average

Source: Authors' calculation based on DHS/MICS/CWIQ data; see appendix J, table J.1.
Note: The graph is a simulation based on a regression model that controls for age, gender, and urban/rural location. HIV/AIDS = human immunodeficiency virus and acquired immunodeficiency disease syndrome.

Figure 6.6 Relationship between Educational Attainment and Exposure to Information Media, Sub-Saharan African Average

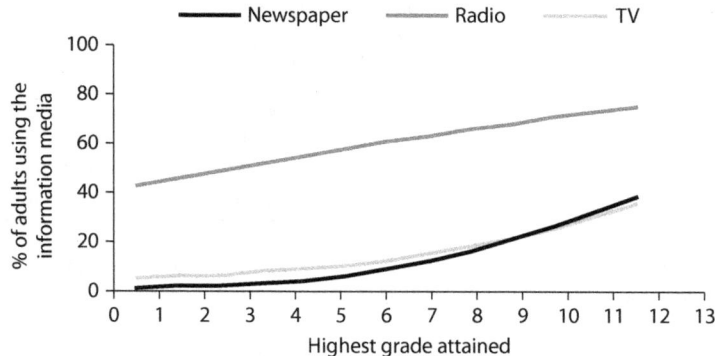

Source: Authors' calculation based on DHS/MICS/CWIQ data; see appendix J, table J.1.
Note: The graph is a simulation based on a regression model that controls for age, gender, and urban/rural location.

education. Even among those with 12 years of education, only 38 percent read newspapers and 36 percent watch television.

Relationship between Education and Social Outcomes by Level of Education

Information about the magnitude of education's impact on social outcomes, such as those discussed above, is crucial to policy makers. It adds perspective on the contribution that different levels of education can make to desired social outcomes. Such information can be a valuable guide to policy formation and spending decisions regarding the allocation of limited resources to different levels and types of education. Table 6.2 summarizes the magnitude of social outcomes by level of education across Sub-Saharan African countries.

Primary and Secondary Education Have Nearly the Same Impact on Social Outcomes

The first two columns in table 6.2 show the change in each social indicator associated with moving from no education to 12 years of education. The last three columns show the percentage share of the total change that primary, lower secondary, and upper secondary education contribute, respectively, in each social indicator.

On the average, across all the 17 social dimensions, primary education accounts for 48 percent of the total change associated with 12 years of education, and secondary education accounts for the remaining 52 percent. There are exceptions: First, primary education accounts for only about a third of the impact on the number of live births. Second, and in contrast, primary education has a particularly strong impact on the use of contraception (60 percent), knowledge about HIV/AIDS (64 percent), and children's enrollment in school (71 percent).

Table 6.2 Social Outcomes by Level of Education, Sub-Saharan African Average

	Simulation of social outcome as a function of highest grade attained		Share contributed to total change in social outcome by education of 0–12 years, by level (percentage)		
	No formal education (0 years)	Upper secondary completed (12 years)	Primary (6 years)	Lower secondary (4 years)	Upper secondary (2 years)
Childbearing					
Age at first birth (years)	18.3	20.1	15.8	47.0	37.2
Months between consecutive births	36.9	40.2	51.2	34.0	14.8
Number of live births by approx. age 30	3.3	2.2	34.3	39.7	26.1
Use of any contraceptive method (%)	27.9	55.2	60.2	29.3	10.6
Prenatal health					
Prenatal consultations (no.)	3.2	5.3	51.9	32.5	15.6
Tetanus vaccines during pregnancy (no.)	1.2	1.6	65.4	24.2	10.4
Vitamin A taken in pregnancy (%)	12.5	19.4	53.4	31.0	15.6
Delivery assisted by skilled personnel (%)	24.9	50.9	50.4	34.2	15.2
Child health and development					
Children sleep under a bed net (%)	14.4	30.2	43.0	34.8	22.2
Children fully vaccinated by age 2 (%)	24.7	39.7	50.6	33.3	16.1
Under-5 mortality rate (per thousand)	159.5	77.2	48.3	33.1	18.6
Children enrolled in school (%)	68.0	95.5	71.4	22.0	6.6
Poverty, HIV/AIDS, and use of media					
Risk of poverty (%)	45.6	13.3	55.1	32.4	12.5
Knowledge about HIV/AIDS (index)	4.9	7.5	63.5	27.1	9.4
Use of radio (%)	43.3	76.0	53.5	32.4	14.1
Use of television (%)	4.9	35.6	23.8	43.6	32.6
Use of newspapers (%)	0.7	38.3	19.3	47.1	33.5
Average of all dimensions			47.7	34.0	18.3

Source: Authors' construction. Results shown are from model "without wealth." For data from model "with wealth" and for country tables, see appendix H.
Note: For childbearing and prenatal health, "highest grade attained" refers to the grade attained by the woman herself. For child health and development, it refers to the grade attained by the child's mother, and for poverty, it refers to the educational attainment of the head of household.

Primary Education Provides Maximum Social Outcomes per Education Dollar

Table 6.3 shows what a year of primary, lower secondary, and upper secondary schooling, respectively, contributes to total social outcome (defined as the average across all the social outcomes, as discussed above).

As seen in row A of the table, each year of primary education contributes 8 percent to the total social outcome, compared with a slightly higher 8.5 percent for each lower secondary year, and 9.2 percent for each upper secondary year. The "benefit-to-cost ratio," defined as the ratio of the contribution to total social outcome of each year of schooling (row A) to the per-student cost per year of schooling (row B) is 69 for primary education. Given the much higher costs of secondary education, it is not surprising to find that the benefit-to-cost

Table 6.3 Contribution to Social Outcomes by Year of Education, Sub-Saharan African Average

	Primary education (6 years)	Lower secondary education (4 years)	Upper secondary education (2 years)
Share that education (0–12 years) contributed to total change in social outcome, by education level (average % across all social dimensions)	47.7	34.0	18.3
A: Contribution to total social outcome per year of schooling (%)	8.0	8.5	9.2
B: Per-student cost per year of schooling (multiples of GDP per capita)	11.5	24.4	57.1
A/B: Benefit-to-cost ratio	69	35	16

Source: Authors' construction from table 6.2 data and unit cost data from appendix E, table E.2.
Note: GDP = gross domestic product.

ratio drops to 35 for lower secondary education and to 16 for upper secondary education.[6]

This analysis implies that, to achieve the highest social impact per education dollar spent, it is much more cost-effective to invest in primary education than in secondary education. Further, as discussed above, the fact that many of the desired social outcomes are related to women's and mothers' education suggests that investing in girls' education yields particularly high returns.[7]

Cross-Country Variations in the Relationship between Education and Social Outcomes

The previous sections looked at the relationship between education and social outcomes across the Sub-Saharan African region as a whole. Here we examine the extent of cross-country variations in the relationship. For illustrative purposes, figure 6.7 shows the extent of the variations by comparing the results from four selected Sub-Saharan African countries on the basis of two of the social outcomes discussed above.[8]

Educational Attainment Associated with Fertility Drop

Panel A in figure 6.7 shows the relationship between women's educational attainment and the number of live births before age 30 in four countries. In the four selected countries—and in all the other Sub-Saharan African countries for which the analysis was performed—women with more education tend to have fewer children.

In Lesotho, the decline in fertility is quite small, probably because fertility in Lesotho is already relatively low among all groups of women. The drop in fertility as a function of educational attainment is steepest in Guinea-Bissau, as indicated by the slope of the curve, while it is more modest in Uganda.

Figure 6.7 Cross-Country Variation in the Relationship between Education, Live Births, and Child Vaccination in Selected Sub-Saharan African countries

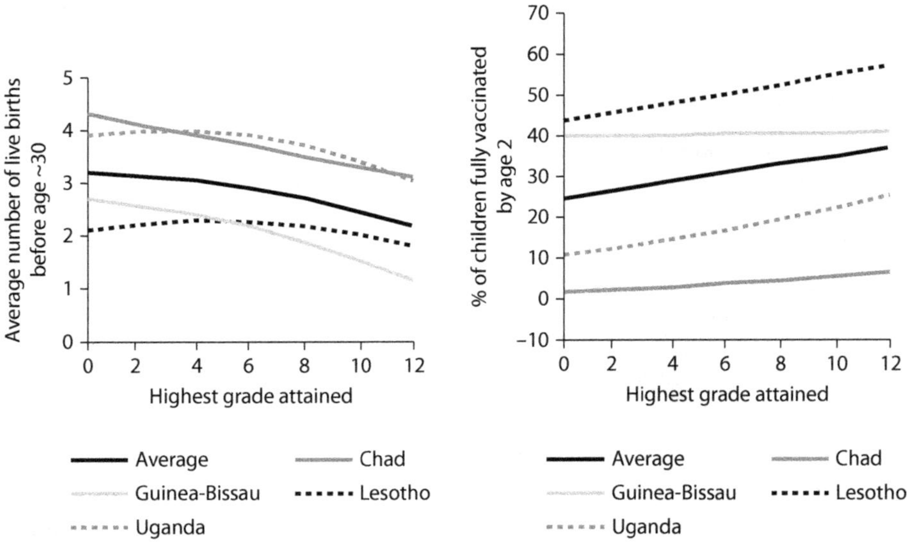

Source: Authors' construction from data in appendix H, tables H.9 and H.16.

Educational Attainment Raises Demand for Child Vaccination in Some, but Not All, Sub-Saharan African Countries

Panel B in figure 6.7 shows the relationship between mothers' educational attainment and child vaccination rates. The chart shows the following pertinent features: First, countries differ greatly in the proportion of children who received childhood vaccines by the age of two—from less than 5 percent of children in Chad to about 50 percent in Lesotho.

Second, there are large differences between countries in the relationship between mothers' education and child vaccination rates. As reflected by the slopes of the curves in Lesotho and Uganda, for example, there is a 13–15 percentage point difference between mothers with no schooling and those with 12 years of schooling. In contrast, there is virtually no difference between these two groups in Guinea-Bissau. Although not shown here, in a few countries, especially Swaziland and Togo, child vaccination rates appear to decline slightly as a function of mothers' educational attainment.

Effectiveness of Education Systems at Generating Social Outcomes

Link with Education Systems' Effectiveness at Generating Student Learning

Is there a link between student learning outcomes (academic performance) of a country's education system and improvements in desired social outcomes per additional year of schooling? In particular, we examine the relationship between learning outcomes, as measured by the Africa Student Learning Index (ASLI)

Social Outcomes

score (discussed in detail in chapter 5) and improvement in social outcomes (measured by the magnitude of the overall change in social outcomes associated with 6 years of primary schooling).

The quality of schools and change in social outcomes appear to be unrelated. Figure 6.8 shows the scatterplot of the ASLI scores for countries in the region against the index capturing the magnitude of the overall change in social outcomes associated with 6 years of primary schooling. These two indicators measure, in a sense, the academic and social "quality" of primary education in the Sub-Saharan African countries.

The scatterplot and the regression line in figure 6.8 show the absence of a statistically significant relationship between the two measures, suggesting that the academic and social dimensions of school quality are probably uncorrelated (R^2 is only 0.006). Overall, this result implies that an education system that performs well in terms of student learning does not necessarily generate large gains in desired social outcomes—possibly meaning simply that the exposure to formal schooling alone is what counts toward generating desired social outcomes.

Link with Countries' Average Level of Social Outcomes

Figure 6.9 shows scatterplots of the improvements in selected social outcomes (women's contraceptive use, skilled assistance in delivery, under-five mortality, and awareness of HIV/AIDS) resulting from 6 years of primary schooling against average levels of the same outcomes across Sub-Saharan African countries.

Education May Raise Demand for Certain Health Services

Panel A in figure 6.9 shows that the difference in contraceptive use between women without formal schooling and women with 6 years of schooling tends to be larger in countries where contraceptive use is generally quite high than in countries where contraceptive use is uncommon.

Figure 6.8 Relationship between Effectiveness at Generating Social Outcomes and ASLI Scores in Sub-Saharan African Countries

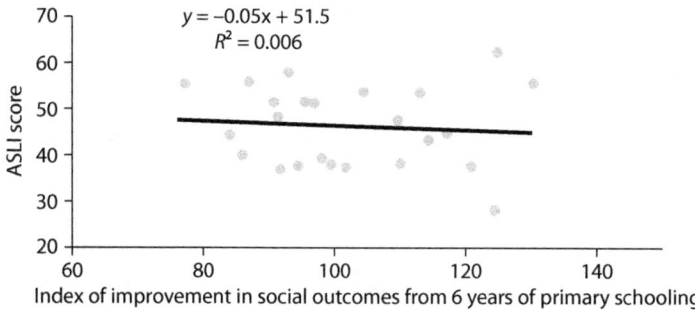

Sources: Authors' construction from index of improvement in social outcomes from six years of primary schooling, as calculated in appendix H, table H.23. The Africa Student Learning Index (ASLI) data are from chapter 5, table 5.1.

Figure 6.9 Relationship between National Average Social Outcome Indicators and Change in Indicators from Six Years of Primary Education, Sub-Saharan African Countries

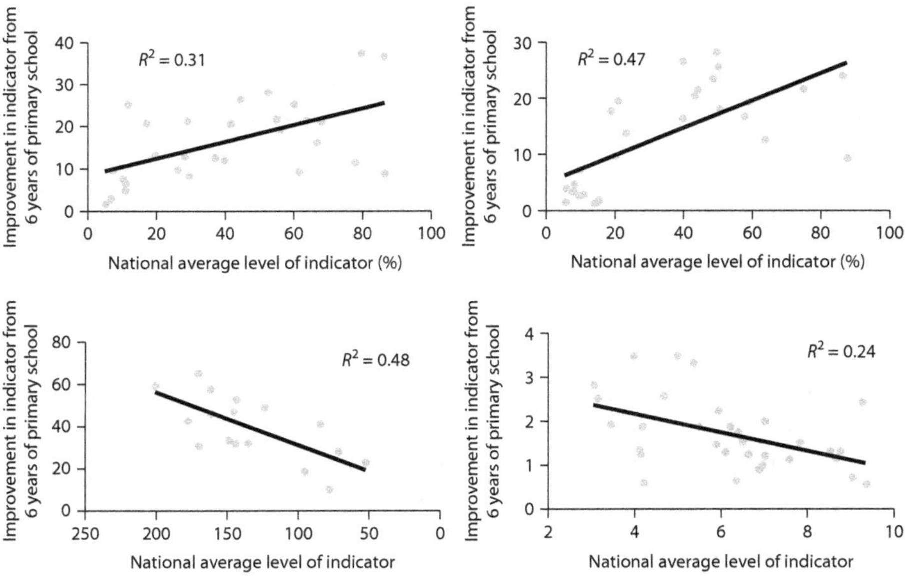

Source: Authors' construction based on data in appendix H.
Note: Values on the horizontal axes are shown in reverse order for under-five mortality because the lower this indicator is, the better. In the three other indicators shown, the higher they are, the better. HIV/AIDS = human immunodeficiency virus/acquired immune deficiency syndrome.

Panel B paints a similar picture for skilled assistance in delivery. These findings suggest that schooling contributes toward greater acceptance of health services such as contraceptive provision and the skilled assistance with delivery. Such findings, in turn, also imply that as countries promote and invest in the expansion of these services as well as in education, they should prepare for the rise in the demand for these services.

Magnitude of Education-Induced Change in Social Outcomes May Change as Countries Progress

Panel C shows a somewhat different pattern of the relationship between education and the change in under-five mortality. In particular, the difference in child mortality rates between mothers with no schooling and mothers with 6 years of schooling tends to be greater in countries with high average child mortality rates than in countries with low child mortality rates. This result suggests that as a country progresses along its development path and successfully addresses child mortality, the difference between mothers with no education and mothers with education may be expected to decline over time.

Panel D shows that the difference in HIV/AIDS awareness between adults with no schooling and adults with 6 years of schooling also tends to diminish as the overall level of awareness grows in a country.

Issues for Policy Development

A full course of schooling for all children, particularly girls, can improve desired health and welfare outcomes for future generations. This chapter shows that education in the Sub-Saharan African region can and does yield substantial positive social outcomes. Educational attainment is associated with better health and welfare in adulthood, especially for girls. Although the monetary benefits of the social outcomes discussed here have not been quantified, it is nevertheless evident that the returns on investment in basic education extend far beyond the traditional measure of higher earnings. This finding further stresses the importance of providing schooling to all children.

Demand for health services may grow as more girls (and boys) graduate. The above discussion indicates that women who completed primary or secondary schooling are more likely than women with no schooling to take advantage of certain health services. As the number of girls completing the full course of schooling in the Sub-Saharan African region grows, the health sector may be pressured to increase the supply of health services—pressure that will, in turn, have implications for planning and financing in the health sector.

More information is needed on the importance of teaching life skills. In terms of the implications for education policy, it is important to increase our understanding of how education systems can be designed and managed to produce the largest possible social benefits in addition to academic learning. Although the link between student learning (the academic performance of countries' education systems) and change in social outcomes appears to be weak, changes in social outcomes may be larger in countries that place more emphasis on teaching life skills. More research is clearly needed on the relationship between curriculum content, particularly regarding the teaching of life skills, and desired social outcomes.

Notes

1. Appendix J, table J.1, provides a list of the household surveys used for this chapter.
2. In this chapter, logit models are used whenever the dependent variable is binary (such as poor/nonpoor). Linear models are used when the dependent variable is continuous (such as months between consecutive births).
3. To allow for nonlinear effects, age squared and highest grade attained are also included whenever they are statistically significant and improve the coefficient of determination (R^2). These three control variables (age, gender, and location) are included in all regressions of this chapter where applicable. Further, a wealth variable was included as a control variable in the logit regressions, except in the regression for risk of poverty, but it was dropped from the final regression runs because it did not result in any significant changes in the estimates and, more importantly,

there was the possibility that it would give rise to various estimation problems. The rest of the discussion in this chapter is based on logit regressions that excluded the wealth variable. Appendix H shows results for both regressions—with and without wealth as a control variable. Also see appendix H for a discussion of this estimation problem.

4. Reductions in maternal and infant mortality are key MDG goals. For a list of all the goals, see appendix K.

5. According to the U.S. Centers for Disease Control and Prevention (CDC), ideally, pregnant women with an uncertain or incomplete history of tetanus vaccinations should receive a series of three vaccinations (two during pregnancy and one postpartum) to protect against maternal and neonatal tetanus. Women who have completed a series of vaccinations in the past may not need new vaccinations or only need a booster dose.

6. Because the benefits have not been expressed in monetary terms, this is not an actual benefit-cost ratio. It does, nevertheless, enable us to compare the cost-effectiveness of the three levels of education.

7. Available research literature focuses on the impact of mothers' education rather than fathers' because it is generally believed that mothers exert greater influence on their children's welfare. Handa (1999) examined the impact of fathers' education on children's height in Jamaica and found that fathers' level of education did not matter (although mothers' education did), but the presence of a father in the family did have a large positive impact on children's height.

8. Detailed data for all countries and all social dimensions are provided in appendix H.

References

Ferré, C. 2009. "Age at First Child: Does Education Delay Fertility Timing? The Case of Kenya." Policy Research Working Paper 4833, World Bank, Washington, DC.

Glewwe, P. 1999. "Why Does Mother's Schooling Raise Child Health in Developing Countries: Evidence from Morocco." *Journal of Human Resources* 34 (1): 124–59.

Handa, S. 1999. "Maternal Education and Child Height." *Economic Development and Cultural Change* 47 (2): 421–39.

Haveman, R., and B. Wolfe. 1984. "Schooling and Economic Well-Being: The Role of Nonmarket Effects." *Journal of Human Resources* 19 (3): 377–407.

Khan, Q., S. E. Zayed, and Y. Stopnitzky. 2006. "Reaping the Benefits of Girls' Secondary Education in Bangladesh: Impact on Fertility and Malnutrition." Presentation, World Bank, Washington, DC.

Schultz, T. P. 2002. "Why Governments Should Invest More to Educate Girls." *World Development* 30 (2): 207–25.

World Bank. 2002. *Education and HIV/AIDS: A Window of Hope.* Washington, DC: World Bank.

CHAPTER 7

Education and Employment

In the previous chapters, we examined the performance of the education systems in Sub-Saharan Africa in light of the Millennium Development Goals (MDGs), particularly in terms of the objectives of universal primary completion and gender parity. The focus was primarily on primary or basic education rather than on postbasic education. The present discussion focuses on the performance of the education system in terms of its ability to meet the demands of the respective national labor markets.

This shift in emphasis naturally leads to a shift in focus towards postbasic education. How well secondary school completers and higher education graduates fare in the labor market, in terms of finding jobs that match their skills, is central to the success of national education policies at the postbasic level.

Here, we look first at the pattern of employment across a sample of 23 Sub-Saharan African countries.[1] This examination is complemented by an assessment of the trends in labor productivity within the main sectors of the 23 Sub-Saharan African economies. Next, the analysis examines the quantitative match between the demand for, and supply of, workers with postbasic education. Not surprisingly, the study finds a close link between the level of economic development and job opportunities for highly skilled workers.

Data collected in labor market or household surveys[2] in the 23 countries across the region constitute the main source of information for this analysis. These surveys were all carried out between 2001 and 2005. Although they did not use identical questionnaires, it is possible to generate a variable describing the respondents' employment status that is comparable across the 23 countries.[3] The surveys also provide information on respondents' educational attainment, allowing for a comprehensive analysis of the relationship between education and employment.

Cross-Country Analysis of the Pattern of Employment

The countries in the sample are at different stages of economic development. Although all are low-income countries,[4] there is a wide range of per capita income across the 23 countries—from a low of US$85 in Burundi to a high of US$946 in the Republic of Congo (2003 data, current US$). The 23 countries are clearly at different stages of economic development, but they are all characterized by economic dualism.

In Sample Countries, Formal and Informal Sectors Coexist

All 23 countries are dualistic economies marked by the coexistence of a modern or formal sector and a traditional, or more backward, informal sector (Fields 2007). The modern or formal sector is characterized by the payment of taxes and the registration of workers under some social security scheme. It consists of a public component, made up of the civil service and public companies, and a private component.

The informal sector, on the other hand, is highly heterogeneous, precluding a clear definition. Nevertheless, in the context of the Sub-Saharan African region, the informal sector can be conveniently subdivided into farm and nonfarm sectors. The former typically consists of subsistence farming. The latter typically consists of household or nonhousehold small manufacturing, handicrafts, repairs, construction, trade, and community and personal services. The informal sector as a whole includes both nonwage employment (such as self-employment and work in family farms or businesses) and wage employment (such as regular and casual work, including subcontract and home-based work) (Blunch, Canagarajah, and Raju 2001).

About 86 Percent of Those Aged 15–59 Are Economically Active

Table 7.1 shows the employment status of 15- to 59-year-olds, excluding individuals who were still in school during the survey period, across the Sub-Saharan African region as a whole. In about 2003, out of every 100 persons in the working-age population, 86 were economically active, and the remaining 14 were not in the labor force for reasons other than schooling. Out of every 86 economically active persons, 79 were gainfully employed, and 7 were unemployed.[5]

Table 7.1 Employment Status Distribution per 100 Working-Age Population, Aggregate for 23 Sub-Saharan African Countries, ca. 2003

Total 15–59 population, not in school 100	Not active 14.0				
	Economically active 86.0	Unemployed 6.9			
		Employed 79.1	Informal sector 71.0	Farming 51.3	
				Nonfarm 19.6	Skilled 4.8
			Formal sector 8.2	Private (modern) 4.3	
				Public 3.9	Unskilled 3.4

Source: Authors' analysis of labor market surveys; see appendix I, table I.2.
Note: Sample population is the 15–59 age group who were not in school at the time of survey.

Education and Employment

Informal Sector Employs More Workers than Formal Sector

Table 7.1 also provides a further breakdown of employment into the formal and informal sectors. Out of every 79 persons who were gainfully employed, 71 worked in the informal sector and the remaining 8 worked in the formal sector. Within the informal sector, farming is by far the largest employer, employing more than twice as many (51 out of every 71 persons) of the gainfully employed as the nonfarm sector employs (20 persons).

Main Employer Is Farming in Most Countries, Informal Nonfarm Sector in Others

Figure 7.1 shows the composition of employment by sector in each of the 23 Sub-Saharan African sample countries. Farming remains the main economic activity in many of the countries, but not in all. In Burundi and Rwanda, farming accounts for as much as 89 percent of employment, compared with only 22 percent in Lesotho. The formal sector is fairly small in all 23 countries.

Farm Employment Tends to Decline with Rising Per Capita GDP

Figure 7.2 shows a robust negative relationship (the coefficient of determination, R^2, is 0.58) between farm employment (as a proportion of total employment) and the level of economic development (proxied by per capita gross domestic product (GDP)) across the 23 Sub-Saharan African countries. The higher the level of per capita GDP, the less important farming is as a source of employment.

Figure 7.1 Employment by Sector in 23 Sub-Saharan African Countries, ca. 2003

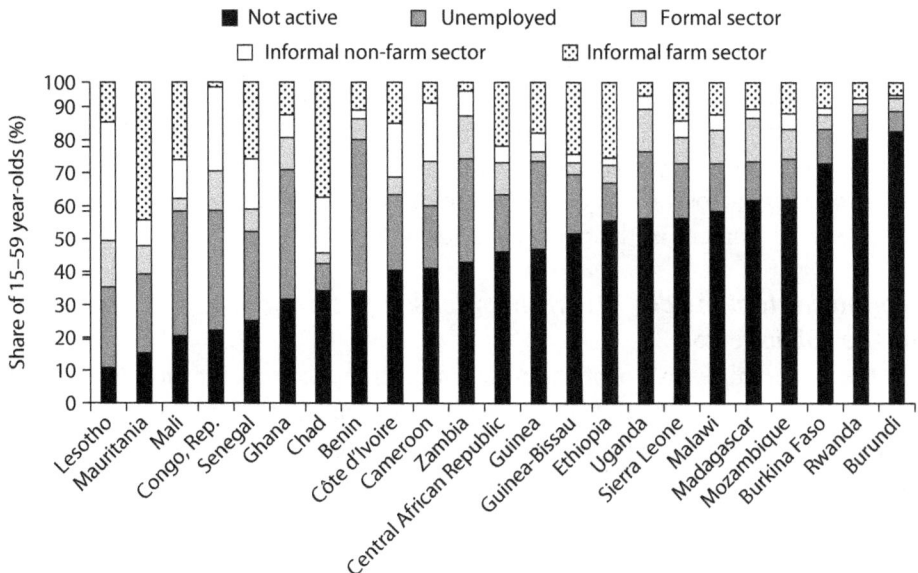

Source: Authors' analysis of labor market surveys. For the data set of employment by sector, see appendix I, table I.2. For a country-specific list of the labor market surveys used, see appendix J, table J.2.
Note: Sample population is the 15–59 age group who were not in school at the time of survey.

Figure 7.2 Farm Employment by Per Capita GDP in 23 Sub-Saharan African Countries, ca. 2003

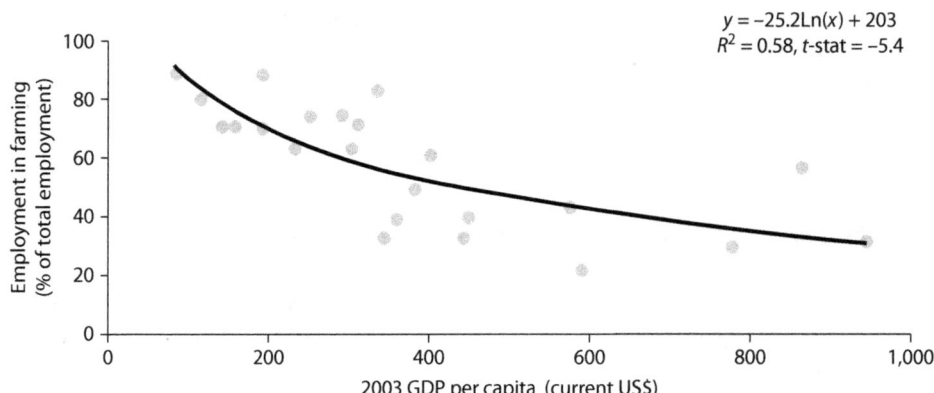

Sources: Authors' construction from analysis of labor market surveys (see appendix J, table J.2) and GDP per capita data from DDP database.
Note: GDP = gross domestic product.

Farm Employment Appears to Decline Over Time

Economic growth aside, in almost all developing countries, rapid population growth accompanied by rapid urbanization from very low levels are contributing to a decline in farm employment relative to total employment as an increasing proportion of the labor force seeks work outside the agricultural sector (UNCTAD 2006). Increasing competition for a fixed amount of farm land also contributes to this trend (UNCTAD 2006). Failed agricultural policies or regional conflict are also common causes of the migration of rural workers to urban areas (UN-HABITAT 2004).

Among Sub-Saharan African countries, in addition to the decline associated with economic growth, farm employment as a share of total employment declines by about half a percentage point every year (Mingat and Ndem 2007). Household survey data lend support, showing a decline in the proportion of farm workers across age cohorts—from about 71 percent in the cohort aged 50–59 to 61 percent in the cohort aged 25–34.

Formal Sector Provides 10 Percent of Jobs, Half of which Are in the Public Sector

In the 23 countries as a whole, the formal sector accounts for only 10 percent of total employment. But the share of formal sector employment varies greatly—from around 4 percent in Burundi, Guinea, and Rwanda; to more than 17 percent in Cameroon, Mauritania, and the Republic of Congo; to a high of 28 percent in Lesotho.

About half of formal sector jobs are in the public sector. The public sector (including public companies) accounts for 4.9 percent of total employment in the 23 countries as a whole, but it makes up almost 50 percent of all formal sector jobs. However, the size of public sector employment varies quite substantially across countries—ranging from 2 percent to 3 percent of total employment in Burkina Faso, Burundi, Guinea, Guinea-Bissau, and Rwanda; to 11 percent in Mauritania; and as much as 24 percent of total employment in Lesotho.

Formal and Public Sector Employment Increase with Rising Per Capita GDP, but Cross-Country Variability Is Large

Panel A in Figure 7.3 plots *formal* sector employment as a proportion of total employment against per capita GDP. Panel B plots *public* sector employment as a proportion of total employment against per capita GDP in the 23 Sub-Saharan African countries.

The two charts show positive relationships between the level of economic development (proxied by per capita GDP) and the incidence of formal and public

Figure 7.3 Formal and Public Sector Employment by Per Capita GDP in 23 Sub-Saharan African Countries, ca. 2003

a. Formal Sector

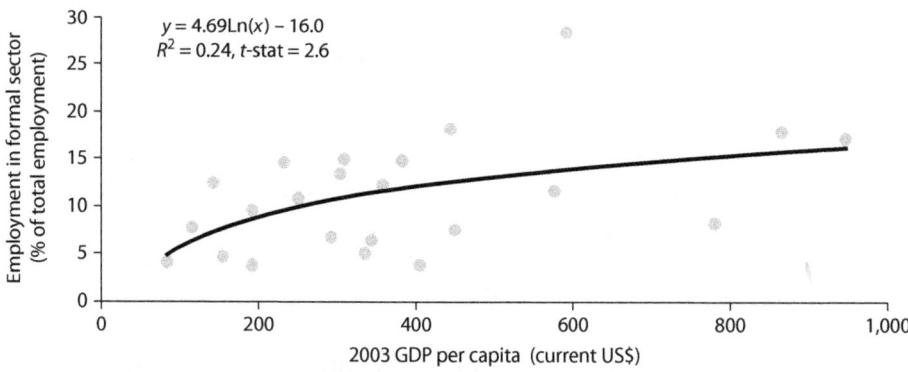

b. Public Sector

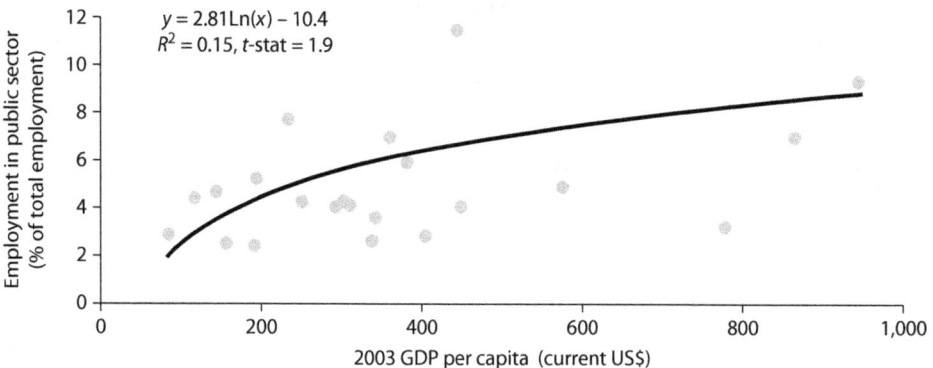

Sources: Authors' construction from analysis of labor market surveys (see appendix J, table J.2) and GDP per capita data from DDP database.
Note: In panel B, Lesotho is off the chart, with its public sector employment of 24 percent, but it is included in the regression. GDP = gross domestic product.

sector employment. Although statistically significant, the relationships are relatively weak, however, because both relationships are characterized by fairly low R^2 and t-statistics.

In particular, per capita GDP explains only 24 percent and 16 percent, respectively, of the variance in the incidence of formal and public sector employment. Both charts also indicate that the shares of formal and public sector employment in total employment are fairly low among the 23 Sub-Saharan African countries, even in countries with relatively high levels of per capita GDP.

Private Sector Employment in the Formal Sector Increases with Rising per capita GDP, but Relationship Is Weak

The private sector (hereafter referred to as the "modern" private sector to distinguish it from the informal private sector) accounts for slightly more than half of formal sector jobs. Modern private sector employment, as a proportion of total employment, is also positively correlated with per capita GDP. However, like formal and public sector employment, the R^2 of the regression is very low (0.15), indicating that factors other than economic growth (as proxied by per capita GDP) influence the modern private sector's share of total employment.

Informal Nonfarm Sector, Employer of Last Resort, Is Region's Fastest Growing Sector

With the share of farm employment declining as the economies develop, but with growth in formal sector employment growing at a relatively modest pace, the unregulated informal nonfarm sector has become an increasingly important source of employment across the Sub-Saharan African region. The sector is now the employer of last resort not only for urban migrants but also for large segments of the rural population (Haggblade, Hazell, and Reardon 2007).

Employment Patterns Evolve Largely through Intergenerational Mobility

Table 7.2 shows how the pattern of employment is likely to change in the farming, formal, and informal nonfarm sectors as per capita GDP increases over time.

Farm employment may increase in absolute terms, but because employment in the formal and informal nonfarm sectors are expected to rise even more

Table 7.2 Simulation of Employment by Sector as a Function of Per Capita GDP, Average Low-Income Sub-Saharan African Country

	GDP per Capita (US$ in 2003 prices)						
	100	200	300	400	500	600	800
Farming (%)	87	69	59	52	46	42	35
Formal sector (%)	6	9	11	12	13	14	15
Informal nonfarm (%)	7	22	30	36	40	44	50
Total (%)	100	100	100	100	100	100	100

Source: Authors' construction based on regression results for farming in figure 7.2 and formal sector in figure 7.3.
Note: Employment in the informal nonfarm sector is calculated as the residual. GDP = gross domestic product.

Education and Employment

rapidly, the farm sector's share of total employment is likely to decline over time. As per capita GDP increases from US$200 to US$400, for example, the faming sector's share of employment may be expected to decline by 17 percentage points.

Formal sector employment may be expected to rise by 3 percentage points, but the bulk of the shift in employment is likely to occur in the informal nonfarm sector because its share in total employment is projected to increase by 14 percentage points. This change in employment pattern occurs partly through intergenerational mobility as the younger generation enters occupations that are different from those of their parents.

Countries with High Unemployment Rates Tend to Have Large Informal Nonfarm Sectors

Figure 7.4 shows a close relationship between the unemployment rate and the share of workers engaged in the informal nonfarm sector. In particular, as the overall unemployment rate increases, employment in the informal nonfarm sector as a proportion of total employment increases because it often functions as the employer of last resort—the only alternative often being unemployment.

Labor Productivity by Economic Sector

Labor productivity strongly influences earnings and serves as an indicator of the relative attractiveness of different sectors to workers seeking to maximize their incomes. Table 7.3 shows the change in labor productivity by sector in the Sub-Saharan African region between 1985 and 2003. Labor productivity is calculated by dividing value added by employment in each of the three main sectors traditionally included in the national GDP accounts and labor statistics: farming, industry, and services.

Figure 7.4 Relation between Informal Nonfarm Sector Employment and Unemployment Rate in 23 Sub-Saharan African Countries, ca. 2003

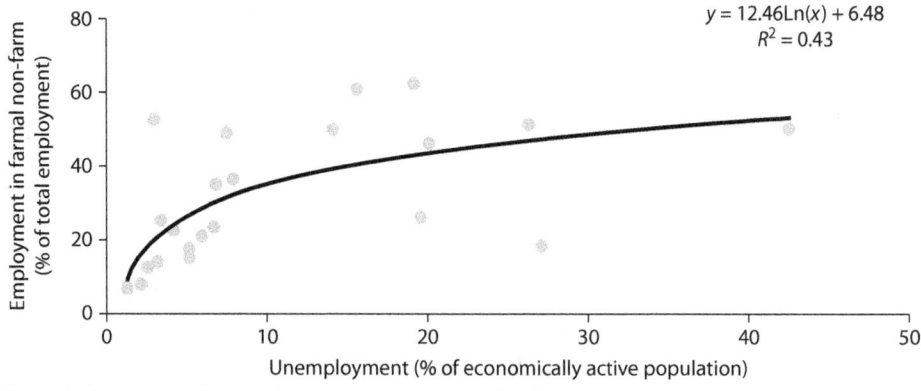

Source: Authors' analysis of labor market surveys; see appendix J, table J.2.

Table 7.3 Apparent Labor Productivity by Sector, Sub-Saharan African Average, 1985–2003

	Annual labor productivity (constant 2003 US$)				
	1985	1990	1995	2000	2003
All sectors	806	819	771	803	802
Farming	300	348	363	451	499
Industry	11,473	13,520	13,290	15,662	15,503
Services[a]	1,299	1,007	847	728	686
Formal	1,939	1,692	1,611	1,365	1,389
Informal nonfarm	913	730	600	550	509

Source: Reproduced from Mingat and Ndem (2007) based on data on value-added by sector and employment by sector; see appendix I, table I.5.
Note: Aggregate for 34 Sub-Saharan African countries. Apparent labor productivity is calculated by dividing the value added of each sector by its labor input.
a. The services sector has been divided into its formal and informal parts by making assumptions about the level of remuneration and employment share of each.

The table shows that labor productivity in the informal nonfarm sector has been declining. In 1985, labor productivity was much higher in the informal nonfarm sector (US$913) than in farming (US$300). This difference is reflected in the migration of workers from farming to nonfarming activities. Since 1985, however, labor productivity in the farming sector has been increasing (to US$499 in 2003) while that in the informal nonfarm sector has been declining (to US$509), to the extent that there is now little difference in labor productivity between the two sectors.

Informal Nonfarm Sector Cannot Absorb Growing Work Force, While Modern Private Sector Has High Labor Productivity but Slow Growth

Declining labor productivity in the informal nonfarm sector suggests that the sector cannot effectively absorb all jobseekers who cannot find work in the relatively more attractive, but highly regulated, formal sector.

The industrial sector—part of the modern formal sector—is characterized by a high and rising level of labor productivity, as shown in table 7.3. That sector, however, only provides employment to the few, and employment in the sector is growing only at a moderate pace.

Macro-Level Labor Market Shows Little Economic Return from Education

Although the Sub-Saharan African regional labor productivity has been on the increase in farming and industry, it has been decreasing in the services sector over the same period, resulting in the weighted average labor productivity across all three sectors remaining at practically the same level since 1985.

At the same time, the average level of schooling has been increasing across the region. However, the rise in education of the labor force appears to have had little impact on average labor productivity—suggesting poor use of human capital in the region.

Quantitative Match between Demand and Supply in the Labor Market

This section analyzes: (a) the educational attainment of the work force in the Sub-Saharan African region; (b) the relationship between education and employment, particularly the type of work, whether formal or informal, public or private; and (c) an analysis of the quantitative match between the demand for and supply of highly skilled workers.

Educational Profile of the Workforce

Figure 7.5 provides a breakdown of the working-age population by highest level of education. Across the 23 Sub-Saharan African countries, an average of 52 percent of the working-age population have received no formal schooling; 30 percent have received only primary education; and 18 percent have received some secondary, technical and vocational education and training (TVET), or higher education. The workforce as a whole is clearly characterized by relatively low average educational attainment.

Figure 7.5 also shows the extent of the cross-country variation in the proportion of the working-age population with some schooling among the 23 Sub-Saharan African countries. In the Republic of Congo, Lesotho, or Zambia, about 85 percent of the 15- to 59-year-olds have had at least some primary schooling. In contrast, only about 20 percent of the working-age population in Burkina Faso, Guinea, or Mali has had at least some primary education.

Figure 7.5 Highest Level of Schooling among Working-Age Population in 23 Sub-Saharan African Countries, ca. 2003

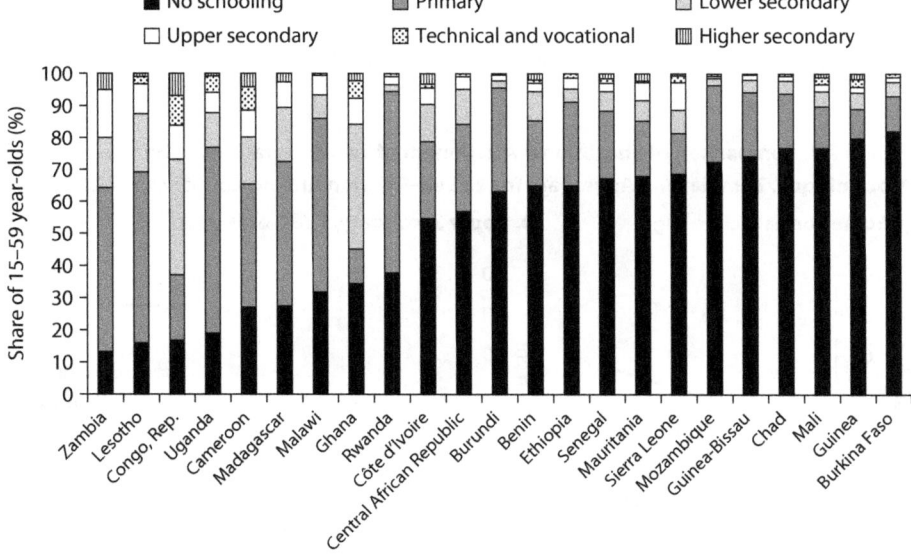

Source: Authors' construction from data in appendix I, table I.1.
Note: Based on sample population in the 15–59 age group who were not in school at the time of survey.

More-Developed Sub-Saharan African Economies Have Better-Educated Workforces

Figure 7.6 plots the share of the working-age population that has attended upper secondary or higher education against the per capita GDP across the 23 Sub-Saharan African countries. The plot shows a positive statistical relationship between the two, but GDP per capita alone explains only 44 percent of the variance in educational attainment (R^2 is 0.44).

Younger Generations More Educated than Older Generations

Figure 7.7 compares the educational attainment of two different generations: the 25- to 34-year-olds and the 50- to 59-year-olds. On the average, while only about a third of the 50- to 59-year-olds have had some formal schooling, more

Figure 7.6 Relationship between Share of Population with Upper Secondary or Higher Education and Per Capita GDP in 23 Sub-Saharan African Countries, ca. 2003

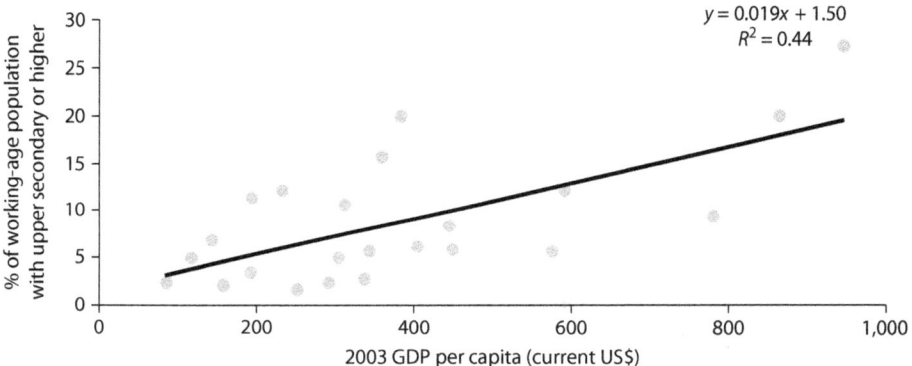

Sources: Authors' construction from analysis of labor market surveys (see appendix J, table J.2) and GDP per capita data from DDP database.
Note: Based on sample population in the 15–59 age group who were not in school at the time of survey. GDP = gross domestic product.

Figure 7.7 Comparison of Educational Attainment of Two Generations in Ghana, Mozambique, Zambia, and Aggregate for 23 Sub-Saharan African Countries, ca. 2003

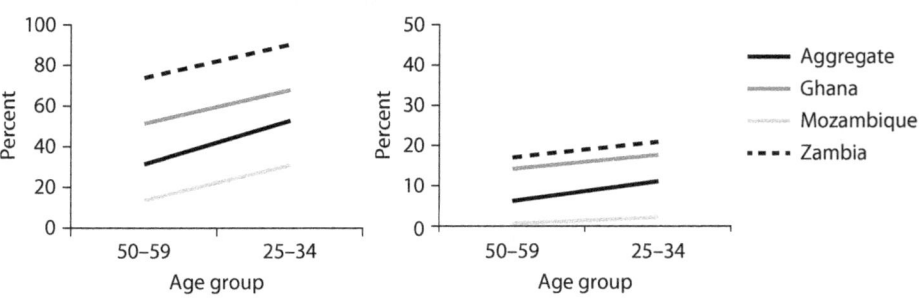

Source: Authors' analysis of labor market surveys for 23 countries; see appendix J, table J.2.
Note: TVET = technical and vocational education and training.

Figure 7.8 Share of Workforce Employed in Formal and Informal Sectors, by Highest Level of Education Attended, ca. 2003

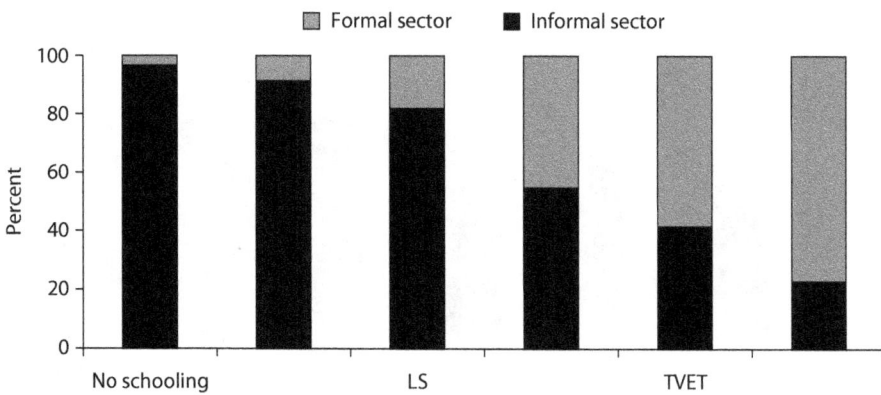

Source: Authors' analysis of labor market surveys (see appendix J, table J.2). For data set, see appendix I, table I.4.
Note: Aggregate for 23 countries. Based on sample population in the 15–59 age group who are employed. LS = lower secondary, TVET = technical and vocational education and training.

than half of the 25- to 34-year-olds have been in school. On the other hand, while 4 percent of the 50- to 59-year-olds have attained upper secondary, TVET, or higher education, 9 percent of the 25- to 34-year-olds have had at least some upper secondary education. The chart also illustrates the extent of the differences between Ghana, Mozambique, and Zambia.

Education and Employment[6]

Figure 7.8 shows the probability of working in the formal or informal sectors of the labor market by highest level of education attended (but not necessarily completed).

Almost 80 Percent of Those with Higher Education Work in Formal Sector

The likelihood of working in the formal sector is only 3 percent for individuals with no schooling, 8 percent for those with only primary education, 18 percent for those with lower secondary education, 45 for upper secondary, 58 percent for TVET, and 77 percent for those who attended higher education.

Clearly, the probability of working in the formal sector improves dramatically with increasing levels of education. Conversely, the probability of working in the informal sector decreases with increasing levels of education.

In Informal Sector, Those with Postbasic Education More Attracted to Nonfarm Work than to Farming

Panel A in figure 7.9 shows the share of informal sector workers engaged in farming and nonfarming activities by highest level of education attended. Among informal sector workers with no schooling, 80 percent work in farming and the remaining 20 percent in the informal nonfarm sector.

Figure 7.9 Shares Working in Farm vs. NonFarm Sectors, and in Public vs. Modern Private Sectors, by Education Level, ca. 2003

a. Informal Sector Workers

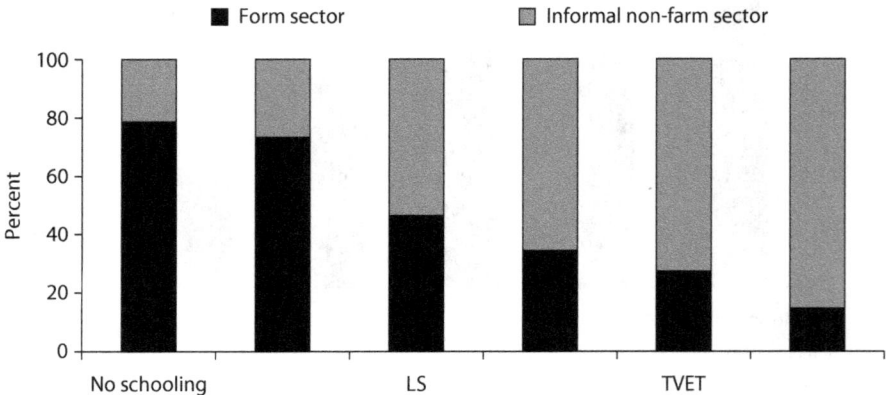

b. Formal Sector Workers

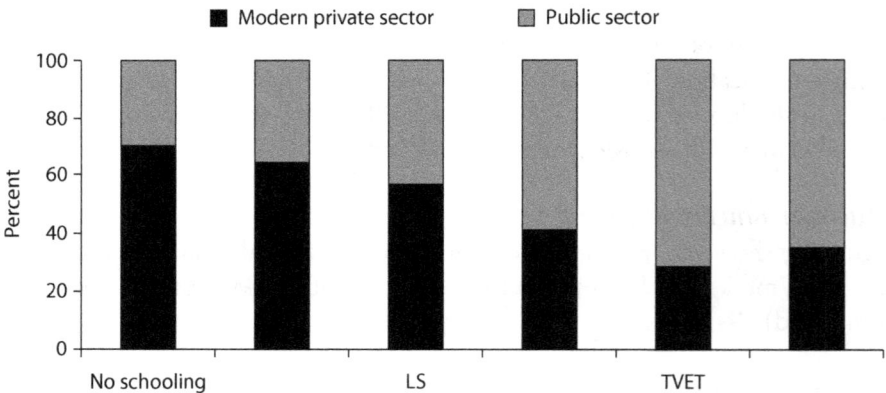

Source: Authors' analysis of labor market surveys; see appendix J, table J.2. For data set, see appendix I, table I.4.
Note: Aggregate for 23 countries. Based on sample population in the 15–59 age group who were employed at the time of the survey. LS = lower secondary, TVET = technical and vocational education and training.

Further up the spectrum, most of the informal sector workers with upper secondary or higher education tend to be engaged in nonfarm work, suggesting that the nonfarm sector offers higher incomes and other nonpecuniary benefits than does farming for those with higher educational attainment. However, the lack of education in rural areas, where farming takes place, may also play a role in explaining this pattern.

Modern Private Sector Has Few Opportunities for the Highly Educated

Panel B in figure 7.9 shows that, among those working in the formal sector, the probability of working in the public sector increases with the level of education, while the likelihood of working in the modern private sector decreases the higher the level of education attended. The fact that the modern private sector accounts for smaller proportions of workers with upper secondary or higher education is a cause for concern, especially because the public sector is not likely to grow rapidly in the coming years.

Young Workers with Postbasic Education Less Likely to Find Formal Sector Jobs than in the Past

With increasing numbers of youths attaining postbasic levels of education and formal sector employment growing only at a moderate pace, young skilled workers are likely to encounter increasing difficulty securing employment in the formal sector in the near future than in the past. Because older generations of workers are already well entrenched in the labor market and are likely to hold on to their formal sector jobs until retirement, the prospects of formal sector employment are not particularly bright for young skilled workers.

Table 7.4 shows that the share of individuals with upper secondary or higher education who work in the formal sector is much lower among those in the 25–34 age group than among the older generations. Among individuals aged 35 years and older, about 75 percent of those with higher education are engaged in the formal sector. In contrast, among those aged 25–34, only 55 percent have formal sector jobs. A similar pattern is observed for those with upper secondary education.

Young Skilled Workers Also More Likely to Be Unemployed

Table 7.4 shows that, across the three age cohorts, similar proportions of those with upper secondary and higher education are engaged in the informal sector. Specifically, for each age cohort, about 45 percent of upper secondary school leavers and about 20 percent of those with higher education are engaged in the informal sector. However, as discussed above, smaller proportions of the youngest cohort (aged 25–34) than older cohorts with upper secondary and higher education are employed in the formal sector.

Table 7.4 Employment Status by Age Group and Highest Level of Schooling Attended, Aggregate for 23 Sub-Saharan African Countries, ca. 2003

percentage

	25–34 years		35–49 years		50–59 years	
	Upper secondary	Higher	Upper secondary	Higher	Upper secondary	Higher
Employed						
Formal sector	36	55	46	76	53	74
Informal sector	46	20	47	19	41	22
Unemployed	18	26	7	6	6	4
Not active	8	3	5	3	9	9
Total	100	100	100	100	100	100

Source: Authors' analysis of labor market surveys; see appendix J, table J.2. For data set, see appendix I, table I.4.
Note: Based on sample population in the 25–59 age group who were not in school at time of survey.

Together, these results imply that young workers with postbasic education are more likely to be unemployed than older workers. In particular, table 7.4 shows the stark contrast between the youngest and older two cohorts in terms of the incidence of unemployment. Among those with upper secondary education, the unemployment rate of the youngest cohort (18 percent) is three times higher than that of the two older cohorts (7 percent and 6 percent, respectively). Similarly, among those with higher education, the unemployment rate of the youngest cohort (26 percent) is about five times higher than that of the two older cohorts (6 percent and 4 percent, respectively).

High Unemployment Suggests Overenrollment in Postbasic Education, a Skills Mismatch, and Low Educational Quality

The difficulty experienced by the younger generation in finding jobs that match their skills may indicate some level of overenrollment in postbasic education compared with the current absorptive capacity of the labor markets in the Sub-Saharan African region.

Beyond a possible quantitative mismatch, there may be other more fundamental reasons for the high rates of unemployment among young workers with postbasic education. Shortages of high-skilled workers within certain fields of study (for example, medicine and engineering) may coexist with high unemployment rates in other fields because the composition of the output of postbasic educational institutions by specialization does not reflect the demands of the labor markets.

Beyond the mismatch between supply and demand, rapid increase in tertiary-level enrollment in the region, coupled with the drop in per-student spending (Brossard and Foko 2007), has resulted in the erosion of the quality of education over time (World Bank 2008), and students are graduating without the required marketable skills.

Match between Demand and Supply in Individual Countries

There are significant differences across labor markets in the Sub-Saharan African region. Unemployment among 25- to 34-year-olds with higher education varies between 1 percent in Lesotho and 48 percent in Mali. In nine of the 23 Sub-Saharan African countries, the unemployment rate for the youngest cohort (aged 25–34) with higher education is less than 10 percent. Lesotho and Malawi, for example, have unemployment rates of only 1 percent and 5 percent, respectively, as shown in table 7.5.

At the other end of the spectrum, nine countries have unemployment rates exceeding 20 percent. In the Republic of Congo, Guinea, and Mali, the unemployment rates exceed 40 percent.

School-to-Work Transition Shows Striking Differences across Countries

The striking difference in labor market outcomes among those with higher education in Guinea and Malawi highlights stark differences in school-to-work transition across the region. In Malawi, 88 percent of 25- to 34-year-olds with higher education

Table 7.5 Employment and Unemployment by Level of Education and Age Group in 23 Sub-Saharan African Countries, ca. 2003

percentage

	Individuals with higher education and formal sector job		Individuals with higher education and informal sector job		Individuals with higher education who are unemployed	
	25–34 years	50–59 years	25–34 years	50–59 years	25–34 years	50–59 years
Benin	74.7	70.5	16.3	25.1	9.0	4.4
Burkina Faso	82.6	91.2	10.4	5.8	7.0	3.0
Burundi	79.1	71.7	9.9	24.4	11.0	4.0
Cameroon	51.2	71.5	12.6	16.6	36.2	11.8
Central African Rep.	56.6	83.6	18.9	9.4	24.6	7.1
Chad	86.0	97.1	4.9	0.0	9.1	2.9
Congo, Rep.	29.1	71.7	27.6	18.4	43.3	9.9
Côte d'Ivoire	34.1	69.4	28.1	25.2	37.8	5.4
Ethiopia	67.1	64.1	23.3	33.3	9.6	2.6
Ghana	64.3	79.9	22.1	18.7	13.6	1.4
Guinea	19.6	80.2	35.3	13.0	45.1	6.8
Guinea-Bissau	—	—	—	—	—	—
Lesotho	76.8	68.9	22.6	8.4	0.6	22.7
Madagascar	59.9	84.6	23.9	15.4	16.2	0.0
Malawi	87.8	67.4	7.0	32.6	5.3	0.0
Mali	41.8	59.6	9.7	40.4	48.5	0.0
Mauritania	57.9	78.6	25.1	17.3	17.0	4.1
Mozambique	92.0	73.7	0.0	26.3	8.0	0.0
Rwanda	54.9	100.0	21.1	0.0	24.0	0.0
Senegal	54.1	80.0	17.8	20.0	28.1	0.0
Sierra Leone	81.8	82.9	9.1	17.1	9.1	0.0
Uganda	68.7	50.0	7.4	50.0	23.9	0.0
Zambia	70.2	66.3	20.8	33.1	9.0	0.7
Simple average	63.2	75.6	17.0	20.5	19.8	3.9
Minimum	19.6	50.0	0.0	0.0	0.6	0.0
Maximum	92.0	100.0	35.3	50.0	48.5	22.7

Source: Authors' analysis of labor market surveys; see appendix J, table J.2. For data set, see appendix I, table I.4.
Note: Based on sample population in the age group 15–59 who were not in school at time of survey. — = not available.

work in the formal sector, 7 percent in the informal sector, and only 5 percent are unemployed (as shown in table 7.5). In Guinea, on the other hand, only 20 percent of the 25- to 34-year-olds with higher education work in the formal sector, and 35 percent in the informal sector, and 45 percent are unemployed.

Although most higher-education graduates in Malawi enter the formal sector soon after leaving school, only one in five in Guinea does so. In both countries, those who do not find work in the formal sector are about equally divided between informal sector employment and unemployment.

Relationship between Higher Education Enrollment and Unemployment

To examine the relationship between higher education enrollment and unemployment among those with higher education, we first examine the relationship between unemployment and the supply of and demand for highly skilled labor.

Table 7.6 Determinants of Unemployment Rate in 25–34 Age Cohort of Higher-Education Graduates: Cross-Country Analysis, ca. 2003

Dependent variable	Model 1: Share of 25-to 34-year-olds with higher education who are unemployed (UR)
Constant	24.45
Explanatory variables	
Natural Logarithm of Proportion of 25- to 34-year-olds with higher education Ln (%H)	8.906*
Share of skilled (higher education) formal sector employment to total employment (EMPQUAL)	−1.629
Number of observations	22
R^2	0.22

Source: UR data from table 7.5; %H data from appendix I, table I.3; and EMPQUAL data in appendix I, table I.4.
Note: All survey data are from around 2003. Guinea-Bissau is excluded for lack of unemployment data.
Significance level: * = 5 percent

The first regression (model 1) in table 7.6 explores the relationship for the cohort aged 25–34. The dependent variable is the unemployment rate of the cohort aged 25–34 with higher education. The supply of highly skilled labor is proxied by the proportion of 25- to 34-year-olds with higher education, and the demand for highly skilled labor is proxied by the proportion of formal sector jobs requiring higher education to total employment.

The Higher the Proportion of Highly Educated Students, the Higher the Unemployment Rate among Highly Educated Individuals<xen>[7]

The regression results in table 7.6 show that the supply of highly skilled labor (proxied by the proportion of 25- to 34-year-olds with higher education) is a significant and positive determinant of the unemployment rate among 25- to 34-year-olds with higher education. This result indicates that unemployment among university dropouts or graduates is worse in countries where higher proportions of students have attended higher education.

The coefficient of the proxy representing the demand for highly skilled labor is negative, as expected, but not statistically significant, indicating that the unemployment rate among 25- to 34-year-olds with higher education is not significantly influenced by the incidence of skilled formal sector jobs in a country.

For Policy Analysis, Higher-Education Enrollment Can Be Expressed as a Function of the Unemployment Rate and Per Capita GDP

The second regression (model 2), in the first column in table 7.7, shows that the proportion of the population with higher education (a measure of the stock of human capital) is statistically correlated with higher-education enrollment per 100,000 population (a measure of the flow of human capital).

The third regression (model 3), in the second column of table 7.7, expresses the proportion of skilled formal sector jobs to total employment as a function of per capita GDP.

Education and Employment

These two regressions (models 2 and 3) can be substituted into the first regression (model 1, in table 7.6) to obtain an expression of higher education enrollment (per 100,000 population) as a function of the unemployment rate among 25–34 year olds with higher education and per capita GDP.[8] This expression is used to simulate higher education enrollment for the Sub-Saharan African region that would be consistent with an unemployment rate of 25 percent among 25- to 34-year-olds who have had higher education, expressed by the curve in figure 7.10.

Simulation Illustrates How Much Higher-Education Enrollment Can Grow with Rising Per Capita GDP without Worsening Unemployment

Figure 7.10 shows how, on the basis of this simple labor market model, countries with higher per capita GDP can sustain a higher level of higher-education enrollment than countries with lower per capita GDP—while keeping the unemployment rate among 25- to 34-year-olds with higher education unchanged at

Table 7.7 Modeling Higher Education Enrollment and Share of Skilled Formal Sector Jobs

Dependent variable	Model 2: Higher education enrollment per 100,000 inhabitants (S)	Model 3: Share of skilled formal sector jobs in total employment (EMPQUAL)
Constant	158.4	1.259
Explanatory variables		
Proportion of 25- to 34-year-olds with some higher education (%H)	45.97*	
2003 GDP per capita (GDPpc)		0.009086*
Number of observations	23	23
R^2	0.46	0.51

Sources: Data on S in appendix B, table B.1; data on %H in appendix I, table I.3; and data on EMPQUAL in appendix I, table I.4.
Note: GDP per capita data are from World Bank and expressed in current US$. Country is the unit of observation in the regressions.
Significance level: * = 1 percent

Figure 7.10 Simulation of Higher-Education Enrollment Associated with 25% Unemployment among 25–34 Year Olds with Higher Education, by Per Capita GDP, in Selected Sub-Saharan African Countries

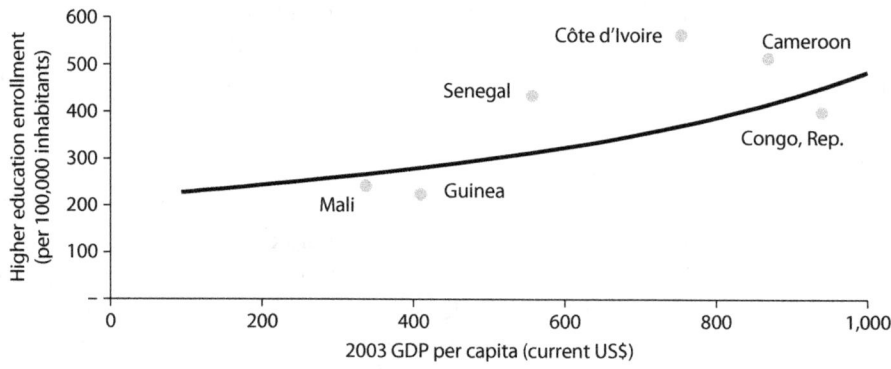

Source: Authors' construction from analysis of labor market surveys (see appendix J, table J.2) and 2003 higher-education enrollment data from UIS Data Centre, Pôle de Dakar UNESCO-BREDA 2007, and selected Country Status Reports. For the full data set, see appendix B, table B.2 (interpolated from 1999 and 2005 data).

25 percent. The simulation also shows that rising per capita GDP leads to only fairly modest increases in higher-education enrollment. This general conclusion may serve as a guide for decision making regarding higher-education enrollment in countries with high or rising unemployment among higher-education graduates.

But the Model Has Clear Limitations at the Country Level

The chart also illustrates how six countries—all with more than 25 percent unemployment among highly educated 25- to 34-year-olds—are placed relative to the curve. If the model had a perfect fit, we would expect these countries to be placed above the curve, indicating a higher enrollment than that consistent with a 25 percent unemployment rate. However, only three of the six countries (Cameroon, Cote d'Ivoire, and Senegal) have university enrollments significantly above that predicted by the curve, while the other three (the Republic of Congo, Guinea, and Mali) have enrollments below the predicted levels. This result implies that job opportunities for highly skilled workers also depend on factors other than just per capita GDP, thus limiting the model's usefulness as a tool for education policy at the national level.

Balancing Quantity and Quality in Higher Education

Producing more higher-education graduates than the labor market can absorb makes little economic sense, particularly when higher education is largely subsidized by public funds. Nevertheless, a certain level of overproduction may be a good long-term investment that can contribute to future economic growth if the graduates are of high quality.

In countries where many skilled workers emigrate, universities may need to train extra workers to meet domestic demand. Emigration of skilled workers is not necessarily a long-term loss to the country because many remit their earnings to the home country. In this context, skilled workers may even be considered an export from the home country.

However, if most recent graduates cannot find gainful employment or cannot find jobs that match their skills, it may be an indication that the education system needs some form of rebalancing, such as shifting its emphasis on quantity to an emphasis on quality. Although the simulation in figure 7.10 has its limitations, it may still be useful insofar as it provides an indication of a more appropriate level of enrollment in higher education, given a country's per capita GDP.

Issues for Policy Development

Rapid expansion in higher education, coupled with moderate growth in suitable employment opportunities in recent years, has resulted in considerable unemployment among recent university graduates in a number of Sub-Saharan African countries. Most of these countries suffer from slow growth of the formal sector, which is traditionally the employer of first resort among highly skilled workers. The relatively faster growing informal sector, on the other hand, cannot effectively absorb the rapidly growing numbers of higher-education graduates.

The above underscores the importance of policies that can foster economic growth and create jobs, especially well-paid jobs, though these policies are largely beyond the control of the ministries of education. In terms of education policy, a few recommendations emerge from the analysis:

- *Collect and share information on employment and education.* As the discussion above shows, examining the relationship between education and employment provides useful information on the performance of the education system in relation to the labor market. Key findings from studies of this nature help guide education policy. Labor market information generated from such studies is often useful to prospective employers and job seekers. Collecting and disseminating information on the relationship between education and employment, including information on job opportunities and earnings, may help reduce some labor market mismatches in the Sub-Saharan African region. For jobseekers, for example, such information may shorten their job searches by directing their attention to sectors that offer the best chances of finding employment.
- *Focus more on quality at the postprimary levels of education.* Although the evidence of declining quality in higher education is mostly anecdotal, evidence of the decline in per-student public sector spending in postprimary education as a result of rapidly growing enrollments is well established. Quality and labor market relevance are key measures of the effectiveness of education at postprimary levels of education. There is a need to strike the right balance between quantity and quality. In this light, decision makers and policymakers in higher-education institutions need to consider the relevance of their programs in meeting and responding to employers' needs to produce students who are employable and whose expectations match available job opportunities.
- *Collect more data on the quality of postprimary levels of education.* The strong focus on the quantitative aspects of postprimary education in this chapter is due, in part, to the lack of qualitative data on secondary, TVET, and higher education. Having access to internationally comparable national-level data on student learning at postprimary levels of education is critical for education policymakers and practitioners. Going forward, school-level data on student learning can be a useful tool for improving accountability and performance in the sector.
- *Use public funding for postprimary education more strategically.* Competing needs for funding in the education sector puts increasing pressure on policymakers and practitioners to make the best use of available and limited resources. In secondary, TVET, and higher education, this pressure may imply the need to focus spending more on high-quality inputs and less on other types of expenditures. It also implies the need to direct spending into areas where there are shortages of skilled workers or into fields of specialization than can be potential drivers of economic growth, such as in science and technology.

Notes

1. The 23 countries are Benin, Burkina Faso, Burundi, Cameroon, the Central African Republic, Chad, the Republic of Congo, Côte d'Ivoire, Ethiopia, Ghana, Guinea, Guinea-Bissau, Lesotho, Madagascar, Malawi, Mali, Mauritania, Mozambique, Rwanda, Senegal, Sierra Leone, Uganda, and Zambia.
2. For a list of the surveys, see appendix J.
3. None of the labor market surveys includes a specific variable characterizing a person's employment status. For the purpose of this analysis, an employment status variable was constructed based on the respondents' answers to several different questions in the surveys. In this process, a substantial effort was devoted to resolving inconsistencies in the data. For example, some individuals may declare, in one question, to work in the civil service and, in another, to be paid weekly or on an irregular basis. Also, whenever data were missing (a frequent occurrence in employment-related questions), answers provided to other questions were used to fill in the gaps.
4. "Low-income countries" are those eligible for lending from the International Development Association (IDA). The IDA threshold changes every year, as do the countries' gross national income(s) (GNI) per capita, so there may be small changes from year to year in this group. However, the 2006 IDA threshold was GNI per capita of less than US$1,065. For the full list of low-income Sub-Saharan African countries, see appendix A, table A.1.
5. The unemployment rate may be calculated by using the economically active population as the denominator: thus, the aggregate unemployment rate in the 23 Sub-Saharan African countries is around 8 percent (7 out of 86).
6. This section is based on appendix I, tables I.3 and I.4, which break down the working-age population by age group, labor market status, and highest level of schooling. The breakdown by age group allows for analyzing differences between different generations.
7. This group includes all who have attained higher education, including some who have not graduated.
8. Higher education enrollment per 100,000 inhabitants = 46.0 * exp(UR/8.91 − 2.51 + 0.00166 * GDPpc) + 158.4.

References

Blunch, N.-H., S. Canagarajah, and D. Raju. 2001. "The Informal Sector Revisited: A Synthesis across Space and Time." Social Protection Discussion Paper 119, World Bank, Washington, DC.

Brossard, M., and B. Foko. 2007. *Coûts et financement de l'enseignement supérieur en Afrique francophone. African Human Development Series.* Washington, DC: World Bank.

DDP (Development Data Platform) (database). World Bank, Washington, DC. http://databank.worldbank.org/ddp/home.do.

Fields, G. 2007. "Dual Economy." Working Paper 17, ILR Collection, Cornell University, Ithaca, NY.

Haggblade, S., P. B. R. Hazell, and T. Reardon, eds. 2007. *Transforming the Rural Nonfarm Economy. Opportunities and Threats in the Developing World.International Food Policy*

Research Institute (IFPRI) Series, World Bank and IFPRI Project. Baltimore: Johns Hopkins University Press.

Mingat, A., and F. Ndem. 2007. "La dimension rurale des scolarisations dans les pays d'Afrique au sud du Sahara: situation actuelle et défis pour le développement de la couverture scolaire au niveau du premier cycle secondaire." Paper presented at seminar of IREDU, CNRS and University of Bourgogne, France.

Pôle de Dakar UNESCO-BREDA (United Nations Educational, Scientific and Cultural Organization, Regional Office for Education in Africa). 2007. "Education for All in Africa: Top Priority for Integrated Sector-Wide Policies." Dakar+7 Report, Pôle de Dakar UNESCO-BREDA, Dakar.

UIS (United Nations Educational, Scientific and Cultural Organization, Institute for Statistics) Data Centre (database). UIS, Montreal. http://stats.uis.unesco.org.

UNCTAD (United Nations Conference on Trade and Development). 2006. *The Least Developed Countries Report 2006: Developing Productive Capacities.* Geneva: UNCTAD Secretariat.

UN-HABITAT (United Nations Human Settlements Program). 2004. "Africa on the Move: An Urban Crisis in the Making." Submission to the Commission for Africa, UN-HABITAT, Nairobi.

World Bank. 2008. *Accelerating Catch-Up: Tertiary Education for Growth in Sub-Saharan Africa.* Directions in Development Series. Washington, DC: World Bank.

APPENDIX A

Definitions and Background Information

Table A.1 Classification of Sub-Saharan African Countries Used in This Report

Low-income countries[a] (2006 GNI per capita ≤ US$1,065)	In sample of 33 low-income countries?[c]	Middle-income countries[b] (2006 GNI per capita > US$1,065)
Angola	No	Botswana
Benin	Yes	Equatorial Guinea
Burkina Faso	Yes	Gabon
Burundi	Yes	Mauritius
Cameroon	Yes	Namibia
Cape Verde	No	Seychelles
Central African Republic	Yes	South Africa
Chad	Yes	Swaziland
Comoros	No	
Congo, Dem. Rep.	Yes	
Congo, Rep.	Yes	
Côte d'Ivoire	Yes	
Eritrea	Yes	
Ethiopia	Yes	
Gambia, The	Yes	
Ghana	Yes	
Guinea	Yes	
Guinea-Bissau	Yes	
Kenya	Yes	
Lesotho	Yes	
Liberia	No	
Madagascar	Yes	
Malawi	Yes	
Mali	Yes	
Mauritania	Yes	
Mozambique	Yes	
Niger	Yes	
Nigeria	Yes	
Rwanda	Yes	
São Tomé and Príncipe	No	
Senegal	Yes	
Sierra Leone	Yes	
Somalia	No	

(table continues on next page)

Table A.1 Classification of Sub-Saharan African Countries Used in This Report *(continued)*

Low-income countries[a] (2006 GNI per capita ≤ US$1,065)	In sample of 33 low-income countries?[c]	Middle-income countries[b] (2006 GNI per capita > US$1,065)
Sudan	Yes	
Tanzania	Yes	
Togo	Yes	
Uganda	Yes	
Zambia	Yes	
Zimbabwe	Yes	

Source: Bruns et al. 2003; DDP database.
Note: GNI = gross national income.
a. Low-income countries are defined in this report as countries eligible for lending from the World Bank Group's International Development Association (IDA). These countries had a 2006 GNI per capita income of less than US$1,065. The threshold changes every year as does the countries' per capita incomes, so there may be small changes from year to year in this group.
b. Middle-income countries are defined in this report as developing countries that are above the threshold to qualify for IDA lending. They are instead eligible for lending from the International Bank for Reconstruction and Development (IBRD).
c. The sample of 33 low-income countries (selected in Bruns et al. 2003) comprises the Sub-Saharan African countries eligible for IDA lending except those with very small populations (Cape Verde, the Comoros, and São Tomé and Príncipe) or highly incomplete data (Angola, Liberia, and Somalia).

Table A.2 Definitions of Student Flow Indicators

Name of indicator	Short form	Definition
Gross intake rate	GIR	Number of new entrants to the first year of that cycle as a share of the population of official entry age.
Gross enrollment rate	GER	Total number of students enrolled in the cycle as a share of the population in the official age group for that cycle.
Primary completion rate	PCR	Number of students in the last grade of primary school, minus the number of repeaters, as a share of the population of official age of attending that grade.
Completion rate	CR	Number of students in the last grade of that cycle, minus the number of repeaters, as a share of the population of official age of attending that grade.
Retention rate	RET	Percentage of students who enroll in a school year and continue to be in school the following years. The retention rate to the last grade of primary can be calculated as PCR/GIR, which is an approximation.
Transition rate	n.a.	Number of new entrants to the first grade of a cycle of education in a given year, expressed as a percentage of the number of pupils enrolled in the final grade of the previous cycle of education in the previous year.
School-life expectancy	SLE	Number of years a child of school entrance age is expected to spend in school, from primary to tertiary levels, including years spent on repetition. It is the sum of the age-specific enrollment rates for the levels specified.

Sources: Adapted from UNESCO Institute for Statistics (UIS) Glossary and the World Bank's EdStats website.
See www.uis.unesco.org/glossary for more calculation methods and other details.
Note: n.a. = not applicable.

Table A.3 Duration of Primary and Secondary Cycles (Standardized) in 47 Sub-Saharan African Countries, 2005

Years of study	1	2	3	4	5	6	7	8	9	10	11	12	13
Angola	P	P	P	P	S1	S1	S1	S1	S2	S2	S2		
Ethiopia	P	P	P	P	S1	S1	S1	S1	S2	S2	S2	S2	
Equatorial Guinea	P	P	P	P	P	S1	S1	S1	S1	S2	S2	S2	
Eritrea	P	P	P	P	P	S1	S1	S1	S2	S2	S2	S2	
Madagascar	P	P	P	P	P	S1	S1	S1	S1	S2	S2	S2	
São Tomé and Príncipe	P	P	P	P	P	P	S1	S1	S2	S2	S2		
Sudan	P	P	P	P	P	P	S1	S1	S2	S2	S2		
Congo, Dem. Rep.	P	P	P	P	P	P	S1	S1	S2	S2	S2	S2	
Kenya	P	P	P	P	P	P	S1	S1	S2	S2	S2	S2	
Guinea-Bissau	P1	P1	P1	P1	P2	P2	S1	S1	S1	S2	S2		
Seychelles	P	P	P	P	P	P	S1	S1	S1	S2	S2		
Cape Verde	P	P	P	P	P	P	S1	S1	S1	S2	S2	S2	
Gambia, The	P	P	P	P	P	P	S1	S1	S1	S2	S2	S2	
Ghana	P	P	P	P	P	P	S1	S1	S1	S2	S2	S2	
Liberia	P	P	P	P	P	P	S1	S1	S1	S2	S2	S2	
Malawi	P	P	P	P	P	P	S1	S1	S1	S2	S2	S2	
Mali	P	P	P	P	P	P	S1	S1	S1	S2	S2	S2	
Nigeria	P	P	P	P	P	P	S1	S1	S1	S2	S2	S2	
Rwanda	P	P	P	P	P	P	S1	S1	S1	S2	S2	S2	
Sierra Leone	P	P	P	P	P	P	S1	S1	S1	S2	S2	S2	
Mauritius	P	P	P	P	P	P	S1	S1	S1	S2	S2	S2	S2
Benin	P	P	P	P	P	P	S1	S1	S1	S1	S2	S2	S2
Burkina Faso	P	P	P	P	P	P	S1	S1	S1	S1	S2	S2	S2
Burundi	P	P	P	P	P	P	S1	S1	S1	S1	S2	S2	S2
Cameroon	P	P	P	P	P	P	S1	S1	S1	S1	S2	S2	S2
Central African Republic	P	P	P	P	P	P	S1	S1	S1	S1	S2	S2	S2
Chad	P	P	P	P	P	P	S1	S1	S1	S1	S2	S2	S2
Comoros	P	P	P	P	P	P	S1	S1	S1	S1	S2	S2	S2
Congo, Rep.	P	P	P	P	P	P	S1	S1	S1	S1	S2	S2	S2
Côte d'Ivoire	P	P	P	P	P	P	S1	S1	S1	S1	S2	S2	S2
Gabon	P	P	P	P	P	P	S1	S1	S1	S1	S2	S2	S2
Guinea	P	P	P	P	P	P	S1	S1	S1	S1	S2	S2	S2
Mauritania	P	P	P	P	P	P	S1	S1	S1	S1	S2	S2	S2
Niger	P	P	P	P	P	P	S1	S1	S1	S1	S2	S2	S2
Senegal	P	P	P	P	P	P	S1	S1	S1	S1	S2	S2	S2
Togo	P	P	P	P	P	P	S1	S1	S1	S1	S2	S2	S2
South Africa	P	P	P	P	P	P	P	S1	S1	S2	S2	S2	
Zambia	P	P	P	P	P	P	P	S1	S1	S2	S2	S2	
Zimbabwe	P	P	P	P	P	P	P	S1	S1	S2	S2	S2	S2
Botswana	P	P	P	P	P	P	P	S1	S1	S1	S2	S2	
Lesotho	P	P	P	P	P	P	P	S1	S1	S1	S2	S2	
Mozambique	P1	P1	P1	P1	P1	P2	P2	S1	S1	S1	S2	S2	
Namibia	P	P	P	P	P	P	P	S1	S1	S1	S2	S2	
Somalia	P	P	P	P	P	P	P	S1	S1	S1	S2	S2	
Swaziland	P	P	P	P	P	P	P	S1	S1	S1	S2	S2	
Uganda	P	P	P	P	P	P	P	S1	S1	S1	S1	S2	S2
Tanzania	P	P	P	P	P	P	P	S1	S1	S1	S1	S2	S2

Source: UIS Data Centre.
Note: The table provides the cycle lengths (standardized) for which UIS education statistics are reported. For a few countries, notably Kenya and Malawi, actual cycle lengths are different. P = Primary. S1 = Lower secondary (ISCED 2A). S2 = Upper secondary (ISCED 3A). ISCED = International Standard Classification of Education.

References

Bruns, B., A. Mingat, and R. Rakotomalala. 2003. *Achieving Universal Primary Education by 2015: A Chance for Every Child*. Washington, DC: World Bank.

DDP (Development Data Platform) (database). World Bank, Washington, DC. http://databank.worldbank.org/ddp/home.do.

EdStats (Education Statistics) (database). World Bank, Washington, DC. http://www.worldbank.org/education/edstats.

UIS (United Nations Educational, Scientific and Cultural Organization, Institute for Statistics) Data Centre (database). UIS, Montreal. http://stats.uis.unesco.org.

APPENDIX B

Enrollment Data

Table B.1 Education Coverage by Level of Education in 47 Sub-Saharan African Countries, ca. 2009

	Pre-primary	Primary				Transition	Lower secondary			Transition	Upper secondary			TVET	Higher
	GER	GER	GIR	PCR	Ret.[a]	(P–LS)	GER	GIR	CR	(LS–US)	GER	GIR	CR	(Students per 100,000 pop.)	
	(%)	(%)	(%)	(%)	(%)	(%)	(%)	(%)	(%)	(%)	(%)	(%)	(%)		
Angola	9	103	132	35	27	—	23	—	—	—	16	—	—	871	294
Benin	13	117	164	65	40	89	59	58	26	82	22	21	15	339	949
Botswana	17	109	113	95	84	100	91	95	88	64	67	56	54	496	883
Burkina Faso	3	78	87	43	50	58	27	25	15	55	10	9	5	164	312
Burundi	10	147	149	52	35	51	29	27	16	61	11	10	4	166	301
Cameroon	26	114	126	73	58	52	50	38	27	97	29	26	15	1,326	912
Cape Verde	61	98	87	87	99	111	101	96	81	96	75	78	52	957	1,698
Central African Rep.	5	89	97	38	39	56	18	21	9	76	8	7	7	96	240
Chad	1	90	115	33	29	92	29	31	17	76	17	13	12	42	187
Comoros	27	119	96	81	85	62	50	50	36	88	37	31	28	—	523
Congo, Dem. Rep.	4	90	112	53	47	87	48	46	33	58	31	19	15	935	591
Congo, Rep.	13	120	113	74	65	71	64	52	44	49	25	21	19	1,028	596
Côte d'Ivoire	4	74	72	46	65	72	36	33	35	53	18	18	14	257	797
Equatorial Guinea	53	82	87	47	54	—	—	—	—	—	—	—	—	—	—
Eritrea	13	48	42	48	114	92	46	44	34	88	21	30	12	33	201
Ethiopia	4	102	150	55	37	79	43	44	29	19	15	6	6	371	337
Gabon	46	144	108	86	80	86	87	74	48	90	46	43	25	377	1,098
Gambia	22	86	93	79	85	86	62	68	59	65	39	38	28	48	402
Ghana	82	105	110	83	75	96	78	79	68	46	35	31	30	210	625
Guinea	11	90	92	55	59	90	43	49	32	67	25	21	21	112	834
Guinea-Bissau	5	120	118	48	41	76	37	37	26	78	19	20	17	65	251
Kenya	51	113	113	91	81	—	90	—	—	—	43	—	—	39	433
Lesotho	18	108	97	73	75	83	51	60	29	77	23	23	18	76	426
Liberia	103	91	112	58	51	75	39	43	35	74	23	26	21	—	408
Madagascar	10	160	197	79	40	58	43	45	26	53	15	14	9	173	349
Malawi	23	119	140	59	42	85	52	50	42	43	17	18	14	35	46
Mali	4	95	96	59	62	81	50	48	37	53	26	19	10	684	603
Mauritania	5	104	115	72	63	32	26	23	18	106	23	19	16	104	385

(table continues on next page)

Table B.1 Education Coverage by Level of Education in 47 Sub-Saharan African Countries, ca. 2009 *(continued)*

	Pre-primary	Primary				Transition	Lower secondary			Transition	Upper secondary			TVET	Higher
	GER	GER	GIR	PCR	Ret.[a]	(P–LS)	GER	GIR	CR	(LS–US)	GER	GIR	CR		(Students per
	(%)	(%)	(%)	(%)	(%)	(%)	(%)	(%)	(%)	(%)	(%)	(%)	(%)		100,000 pop.)
Mauritius	98	100	99	89	90	92	96	82	83	97	81	81	44	1,402	2,012
Mozambique		115	160	57	36	61	32	35	20	50	10	10	7	144	143
Namibia	31	112	98	87	89	90	86	78	59	62	34	37	31	—	925
Niger	3	62	90	40	45	66	17	27	10	37	4	4	3	42	109
Nigeria	16	93	—	—	—	—	34	—	—	—	26	—	—	178	1,009
Rwanda	17	151	191	54	28	54	36	29	22	77	17	17	13	544	552
São Tomé and Príncipe	46	130	118	85	72	67	71	57	43	73	19	31	12	99	440
Senegal	12	84	99	57	57	71	40	40	27	62	16	17	11	197	773
Seychelles	109	106	107	105	98	—	110	—	—	—	98	—	—	—	—
Sierra Leone	5	158	192	88	46	67	50	59	33	55	18	18	11	220	301
Somalia	—	33	—	—	—	—	10	—	8	121	6	9	4	—	—
South Africa	51	105	108	86	80	95	94	82	86	83	96	71	43	788	1,536
Sudan	28	74	83	57	69	83	53	47	43	65	28	28	31	66	630
Swaziland	16	108	103	72	70	109	64	79	44	90	37	40	31	—	506
Tanzania	33	105	99	102	103	53	39	55	24	21	4	5	3	252	137
Togo	7	115	105	61	59	84	51	52	35	55	27	20	9	505	529
Uganda	19	122	153	56	37	64	33	36	24	46	15	11	10	179	352
Zambia	2	113	117	87	74	80	73	69	65	41	31	27	31	463	136
Zimbabwe	—	104	—	81	—	—	59	—	—	—	32	—	5	—	396
Simple average	26	104	115	67	58	77	53	52	37	68	29	25	19	361	572
Truncated average[b]	26	93	96	67	—	—	51	52	37	—	29	25	19	—	—

Sources: Based on most recent UIS data for the 2006–10 period (UIS Data Centre); whenever recent UIS data were unavailable, data from Pôle de Dakar UNESCO-BREDA (2005, 2006; 2007) or World Bank databases, Country Status Reports on Education (all data are from 2005 or later).
Note: GER = gross enrollment rate. GIR = gross intake rate. PCR = primary completion rate. Ret. = retention rate. CR = completion rate. P–LS = primary to lower secondary. LS = lower secondary. LS–US = lower secondary to upper secondary. US = upper secondary. TVET = technical and vocational education and training. — = not available. All indicators are defined in appendix A, table A.2.
a. Retention is here calculated as PCR/GIR.
b. Truncated average: Values larger than 100 are reduced to 100 before computing the average. This statistic may be a better indicator than the simple average of the level of coverage in the region.

Table B.2 Development in Education Coverage over Time in Sample of 33 Low-Income[a] Sub-Saharan African Countries, 1990, 1999, and 2009

	Primary						Lower secondary			Upper secondary			Higher		
	1990	1999		2009			1990	1999	2009	1990	1999	2009	1990	1999	2009
	GER (%)	GER (%)	PCR (%)	GER (%)	GIR (%)	PCR (%)	GER (%)			GER (%)			(Students per 100,000 pop.)		
Benin	59	74	34	117	164	65	13	26	59	5	9	22	210	272	949
Burkina Faso	33	43	23	78	87	43	10	14	27	4	5	10	61	86	312
Burundi	71	60	26	147	149	52	6	10	29	2	2	11	63	77	301
Cameroon	99	84	49	114	126	73	25	26	50	19	19	29	271	394	912
Central African Rep.	66	67	23	89	97	38	11	15	18	5	6	8	128	164	240
Chad	55	63	20	90	115	33	10	15	29	4	9	17	43	65	187

(table continues on next page)

Table B.2 Development in Education Coverage over Time in Sample of 33 Low-Income[a] Sub-Saharan African Countries, 1990, 1999, and 2009 (continued)

	Primary						Lower secondary			Upper secondary			Higher		
	1990	1999			2009		1990	1999	2009	1990	1999	2009	1990	1999	2009
	GER (%)	GER (%)	PCR (%)	GER (%)	GIR (%)	PCR (%)	GER (%)			GER (%)			(Students per 100,000 pop.)		
Congo, Dem. Rep.	71	48	29	90	112	53	14	—	48	11	—	31	211	313	591
Congo, Rep.	117	56	40	120	113	74	50	32	64	17	13	25	441	343	596
Côte d'Ivoire	65	69	38	74	72	46	18	27	36	9	14	18	277	580	797
Eritrea	21	52	34	48	42	48	20	40	46	15	15	21	98	112	201
Ethiopia	32	48	19	102	150	55	13	21	43	11	7	15	67	77	337
Gambia	61	77	53	86	93	79	29	43	62	12	21	39	142	87	402
Ghana	72	75	63	105	110	83	38	55	78	5	18	35	88	250	625
Guinea	34	57	30	90	92	55	9	19	43	4	8	25	89	145	834
Guinea-Bissau	50	70	27	120	118	48	10	22	37	2	11	19	37	37	251
Kenya	94	93	70	113	113	91	35	64	90	15	24	43	143	271	433
Lesotho	112	102	61	108	97	73	32	38	51	13	18	23	127	218	426
Madagascar	94	93	32	160	197	79	21	19	43	9	7	15	298	196	349
Malawi	68	137	67	119	140	59	11	49	52	5	23	17	51	28	46
Mali	25	59	30	95	96	59	11	18	50	2	10	26	62	192	603
Mauritania	50	89	50	104	115	72	16	22	26	14	15	23	274	350	385
Mozambique	64	70	14	115	160	57	6	7	32	1	2	10	30	69	143
Niger	28	31	19	62	90	40	13	8	17	3	4	4	58	66	109
Nigeria	92	88	69	93	—	—	26	26	34	17	22	26	400	575	1,009
Rwanda	71	92	27	151	191	54	1	12	36	1	8	17	60	74	552
Senegal	58	64	41	84	99	57	19	18	40	11	10	16	257	291	773
Sierra Leone	50	62	53	158	192	88	20	22	50	11	10	18	116	146	301
Sudan	52	49	37	74	83	57	—	37	53	19	19	28	251	—	630
Tanzania	67	67	57	105	99	102	6	7	39	1	3	4	25	57	137
Togo	110	112	60	115	105	61	27	47	51	9	14	27	226	288	529
Uganda	69	125	56	122	153	56	18	11	33	4	7	15	99	169	352
Zambia	94	80	63	113	117	87	28	25	73	12	16	31	189	226	136
Zimbabwe	104	100	90	104	—	—	54	65	59	—	31	32	471	342	396
Simple average	67	74	43	105	119	63	19	26	45	8	12	21	163	205	450

Sources: UIS Data Centre for the years shown, supplemented with data from Pôle de Dakar UNESCO-BREDA 2007 and selected Country Status Reports (listed in Overview chapter references). Some data are calculated by interpolation from other years' data.
Note: All indicators are defined in appendix A, table A.2. For Kenya and Malawi, the figures reflect the standardized cycles used by UIS. The 33 low-income Sub-Saharan African countries in the sample were selected in Bruns et al. 2003 from the group of International Development Association (IDA)-eligible or blend countries in Sub-Saharan Africa. They exclude countries with incomplete education data (Angola, Liberia, and Somalia) and those with very small populations (Cape Verde, the Comoros, and São Tomé and Príncipe). — = not available.
a. "Low-income" countries are eligible for lending from IDA; see appendix A, table A.1.

References

Bruns, B., A. Mingat, and R. Rakotomalala. 2003. *Achieving Universal Primary Education by 2015: A Chance for Every Child.* Washington, DC: World Bank.

DDP (Development Data Platform) (database). World Bank, Washington, DC. http://databank.worldbank.org/ddp/home.do.

EdStats (Education Statistics) (database). World Bank, Washington, DC. http://www.worldbank.org/education/edstats.

Pôle de Dakar UNESCO-BREDA (United Nations Educational, Scientific and Cultural Organization, Regional Office for Education in Africa). 2005. "Education for All in Africa: Paving the Way for Action." Dakar+5 Report, Pôle de Dakar UNESCO-BREDA, Dakar.

———. 2006. "Education for All in Africa: Sub-regional Statistics and Analysis." Dakar+6 Report, Pôle de Dakar UNESCO-BREDA, Dakar.

———. 2007. "Education for All in Africa: Top Priority for Integrated Sector-Wide Policies." Dakar+7 Report, Pôle de Dakar UNESCO-BREDA, Dakar.

UIS (United Nations Educational, Scientific and Cultural Organization, Institute for Statistics) Data Centre (database). UIS, Montreal. http://stats.uis.unesco.org.

APPENDIX C

Social Disparities

Table C.1 Gender Disparities by Level of Education and Sub-Saharan African Country, ca. 1990 and 2008

	Year	Primary			Lower secondary	Upper secondary	Higher
		GER F/M	GIR F/M	PCR F/M	GER F/M	GER F/M	GER F/M
Angola	1990	0.92	0.90	0.83	—	—	0.20
	2008	0.85	—	—	0.86	0.74	0.69
Benin	1990	0.50	0.48	0.47	0.43	0.24	0.15
	2008	0.87	0.92	0.73	0.60	0.52	—
Botswana	1990	1.02	1.02	1.21	1.22	0.90	0.73
	2008	0.98	0.98	1.07	1.07	1.03	1.00
Burkina Faso	1990	0.63	0.64	0.58	0.54	0.32	0.30
	2008	0.87	0.92	0.79	0.78	0.60	0.50
Burundi	1990	0.83	0.86	0.86	0.64	0.44	0.36
	2008	0.95	0.94	0.87	0.73	0.66	0.43
Cameroon	1990	0.86	0.89	0.87	0.77	0.53	—
	2008	0.86	0.87	0.84	0.80	0.79	0.79
Cape Verde	1990	0.94	0.95	—	1.02	0.95	—
	2008	0.94	0.99	1.05	1.09	1.10	1.24
Central African Republic	1990	0.64	0.73	0.53	0.42	0.28	0.15
	2008	0.71	0.76	0.61	0.68	0.60	0.33
Chad	1990	0.45	0.60	0.23	0.21	0.12	0.16
	2008	0.70	0.74	0.54	0.41	0.55	0.15
Comoros	1990	—	—	—	—	—	—
	2008	0.88	0.89	0.95	0.75	0.78	0.77
Congo, Dem. Rep.	1990	0.74	0.83	0.59	0.59	0.33	—
	2008	0.83	1.21	0.69	0.58	0.54	0.35
Congo, Rep.	1990	0.90	0.90	0.80	0.83	0.37	0.21
	2008	0.94	0.92	0.95	0.87	0.75	0.19
Côte d'Ivoire	1990	0.71	0.76	0.59	0.51	0.34	0.28
	2008	0.79	0.85	0.69	0.59	—	0.50
Equatorial Guinea	1990	—	—	—	0.61	0.15	0.14
	2008	0.95	0.96	0.95	0.60	0.45	—
Eritrea	1990	0.96	—	—	0.82	0.75	—
	2008	0.82	0.84	0.80	0.72	0.69	0.32
Ethiopia	1990	0.66	0.64	0.47	0.80	0.66	0.22
	2008	0.89	0.89	0.86	0.73	0.69	0.31
Gabon	1990	0.99	1.00	1.11	1.03	0.85	0.44
	2008	0.99	1.00	1.04	—	—	—

(table continues on next page)

Table C.1 Gender Disparities by Level of Education and Sub-Saharan African Country, ca. 1990 and 2008 *(continued)*

		Primary		Lower secondary		Upper secondary	Higher
	Year	GER F/M	GIR F/M	PCR F/M	GER F/M	GER F/M	GER F/M
Gambia, The	1990	0.69	0.74	0.60	0.56	0.43	0.56
	2008	1.06	1.06	1.09	0.97	0.90	0.23
Ghana	1990	0.84	0.89	0.76	0.67	0.49	0.30
	2008	0.99	1.02	0.95	0.92	0.79	0.54
Guinea	1990	0.48	0.49	0.36	0.36	0.20	0.07
	2008	0.85	0.90	0.75	0.62	0.49	0.34
Guinea-Bissau	1990	0.54	—	0.57	0.58	0.23	0.06
	2008	0.67	—	—	—	—	—
Kenya	1990	0.95	0.95	0.83	0.79	0.51	0.42
	2008	0.98	0.96	0.98	0.96	0.90	0.70
Lesotho	1990	1.12	1.02	1.71	1.54	1.21	1.30
	2008	0.99	0.94	1.36	1.37	1.17	1.19
Liberia	1990	—	—	—	—	—	—
	2008	0.90	0.92	0.84	0.97	0.69	—
Madagascar	1990	0.97	1.03	1.03	1.01	0.94	0.82
	2008	0.97	0.98	1.00	0.96	0.89	0.89
Malawi	1990	0.84	0.92	0.78	0.51	—	0.34
	2008	1.03	1.05	1.02	0.89	0.77	0.51
Mali	1990	0.59	0.59	0.64	0.59	0.36	0.15
	2008	0.83	0.87	0.74	0.67	0.58	0.45
Mauritania	1990	0.74	0.75	0.65	0.50	0.46	0.17
	2008	1.07	1.06	1.04	0.89	0.88	0.36
Mauritius	1990	1.00	1.00	0.99	1.05	0.98	0.73
	2008	0.99	1.02	1.01	1.03	0.97	1.17
Mozambique	1990	0.75	0.81	0.65	0.63	0.40	0.33
	2008	0.88	0.94	0.78	0.76	0.70	0.49
Namibia	1990	1.01	1.00	1.21	—	—	1.75
	2008	0.99	1.00	1.13	1.16	1.20	1.32
Niger	1990	0.57	0.61	0.57	0.48	0.25	0.20
	2008	0.78	0.87	0.72	0.63	0.49	0.34
Nigeria	1990	0.79	0.79	0.76	0.76	0.79	0.32
	2008	0.88	0.84	0.81	0.79	0.73	0.70
Rwanda	1990	0.99	0.98	1.00	0.60	0.46	0.23
	2008	1.01	0.97	1.07	0.95	0.84	0.62
São Tomé and Príncipe	1990	—	—	—	0.95	0.82	—
	2008	0.98	1.03	1.05	1.11	0.86	0.93
Senegal	1990	0.74	0.80	0.65	0.56	0.49	—
	2008	1.02	1.05	0.98	0.84	0.67	0.54
Seychelles	1990	—	—	—	0.99	0.94	—
	2008	0.99	0.94	1.06	1.09	1.14	—
Sierra Leone	1990	0.68	—	—	0.59	0.47	0.32
	2008	0.88	0.91	0.74	0.66	0.70	0.40
Somalia	1990	0.50	—	—	—	—	—
	2008	—	—	—	—	0.45	—
South Africa	1990	0.99	0.93	1.12	1.17	1.20	0.83
	2008	0.96	0.93	1.00	0.99	1.08	1.21
Sudan	1990	0.76	0.76	0.81	0.77	0.87	0.88
	2008	0.88	0.89	0.88	0.91	0.90	1.25

(table continues on next page)

Table C.1 Gender Disparities by Level of Education and Sub-Saharan African Country, ca. 1990 and 2008 *(continued)*

		Primary		Lower secondary		Upper secondary	Higher
	Year	GER F/M	GIR F/M	PCR F/M	GER F/M	GER F/M	GER F/M
Swaziland	1990	0.98	0.99	1.09	1.01	0.88	0.76
	2004	0.93	0.96	0.93	0.88	0.94	0.97
Tanzania	1990	0.99	0.99	1.03	0.76	0.29	0.19
	2008	0.99	0.99	0.96	—	—	0.48
Togo	1990	0.65	0.76	0.47	0.37	0.19	0.16
	2008	0.86	0.94	0.72	0.57	0.42	—
Uganda	1990	0.69	0.86	0.61	0.62	0.40	0.38
	2008	1.01	1.01	0.97	0.87	0.75	0.80
Zambia	1990	0.91	0.99	0.76	0.68	0.53	0.38
	2008	0.98	1.04	0.89	0.88	0.78	—
Zimbabwe	1990	0.99	1.00	0.94	0.99	0.75	0.50
	2008	0.99	0.97	0.96	0.99	0.87	0.63
Simple average	**1990**	**0.80**	**0.84**	**0.78**	**0.73**	**0.56**	**0.42**
Sub-Saharan Africa	**2008**	**0.92**	**0.95**	**0.91**	**0.85**	**0.78**	**0.65**

Sources: Most data are from UNESCO Institue for Statistics Data Centre for the years indicated. For a few countries, data are from Pôle de Dakar UNESCO-BREDA 2007.
Note: GER = gross enrollment rate, GIR = gross intake rate, PCR = primary completion rate, — = not available.

References

Pôle de Dakar UNESCO-BREDA (United Nations Educational, Scientific and Cultural Organization, Regional Office for Education in Africa). 2007. "Education for All in Africa: Top Priority for Integrated Sector-Wide Policies." Dakar+7 Report, Pôle de Dakar UNESCO-BREDA, Dakar.

UIS (United Nations Educational, Scientific and Cultural Organization, Institute for Statistics) Data Centre (database). UIS, Montreal. http://stats.uis.unesco.org.

APPENDIX D

Out-of-School Children

Table D.1 Number and Proportion of Out-of-School Children in 33 Low-Income Sub-Saharan African Countries, 2003

	Out of school in cohort entering grade one (% of population)	Out of school in cohort entering grade six (% of population)	Primary school-age cohort		
			Population (million)	Out of school	
				(million)	(% of population)
Benin	9	58	1.2	0.40	34
Burkina Faso	42	71	2.2	1.20	57
Burundi	26	67	1.3	0.60	47
Cameroon	8	34	2.7	0.60	21
Central African Rep.	37	79	0.6	0.40	58
Chad	20	64	1.5	0.60	42
Congo, Dem. Rep.	24	59	10.1	4.20	42
Congo, Rep.	29	46	0.6	0.20	38
Côte d'Ivoire	27	50	2.5	1.00	39
Eritrea	40	64	0.8	0.40	52
Ethiopia	18	69	12.0	5.20	44
Gambia, The	19	39	0.2	0.07	29
Ghana	19	36	3.2	0.90	28
Guinea	14	53	1.3	0.40	34
Guinea-Bissau	7	69	0.2	0.08	38
Kenya	8	24	5.1	0.80	16
Lesotho	8	28	0.4	0.06	18
Madagascar	10	60	2.8	1.00	35
Malawi	10	37	2.0	0.50	24
Mali	40	63	2.2	1.10	52
Mauritania	10	50	0.5	0.10	30
Mozambique	4	49	2.9	0.80	27
Niger	36	65	2.2	1.10	51
Nigeria	21	40	23.3	7.10	31
Rwanda	14	63	1.4	0.60	39
Senegal	25	56	1.8	0.70	41
Sierra Leone	37	65	0.9	0.40	51
Sudan	28	45	4.6	1.70	37
Tanzania	5	42	6.2	1.50	24
Togo	14	36	0.9	0.20	25

(table continues on next page)

Table D.1 Number and Proportion of Out-of-School Children in 33 Low-Income Sub-Saharan African Countries, 2003 *(continued)*

	Out of school in cohort entering grade one (% of population)	Out of school in cohort entering grade six (% of population)	Primary school-age cohort		
			Population (million)	Out of school	
				(million)	(% of population)
Uganda	7	27	4.4	0.80	17
Zambia	13	32	1.8	0.40	23
Zimbabwe	3	12	2.2	0.20	8
Aggregate/population-weighted average	18.5	47.9	105.8	35.2	33.3

Sources: Authors' calculation based on population data from UN 2007; GIR and PCR data from UNESCO Institute for Statistics Data Centre; and access rates from household surveys, as reported in Country Status Reports (listed in Overview chapter references).
Note: GIR = gross intake rate, PCR = primary completion rate. "Low-income" countries in this table (from the sample selected in Bruns, Mingat, and Rakotomalala 2003) comprise all the International Development Agency (IDA)-eligible or blend countries in Sub-Saharan Africa, except those with very small populations (Cape Verde, Comoros, São Tomé and Príncipe) or incomplete data (Angola, Liberia and Somalia); see appendix A, table A.1.

Table D.2 Characteristics of Out-of-School Children in 30 Low-Income Sub-Saharan African Countries, ca. 2003

	Out-of-school children by gender (%)		Out-of-school children by location (%)		Out-of-school children by wealth quintile (%)				
	Female	Male	Rural	Urban	Poorest 20%	Q2	Q3	Q4	Richest 20%
Benin	59.2	40.5	75.9	24.1	33.6	25.6	19.0	12.4	0.1
Burkina Faso	51.4	48.6	95.7	4.3	25.0	23.0	29.3	16.6	6.1
Burundi	53.2	46.8	95.6	4.4	20.1	21.9	20.6	23.5	13.9
Cameroon	59.1	40.9	82.0	18.0	37.0	36.0	13.2	9.6	4.2
Central African Republic	53.7	46.3	77.1	22.9	27.8	24.0	24.1	13.3	10.7
Chad	58.1	41.9	82.4	17.6	35.3	19.8	14.2	16.4	14.3
Congo, Dem. Rep.	58.6	41.4	84.1	15.9	25.9	28.1	24.1	16.2	5.7
Côte d'Ivoire	55.1	44.9	62.7	37.3	30.8	22.9	23.2	16.2	7.0
Ethiopia	51.8	48.2	96.5	3.5	29.9	23.4	19.9	18.8	7.9
Gambia, The	53.2	46.8	78.5	21.5	33.0	20.6	22.9	16.1	5.7
Ghana	45.8	54.2	78.0	22.0	45.2	25.1	15.3	10.8	3.6
Guinea	56.3	43.7	91.4	8.6	33.5	25.6	19.2	14.8	6.9
Guinea-Bissau	53.2	46.8	81.2	18.8	23.6	24.2	24.6	19.9	7.7
Kenya	44.0	56.0	91.9	8.1	60.2	14.7	10.9	8.5	5.9
Lesotho	39.9	60.1	88.4	11.6	35.0	27.9	17.9	11.4	7.7
Madagascar	47.2	52.8	92.5	7.5	30.3	38.4	17.8	13.0	0.5
Malawi	47.7	52.3	95.4	4.6	34.0	23.5	13.5	21.7	7.4
Mali	55.8	44.2	88.2	11.8	25.9	27.2	21.9	18.6	6.4
Mozambique	56.7	43.3	84.0	16.0	28.4	30.3	24.7	13.0	3.6
Niger	57.4	42.6	93.7	6.3	24.7	20.6	24.5	21.2	9.0
Nigeria	62.2	37.8	78.8	21.2	37.3	32.0	21.0	7.5	2.1

(table continues on next page)

Table D.2 Characteristics of Out-of-School Children in 30 Low-Income Sub-Saharan African Countries, ca. 2003 *(continued)*

	Out-of-school children by gender (%)		Out-of-school children by location (%)		Out-of-school children by wealth quintile (%)				
	Female	Male	Rural	Urban	Poorest 20%	Q2	Q3	Q4	Richest 20%
Rwanda	48.0	51.7	92.8	7.2	16.3	29.0	21.6	22.5	10.4
Senegal	53.6	46.4	78.5	21.5	25.7	27.1	25.2	13.6	8.4
Sierra Leone	49.1	50.8	82.8	17.2	28.0	23.2	19.2	19.5	10.1
Sudan	50.1	49.9	68.5	31.5	39.4	26.8	19.1	10.6	4.2
Tanzania	49.4	50.6	86.5	13.5	23.1	26.6	30.2	14.8	5.3
Togo	58.5	41.5	82.4	17.6	34.9	27.0	19.2	12.2	6.8
Uganda	46.3	53.7	91.7	8.3	35.2	29.0	17.4	10.6	7.8
Zambia	50.6	49.4	80.1	19.9	35.1	24.4	19.7	15.0	5.8
Zimbabwe	48.3	51.7	88.4	11.6	39.6	14.4	22.5	17.3	6.3
Aggregate	53.2	46.8	84.0	16.0	29.9	25.3	21.9	15.6	7.3

Source: Authors' analysis of household survey data for 30 Sub-Saharan African countries; see appendix J, table J.1.
Note: The table is based on school-age children not enrolled in school. Q = quintile.

Table D.3 Extent of Social Disparities between Children In and Out of School in 30 Sub-Saharan African Countries, ca. 2003

	Index of disparity			
	Location (rural)	Wealth (Q1+2)[a]	Gender (female)	Total[b]
Benin	1.15	1.48	1.18	2.02
Burkina Faso	1.13	1.20	1.03	1.39
Burundi	1.02	1.05	1.06	1.14
Cameroon	1.26	1.83	1.18	2.72
Central African Republic	1.27	1.30	1.07	1.77
Chad	1.09	1.38	1.16	1.75
Congo, Dem. Rep.	1.20	1.35	1.17	1.89
Côte d'Ivoire	1.26	1.34	1.10	1.86
Ethiopia	1.10	1.33	1.04	1.52
Gambia, The	1.21	1.34	1.06	1.72
Ghana	1.26	1.76	0.92	2.02
Guinea	1.29	1.48	1.13	2.15
Guinea-Bissau	1.31	1.20	1.06	1.67
Kenya	1.08	1.87	0.88	1.77
Lesotho	1.09	1.57	0.80	1.36
Madagascar	1.15	1.72	0.94	1.86
Malawi	1.09	1.44	0.95	1.50
Mali	1.14	1.33	1.12	1.69
Mozambique	1.27	1.47	1.13	2.11
Niger	1.12	1.13	1.15	1.46
Nigeria	1.19	1.73	1.24	2.57
Rwanda	1.06	1.13	0.96	1.15
Senegal	1.25	1.32	1.07	1.76
Sierra Leone	1.15	1.28	0.98	1.45
Sudan	1.44	1.65	1.00	2.39
Tanzania	1.08	1.24	0.99	1.32

(table continues on next page)

Table D.3 Extent of Social Disparities between Children In and Out of School in 30 Sub-Saharan African Countries, ca. 2003 *(continued)*

	Index of disparity			
	Location (rural)	Wealth (Q1+2)[a]	Gender(female)	Total[b]
Togo	1.20	1.55	1.17	2.17
Uganda	1.03	1.61	0.93	1.53
Zambia	1.26	1.49	1.01	1.90
Zimbabwe	1.15	1.35	0.97	1.50
Aggregate 30 countries	1.19	1.38	1.06	1.75

☐ = bottom 33 percent of the indicator (column heading)
☐ = middle 33 percent
■ = top 33 percent.

Source: Authors' analysis of household survey data for 30 countries; see appendix J, table J.1.
Note: The table is constructed by comparing school-age children in and out of school. Q = quintile.
a. Q1 + 2 = poorest 40 percent of households.
b. The indicator for the overall level of disparities is computed as the product of the three others.

References

Bruns, B., A. Mingat, and R. Rakotomalala. 2003. *Achieving Universal Primary Education by 2015: A Chance for Every Child.* Washington, DC: World Bank.

UIS (United Nations Educational, Scientific and Cultural Organization, Institute for Statistics) Data Centre (database). UIS, Montreal. http://stats.uis.unesco.org.

UN (United Nations). 2007. *Demographic Yearbook.* New York: UN.

APPENDIX E

Education Expenditure

Table E.1 Public Spending (Capital and Recurrent) on Education in Sub-Saharan African Countries, ca. 2005

	Public spending on education (% of GDP)	Total public spending (% of GDP)	Public spending on education (% of total public spending)
Low-income countries[a]			
Angola	2.4	—	—
Benin	4.4	26	17
Burkina Faso	4.2	26	16
Burundi	5.1	29	18
Cameroon	3.1	19	16
Cape Verde	6.8	27	25
Central African Republic	1.4	—	—
Chad	1.9	19	10
Comoros	3.8	16	24
Congo, Rep.	1.9	23	8
Côte d'Ivoire	4.6	—	—
Eritrea	5.3	—	—
Ethiopia	6.0	34	18
Gambia, The	2.8	31	9
Ghana	5.4	—	—
Guinea	1.6	—	—
Kenya	7.3	41	18
Lesotho	13.8	46	30
Madagascar	3.2	13	25
Malawi	5.8	—	—
Mali	4.1	28	15
Mauritania	2.3	28	8
Mozambique	4.3	19	23
Niger	3.4	19	18
Rwanda	3.8	31	12
Senegal	5.4	29	19
Sierra Leone	3.8	—	—
Togo	2.6	19	14
Uganda	5.2	29	18
Zambia	2.8	19	15
Low-income average	4.3	25	17

(table continues on next page)

Table E.1 Public Spending (Capital and Recurrent) on Education in Sub-Saharan African Countries, ca. 2005 *(continued)*

	Public spending on education (% of GDP)	Total public spending (% of GDP)	Public spending on education (% of total public spending)
Middle-income countries[b]			
Botswana	9.7	45	22
Equatorial Guinea	0.6	15	4
Mauritius	4.4	31	14
Namibia	6.9	35	20
South Africa	5.3	30	18
Swaziland	7.0	35	20
Middle-income average	5.7	35	16

Source: Education spending data are from UNESCO Institute for Statistics Data Centre. Total public spending (middle column) is computed from the other two columns.
Note: For lack of expenditure data, table does not include Congo, Dem. Rep., Gabon, Guinea-Bissau, Liberia, Nigeria, São Tomé and Príncipe, Seychelles, Somalia, Sudan, Tanzania, and Zimbabwe. GDP = gross domestic product, — = not available.
a. "Low-income" countries are eligible for lending from International Development Agency (IDA); see appendix A, table A.1.
b. "Middle-income" countries are eligible for lending from International Bank for Reconstruction and Development (IBRD); see appendix A, table A.1.

Table E.2 Public Recurrent Spending per Student per Year in Sub-Saharan African Countries, by Education Level, ca. 2003

	Primary (% of GDP per capita)	Lower secondary (% of GDP per capita)	Upper secondary (% of GDP per capita)	Secondary (all) (% of GDP per capita)	Higher education	
					(% of GDP per capita)	(2005 US$ current prices)[a]
Low-income countries[b]						
Angola	7.8	—	—	—	65.5	1,348
Benin	10.8	15.2	41.2	19.3	148.9	756
Burkina Faso	19.2	39.0	84.0	47.0	550.0	2,151
Burundi	15.1	41.6	135.5	60.2	718.7	762
Cameroon	7.1	31.6	37.1	33.1	83.5	863
Cape Verde	18.0	—	—	21.7	284.9	5,527
Central African Republic	7.3	15.2	24.7	17.0	165.4	561
Chad	7.1	26.7	35.8	29.2	412.0	2,311
Comoros	12.2	—	—	30.3	129.9	838
Congo, Dem. Rep.	2.8	—	—	14.1	56.7	70
Congo, Rep.	8.1	12.7	36.8	17.0	220.8	2,811
Côte d'Ivoire	17.5	35.0	72.0	48.0	137.1	1,234
Eritrea	11.8	—	—	35.7	445.1	979
Ethiopia	12.0	—	—	32.0	1,082.0	1,699
Gambia, The	13.2	—	—	19.0	229.7	698
Ghana	17.6	—	—	43.5	372.0	1,804
Guinea	9.0	13.4	17.6	14.0	231.0	809

(table continues on next page)

Table E.2 Public Recurrent Spending per Student per Year in Sub-Saharan African Countries, by Education Level, ca. 2003 *(continued)*

	Primary (% of GDP per capita)	Lower secondary (% of GDP per capita)	Upper secondary (% of GDP per capita)	Secondary (all) (% of GDP per capita)	Higher education (% of GDP per capita)	Higher education (2005 US$ current prices)[a]
Guinea-Bissau	7.2	—	—	13.8	121.1	230
Kenya	9.0	—	—	22.0	266.1	1,456
Lesotho	18.0	—	—	43.0	803	6,488
Madagascar	8.3	26.7	64.0	35.9	189.4	513
Malawi	11.0	—	—	77.0	1,760.0	2,834
Mali	11.1	26.5	117.1	40.3	192.9	756
Mauritania	12.0	—	—	49.0	120.0	724
Mozambique	10.2	21.6	72.0	32.4	791.1	2,650
Niger	20.0	49.0	157.0	61.0	515.0	1,257
Nigeria	14.4	20.1	25.0	21.0	111.0	835
Rwanda	8.1	47.4	64.3	58.6	786.9	1,873
Senegal	13.9	14.7	70.3	19.5	257.0	1,817
Sierra Leone	9.2	26.8	29.1	28.0	278.3	601
Sudan	7.9	—	—	17.8	110.0	836
Tanzania	12.5	—	—	43.6	530.0	1,675
Togo	10.0	14.0	31.0	17.0	197.0	705
Uganda	9.8	—	—	34.9	194.1	588
Zambia	7.1	—	—	19.3	163.8	1,021
Zimbabwe	16.2	—	—	24.2	201.3	521
Simple average low-income	11.5	26.5	61.9	32.6	358.9	1,461
Middle-income countries[c]						
Botswana	6.1	—	—	5.7	90.5	5,291
Gabon	4.7	—	—	13.9	52.4	3,050
Mauritius	9.0	—	—	14.0	48.7	2,464
Namibia	21.0	—	—	25.2	93.5	2,820
Seychelles	14.5	—	—	17.7	—	—
South Africa	14.3	—	—	17.7	53.2	2,718
Swaziland	11.2	—	—	28.9	245.9	5,936
Simple average middle-income	11.5		33.4[a]	17.6	97.4	3,713
Simple average Sub-Saharan Africa	11.5	24.4[a]	57.1[a]	30.1	321.6	1,783

Sources: Data are from Country Status Reports (listed in Overview chapter references) whenever unit costs are broken down by lower and upper secondary. For remaining countries, data are from UNESCO Institute for Statistics Data Centre or Pôle de Dakar UNESCO-BREDA 2005.
Note: For lack of expenditure data, table omits Liberia, São Tomé and Príncipe, and Somalia. — = not available.
a. Estimated.
b. "Low-income" countries are eligible for lending from International Development Agency (IDA); see appendix A, table A.1.
c. "Middle-income" countries are eligible for lending from International Bank for Reconstruction and Development (IBRD); see appendix A, table A.1.

Figure E.1 Ranking of Sub-Saharan African Countries by Public Recurrent Spending Per Student in Secondary and Higher Education, ca. 2003

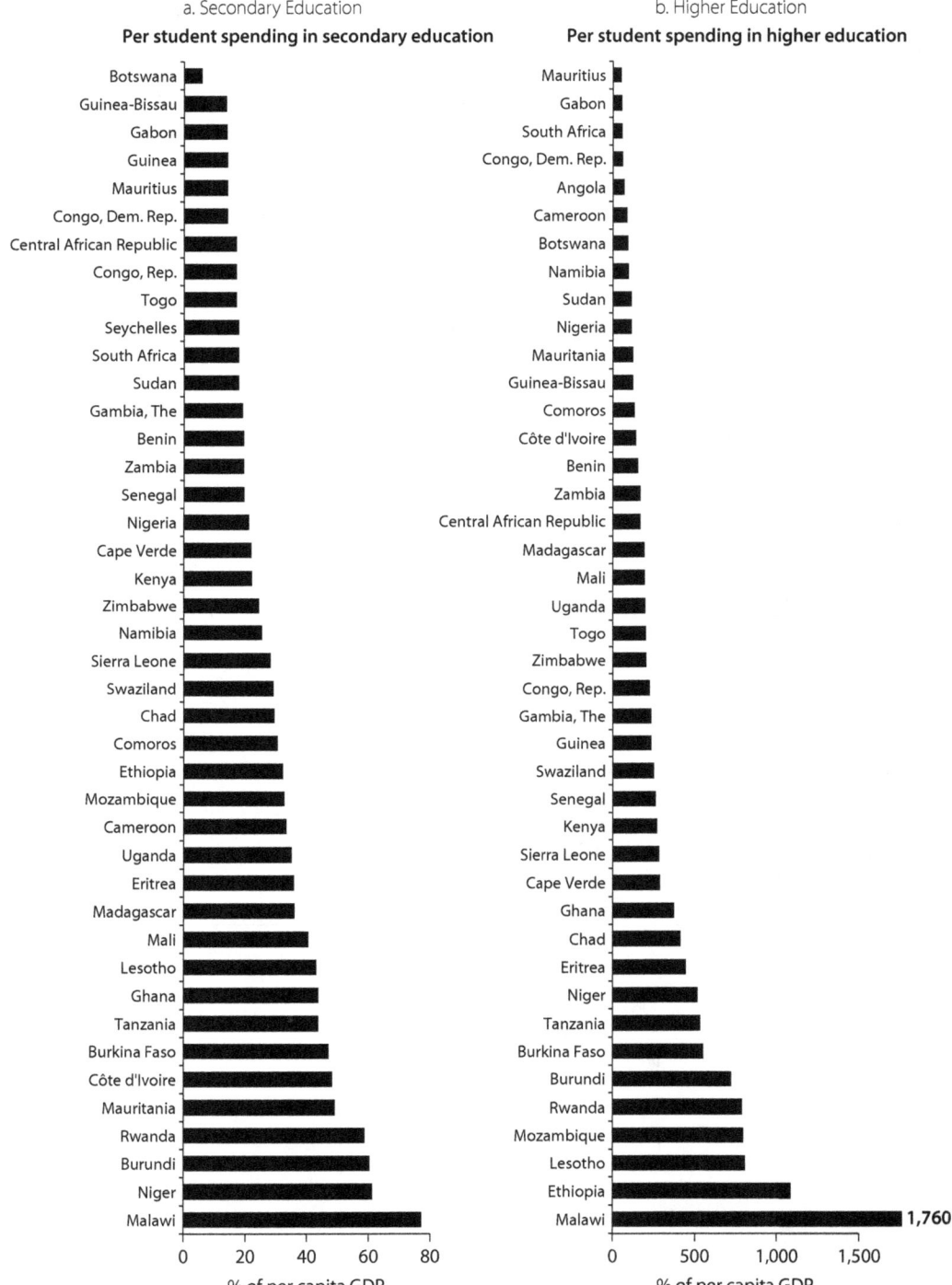

Sources: Data are from Country Status Reports (listed in Overview chapter references), UNESCO Institute for Statistics Data Centre, or Pôle de Dakar UNESCO-BREDA 2007.
Note: Equatorial Guinea, Liberia, São Tomé and Príncipe, and Somalia are omitted for lack of data. GDP = gross domestic product.

Figure E.2 Lorenz Curve and Calculation of Equity Indicators in Distribution of Public Education Spending in Burundi

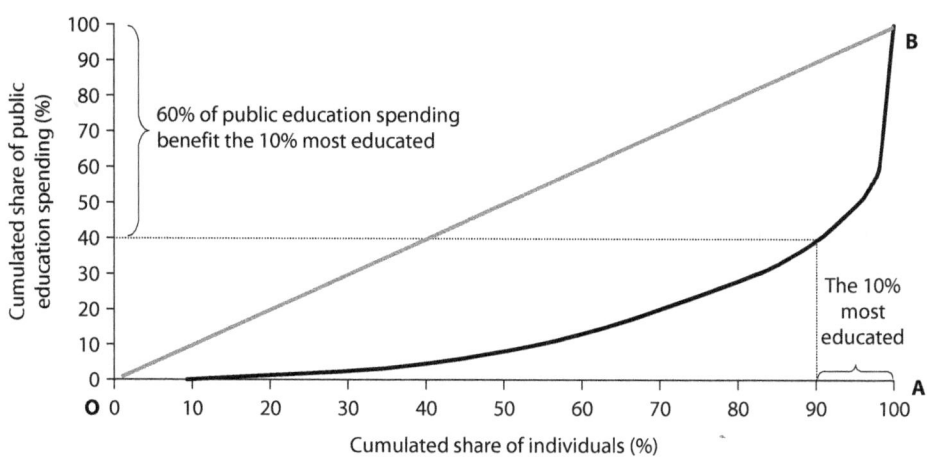

Source: Reproduced from World Bank 2007.
Note: (1) The data needed to draw up the Lorenz curve are the distribution of a cohort according to highest educational attainment (share of a cohort who never enroll, reach grade 1, grade 2, grade 3,..., grade 12, higher education) and data on per-student spending at each level of education. (2) The share of education spending received by the 10 percent most educated can be derived graphically from the Lorenz curve as shown. (3) The Gini coefficient can be calculated as the ratio between (a) the area between the diagonal OB and the Lorenz curve, and (b) the area of the triangle OAB.

References

Bruns, B., A. Mingat, and R. Rakotomalala.. 2003. *Achieving Universal Primary Education by 2015: A Chance for Every Child.* Washington, DC: World Bank.

Pôle de Dakar UNESCO-BREDA (United Nations Educational, Scientific and Cultural Organization, Regional Office for Education in Africa). 2005. "Education for All in Africa: Paving the Way for Action." Dakar+5 Report, Pôle de Dakar UNESCO-BREDA, Dakar.

———. 2007. "Education for All in Africa: Top Priority for Integrated Sector-Wide Policies." Dakar+7 Report, Pôle de Dakar UNESCO-BREDA, Dakar.

UIS (United Nations Educational, Scientific and Cultural Organization, Institute for Statistics) Data Centre (database). 2010. UIS, Montreal. http://stats.uis.unesco.org.

World Bank. 2007. *Le système éducatif Burundais: Diagnostic et perspectives pour une nouvelle politique éducative dans le contexte de l'éducation primaire gratuite pour tous.* Africa Human Development Series. World Bank Working Paper 109, World Bank, Washington, DC.

APPENDIX F

Gross Enrollment Rate (GER) and Its Underlying Components

Consider the following set of accounting identities for primary education:

$$\frac{PEP}{GDP} = \frac{PEP}{TPOP} \cdot \frac{TPOP}{GDP} \tag{F.1}$$

$$= \frac{PEP}{E} = \frac{E}{SAPOP} \cdot \frac{SAPOP}{TPOP} \cdot \frac{TPOP}{GDP} \tag{F.2}$$

$$= US \cdot GER \cdot DR \cdot \frac{1}{PCGDP} \tag{F.3}$$

$$= \frac{US}{PCGDP} \cdot GER \cdot DR \tag{F.4}$$

where PEP refers to recurrent public expenditure on primary education;
GDP, to gross domestic product;
TPOP, to total population;
E, to total enrollments in primary education;
SAPOP, to the school-age population;
US, to spending per primary pupil;
GER, to the primary gross enrollment ratio;
DR, to the ratio of the school-age population to the total population; and
PCGDP, to per capita GDP.

Rearranging the terms in the first (F.1) and last (F.4) equations, and renaming US/PCGDP as USR (to stand for unit spending relative to per capita GDP), we obtain an expression that relates the GER to its underlying components, as follows:

$$GER = \frac{PEP}{GDP} \cdot \frac{1}{USR} \cdot \frac{1}{DR} \tag{F.5}$$

Equation (F.5) above makes the relatively obvious statement that the GER would be higher, the larger the volume of recurrent public spending on primary education relative to GDP, the smaller the spending per student relative to GDP, and the smaller the share of the school-age population relative to the total population.

The foregoing disaggregation can be further developed by decomposing the unit spending. In particular, US and USR can be expressed as follows:

$$\text{US} = \frac{\text{ATS}}{\text{PTR}} \cdot (1+\alpha) \tag{F.6}$$

$$\text{USR} = \frac{\text{US}}{\text{PCGDP}} = \frac{\text{ATS}}{\text{PCGDP}} \cdot \frac{1}{\text{PTR}} \cdot (1+\alpha) \tag{F.7}$$

$$= \text{ATSR} \cdot \frac{1}{\text{PTR}} \cdot (1+\alpha) \tag{F.8}$$

where ATS and ATSR refer to average teacher salaries expressed in absolute terms and relative to per capita GDP;
PTR, to the ratio of pupils to teachers in primary education; and
α, to all expenditure other than teacher salaries as a proportion of the teacher salary bill.

Plugging this expression for USR into the earlier equation for the GER, we obtain another formulation of the relationship between the GER and its underlying components, as follows:

$$\text{GER} = \frac{\text{PEP}}{\text{GDP}} \cdot \frac{1}{1+\alpha} \cdot \frac{1}{\text{ATSR}} \cdot \text{PTR} \cdot \frac{1}{\text{DR}} \tag{F.9}$$

APPENDIX G

Student Learning

Table G.1 PASEC and SACMEQ Scores and Their Transformation to the MLA Scale in Sub-Saharan African Countries, 1996–2009

	Original scores			Step 1[a]		Step 2[b]	
	MLA	PASEC	SACMEQ	PASEC standardized	SACMEQ standardized	PASEC on MLA scale	SACMEQ on MLA scale
Low-income countries[c]							
Benin	n.a.	30.4	n.a.	41.1	n.a.	38.0	n.a.
Burkina Faso	n.a.	36.0	n.a.	47.3	n.a.	43.7	n.a.
Burundi	48.7	n.a.	n.a.	n.a.	n.a.	n.a.	n.a.
Cameroon	n.a.	46.0	n.a.	58.4	n.a.	54.0	n.a.
Chad	n.a.	31.0	n.a.	41.7	n.a.	38.6	n.a.
Congo, Rep.	n.a.	34.5	n.a.	45.7	n.a.	42.2	n.a.
Côte d'Ivoire	n.a.	46.1	n.a.	58.8	n.a.	54.1	n.a.
Gambia, The	40.4	n.a.	n.a.	n.a.	n.a.	n.a.	n.a.
Guinea	n.a.	40.1	n.a.	51.9	n.a.	48.0	n.a.
Kenya	n.a.	n.a.	555	n.a.	61.2	n.a.	62.8
Lesotho	n.a.	n.a.	449	n.a.	38.8	n.a.	39.8
Madagascar	49.2	41.3	n.a.	53.3	n.a.	49.2	n.a.
Malawi	39.0	n.a.	431	n.a.	34.9	n.a.	35.8
Mali	47.7	35.0	n.a.	46.2	n.a.	42.7	n.a.
Mauritania	n.a.	19.8	n.a.	29.3	n.a.	27.1	n.a.
Mozambique	n.a.	n.a.	523	n.a.	n.a.	n.a.	56.0
Niger	39.2	29.5	n.a.	40.1	n.a.	37.1	n.a.
Nigeria	28.6	n.a.	n.a.	n.a.	n.a.	n.a.	n.a.
Senegal	43.3	38.4	n.a.	50.0	n.a.	46.2	n.a.
Tanzania	n.a.	n.a.	534	n.a.	56.8	n.a.	58.3
Togo	n.a.	44.0	n.a.	56.2	n.a.	52.0	n.a.
Uganda	53.7	n.a.	494	n.a.	48.4	n.a.	49.7
Zambia	39.5	n.a.	438	n.a.	36.4	n.a.	37.3
Zimbabwe	n.a.	n.a.	505	n.a.	50.6	n.a.	51.9
Average low-income	42.9	36.3	491	47.7	46.7	44.1	49.0
Middle-income countries[d]							
Botswana	49.5	n.a.	517	n.a.	53.2	n.a.	54.6
Gabon	n.a.	48.3	n.a.	60.9	n.a.	56.3	n.a.
Mauritius	59.8	55.7	561	69.2	62.4	64.0	64.1
Namibia	n.a.	n.a.	440	n.a.	36.8	n.a.	37.8
Seychelles	n.a.	n.a.	568	n.a.	64.1	n.a.	65.7

(table continues on next page)

Table G.1 PASEC and SACMEQ Scores and Their Transformation to the MLA Scale in Sub-Saharan African Countries, 1996–2009 (continued)

	Original scores			Step 1[a]		Step 2[b]	
	MLA	PASEC	SACMEQ	PASEC standardized	SACMEQ standardized	PASEC on MLA scale	SACMEQ on MLA scale
South Africa	n.a.	n.a.	489	n.a.	47.3	n.a.	48.5
Swaziland	n.a.	n.a.	523	n.a.	54.5	n.a.	55.9
Avg. middle-income	54.7	52.0	516	65.1	53.1	60.2	54.4
Average Sub-Saharan Africa	44.9	38.4	502	50	50	46.2	51.3

Shaded cells mark countries that have more than one test score.

Source: Authors' construction based on MLA, PASEC, and SACMEQ scores in literacy and numeracy.

Note: MLA tests students in grade four, PASEC in grade five, and SACMEQ in grade six. MLA also tests in life skills, but those scores are not used here. All scores are from after 1995. The following countries use none of the three student tests shown and thus are excluded from the table: Congo, Dem. Rep., Guinea-Bissau, Liberia, São Tomé and Príncipe, Seychelles, Somalia, Sudan, and Tanzania. PASEC = Program for the Analysis of Education Systems of CONFEMEN, CONFEMEN = Conference of Ministers of Education of French-Speaking Countries, SACMEQ = Southern Africa Consortium for Monitoring Educational Quality, MLA = Measurement of Learning Achievement, n.a. = not applicable (test not used in a particular country).

a. In step 1, PASEC and SACMEQ scores are standardized to a distribution with mean 50 and a standard deviation of 10 (which is approximately similar to the distribution of MLA scores).

b. In step 2, the standardized PASEC scores are multiplied with a constant that is calibrated so that the mean PASEC score becomes the same as the MLA score in the five countries that have both PASEC and MLA (Madagascar, Mali, Niger, Mauritius, and Senegal). Similarly, the adjustment of the standardized SACMEQ scores in step 2 is based on the five countries that have both SACMEQ and MLA (Botswana, Malawi, Mauritius, Uganda, and Zambia).

c. "Low-income" countries are eligible for lending from International Development Agency (IDA); see appendix A, table A.1.

d. "Middle-income" countries are eligible for lending from International Bank for Reconstruction and Development (IBRD); see appendix A, table A.1.

APPENDIX H

Social Outcomes

On Including Wealth in Regressions

The level of income or wealth can clearly influence the degree to which pregnant women and children under five have access to health care and other services. Thus, ideally we would include some measure of wealth or income among the explanatory variables in the regressions. In fact, if we leave out an important variable, our coefficient estimates are likely to be biased because the other variables will capture some of the effect of the omitted variable. Schooling and income or wealth are closely correlated; therefore, if wealth were omitted, the coefficient to schooling would capture some of the effect of wealth (as a result, the coefficient to schooling would be upward-biased), and we would overestimate the pure impact of education.

On the other hand, if we include both education and wealth as explanatory variables in the regressions, the high correlation between the two will cause the coefficients to be unreliable (high correlation, also called multicollinearity, causes higher variance of the coefficient estimates).

Thus, we are presented with a classical problem when two explanatory variables are so closely correlated: the coefficients will be biased if we include both, and unreliable if we omit one of them. To solve this, the regressions were carried out twice—with and without the wealth variable. The results of both specifications are shown in the tables below. Because the difference in the coefficient estimates in most cases turned out to be very small, however, the charts presented in chapter 5 show only one of the specifications: in this case, we based the charts on the *without wealth* regressions. (See sections on multicollinearity and omitted variable bias in an econometrics textbook, such as Verbeek 2008.)

Reference

Verbeek, M. 2008. *A Guide to Modern Econometrics*, 3rd ed. New York: John Wiley and Sons.

Table H.1 Education and Risk of Being Poor in Sub-Saharan African Countries, without Wealth as Control

	Highest grade attained (head of household)												
	0	1	2	3	4	5	6	7	8	9	10	11	12
Probability of being in two lowest (40% poorest) income quintiles (%)	45.9	42.9	40.0	37.0	33.9	30.9	28.0	25.2	22.4	19.9	17.4	15.4	13.3

Source: Authors' calculation based on the household survey (DHS/MICS/CWIQ) database; see appendix J, table J.1.

Table H.2 Education and Childbearing Behavior in Sub-Saharan African Countries, with and without Wealth as Control

	Highest grade attained (woman)												
	0	1	2	3	4	5	6	7	8	9	10	11	12
Age at first birth													
Model without wealth	18.3	18.3	18.3	18.3	18.4	18.5	18.5	18.7	18.9	19.1	19.4	19.7	20.1
Model with wealth	18.4	18.3	18.3	18.3	18.3	18.4	18.5	18.7	18.8	19.1	19.3	19.6	19.9
Months between last two consecutive 6 births													
Model without wealth	36.9	37.2	37.6	37.8	38.1	38.4	38.6	38.9	39.2	39.5	39.8	40.0	40.2
Model with wealth	37.1	37.3	37.5	37.7	37.8	38.0	38.2	38.4	38.6	38.8	39.0	39.2	39.4
Number of live births to date													
Model without wealth	3.30	3.25	3.20	3.13	3.07	2.99	2.92	2.81	2.71	2.59	2.47	2.32	2.17
Model with wealth	3.24	3.20	3.17	3.12	3.07	2.99	2.92	2.82	2.73	2.61	2.50	2.36	2.23
Share of women using any contraceptive method frequently (%)													
Model without wealth	27.9	30.8	33.7	36.5	39.3	41.8	44.3	46.5	48.6	50.5	52.3	53.7	55.2
Model with wealth	29.0	31.6	34.2	36.7	39.2	41.3	43.5	45.3	47.0	48.4	49.8	50.7	51.6

Source: Authors' calculation based on the household survey (DHS/MICS/CWIQ) database; see appendix J, table J.1.

Table H.3 Education and Maternal Health in Sub-Saharan African Countries, with and without Wealth as Control

	Highest grade attained (woman)												
	0	1	2	3	4	5	6	7	8	9	10	11	12
Number of prenatal consultations during pregnancy													
Model without wealth	3.17	3.36	3.55	3.73	3.91	4.09	4.27	4.45	4.62	4.79	4.96	5.13	5.30
Model with wealth	3.36	3.51	3.67	3.82	3.96	4.11	4.25	4.39	4.53	4.66	4.79	4.92	5.04
Number of tetanus vaccines during pregnancy													
Model without wealth	1.15	1.21	1.26	1.31	1.36	1.39	1.43	1.46	1.49	1.51	1.53	1.56	1.58
Model with wealth	1.18	1.23	1.27	1.31	1.35	1.39	1.42	1.44	1.47	1.48	1.50	1.51	1.52
Probability of receiving vitamin A during pregnancy (%)													
Model without wealth	12.5	13.1	13.7	14.4	15.0	15.6	16.2	16.7	17.3	17.8	18.3	18.9	19.4
Model with wealth	12.8	13.3	13.8	14.3	14.9	15.4	15.8	16.3	16.7	17.1	17.5	17.8	18.1
Probability of last delivery being assisted by skilled attendant (%)													
Model without wealth	24.9	26.9	29.0	31.2	33.4	35.7	38.0	40.3	42.6	44.7	46.9	48.9	50.9
Model with wealth	27.4	29.1	30.8	32.6	34.4	36.2	37.9	39.7	41.4	43.1	44.8	46.4	47.9

Source: Authors' calculation based on the household survey (DHS/MICS/CWIQ) database; see appendix J, table J.1.

Social Outcomes

Table H.4 Education and Child Health and Development in Sub-Saharan African Countries, with and without Wealth as Control

	Highest grade attained (mother)												
	0	1	2	3	4	5	6	7	8	9	10	11	12
Share of children who sleep under a bed net (%)													
Model without wealth	14.4	15.5	16.5	17.6	18.7	19.9	21.1	22.4	23.7	25.2	26.7	28.4	30.2
Model with wealth	15.2	15.9	16.5	17.3	18.1	19.0	19.9	20.9	21.9	23.0	24.1	25.3	26.6
Share of children fully vaccinated by age 2 (%)													
Model without wealth	24.7	26.0	27.2	28.5	29.7	31.0	32.3	33.5	34.7	36.0	37.2	38.5	39.7
Model with wealth	25.4	26.4	27.4	28.4	29.5	30.5	31.5	32.5	33.5	34.5	35.4	36.4	37.3
Mortality rate of children under 5 (per thousand)													
Model without wealth	159.5	153.1	146.8	140.1	133.4	126.6	119.8	113.1	106.4	99.5	92.5	84.9	77.2
Model with wealth	155.1	149.6	144.1	138.5	132.9	127.2	121.5	115.7	109.8	103.9	98.0	91.9	85.9
Share of children who have ever been enrolled in school by age 9–11 (%)													
Model without wealth	68.0	72.2	76.4	79.6	82.8	85.3	87.7	89.4	91.2	92.5	93.7	94.6	95.5
Model with wealth	72.4	75.5	78.6	81.1	83.5	85.4	87.4	88.9	90.4	91.5	92.7	93.6	94.4

Source: Authors' calculation based on the household survey (DHS/MICS/CWIQ) database; see appendix J, table J.1.

Table H.5 Education, Knowledge about HIV/AIDS, and Use of Information Media in Sub Saharan Africa Countries, with and without Wealth as Control

	Highest grade attained (any adult)												
	0	1	2	3	4	5	6	7	8	9	10	11	12
Index of knowledge about HIV/AIDS													
Model without wealth	4.85	5.18	5.50	5.79	6.07	6.31	6.56	6.76	6.96	7.12	7.28	7.41	7.54
Model with wealth	5.09	5.38	5.68	5.93	6.19	6.40	6.61	6.79	6.96	7.10	7.23	7.33	7.42
Share of adults who read newspapers frequently (%)													
Model without wealth	0.7	1.2	1.7	2.7	3.8	5.9	8.0	11.6	15.3	20.5	25.7	32.0	38.3
Model with wealth	0.9	1.3	1.8	2.8	3.8	5.6	7.5	10.5	13.6	17.9	22.2	27.4	32.6
Share of adults who listen to radio frequently (%)													
Model without wealth	43.3	46.3	49.3	52.2	55.2	58.0	60.8	63.6	66.3	68.8	71.4	73.7	76.0
Model with wealth	47.2	49.5	51.9	54.0	56.2	58.2	60.2	62.0	63.9	65.6	67.3	68.9	70.5
Share of adults who watch TV frequently (%)													
Model without wealth	4.9	5.6	6.4	7.5	8.6	10.4	12.2	15.0	17.7	21.7	25.6	30.6	35.6
Model with wealth	5.3	5.9	6.6	7.5	8.5	9.8	11.1	12.9	14.7	17.3	19.8	23.2	26.5

Source: Authors' calculation based on the household survey (DHS/MICS/CWIQ) database; see appendix J, table J.1.
Note: HIV/AIDS = human immunodeficiency virus/acquired immunodeficiency syndrome.

Table H.6 Relation between Education and Probability of Being in the 40 Percent Poorest, by Country
percentage

	Highest grade attained (mother)						
	0	2	4	6	8	10	12
Angola	57.0	45.6	34.6	25.0	17.4	11.8	7.8
Benin	52.9	41.3	30.7	21.7	14.8	9.8	6.4
Burkina Faso	32.8	25.7	19.7	14.8	10.9	8.0	5.8
Burundi	47.0	38.2	30.0	23.0	17.2	12.6	9.1

(table continues on next page)

Table H.6 Relation between Education and Probability of Being in the 40 Percent Poorest, by Country
percentage (continued)

	Highest grade attained (mother)						
	0	2	4	6	8	10	12
Cameroon	53.9	48.7	41.7	33.3	24.3	16.1	9.6
Central African Republic	53.3	48.2	42.4	36.2	29.9	23.7	18.1
Chad	47.8	38.4	29.8	22.4	16.4	11.8	8.4
Congo, Dem. Rep.	47.9	44.0	40.2	36.4	32.9	29.5	26.4
Côte d'Ivoire	46.5	41.3	36.4	31.7	27.3	23.4	19.9
Equatorial Guinea	58.1	52.1	46.0	40.1	34.5	29.2	24.5
Ethiopia	27.3	22.9	19.0	15.6	12.8	10.4	8.4
Gabon	50.7	52.8	52.3	49.2	43.6	35.6	26.3
Gambia, The	42.4	34.8	27.9	21.9	16.9	12.9	9.7
Ghana	43.1	36.2	29.9	24.2	19.4	15.3	11.9
Guinea	41.6	39.3	37.0	34.9	32.7	30.7	28.7
Guinea-Bissau	38.1	41.4	39.8	33.7	24.1	14.1	6.4
Kenya	49.6	43.3	36.7	30.1	23.7	18.0	13.1
Lesotho	55.5	44.7	34.4	25.4	18.1	12.5	8.5
Malawi	51.7	45.8	40.1	34.6	29.5	24.8	20.7
Mali	35.8	30.5	25.7	21.4	17.7	14.5	11.8
Mozambique	52.3	43.8	33.8	23.5	14.6	8.0	3.9
Namibia	35.8	31.5	27.4	23.7	20.3	17.3	14.7
Niger	40.4	34.8	29.7	25.0	20.8	17.2	14.1
Nigeria	51.9	46.4	39.9	32.9	25.9	19.3	13.6
Rwanda	43.8	38.7	33.7	29.2	25.0	21.2	17.8
São Tomé and Príncipe	54.3	47.7	38.9	28.8	18.9	10.9	5.5
Senegal	35.7	29.4	23.8	18.9	14.9	11.6	8.9
Sierra Leone	43.1	37.7	32.6	27.8	23.6	19.8	16.4
Sudan	48.3	34.6	24.4	17.5	13.2	10.5	8.9
Swaziland	57.9	54.8	49.3	41.7	32.4	22.7	14.1
Tanzania	41.3	36.6	32.2	28.0	24.2	20.8	17.7
Togo	44.6	36.6	30.2	25.4	21.9	19.5	18.0
Uganda	57.0	50.9	44.1	36.6	29.1	22.0	15.8
Zambia	52.5	49.0	43.3	35.8	27.2	18.7	11.5
Zimbabwe	14.9	12.3	10.1	8.2	6.7	5.4	4.4
Average	45.9	40.0	33.9	28.0	22.4	17.4	13.3

Source: Authors' calculation based on the household survey (DHS/MICS/CWIQ) database; see appendix J, table J.1.
Note: Based on model without wealth as a control variable.

Table H.7 Relation between Education and Woman's Age at First Birth, by Country

	Highest grade attained (women aged 15–49)						
	0	2	4	6	8	10	12
Benin	18.8	19.1	19.5	20.0	20.7	21.5	22.5
Burkina Faso	18.6	18.5	18.6	19.0	19.6	20.5	21.6
Cameroon	18.1	18.1	18.2	18.2	18.3	18.3	18.3
Central African Republic	18.6	18.6	18.5	18.6	18.8	19.2	19.6
Chad	17.4	17.7	17.9	18.3	18.7	19.1	19.6
Congo, Dem. Rep.	18.9	18.8	18.7	19.0	19.6	20.7	22.1

(table continues on next page)

Social Outcomes

Table H.7 Relation between Education and Woman's Age at First Birth, by Country (continued)

	Highest grade attained (women aged 15–49)						
	0	2	4	6	8	10	12
Equatorial Guinea	17.9	18.1	18.2	18.2	18.4	18.9	19.6
Ethiopia	18.1	18.1	18.2	18.2	18.2	18.3	18.3
Gabon	17.0	17.4	17.7	17.8	18.0	18.2	18.6
Gambia, The	19.6	19.6	19.7	19.7	19.7	19.7	19.8
Ghana	19.0	19.1	19.2	19.1	19.4	19.9	20.6
Guinea-Bissau	18.4	18.4	18.5	18.5	18.5	18.6	18.6
Kenya	18.0	17.9	18.1	18.2	18.5	19.4	20.5
Malawi	18.0	18.1	18.1	18.2	18.7	19.4	20.3
Mali	17.8	17.7	17.9	18.2	18.8	19.6	20.6
Mozambique	17.9	17.7	17.8	18.4	19.3	20.6	22.3
Namibia	18.9	18.9	18.9	19.0	19.6	20.3	21.4
Niger	17.9	18.0	18.0	18.1	18.2	18.3	18.4
Nigeria	17.5	17.7	18.0	18.5	19.0	19.6	20.3
Rwanda	20.2	20.2	20.3	20.3	20.3	20.4	20.4
São Tomé and Príncipe	18.9	19.0	19.0	19.1	19.1	19.1	19.2
Swaziland	18.2	18.0	17.9	18.3	18.7	19.5	20.6
Tanzania	18.0	17.7	17.7	18.2	19.0	20.2	21.9
Uganda	17.8	17.7	17.7	18.0	18.4	18.9	19.7
Zambia	17.8	17.8	17.9	17.9	18.4	19.1	20.0
Zimbabwe	17.1	17.1	17.2	17.2	17.2	17.3	17.3
Average	18.3	18.3	18.4	18.5	18.9	19.4	20.1

Source: Authors' calculation based on the household survey (DHS/MICS/CWIQ) database; see appendix J, table J.1.
Note: Based on model without wealth as a control variable.

Table H.8 Relation between Education and Months between Last Two Consecutive Births, by Country

	Highest grade attained (women aged 15-49)						
	0	2	4	6	8	10	12
Benin	37.4	38.7	40.0	41.2	42.5	43.8	45.0
Burkina Faso	39.7	40.8	41.5	41.9	41.8	41.4	40.6
Ethiopia	34.9	35.4	35.9	36.4	36.9	37.4	37.9
Gabon	35.1	36.4	37.8	39.1	40.4	41.7	43.1
Ghana	42.7	43.3	43.8	44.4	44.9	45.5	46.0
Kenya	36.2	36.9	37.7	38.5	39.3	40.1	40.8
Mali	34.9	36.1	37.2	38.3	39.5	40.6	41.8
Mozambique	37.5	38.9	40.4	40.8	43.3	44.8	46.3
Namibia	42.3	42.6	42.9	43.3	43.6	44.0	44.3
Nigeria	35.2	35.3	35.4	35.5	35.5	35.6	35.7
Rwanda	34.4	34.3	34.1	34.0	33.9	33.8	33.6
Tanzania	36.4	36.8	37.2	37.6	38.0	38.4	38.8
Uganda	33.4	33.3	33.1	33.0	32.8	32.7	32.6
Zambia	36.9	36.9	36.9	36.9	36.9	36.9	36.9
Zimbabwe	36.9	37.5	38.0	38.5	39.1	39.6	40.2
Average	36.9	37.6	38.1	38.6	39.2	39.8	40.2

Source: Authors' calculation based on the household survey (DHS/MICS/CWIQ) database; see appendix J, table J.1.
Note: Based on model without wealth as a control variable.

Table H.9 Relation between Education and Number of Live Births to Date, by Country
average per woman, age 15–49

	Highest grade attained (women aged 15–49)						
	0	2	4	6	8	10	12
Angola	2.85	2.83	2.82	2.80	2.58	2.23	1.74
Benin	3.49	3.32	3.11	2.85	2.56	2.23	1.86
Burkina Faso	3.63	3.46	3.29	3.12	2.95	2.78	2.61
Burundi	2.64	2.52	2.40	2.28	2.16	2.05	1.93
Cameroon	3.31	3.14	2.97	2.80	2.63	2.48	2.28
Central African Republic	3.15	3.15	3.12	3.10	3.03	2.84	2.58
Chad	4.32	4.14	3.93	3.78	3.60	3.42	3.24
Congo, Dem. Rep.	3.06	3.04	3.04	3.02	2.84	2.51	2.03
Equatorial Guinea	2.89	2.87	2.85	2.83	2.73	2.50	2.19
Ethiopia	3.11	3.14	3.08	2.95	2.75	2.47	2.11
Gabon	3.00	3.00	3.02	2.97	2.81	2.56	2.21
Gambia, The	2.99	2.83	2.66	2.50	2.34	2.18	2.01
Ghana	3.14	2.95	2.76	2.57	2.38	2.19	2.00
Guinea-Bissau	2.72	2.60	2.42	2.19	1.90	1.55	1.15
Kenya	4.23	3.92	3.62	3.31	3.01	2.71	2.40
Lesotho	2.35	2.34	2.32	2.29	2.19	2.02	1.79
Malawi	3.53	3.63	3.62	3.49	3.26	2.91	2.44
Mali	3.94	3.71	3.49	3.27	3.05	2.83	2.61
Mozambique	3.65	3.64	3.50	3.23	2.81	2.26	1.58
Namibia	3.21	2.96	2.72	2.48	2.23	1.99	1.75
Niger	3.41	3.27	3.17	3.12	3.11	3.11	3.10
Nigeria	4.14	3.86	3.59	3.31	3.04	2.76	2.48
Rwanda	3.07	2.92	2.77	2.61	2.46	2.31	2.16
São Tomé and Príncipe	3.04	2.92	2.65	2.38	2.11	1.83	1.56
Sierra Leone	2.67	2.52	2.37	2.22	2.07	1.92	1.77
Swaziland	3.39	3.17	2.95	2.73	2.51	2.29	2.07
Tanzania	3.39	3.44	3.39	3.23	2.96	2.58	2.10
Uganda	3.94	4.03	4.02	3.92	3.72	3.43	3.04
Zambia	3.54	3.53	3.58	3.50	3.27	2.90	2.39
Zimbabwe	3.34	3.10	2.86	2.62	2.37	2.13	1.89
Average	3.30	3.20	3.07	2.92	2.71	2.47	2.17

Source: Authors' calculation based on the household survey (DHS/MICS/CWIQ) database; see appendix J, table J.1.
Note: Based on model without wealth as a control variable.

Table H.10 Relation between Education and Probability of Using any Contraceptive Method Frequently, by Country
percentage

	Highest grade attained (women aged 22–44)						
	0	2	4	6	8	10	12
Angola	1.9	3.9	7.1	11.6	17.2	23.1	28.4
Benin	47.2	56.2	64.9	72.6	79.2	84.6	88.7
Burkina Faso	42.1	54.1	63.6	70.4	74.9	77.3	78.2
Burundi	12.0	16.4	20.9	25.2	28.8	31.4	32.8
Cameroon	20.1	27.0	34.1	40.9	46.8	51.6	55.3
Central African Republic	24.1	26.7	29.5	32.5	35.6	38.9	42.2
Chad	7.2	14.4	23.6	32.5	39.0	42.0	41.0
Congo, Dem. Rep.	24.4	28.3	32.5	37.1	41.9	46.8	51.8
Equatorial Guinea	5.8	7.1	8.7	10.7	13.0	15.7	18.9

(table continues on next page)

Social Outcomes   225

Table H.10 Relation between Education and Probability of Using any Contraceptive Method Frequently, by Country *(continued)*

	Highest grade attained (women aged 22–44)						
	0	2	4	6	8	10	12
Ethiopia	11.6	17.8	25.1	32.4	38.9	43.9	47.3
Gabon	42.2	57.4	70.0	79.0	85.1	89.0	91.5
Gambia, The	4.4	4.9	5.5	6.1	6.8	7.6	8.5
Ghana	42.8	50.5	57.6	63.9	69.3	73.7	77.3
Guinea-Bissau	5.5	6.4	7.4	8.5	9.8	11.3	12.9
Kenya	34.4	49.6	62.6	72.1	78.4	82.3	84.3
Lesotho	1.5	3.0	5.5	9.1	13.7	18.7	23.3
Malawi	53.0	59.5	64.9	69.2	72.5	74.9	76.5
Mali	23.0	30.0	37.3	44.5	51.4	57.5	62.8
Mozambique	56.0	62.3	69.7	77.5	84.6	90.4	94.6
Namibia	62.2	66.3	70.1	73.7	77.0	80.0	82.7
Niger	15.2	20.1	24.0	25.0	26.4	26.0	26.0
Nigeria	16.3	24.3	33.5	42.8	51.3	58.5	64.1
Rwanda	30.4	34.2	38.2	42.4	46.8	51.1	55.5
São Tomé and Príncipe	18.0	23.6	27.9	31.0	30.0	31.0	31.0
Sierra Leone	9.7	11.6	13.7	16.2	19.1	22.3	25.9
Tanzania	35.9	42.2	48.6	55.2	61.5	67.5	73.0
Uganda	34.6	41.6	49.0	56.5	63.6	70.2	76.0
Zambia	52.2	57.2	60.3	61.5	62.0	62.0	62.0
Zimbabwe	75.7	79.6	82.6	84.6	86.1	87.0	87.4
Average	27.9	33.7	39.3	44.3	48.6	52.3	55.2

Source: Authors' calculation based on the household survey (DHS/MICS/CWIQ) database; see appendix J, table J.1.
Note: Based on model without wealth as a control variable.

Table H.11 Relation between Education and Number of Prenatal Consultations during Pregnancy, by Country

	Highest grade attained (women aged 15–49)						
	0	2	4	6	8	10	12
Benin	4.31	4.81	5.31	5.82	6.32	6.83	7.33
Burkina Faso	2.15	2.28	2.45	2.67	2.93	3.23	3.57
Chad	1.29	1.88	2.35	2.70	2.94	3.05	3.05
Ethiopia	0.84	1.20	1.61	2.06	2.56	3.10	3.68
Gabon	4.04	4.22	4.40	4.57	4.75	4.93	5.11
Ghana	4.77	5.10	5.44	5.78	6.11	6.45	6.78
Kenya	2.96	3.29	3.62	3.95	4.28	4.61	4.94
Malawi	3.70	3.87	4.05	4.23	4.40	4.58	4.75
Mali	2.17	2.62	3.08	3.56	4.05	4.56	5.08
Mozambique	3.17	3.69	4.14	4.51	4.81	5.03	5.17
Namibia	4.26	4.61	4.95	5.30	5.64	5.99	6.33
Nigeria	2.63	4.01	5.25	6.37	7.34	8.19	8.89
Rwanda	2.23	2.19	2.22	2.32	2.50	2.75	3.07
Tanzania	4.44	4.67	4.89	5.12	5.35	5.58	5.81
Uganda	2.99	3.31	3.63	3.94	4.26	4.58	4.90
Zambia	4.22	4.49	4.75	5.02	5.28	5.54	5.81
Zimbabwe	3.69	4.03	4.37	4.71	5.06	5.40	5.74
Average	3.17	3.55	3.91	4.27	4.62	4.96	5.30

Source: Authors' calculation based on the household survey (DHS/MICS/CWIQ) database; see appendix J, table J.1.
Note: Based on model without wealth as a control variable.

Table H.12 Relation between Education and Number of Tetanus Vaccinations during Last Pregnancy, by Country

	Highest grade attained (women aged 15–49)						
	0	2	4	6	8	10	12
Benin	1.36	1.42	1.49	1.56	1.63	1.70	1.77
Burkina Faso	1.15	1.27	1.37	1.42	1.42	1.42	1.43
Chad	0.72	1.03	1.26	1.34	1.43	1.35	1.35
Ethiopia	0.52	0.72	0.90	1.04	1.15	1.24	1.29
Gabon	1.46	1.49	1.53	1.56	1.60	1.64	1.67
Ghana	1.35	1.39	1.44	1.48	1.53	1.57	1.62
Kenya	1.27	1.34	1.41	1.49	1.56	1.63	1.71
Malawi	1.66	1.70	1.74	1.77	1.81	1.85	1.88
Mali	0.90	1.03	1.13	1.22	1.28	1.32	1.33
Mozambique	1.39	1.61	1.76	1.83	1.85	1.84	1.85
Nigeria	0.67	0.97	1.23	1.45	1.65	1.81	1.93
Rwanda	0.98	1.02	1.06	1.10	1.14	1.18	1.22
Tanzania	1.58	1.63	1.69	1.74	1.79	1.85	1.90
Uganda	1.13	1.20	1.27	1.34	1.41	1.47	1.54
Zambia	1.03	1.06	1.08	1.11	1.13	1.16	1.19
Zimbabwe	1.30	1.34	1.39	1.44	1.48	1.53	1.58
Average	1.15	1.26	1.36	1.43	1.49	1.53	1.58

Source: Authors' calculation based on the household survey (DHS/MICS/CWIQ) database; see appendix J, table J.1.
Note: Based on model without wealth as a control variable.

Table H.13 Relation between Education and Probability of Receiving Vitamin A during Last Pregnancy, by Country

percentage

	Highest grade attained (women aged 15–49)						
	0	2	4	6	8	10	12
Angola	5.9	6.3	6.8	7.4	7.9	8.5	9.2
Benin	17.6	20.2	23.1	26.3	29.8	33.5	37.4
Burkina Faso	17.0	20.1	22.2	23.1	23.0	23.0	24.0
Burundi	7.2	6.4	5.6	5.0	4.4	3.8	3.4
Cameroon	2.4	2.4	2.4	2.4	2.3	2.3	2.3
Central African Republic	12.9	15.6	17.5	18.5	18.4	18.0	19.0
Congo, Dem. Rep.	6.2	6.9	7.7	8.5	9.5	10.5	11.7
Côte d'Ivoire	19.4	19.3	19.3	19.2	19.2	19.1	19.1
Equatorial Guinea	6.2	6.7	7.2	7.8	8.4	9.0	9.7
Ethiopia	10.8	13.9	16.7	18.9	20.4	20.8	20.3
Gambia, The	3.4	3.3	3.2	3.1	3.0	2.9	2.8
Ghana	44.6	44.5	44.4	44.3	44.2	44.1	44.0
Guinea-Bissau	9.6	9.7	9.7	9.8	9.9	10.0	10.0
Kenya	10.0	11.0	12.0	13.1	14.3	15.6	17.0
Lesotho	1.9	2.1	2.3	2.5	2.8	3.0	3.3
Malawi	38.0	40.3	42.6	44.9	47.3	49.7	52.1
Mali	16.8	18.0	19.4	20.8	22.3	23.9	25.5
Mozambique	16.5	21.2	25.6	29.4	32.3	34.0	34.5
Namibia	26.8	28.9	31.0	33.2	35.4	37.8	40.2
Niger	5.6	7.4	8.9	9.0	9.9	9.0	9.0
Nigeria	10.7	15.5	21.3	27.4	33.4	38.9	43.4

(table continues on next page)

Social Outcomes

Table H.13 Relation between Education and Probability of Receiving Vitamin A during Last Pregnancy, by Country (continued)

	\multicolumn{7}{c}{Highest grade attained (women aged 15–49)}
	0	2	4	6	8	10	12
Rwanda	12.6	13.4	14.3	15.2	16.2	17.1	18.2
Senegal	9.1	8.9	8.7	8.6	8.4	8.2	8.0
Sudan	6.4	6.8	7.2	7.7	8.2	8.7	9.3
Swaziland	4.0	4.0	4.0	4.0	4.0	4.0	4.0
Togo	5.8	5.4	5.1	4.8	4.5	4.3	4.0
Uganda	6.2	7.8	9.6	11.9	14.6	17.7	21.4
Zambia	15.5	18.6	22.2	26.3	30.8	35.8	41.0
Average	12.5	13.7	15.0	16.2	17.3	18.3	19.4

Source: Authors' calculation based on the household survey (DHS/MICS/CWIQ) database; see appendix J, table J.1.
Note: Based on model without wealth as a control variable

Table H.14 Relation between Education and Probability that Last Delivery Was Assisted by Skilled Attendant, by Country
percentage

	Highest grade attained (women aged 15–49)						
	0	2	4	6	8	10	12
Angola	5.8	8.3	10.8	13.1	14.9	15.8	15.7
Benin	64.3	73.1	80.4	86.1	90.3	93.4	95.5
Burkina Faso	41.7	51.5	61.2	70.0	77.6	83.7	88.4
Burundi	6.0	7.3	8.8	10.7	12.9	15.4	18.4
Central African Republic	5.8	7.2	8.4	9.3	9.8	9.7	10.0
Chad	5.0	6.1	7.4	9.0	10.9	13.2	15.0
Congo, Dem. Rep.	5.2	6.1	7.2	8.5	10.0	11.8	13.8
Côte d'Ivoire	57.8	62.3	66.5	70.5	74.1	77.5	80.6
Equatorial Guinea	12.8	13.2	13.6	14.1	14.5	15.0	15.5
Gabon	76.2	79.7	82.8	85.5	87.9	89.9	91.6
Gambia, The	14.0	14.5	15.1	15.6	16.2	16.8	17.4
Ghana	37.5	43.8	50.4	56.9	63.3	69.2	74.5
Guinea	45.8	52.0	58.1	63.9	69.4	74.4	78.8
Guinea-Bissau	9.9	10.8	11.8	12.8	13.9	15.1	16.3
Kenya	12.4	17.9	25.2	34.1	44.3	55.0	65.2
Lesotho	6.0	6.8	7.7	8.7	9.8	11.0	12.4
Malawi	44.3	49.9	55.6	61.1	66.4	71.3	75.7
Mali	16.5	19.7	25.3	34.2	46.9	62.5	77.7
Mozambique	12.9	19.2	26.0	32.5	37.7	41.2	42.8
Namibia	55.8	64.9	73.0	79.9	85.4	89.5	92.6
Niger	5.0	5.5	6.0	6.5	7.1	7.7	8.4
Nigeria	14.8	21.8	30.8	41.5	53.2	64.5	74.4
Rwanda	13.6	17.4	22.0	27.4	33.6	40.4	47.6
Swaziland	13.0	13.6	14.2	14.9	15.5	16.2	16.9
Tanzania	25.0	30.0	35.5	41.5	47.6	53.9	60.1
Togo	33.8	40.3	47.3	54.3	61.2	67.6	73.5
Uganda	11.4	14.1	17.4	21.2	25.5	30.4	35.8
Zambia	20.4	27.7	36.4	46.1	56.2	65.7	74.1
Zimbabwe	48.4	56.8	64.8	72.1	78.3	83.5	87.6
Average	24.9	29.0	33.4	38.0	42.6	46.9	50.9

Source: Authors' calculation based on the household survey (DHS/MICS/CWIQ) database; see appendix J, table J.1.
Note: Based on model without wealth as a control variable.

Table H.15 Relation between Education and Probability that Children Sleep under a Bed Net, by Country

percentage

	Highest grade attained (mother)						
	0	2	4	6	8	10	12
Angola	5.3	7.7	11.0	15.5	21.5	29.0	37.8
Benin	32.5	37.8	43.3	49.0	54.7	60.3	65.6
Burkina Faso	22.2	24.6	27.1	29.9	32.8	35.8	38.9
Cameroon	9.4	10.0	10.7	11.4	12.1	12.9	13.7
Central African Republic	25.5	27.4	30.2	34.1	39.1	45.4	52.8
Congo, Dem. Rep.	8.1	9.4	11.0	12.8	14.0	16.0	19.6
Côte d'Ivoire	8.7	9.5	10.3	11.1	12.0	13.0	14.0
Equatorial Guinea	15.8	17.6	19.6	21.8	24.1	26.6	29.2
Gambia, The	41.0	41.9	42.0	43.0	43.0	43.0	43.0
Ghana	15.0	16.0	16.4	16.1	15.7	16.0	17.0
Kenya	9.0	10.0	11.0	12.0	13.0	16.0	20.0
Mali	24.0	31.1	39.2	48.0	56.9	65.4	73.0
Mozambique	6.6	9.6	13.6	19.0	25.8	34.1	43.5
Niger	15.4	16.4	17.6	18.7	20.0	21.3	22.6
Nigeria	5.0	7.9	7.2	6.0	6.1	5.7	7.0
Rwanda	1.2	1.8	2.8	4.3	6.5	9.7	14.2
São Tomé and Príncipe	26.0	32.9	40.5	48.6	56.8	64.7	71.8
Senegal	12.7	13.7	14.8	16.0	17.3	18.6	20.0
Sudan	23.1	23.0	22.9	22.8	22.7	22.6	22.6
Togo	9.0	11.0	14.0	15.0	16.0	16.0	16.5
Uganda	6.2	7.5	9.0	10.9	13.1	15.7	18.6
Zambia	9.9	12.1	14.7	17.7	21.2	25.2	29.7
Zimbabwe	0.7	0.9	1.1	1.3	1.7	2.1	2.6
Average	14.4	16.5	18.7	21.1	23.7	26.7	30.2

Source: Authors' calculation based on the household survey (DHS/MICS/CWIQ) database; see appendix J, table J.1.
Note: Based on model without wealth as a control variable.

Table H.16 Relation between Education and Probability that Children Are Fully Vaccinated by Age 2, by Country

percentage

	Highest grade attained (mother)						
	0	2	4	6	8	10	12
Angola	11.0	14.6	17.6	19.4	20.0	21.0	21.0
Benin	40.0	43.6	47.3	51.0	54.7	58.4	61.9
Burkina Faso	29.2	36.2	42.1	46.6	49.5	50.6	50.1
Burundi	30.2	34.2	38.4	42.9	47.4	52.0	56.5
Cameroon	17.1	20.1	23.3	27.0	30.9	35.2	39.7
Central African Republic	7.5	9.0	10.7	12.7	15.0	17.7	20.7
Chad	3.8	4.6	5.7	7.0	8.5	10.3	12.5
Congo, Dem. Rep.	1.3	1.5	1.8	2.2	2.6	3.1	3.6
Côte d'Ivoire	50.2	56.6	62.8	68.6	73.8	78.5	82.5
Equatorial Guinea	7.2	8.6	10.3	12.2	14.4	16.9	19.7
Ethiopia	3.8	4.8	6.2	7.9	10.0	12.6	15.8
Gabon	13.7	14.8	15.9	17.1	18.4	19.8	21.2
Gambia, The	62.7	62.9	63.2	63.4	63.6	63.8	64.1
Ghana	25.8	32.0	33.9	38.4	43.1	47.9	52.8

(table continues on next page)

Table H.16 Relation between Education and Probability that Children Are Fully Vaccinated by Age 2, by Country *(continued)*

	Highest grade attained (mother)						
	0	2	4	6	8	10	12
Guinea-Bissau	39.8	40.5	41.2	41.9	42.6	43.4	44.1
Kenya	17.4	21.3	25.9	32.0	36.6	42.6	48.8
Lesotho	39.9	43.4	46.9	50.5	54.0	57.5	61.0
Malawi	24.8	27.5	30.4	33.4	36.5	39.8	43.2
Mali	17.9	21.0	24.5	28.4	32.6	37.1	41.8
Mozambique	30.5	39.0	46.2	51.8	55.4	57.2	57.2
Namibia	42.4	46.2	49.9	53.7	57.4	61.1	64.6
Niger	9.0	10.8	12.9	15.3	18.2	21.4	25.0
Nigeria	1.0	1.8	2.8	4.2	5.7	7.2	8.5
Rwanda	72.9	75.3	77.5	79.6	81.6	83.4	85.0
São Tomé and Príncipe	26.2	31.5	37.3	43.5	49.9	56.4	62.6
Sierra Leone	23.4	25.0	26.8	28.5	30.4	32.3	34.3
Sudan	6.8	6.9	7.0	7.1	7.2	7.3	7.4
Swaziland	41.6	40.5	39.4	38.3	37.2	36.1	35.0
Tanzania	22.4	27.2	32.8	38.8	45.2	51.7	58.2
Togo	25.1	25.3	25.6	25.8	26.1	26.3	26.6
Uganda	11.3	13.1	15.1	17.4	20.0	22.8	25.8
Zambia	3.0	3.0	3.1	3.2	3.2	3.3	3.4
Zimbabwe	55.6	55.4	55.2	55.1	54.9	54.7	54.5
Average	24.7	27.2	29.7	32.3	34.7	37.2	39.7

Source: Authors' calculation based on the household survey (DHS/MICS/CWIQ) database; see appendix J, table J.1.
Note: Based on model without wealth as a control variable.

Table H.17 Relation between Education and Mortality Rate of Children under 5, by Country
number per thousand

	Highest grade attained (mother)						
	0	2	4	6	8	10	12
Benin	141.2	124.7	108.2	91.7	75.3	58.8	42.3
Burkina Faso	158.2	146.9	135.6	124.3	113.0	101.7	90.4
Chad	173.0	169.0	165.0	142.0	135.0	125.0	93.2
Ethiopia	172.3	152.9	133.8	114.2	94.8	75.5	56.1
Gabon	90.8	87.4	83.9	80.5	77.0	73.5	70.1
Ghana	113.9	107.6	101.4	95.0	88.8	82.5	76.2
Kenya	139.8	126.0	109.0	98.3	84.5	70.6	56.8
Malawi	209.6	198.7	184.4	166.6	145.5	120.9	92.8
Mali	212.2	192.3	178.3	152.5	132.6	112.8	92.9
Mozambique	162.3	144.6	129.5	109.1	91.4	73.7	56.0
Namibia	83.5	75.8	65.1	60.3	52.6	44.9	37.1
Nigeria	221.4	199.5	175.3	155.7	133.7	111.8	89.9
Rwanda	196.2	180.7	164.5	149.8	134.3	118.8	103.4
Tanzania	173.3	162.6	151.2	141.2	130.5	119.8	109.1
Uganda	177.6	161.8	144.7	130.3	114.6	98.9	83.1
Zambia	172.2	161.4	144.0	139.7	128.8	118.0	107.1
Zimbabwe	113.4	104.0	93.9	85.1	75.6	66.1	56.7
Average	159.5	146.8	133.4	119.8	106.4	92.5	77.2

Source: Authors' calculation based on the household survey (DHS/MICS/CWIQ) database; see appendix J, table J.1.
Note: Based on model without wealth as a control variable.

Table H.18 Relation between Education and Probability that Children Aged 9–11 Have Ever Attended School, by Country
percentage

	Highest grade attained (mother)						
	0	2	4	6	8	10	12
Benin	69.3	80.8	88.7	93.6	96.5	98.1	99.0
Burkina Faso	37.4	48.4	59.5	69.8	78.4	85.0	89.9
Ethiopia	35.1	45.5	56.4	66.7	75.6	82.8	88.2
Gabon	96.8	97.7	98.4	98.9	99.2	99.4	99.6
Ghana	73.0	80.4	86.2	90.5	93.5	95.6	97.1
Kenya	62.9	77.3	87.2	93.2	96.5	98.2	99.1
Malawi	80.9	88.8	93.7	96.6	98.1	99.0	99.5
Mali	42.2	52.1	61.9	70.8	78.3	84.4	88.9
Mozambique	69.4	87.1	95.3	98.4	99.4	99.8	99.9
Namibia	76.9	84.1	89.4	93.0	95.5	97.1	98.2
Nigeria	59.3	72.3	82.4	89.4	93.8	96.4	98.0
Rwanda	85.1	88.2	90.8	92.8	94.5	95.7	96.7
Tanzania	57.2	62.0	66.6	70.9	74.8	78.4	81.5
Uganda	88.3	91.9	94.5	96.3	97.5	98.3	98.9
Zambia	58.3	68.1	76.5	83.3	88.4	92.1	94.7
Zimbabwe	95.5	97.0	98.0	98.7	99.1	99.4	99.6
Average	68.0	76.4	82.8	87.7	91.2	93.7	95.5

Source: Authors' calculation based on the household survey (DHS/MICS/CWIQ) database; see appendix J, table J.1.
Note: Based on model without wealth as a control variable.

Table H.19 Relation between Education and Index of Knowledge of HIV/AIDS, by Country

	Highest grade attained (adult aged 22–44 years)						
	0	2	4	6	8	10	12
DHS							
Benin	5.77	6.28	6.80	7.31	7.83	8.34	8.86
Burkina Faso	7.31	7.91	8.42	8.83	9.15	9.37	9.49
Chad	5.94	6.63	7.22	7.69	8.05	8.29	8.42
Ethiopia	6.29	7.11	7.78	8.31	8.68	8.91	8.99
Gabon	4.36	4.81	5.26	5.67	6.02	6.33	6.58
Ghana	7.26	7.67	8.06	8.42	8.76	9.08	9.37
Kenya	6.13	7.07	7.88	8.58	9.15	9.60	9.93
Malawi	8.92	9.11	9.30	9.49	9.68	9.80	10.06
Mali	5.42	5.96	6.46	6.91	7.30	7.65	7.94
Mozambique	4.94	5.78	6.53	7.19	7.76	8.25	8.64
Namibia	6.65	7.09	7.54	7.98	8.43	8.88	9.34
Nigeria	5.87	6.16	6.50	6.87	7.30	7.76	8.27
Rwanda	8.47	8.72	8.96	9.20	9.44	9.69	9.93
Tanzania	5.92	6.22	6.53	6.83	7.13	7.44	7.74
Uganda	7.60	7.99	8.38	8.77	9.17	9.56	9.95
Zambia	7.17	7.61	8.05	8.49	8.93	9.37	9.81
Zimbabwe	4.87	5.32	5.73	6.13	6.50	6.84	7.16
Average DHS	6.41	6.91	7.38	7.80	8.19	8.54	8.85

(table continues on next page)

Table H.19 Relation between Education and Index of Knowledge of HIV/AIDS, by Country *(continued)*

	Highest grade attained (adult aged 22–44 years)						
	0	2	4	6	8	10	12
MICS							
Angola	1.49	2.75	3.92	5.00	5.98	6.88	7.69
Burundi	6.76	7.30	7.68	7.91	7.94	7.95	7.96
Cameroon	1.94	3.20	4.31	5.28	6.10	6.78	7.31
Central African Republic	2.86	3.85	4.71	5.45	6.06	6.54	6.90
Congo, Dem. Rep.	3.60	3.78	3.98	4.20	4.44	4.70	4.98
Equatorial Guinea	2.84	3.26	3.68	4.10	4.51	4.93	5.35
Gambia, The	2.09	2.85	3.50	4.02	4.44	4.73	4.91
Guinea-Bissau	1.78	2.84	3.79	4.61	5.32	5.90	6.37
Lesotho	1.24	2.50	3.67	4.75	5.74	6.64	7.44
Niger	3.46	4.43	5.06	5.35	5.31	4.93	4.21
São Tomé and Príncipe	4.36	5.33	5.96	6.25	6.21	5.83	5.11
Senegal	4.25	5.22	5.85	6.14	6.10	5.72	5.00
Sierra Leone	3.47	3.93	4.38	4.84	5.29	5.75	6.20
Sudan	1.03	1.99	2.83	3.56	4.16	4.65	5.02
Swaziland	5.48	5.65	5.86	6.13	6.46	6.83	7.26
Togo	6.13	6.62	7.03	7.35	7.59	7.74	7.81
Average MICS	3.30	4.09	4.76	5.31	5.73	6.03	6.22
Overall Average	4.85	5.50	6.07	6.56	6.96	7.28	7.54

Source: Authors' calculation based on the household survey (DHS/MICS/CWIQ) database; see appendix J, table J.1.
Note: Based on model without wealth as a control variable. HIV/AIDS = human immunodeficiency virus/acquired immunodeficiency syndrome, DHS = Demographic and Health Survey, MICS = Multiple Indicator Cluster Survey.

Table H.20 Relation between Education and Probability of Reading Newspapers Frequently, by Country

percentage

	Highest grade attained (mother)						
	0	2	4	6	8	10	12
Benin	0.5	1.3	3.2	7.0	13.1	21.3	30.3
Burkina Faso	0.4	1.5	4.8	12.4	25.3	40.8	54.1
Chad	0.2	0.8	2.5	6.2	13.2	23.0	33.7
Ethiopia	0.1	0.3	1.0	2.4	4.8	7.9	10.6
Gabon	2.1	5.6	13.0	25.3	40.6	55.3	66.7
Ghana	0.1	0.3	0.8	2.0	5.0	12.2	26.8
Kenya	1.1	2.2	4.4	8.6	16.2	28.3	44.7
Malawi	0.7	1.5	3.1	6.3	12.5	23.1	38.8
Mali	0.5	1.7	5.2	12.9	25.5	40.2	53.1
Mozambique	0.0	0.3	1.2	4.2	11.4	23.8	38.1
Namibia	3.9	6.3	10.5	17.8	29.7	46.3	65.1
Nigeria	0.7	1.3	2.5	4.8	9.0	16.2	27.3
Rwanda	0.7	1.3	2.3	4.1	7.1	11.9	19.5
Tanzania	0.6	1.1	2.1	3.9	7.2	12.7	21.5
Uganda	0.4	1.4	3.7	9.0	18.6	32.2	47.0
Zambia	0.0	0.2	0.7	2.2	6.2	14.7	28.5
Zimbabwe	0.7	1.5	3.3	7.0	14.2	26.9	45.0
Average	0.7	1.7	3.8	8.0	15.3	25.7	38.3

Source: Authors' calculation based on the household survey (DHS/MICS/CWIQ) database; see appendix J, table J.1.
Note: Based on model without wealth as a control variable.

Table H.21 Relation between Education and Probability of Listening to the Radio Frequently, by Country

percentage

	Highest grade attained (mother)						
	0	2	4	6	8	10	12
Benin	67.0	71.1	74.8	78.2	81.3	84.0	86.4
Burkina Faso	60.4	68.5	74.3	78.3	80.9	82.2	82.6
Chad	20.6	24.3	29.9	37.9	48.6	61.2	74.0
Ethiopia	6.3	8.8	12.2	16.6	22.3	29.2	37.2
Gabon	59.4	65.1	70.4	75.2	79.5	83.1	86.3
Ghana	69.4	74.5	79.1	83.0	86.3	89.1	91.4
Kenya	46.5	59.8	70.8	79.0	84.7	88.6	91.2
Malawi	43.8	49.4	54.9	60.3	65.5	70.3	74.7
Mali	65.4	69.7	73.6	77.2	80.4	83.3	85.8
Mozambique	40.7	49.1	56.7	63.0	68.1	72.0	74.8
Namibia	54.7	60.7	66.3	71.6	76.3	80.4	83.9
Nigeria	58.4	62.9	67.2	71.2	74.9	78.3	81.3
Rwanda	29.5	35.6	42.2	49.1	56.1	62.8	69.1
Tanzania	21.1	25.5	30.6	36.1	42.1	48.3	54.6
Uganda	35.8	44.1	52.7	61.2	69.0	75.9	81.7
Zambia	23.6	29.7	36.7	44.3	52.2	59.9	67.2
Zimbabwe	33.0	39.1	45.5	52.1	58.6	64.9	70.6
Average	43.3	49.3	55.2	60.8	66.3	71.4	76.0

Source: Authors' calculation based on the household survey (DHS/MICS/CWIQ) database; see appendix J, table e: Auth J.1.
Note: Based on model without wealth as a control variable.

Table H.22 Relation between Education and Probability of Watching TV Frequently, by Country

percentage

	Highest grade attained (mother)						
	0	2	4	6	8	10	12
Benin	10.0	14.6	20.9	29.0	38.6	49.2	59.9
Burkina Faso	2.4	4.8	9.1	15.8	25.0	35.9	47.1
Chad	2.7	3.5	4.5	5.8	7.5	9.5	12.1
Ethiopia	0.2	0.4	0.8	1.5	2.4	3.6	4.8
Gabon	42.0	45.5	49.9	55.3	61.4	68.0	74.6
Ghana	4.6	5.4	6.8	9.3	13.3	19.9	30.4
Kenya	3.6	4.8	6.7	10.0	15.6	24.8	38.8
Malawi	0.6	1.2	2.5	5.0	9.7	18.1	31.1
Mali	2.2	3.9	6.7	11.4	18.6	29.0	42.1
Mozambique	1.9	3.7	7.0	13.1	23.1	37.4	54.4
Namibia	6.2	10.1	12.4	18.7	28.6	42.7	59.7
Nigeria	1.9	2.9	4.5	7.0	11.2	17.8	27.9
Rwanda	0.8	1.3	2.0	3.2	5.0	7.8	12.0
Tanzania	0.6	0.9	1.4	2.2	3.4	5.1	7.6
Uganda	0.5	1.3	3.5	7.9	15.7	26.5	38.7
Zambia	0.5	1.0	2.0	3.9	7.5	13.8	24.1
Zimbabwe	2.2	3.4	5.4	9.0	15.2	25.4	40.6
Average	4.9	6.4	8.6	12.2	17.7	25.6	35.6

Source: Authors' calculation based on the household survey (DHS/MICS/CWIQ) database; see appendix J, table J.1.
Note: Based on model without wealth as a control variable.

Social Outcomes

Table H.23 Construction of Index of Improvement in Social Outcomes from Six Years of Primary School, 36 Sub-Saharan African Countries

	Woman's age at first birth (example)				Index of improvement in social outcomes from six yrs. of schooling	
			Improvement in social outcomes 0–6 years		Average of (a) across 17 social outcomes	
	No schooling (yrs.)	Six years of primary school completed (yrs.)	Absolute[a]	Standardized (mean 0, standard deviation 1)(a)	Absolute[b]	Standardized (mean 100, standard deviation 0)
Angola	—	—	—	—	0.05	103.5
Benin	18.8	20.0	1.2	2.8	0.67	120.7
Burkina Faso	18.6	19.0	0.4	0.3	0.44	114.2
Burundi	—	—	—	—	−0.39	91.2
Cameroon	18.1	18.2	0.1	−0.6	0.39	112.9
Central African Republic	18.6	18.6	0.0	−0.9	−0.25	95.0
Chad	17.4	18.3	0.9	1.9	0.28	109.9
Congo, Dem. Rep.	18.9	19.0	0.1	−0.6	−0.80	79.7
Côte d'Ivoire	—	—	—	—	0.08	104.3
Equatorial Guinea	17.9	18.2	0.3	0.0	−0.71	82.3
Ethiopia	18.1	18.2	0.1	−0.6	0.21	107.7
Gabon	17.0	17.8	0.8	1.6	−0.54	86.8
Gambia, The	19.6	19.7	0.1	−0.6	−0.58	85.8
Ghana	19.0	19.1	0.1	−0.6	−0.13	98.4
Guinea	—	—	—	—	0.27	109.5
Guinea-Bissau	18.4	18.5	0.1	−0.6	−0.66	83.7
Kenya	18.0	18.2	0.2	−0.3	0.81	124.7
Lesotho	—	—	—	—	−0.15	97.9
Madagascar	—	—	—	—	−0.93	76.0
Malawi	18.0	18.2	0.2	−0.3	−0.37	91.6
Mali	17.8	18.2	0.4	0.3	0.54	117.0
Mozambique	17.9	18.4	0.5	0.6	1.01	130.2
Namibia	18.9	19.0	0.1	−0.6	−0.01	101.6
Niger	17.9	18.1	0.2	−0.3	−0.27	94.3
Nigeria	17.5	18.5	1.0	2.2	0.80	124.3
Rwanda	20.2	20.3	0.1	−0.6	−0.49	88.4
São Tomé and Príncipe	18.9	19.1	0.2	−0.3	0.91	127.3
Senegal	—	—	—	—	−0.65	83.9
Sierra Leone	—	—	—	—	−0.47	89.0
Sudan	—	—	—	—	0.52	116.6
Swaziland	18.2	18.3	0.1	−0.6	−0.90	77.0
Tanzania	18.0	18.2	0.2	−0.3	−0.33	92.8
Togo	—	—	—	—	−0.24	95.3
Uganda	17.8	18.0	0.2	−0.3	−0.19	96.7
Zambia	17.8	17.9	0.1	−0.6	−0.10	99.3
Zimbabwe	17.1	17.2	0.1	−0.6	−0.41	90.6
Regional average	18.3	18.5	0.3	0.0 ($\sigma = 1.0$)	−0.07	100.0 ($\sigma = 15$)

Source: Authors' calculation based on DHS/MICS/CWIQ household surveys; see appendix J, table J.1, and appendix H, table H.7.
Note: — = not available.
a. Calculated as (6y-level) − (0y-level), when the social outcome indicator is better, the higher that indicator is (for example, vaccination); and as (0y-level) − (6y-level) when the social outcome indicator is better, the lower that indicator is (for example, mortality rate).
b. Calculated as the average of the columns (a) across all 17 social indicators (only age at first birth shown here).

APPENDIX I

Education and Employment

Table I.1 Distribution of Population by Age Group and Highest Level of Schooling Attained in 23 Sub-Saharan African Countries, ca. 2003

		15–59 years (not in school)						25–34 years (not in school)					
		No schooling	Primary	Lower secondary	Upper secondary	TVET	Higher	No schooling	Primary	Lower secondary	Upper secondary	TVET	Higher
Benin	(000)	1,880	594	259	81	31	52	—	—	—	—	—	—
	(%)	64.9	20.5	9.0	2.8	1.1	1.8	62.1	21.4	10.9	2.4	0.9	2.4
Burkina Faso	(000)	4,296	588	227	87	17	42	—	—	—	—	—	—
	(%)	81.7	11.2	4.3	1.6	0.3	0.8	78.7	10.5	6.0	3.3	0.4	1.1
Burundi	(000)	1,932	997	60	56	0	16	—	—	—	—	—	—
	(%)	63.1	32.6	2.0	1.8	0.0	0.5	63.7	29.8	2.4	3.4	0.0	0.7
Cameroon	(000)	1,898	2,696	1,047	587	526	286	—	—	—	—	—	—
	(%)	27.0	38.3	14.9	8.3	7.5	4.1	20.8	33.7	17.3	12.4	9.2	6.7
Central African Republic	(000)	1,064	513	208	71	2	19	—	—	—	—	—	—
	(%)	56.7	27.3	11.1	3.8	0.1	1.0	51.8	27.3	14.3	5.2	0.1	1.3
Chad	(000)	2,295	510	112	46	6	19	—	—	—	—	—	—
	(%)	76.8	17.1	3.8	1.5	0.2	0.6	74.2	17.9	4.8	2.2	0.1	0.8
Congo, Rep.	(000)	258	323	562	172	144	108	—	—	—	—	—	—
	(%)	16.5	20.6	35.9	11.0	9.2	6.9	9.3	17.1	42.4	13.5	10.3	7.5
Côte d'Ivoire	(000)	4,443	1,958	971	413	86	271	—	—	—	—	—	—
	(%)	54.6	24.0	11.9	5.1	1.1	3.3	46.5	25.9	14.7	6.6	0.9	5.5
Ethiopia	(000)	18,604	7,540	1,177	1,013	215	136	—	—	—	—	—	—
	(%)	64.9	26.3	4.1	3.5	0.8	0.5	60.2	27.7	4.9	5.6	1.0	0.5
Ghana	(000)	2,693	816	3,065	635	416	179	—	—	—	—	—	—
	(%)	34.5	10.5	39.3	8.1	5.3	2.3	31.9	10.7	39.8	10.1	5.2	2.3
Guinea	(000)	3,050	355	195	67	95	65	—	—	—	—	—	—
	(%)	79.7	9.3	5.1	1.8	2.5	1.7	76.4	10.7	6.3	2.4	2.7	1.4
Guinea-Bissau	(000)	168	45	9	4	0	1	—	—	—	—	—	—
	(%)	74.3	19.8	4.0	1.7	0.0	0.3	72.3	20.2	4.5	2.9	0.0	0.2
Lesotho	(000)	143	483	167	83	19	10	—	—	—	—	—	—
	(%)	15.8	53.3	18.5	9.2	2.1	1.1	11.5	47.8	24.1	12.4	3.1	1.1
Madagascar	(000)	2,081	3,457	1,297	631	0	191	—	—	—	—	—	—
	(%)	27.2	45.2	16.9	8.2	0.0	2.5	23.1	43.4	20.8	10.2	0.0	2.6
Malawi	(000)	1,819	3,090	415	332	36	16	—	—	—	—	—	—
	(%)	31.9	54.1	7.3	5.8	0.6	0.3	28.8	52.6	8.1	9.2	0.8	0.4
Mali	(000)	3,267	548	202	91	96	48	—	—	—	—	—	—
	(%)	76.8	12.9	4.7	2.2	2.3	1.1	75.6	13.1	4.4	2.2	3.2	1.5
Mauritania	(000)	660	172	59	57	3	22	—	—	—	—	—	—
	(%)	67.8	17.7	6.1	5.9	0.4	2.2	59.7	20.0	6.6	10.2	0.4	3.1

(table continues on next page)

Table I.1 Distribution of Population by Age Group and Highest Level of Schooling Attained in 23 Sub-Saharan African Countries, ca. 2003 (continued)

		15–59 years (not in school)						25–34 years (not in school)					
		No schooling	Primary	Lower secondary	Upper secondary	TVET	Higher	No schooling	Primary	Lower secondary	Upper secondary	TVET	Higher
Mozambique	(000)	5,160	1,710	156	58	49	9	—	—	—	—	—	—
	(%)	72.3	23.9	2.2	0.8	0.7	0.1	72.3	23.9	2.2	0.8	0.7	0.1
Rwanda	(000)	1,320	2,000	78	82	27	8	—	—	—	—	—	—
	(%)	37.6	56.9	2.2	2.3	0.8	0.2	30.5	59.5	2.9	4.8	1.9	0.4
Senegal	(000)	2,908	910	275	116	61	60	—	—	—	—	—	—
	(%)	67.2	21.0	6.3	2.7	1.4	1.4	64.1	20.6	7.3	4.2	1.8	1.9
Sierra Leone	(000)	1,491	269	163	191	40	18	—	—	—	—	—	—
	(%)	68.6	12.4	7.5	8.8	1.8	0.8	60.4	12.3	9.4	12.6	3.0	2.3
Uganda	(000)	1,782	5,464	1,048	599	495	69	—	—	—	—	—	—
	(%)	18.8	57.8	11.1	6.3	5.2	0.7	16.0	57.5	11.8	7.0	6.7	0.8
Zambia	(000)	576	2,231	700	650	0	225	—	—	—	—	—	—
	(%)	13.1	50.9	16.0	14.8	0.0	5.1	9.5	49.0	20.7	14.9	0.0	6.0
Weighted ave.	(%)	51.5	30.1	10.1	4.9	1.9	1.5	46.7	30.5	11.7	6.7	2.4	2.0
Minimum	(%)	13.1	9.3	2.0	0.8	0.0	0.1	9.3	10.5	2.2	0.8	0.0	0.1
Maximum	(%)	81.7	57.8	39.3	14.8	9.2	6.9	78.7	59.5	42.4	14.9	10.3	7.5

Source: Authors' analysis of labor market surveys; see appendix J, table J.2.
Note: Table is based on population not in school at the time of survey. The "highest level of schooling attained" does not necessarily mean it was completed. TVET = Technical and Vocational Education and Training. — = not available.

Table I.2 Distribution of Population by Employment Status and Sector in 23 Sub-Saharan African Countries, ca. 2003

		Population aged 15–59	Employed in formal sector				Employed in informal sector			Total employed[a]	Unemployed	Not active
			Public	Private	Total	Skilled	Farming	Nonfarm	Total			
Benin	(000)	2,898	106	87	193	96	1,021	1,356	2,377	2,570	78	250
	(%)	—	4.1	3.4	7.5	3.7	39.7	52.8	92.5	100	2.9	8.6
Burkina Faso	(000)	5,256	124	113	237	103	3,922	573	4,495	4,732	124	401
	(%)	—	2.6	2.4	5.0	2.2	82.9	12.7	95.0	100	2.6	7.6
Burundi	(000)	3,062	84	36	120	49	2,599	193	2,792	2,912	37	112
	(%)	—	2.9	1.3	4.1	1.7	89.3	6.6	95.9	100	1.3	3.7
Cameroon	(000)	7,038	370	575	945	503	2,968	1,393	4,361	5,306	1,292	440
	(%)	—	7.0	10.8	17.8	9.5	55.9	26.3	82.2	100	19.6	6.3
Central African Republic	(000)	1,877	60	128	189	41	890	331	1,221	1,409	101	367
	(%)	—	4.3	9.1	13.4	2.9	63.1	23.5	86.6	100	6.7	19.6
Chad	(000)	2,988	57	37	94	35	1,045	260	1,305	1,399	520	1,069
	(%)	—	4.1	2.7	6.7	2.5	74.7	18.6	93.3	100	27.1	35.8
Congo, Rep.	(000)	1,567	106	87	193	135	360	584	944	1,137	405	25
	(%)	—	9.3	7.7	17.0	11.8	31.6	51.4	83.0	100	26.2	1.6

(table continues on next page)

Table I.2 Distribution of Population by Employment Status and Sector in 23 Sub-Saharan African Countries, ca. 2003 *(continued)*

		Population aged 15–59	Employed in formal sector				Employed in informal sector			Total employed[a]	Unemployed	Not active
			Public	Private	Total	Skilled	Farming	Nonfarm	Total			
Côte d'Ivoire	(000)	8,142	187	279	466	294	3,360	1,926	5,287	5,753	1,357	1,032
	(%)	—	3.3	4.8	8.1	5.1	58.4	33.4	91.9	100	19.1	12.7
Ethiopia	(000)	28,684	950	701	1,651	575	16,335	3,391	19,725	21,376	580	6,728
	(%)	—	4.4	3.3	7.7	2.7	76.5	15.9	92.3	100	2.6	23.5
Ghana	(000)	7,804	453	346	799	453	2,529	3,156	5,684	6,483	525	795
	(%)	—	7.0	5.3	12.3	7.0	39.0	48.7	87.7	100	7.5	10.2
Guinea	(000)	3,828	86	30	116	82	1,838	1,050	2,888	3,005	221	603
	(%)	—	2.9	1.0	3.9	2.7	61.2	34.9	96.1	100	6.9	15.7
Guinea-Bissau	(000)	227	4	4	8	2	120	43	162	170	6	51
	(%)	—	2.6	2.1	4.7	0.9	70.3	25.0	95.3	100	3.4	22.3
Lesotho	(000)	905	110	20	130	41	99	229	328	457	338	109
	(%)	—	24.0	4.3	28.3	8.9	21.6	50.1	71.7	100	42.5	12.1
Madagascar	(000)	7,657	279	737	1,016	386	4,837	944	5,781	6,797	223	636
	(%)	—	4.1	10.8	15.0	5.7	71.2	13.9	85.0	100	3.2	8.3
Malawi	(000)	5,707	228	379	608	178	3,420	839	4,259	4,867	262	578
	(%)	—	4.7	7.8	12.5	3.7	70.3	17.2	87.5	100	5.1	10.1
Mali	(000)	4,253	98	77	175	81	884	1,666	2,551	2,726	506	1,021
	(%)	—	3.6	2.8	6.4	3.0	32.4	61.1	93.6	100	15.6	24.0
Mauritania	(000)	974	55	32	87	33	154	238	392	479	78	417
	(%)	—	11.5	6.7	18.1	6.9	32.1	49.7	81.9	100	14.1	42.8
Mozambique	(000)	7,141	259	404	663	84	4,542	913	5,455	6,119	335	687
	(%)	—	4.2	6.6	10.8	1.4	74.2	14.9	89.2	100	5.2	9.6
Rwanda	(000)	3,516	79	44	123	57	2,909	250	3,159	3,281	71	163
	(%)	—	2.4	1.3	3.7	1.7	88.6	7.6	96.3	100	2.1	4.6
Senegal	(000)	4,329	129	176	305	113	1,120	1,204	2,324	2,630	665	1,035
	(%)	—	4.9	6.7	11.6	4.3	42.6	45.8	88.4	100	20.2	23.9
Sierra Leone	(000)	2,173	94	79	173	104	1,255	371	1,626	1,799	114	260
	(%)	—	5.2	4.4	9.6	5.8	69.8	20.6	90.4	100	6.0	12.0
Uganda	(000)	9,457	673	590	1,262	467	5,443	1,983	7,426	8,688	370	399
	(%)	—	7.7	6.8	14.5	5.4	62.6	22.8	85.5	100	4.1	4.2
Zambia	(000)	4,381	233	346	579	355	1,929	1,418	3,347	3,926	338	117
	(%)	—	5.9	8.8	14.7	9.0	49.1	36.1	85.3	100	7.9	2.7
Total	(000)	123,864	4,826	5,307	10,133	4,266	63,578	24,312	87,890	98,022	8,545	17,296
Weighted ave.	(%)	—	4.9	5.4	10.3	4.4	64.9	24.8	89.7	100	8.0	14.0

Source: Authors' analysis of labor market surveys; see appendix J, table J.2.

Note: Table is based on population not in school at the time of survey. Percentage (%) rows for each country show the proportion of *employed* except for two columns: (a) the "unemployed" column, which gives the percentage of unemployed in the active population (employed and unemployed), and (b) the "not active" column, which gives the percentage of not active in the total population, aged 15–59, who were not in school at the time of the survey.

a. The percentage of "total employed" comprises the percentages of (a) the "total" (public and private) employed in the formal sector and (b) the "total" employed in the informal sector.

Table I.3 Workforce Distribution by Age Group, Highest Level of Schooling, and Employment Status, Aggregate for 23 Sub-Saharan African Countries, ca. 2003

percentage

Highest level attained	No schooling					Primary					Lower secondary					Upper secondary					Technical/vocational					Higher education					Total				
Age group in survey	15–59	25–34	35–49	50–59	15–59	25–34	35–49	50–59	15–59	25–34	35–49	50–59	15–59	25–34	35–49	50–59	15–59	25–34	35–49	50–59	15–59	25–34	35–49	50–59	15–59	25–34	35–49	50–59	15–59	25–34	35–49	50–59
Formal sector	**15.4**	12.0	19.3	**25.4**	**23.7**	21.9	22.9	**16.9**	17.0	17.1	17.1	**20.0**	23.9	22.5	14.6	**10.8**	12.1	11.4	11.7	**11.5**	11.2	15.2	14.4	**100**	100	100	100
Public	**9.5**	7.7	13.2	**19.0**	**18.2**	16.8	16.7	**15.2**	13.5	15.3	18.2	**24.7**	28.4	26.9	17.5	**16.1**	18.4	14.7	15.9	**15.5**	13.7	19.3	18.5	**100**	100	100	100
Private	**20.7**	15.5	17.5	**27.8**	**28.1**	28.0	31.5	**18.4**	19.9	19.2	15.6	**15.8**	20.2	17.5	10.6	**6.0**	7.1	7.5	5.9	**7.8**	9.2	10.4	8.7	**100**	100	100	100
Informal sector	**54.2**	49.5	57.7	71.3	**32.6**	**33.8**	27.9	20.7	**9.1**	11.0	9.4	5.4	**2.8**	4.0	3.4	1.3	**0.9**	1.1	1.2	0.8	**0.4**	0.5	0.5	0.5	**100**	100	100	100
Nonfarm	**40.6**	34.7	43.7	61.3	**31.5**	**32.1**	26.9	21.3	**17.5**	20.1	17.2	10.2	**6.7**	8.9	7.5	3.3	**2.4**	2.7	3.0	2.3	**1.2**	1.5	1.7	1.6	**100**	100	100	100
Farming	**59.3**	56.2	63.3	74.1	**33.0**	**34.5**	28.3	20.5	**5.9**	6.9	6.2	4.1	**1.4**	1.8	1.7	0.8	**0.3**	0.4	0.4	0.4	**0.1**	0.1	0.1	0.2	**100**	100	100	100
Employed	**50.1**	45.1	51.8	65.9	**31.9**	**32.6**	27.1	20.9	**9.9**	11.7	10.3	6.6	**4.6**	6.3	5.8	2.7	**1.9**	2.4	2.5	1.9	**1.5**	1.8	2.4	2.0	**100**	100	100	100
Unemployed	**31.3**	27.6	41.7	55.7	**30.4**	**24.5**	25.2	23.0	**18.3**	19.3	15.8	11.2	**12.3**	16.0	9.2	4.4	**4.4**	5.6	5.0	3.3	**3.4**	7.1	3.1	2.4	**100**	100	100	100
Active[a]	**48.6**	43.7	51.4	65.5	**31.7**	**32.0**	27.0	21.0	**10.6**	12.3	10.6	6.8	**5.2**	7.1	6.0	2.8	**2.1**	2.7	2.6	2.0	**1.7**	2.2	2.4	2.0	**100**	100	100	100
Not active[b]	**69.2**	67.1	77.1	82.7	**19.9**	**20.4**	14.2	10.2	**6.9**	7.5	5.1	3.7	**3.2**	4.0	2.5	1.5	**0.5**	0.5	0.7	0.8	**0.4**	0.4	0.5	1.0	**100**	100	100	100
Total population	**51.5**	46.7	54.4	68.2	**30.1**	**30.5**	25.5	19.3	**10.1**	11.7	9.9	6.3	**4.9**	6.7	5.6	2.6	**1.9**	2.4	2.3	1.8	**1.5**	2.0	2.2	1.8	**100**	100	100	100

Source: Authors' construction based on analysis of labor market surveys for 23 Sub-Saharan African countries; see appendix J, table J.2.

Note: Table is based on population not in school at the time of survey. The "highest level [of schooling] attained" does not necessarily mean it was completed.

a. "Active" designates the sum of employed and unemployed in the workforce.
b. "Not active" designates those *outside* the workforce (not employed and not seeking employment).

Table I.4 Workforce Employment Status, by Generation and Highest Level of Schooling, Aggregate for 23 Sub-Saharan African Countries, ca. 2003

percentage

Highest level attained	No schooling				Primary				Lower secondary				Upper secondary				Technical/vocational				Higher education				Total			
Age group in survey	15–59	25–34	35–49	50–59	15–59	25–34	35–49	50–59	15–59	25–34	35–49	50–59	15–59	25–34	35–49	50–59	15–59	25–34	35–49	50–59	15–59	25–34	35–49	50–59	15–59	25–34	35–49	50–59
Formal sector	**3.0**	2.9	2.8	3.0	**7.6**	8.0	9.9	11.0	**15.2**	14.8	19.7	25.4	**36.4**	36.0	46.0	53.4	**48.2**	49.0	54.0	59.6	**64.5**	54.6	75.9	73.6	**9.5**	10.7	12.2	10.1
Public	**0.9**	0.8	0.9	1.2	**2.7**	2.7	4.1	4.7	**6.5**	5.2	9.5	15.7	**21.4**	19.1	29.7	37.2	**34.1**	33.0	37.7	47.2	**41.6**	29.6	52.2	55.1	**4.5**	4.8	6.6	5.9
Private	**2.1**	2.1	1.9	1.8	**4.9**	5.2	5.8	6.3	**8.7**	9.6	10.2	9.7	**15.0**	16.9	16.3	16.1	**14.1**	16.0	16.3	12.4	**22.9**	25.0	23.7	18.6	**5.0**	6.0	5.6	4.2
Informal sector	**91.8**	92.0	93.6	94.1	**84.7**	86.0	86.0	85.2	**70.9**	72.8	73.7	68.9	**44.8**	46.2	47.2	41.2	**35.3**	34.4	37.4	34.6	**19.5**	19.9	18.5	22.2	**82.5**	81.4	83.4	86.4
Nonfarm	**19.1**	20.2	20.5	17.6	**22.7**	25.6	23.9	19.1	**37.8**	41.5	39.1	28.3	**29.3**	31.9	30.0	22.4	**25.6**	25.7	28.3	21.9	**16.6**	17.9	16.2	15.4	**22.8**	25.5	24.1	18.8
Farming	**72.8**	71.9	73.1	76.5	**62.1**	60.4	62.0	66.1	**33.1**	31.4	34.5	40.6	**15.5**	14.3	17.2	18.8	**9.7**	8.7	9.0	12.7	**2.9**	2.0	2.2	6.9	**59.7**	55.9	59.3	67.6
Employed	**94.8**	95.0	96.4	97.1	**92.3**	93.9	95.9	96.2	**86.1**	87.6	93.4	94.3	**81.2**	82.2	93.2	94.5	**83.5**	83.4	91.4	94.2	**84.0**	74.4	94.4	95.8	**92.0**	92.1	95.6	96.5
Unemployed	**5.2**	5.0	3.6	2.9	**7.7**	6.1	4.1	3.8	**13.9**	12.4	6.6	5.7	**18.8**	17.8	6.8	5.5	**16.5**	16.6	8.6	5.8	**16.0**	25.6	5.6	4.2	**8.0**	7.9	4.4	3.5
Active[a]	**100**	100	100	100	**100**	100	100	100	**100**	100	100	100	**100**	100	100	100	**100**	100	100	100	**100**	100	100	100	**100**	100	100	100
Not active[b]	**18.8**	18.4	16.6	18.9	**9.2**	8.6	6.5	8.3	**9.5**	8.2	6.0	9.2	**9.0**	7.7	5.3	9.1	**3.7**	2.7	3.2	6.9	**3.7**	2.8	2.7	8.5	**14.0**	12.8	11.7	15.6
Total population	**100**	100	100	100	**100**	100	100	100	**100**	100	100	100	**100**	100	100	100	**100**	100	100	100	**100**	100	100	100	**100**	100	100	100

Source: Authors' construction based on analysis of labor market surveys for 23 countries; see appendix J, table J2.

Note: Table is based on population not in school at the time of survey. The "highest level [of schooling] attained" does not necessarily mean it was completed.

a. "Active" designates the sum of employed and unemployed in the workforce.

b. "Not active" designates those *outside* the workforce (not employed and not seeking employment).

Table I.5 Employment by Sector in Mostly Low-Income Sub-Saharan African Countries, 1985 and 2003

	Agriculture					Industry					Services				
	Number (000)		Index	% of total		Number (000)		Index	% of total		Number (000)		Index	% of total	
	1985	2003	2003	1985	2003	1985	2003	2003	1985	2003	1985	2003	2003	1985	2003
Angola	2,500	2,820	112.8	65.2	45.1	170	170	100.1	4.4	2.7	1,162	3,257	280.2	30.3	52.1
Benin	1,011	1,105	109.3	63.3	38.4	41	40	96.8	2.6	1.4	545	1,734	318.0	34.1	60.2
Burkina Faso	2,626	3,601	137.1	83.1	71.2	103	101	97.5	3.3	2.0	429	1,359	316.6	13.6	26.9
Burundi	2,092	2,814	134.5	91.0	88.1	87	77	88.6	3.8	2.4	119	302	253.6	5.2	9.5
Cameroon	2,040	1,886	92.4	57.6	32.3	151	147	97.2	4.3	2.5	1,348	3,811	282.6	38.1	65.2
Cape Verde	55	15	27.7	57.6	10.3	7.1	6.8	95.4	7.4	4.6	34	126	376.3	35.0	85.1
Central African Rep.	668	700	104.8	58.0	40.5	30	27	90.1	2.6	1.6	454	1,000	220.3	39.4	57.9
Chad	1,493	1,984	132.9	75.6	61.0	48	48	100.2	2.4	1.5	433	1,219	281.2	22.0	37.5
Comoros	99	102	102.8	70.5	44.7	1.6	1.6	100.3	1.1	0.7	40	124	311.7	28.4	54.6
Congo, Rep.	303	114	37.7	39.7	7.9	18	18	102.2	2.3	1.2	441	1,316	298.0	58.0	90.9
Côte d'Ivoire	1,936	1,953	100.9	55.1	31.1	90	87	96.7	2.6	1.4	1,490	4,245	285.0	42.4	67.5
Eritrea	900	1,042	115.8	78.8	69.2	32	32	101.5	2.8	2.2	210	432	205.5	18.4	28.6
Ethiopia	17,100	21,986	128.6	86.6	76.1	35	41	117.1	0.2	0.1	2,600	6,867	264.1	13.2	23.8
Gambia, The	188	117	62.0	62.5	20.0	2.8	3.4	121.6	0.9	0.6	110	463	419.8	36.6	79.4
Ghana	3,360	2,470	73.5	61.2	27.8	130	131	101.3	2.4	1.5	2,005	6,279	313.2	36.5	70.7
Guinea	1,650	2,022	122.6	66.6	49.7	46	46	99.0	1.9	1.1	780	2,004	257.0	31.5	49.2
Guinea-Bissau	255	303	118.8	72.8	53.3	8.3	8.0	95.8	2.4	1.4	87	257	295.0	24.9	45.2
Kenya	5,980	9,448	158.0	78.5	67.5	202	202	100.1	2.6	1.4	1,434	4,337	302.5	18.8	31.0
Lesotho	406	367	90.6	73.5	56.7	18	18	100.4	3.3	2.8	128	262	204.8	23.2	40.5
Madagascar	3,270	4,048	123.8	74.8	53.7	83	94	114.0	1.9	1.2	1,019	3,392	332.8	23.3	45.0
Malawi	2,653	4,042	152.3	85.6	73.3	93	96	102.6	3.0	1.7	353	1,378	390.1	11.4	25.0
Mali	2,559	2,406	94.0	80.6	49.1	26	27	102.6	0.8	0.6	591	2,471	417.8	18.6	50.4
Mauritania	410	401	97.7	60.2	37.8	6.5	7.2	110.5	1.0	0.7	264	651	246.6	38.8	61.5
Niger	2,355	3,842	163.1	83.0	74.2	26	27	105.1	0.9	0.5	456	1,311	287.6	16.1	25.3
Nigeria	17,641	12,003	68.0	63.4	27.4	714	694	97.2	2.6	1.6	9,448	31,120	329.4	34.0	71.0
Rwanda	2,268	2,729	120.4	92.1	72.3	56	59	106.1	2.3	1.6	139	987	707.8	5.7	26.1
São Tomé and Príncipe	17	5.7	32.4	56.4	13.1	0.5	0.5	100.6	1.5	1.1	13	37	284.1	42.1	85.8
Senegal	1,395	1,458	104.5	55.2	34.9	83	95	114.9	3.3	2.3	1,052	2,628	249.9	41.6	62.9
Sudan	5,187	3,671	70.8	73.3	38.8	134	157	116.8	1.9	1.7	1,754	5,634	321.3	24.8	59.5
Swaziland	132	197	149.2	68.7	62.5	3.2	3.5	108.5	1.7	1.1	57	114	200.8	29.7	36.3
Tanzania	8,039	11,132	138.5	79.1	62.9	230	236	102.5	2.3	1.3	1,892	6,338	334.9	18.6	35.8
Togo	781	833	106.6	65.4	38.4	55	53	96.9	4.6	2.4	359	1,286	358.6	30.0	59.2
Zambia	1,434	2,040	142.3	52.6	44.6	90	95	105.9	3.3	2.1	1,202	2,444	203.3	44.1	53.4
Zimbabwe	2,089	2,391	114.5	67.3	43.8	139	146	105.3	4.5	2.7	875	2,924	334.1	28.2	53.5

Source: Table is reproduced from Mingat and Ndem 2007.

Reference

Mingat, A., and F. Ndem. 2007. "La dimension rurale des scolarisations dans les pays d'Afrique au sud du Sahara: situation actuelle et défis pour le développement de la couverture scolaire au niveau du premier cycle secondaire." Paper presented by IREDU, CNRS, and University of Bourgogne, France for the Agence Francaise de Développement.

APPENDIX J

Lists of Surveys

Table J.1 List of Household Surveys Used for Chapter 6, "Social Outcomes"

Country	Name of survey	Abbreviation	Year
Angola	Multiple Indicator Cluster Survey	MICS	2001
Benin	Demographic and Health Survey	DHS	2001
Burkina Faso	Demographic and Health Survey	DHS	2003
Burundi	Multiple Indicator Cluster Survey	MICS	2000
Cameroon	Multiple Indicator Cluster Survey	MICS	2000
Central African Republic	Multiple Indicator Cluster Survey	MICS	2000
Chad	Demographic and Health Survey	DHS	2004
Congo, Dem. Rep.	Multiple Indicator Cluster Survey	MICS	2001
Côte d'Ivoire	Multiple Indicator Cluster Survey	MICS	2000
Ethiopia	Demographic and Health Survey	DHS	2000
Equatorial Guinea	Multiple Indicator Cluster Survey	MICS	2000
Gabon	Demographic and Health Survey	DHS	2000
Gambia, The	Multiple Indicator Cluster Survey	MICS	2000
Ghana	Demographic and Health Survey	DHS	2003
Guinea	Core Welfare Indicators Questionnaire	CWIQ	2002
Guinea-Bissau	Multiple Indicator Cluster Survey	MICS	2000
Kenya	Demographic and Health Survey	DHS	2003
Lesotho	Multiple Indicator Cluster Survey	MICS	2000
Madagascar	Multiple Indicator Cluster Survey	MICS	2000
Malawi	Demographic and Health Survey	DHS	2000
Mali	Demographic and Health Survey	DHS	2001
Mozambique	Demographic and Health Survey	DHS	2003
Namibia	Demographic and Health Survey	DHS	2000
Niger	Multiple Indicator Cluster Survey	MICS	2000
Nigeria	Demographic and Health Survey	DHS	2003
Rwanda	Demographic and Health Survey	DHS	2000
São Tomé and Príncipe	Multiple Indicator Cluster Survey	MICS	2000
Senegal	Multiple Indicator Cluster Survey	MICS	2000
Sierra Leone	Multiple Indicator Cluster Survey	MICS	2000
Sudan	Multiple Indicator Cluster Survey	MICS	2000
Swaziland	Multiple Indicator Cluster Survey	MICS	2000
Tanzania	Demographic and Health Survey	DHS	1999
Togo	Multiple Indicator Cluster Survey	MICS	2000
Uganda	Demographic and Health Survey	DHS	2001
Zambia	Demographic and Health Survey	DHS	2002
Zimbabwe	Demographic and Health Survey	DHS	1999

Source: Authors' compilation.
Note: Generally, the most recently completed survey at the time of analysis was used, with preference given to the DHS.

Table J. 2 List of Labor Market Surveys Used for Chapter 7, "Education and Employment"

Country	Name of survey	Abbreviation	Year
Benin	Core Welfare Indicators Questionnaire	CWIQ	2003
Burkina Faso	Core Welfare Indicators Questionnaire	CWIQ	2002
Burundi	Core Welfare Indicators Questionnaire	CWIQ	2002
Cameroon	Enquête Camerounaise Auprès des Ménages	ECAM II	2001
Central African Republic	Recensement Général de la Population et de l'Habitat	RGPH	2003
Chad	Enquête sur la Consommation des Ménages et le Secteur Informel au Tchad	ECOSIT	2002
Congo, Rep.	Questionnaire Unifié sur les Indicateurs de Développement	ECOM	2005
Côte d'Ivoire	Enquête Niveau de Vie des Ménages	n.a.	2002
Ethiopia	Welfare Monitoring Survey Questionnaire	WMS	2004
Ghana	Core Welfare Indicators Questionnaire	CWIQ	2003
Guinea	Core Welfare Indicators Questionnaire	CWIQ	2002
Guinea-Bissau	Core Welfare Indicators Questionnaire	CWIQ	2002
Lesotho	Core Welfare Indicators Questionnaire	CWIQ	2002
Madagascar	Enquête auprès des ménages	n.a.	2001
Malawi	Core Welfare Indicators Questionnaire	CWIQ	2002
Mali	Enquête Permanente Emploi Auprès des Ménages	EPAM	2004
Mauritania	Core Welfare Indicators Questionnaire	CWIQ	2005
Mozambique	Core Welfare Indicators Questionnaire	CWIQ	2002
Rwanda	Core Welfare Indicators Questionnaire	CWIQ	2001
Senegal	Core Welfare Indicators Questionnaire	CWIQ	2001
Sierra Leone	Integrated Household Survey	SLIHS	2003
Uganda	Socio-Economic Survey Questionnaire	UNHS	2002
Zambia	Living Conditions Monitoring Survey III	LCMS III	2002

Source: Authors' compilation.
Note: n.a. = not applicable.

APPENDIX K

The Millennium Development Goals

Table K.1 Millennium Development Goals

Goal #1 Eradicate extreme poverty and hunger
Target 1.A: Halve, between 1990 and 2015, the proportion of people whose income is less than $1 a day
Target 1.B: Achieve full and productive employment and decent work for all, including women and young people
Target 1.C: Halve, between 1990 and 2015, the proportion of people who suffer from hunger

Goal #2 Achieve universal primary education
Target 2.A: Ensure that, by 2015, children everywhere, boys and girls alike, will be able to complete a full course of schooling

Goal #3 Promote gender equality and empower women
Target 3.A: Eliminate gender disparity in primary and secondary education, preferably by 2005, and in all levels of education no later than 2015

Goal #4 Reduce child mortality
Target 4.A: Reduce by two-thirds, between 1990 and 2015, the under-five mortality rate

Goal #5 Improve maternal health
Target 5.A: Reduce by three-quarters the maternal mortality ratio
Target 5.B: Achieve universal access to reproductive health

Goal #6 Combat HIV/AIDS, malaria, and other diseases
Target 6.A: Have halted by 2015 and begun to reverse the spread of HIV/AIDS
Target 6.B: Achieve, by 2010, universal access to treatment for HIV/AIDS for all those who need it
Target 6.C: Have halted by 2015 and begun to reverse the incidence of malaria and other major diseases

Goal #7 Ensure environmental sustainability
Target 7.A: Integrate the principles of sustainable development into country policies and programs and reverse the loss of environmental resources
Target 7.B: Reduce biodiversity loss, achieving, by 2010, a significant reduction in the rate of loss
Target 7.C: Halve, by 2015, the proportion of people without sustainable access to safe drinking water and basic sanitation
Target 7.D: By 2020, have achieved a significant improvement in the lives of at least 100 million slum dwellers

(table continues on next page)

Table K.1 Millennium Development Goals *(continued)*

Goal #8	**Develop a global partnership for development**
	Target 8.A: Develop further an open, rule-based, predictable, nondiscriminatory trading and financial system (includes a commitment to good governance, development, and poverty reduction—both nationally and internationally)
	Target 8.B: Address the special needs of the least developed countries (includes tariff-and quota-free access for exports, enhanced program of debt relief for HIPC and cancellation of official bilateral debt, and more generous ODA for countries committed to poverty reduction)
	Target 8.C: Address the special needs of landlocked developing countries and small island developing states (through the Program of Action for the Sustainable Development of Small Island Developing States and 22nd General Assembly provisions)
	Target 8.D: Deal comprehensively with the debt problems of developing countries (through national and international measures to make debt sustainable in the long term)
	Target 8.E: In cooperation with pharmaceutical companies, provide access to affordable essential drugs in developing countries
	Target 8.F: In cooperation with the private sector, make available the benefits of new technologies, especially information and communications

Source: United Nations Development Programme, www.undp.org/mdg.
Note: For a detailed assessment of progress toward the six Education for All (EFA) goals, which include the education MDGs, see UNESCO 2008. For more about progress toward the education goals, but with a focus on Africa, see Pôle de Dakar UNESCO-BREDA 2007. HIPC = heavily indebted poor countries. ODA = official development assistance.

References

Pôle de Dakar UNESCO-BREDA (UNESCO Regional Office for Education in Africa). 2007. *Education for All in Africa: Top Priority for Integrated Sector-Wide Policies.* Dakar+7 Report. Dakar: Pôle de Dakar UNESCO-BREDA.

UNESCO (United Nations Educational, Scientific and Cultural Organization). 2008. *Education for All by 2015: Will We Make It?* Education for All (EFA) Global Monitoring Report. Paris: UNESCO.

www.ingramcontent.com/pod-product-compliance
Lightning Source LLC
Chambersburg PA
CBHW081219170426
43198CB00017B/2659